MODERN URBAN GIRLS | STEFAN SOELL

STEFAN SOELL

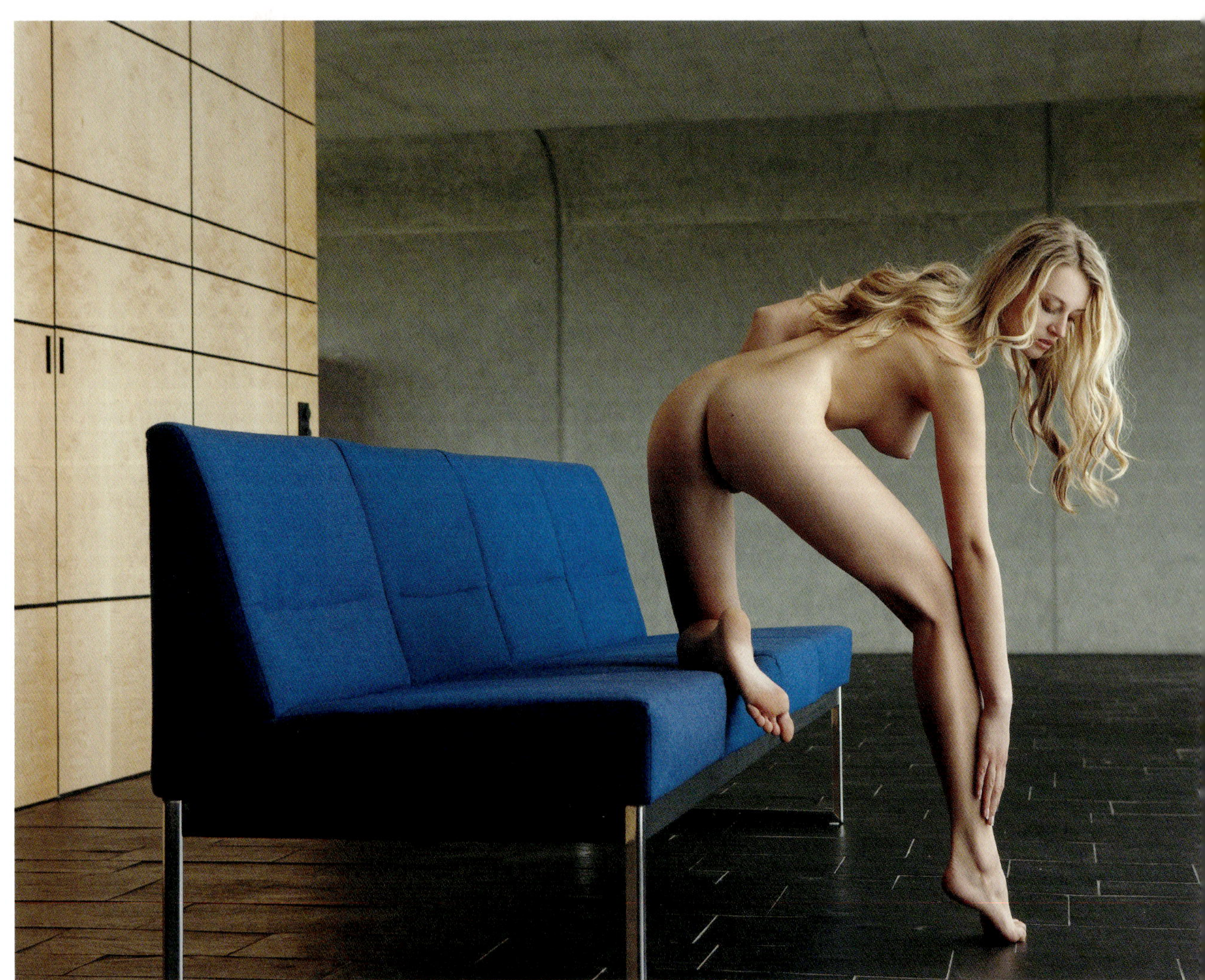

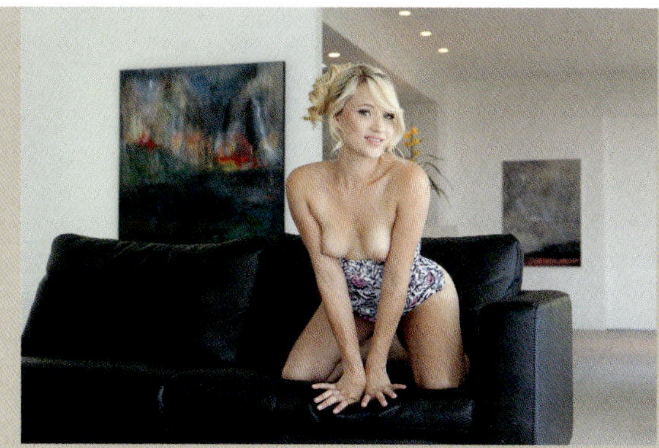

modern urban girls

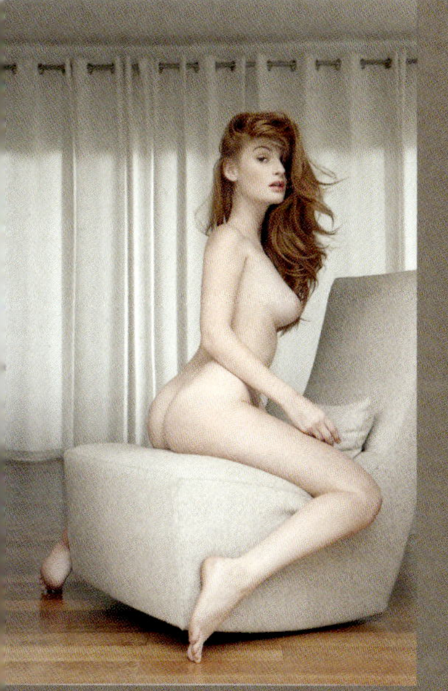

EDITION Skylight

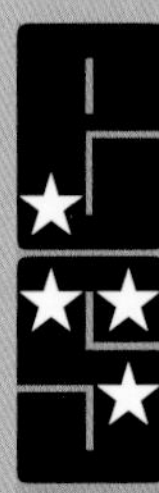

3rd Edition in Paperback, revised and enlarged 2023
2nd Edition in Paperback, revised and enlarged 2021
1st Edition © 2012 by Edition Skylight

EDITION SKYLIGHT
Rosengartenstrasse 13B
CH-8608 Bubikon / Zürich
Switzerland

info@edition-skylight.com
www.edition-skylight.com

ISBN 978-3-03766-675-3

Bibliographic information published by
Die Deutsche Bibliothek
Die Deutsche Bibliothek lists this publication in the
Deutsche Nationalbibliografie; detailed bibliographic data are
available in the Internet at http://dnb.ddb.de

Design: Weiß-Freiburg – Grafik und Buchgestaltung
Übersetzung: Eugene Edwards

Printed in Bosnia and Herzegovina

fan Soell, your latest volume of erotic photos brings together two forms of
pression that could hardly be more different from an aesthetic point of view.
usually, you combine minimalist, cool architecture with hot eroticism. How
you come across this unusual but fascinating idea? ■ **Stefan Soell:** after
oine Glow" and "Volcanic Girls", my first two erotic books, which show na-
ladies in romantic outdoor settings, I knew I had had enough of romance. I
rted to look for new and unusual settings for my erotic productions.

contrast to the previous erotic photos, which were shot out of doors and
in the countryside, these were taken largely indoors. What is the funda-
ntal difference between taking photos indoors compared with sessions in
countryside? ■ It may sound odd, but erotic photographs taken inside
e greater natural atmosphere and emotion. This is also because the models
one hundred percent safe from prying eyes, and so pose more freely and
nhibitedly.

eaking of models, my guess is that these shapely bodies, this fabulous
ount of beauty, is probably not something you see present in your studio
ry day. Can you imagine the secret question people who see these images
st frequently want to ask? ■ Hmm, I can quite easily imagine it, but can
u be specific?

ll, the question naturally is how you find all these beautiful girls, and how
u get them to strip off in front of the camera and pose, sometimes really
te provocatively? ■ with regard to this volume, I searched long and hard
three whole years to find the most perfect models. Of the more than 30
erent ones you see here, 16 are genuinely new discoveries; they have never
sed for me before. In addition, I make sure I only work with models that are
lly new for the sake of my future audience. Sometimes the amount of work
olved is like looking for a needle in a haystack.

this end, you have had to travel around the world quite a bit, as you have
d me. But to be specific, where do you find them? ■ about half the girls are
erican. In the States the modelling business is more open and communica-
e than in Europe, despite the reputed prudishness of the Americans. But in
stern Europe there are always plenty of special scouts around, boy scouts
whatever you call them, whose job it is to find particular kinds of female
aracters.

u mention character, but first and foremost the models need a gorgeous
dy, don't they? Also a pretty face and maybe also great hair? ■ it's not as
ple as that, because I am always interested in the person as a whole. For
, that means having a strong presence, a powerful charisma as well as con-
ant looks that captivate the viewer and draw them inexorably into the picture.

's briefly stay with the face and hair (we can come to the body later on). De-
e their obvious eroticism, your photos have a strong similarity to the most
nanding modern fashion shots seen in expensive glossy magazines. Apart
m the choice of models, how do you achieve this effect? ■ Of course, I work

under 100% professional conditions, and this means that hair and makeup
specialists provide the perfect look; stylists provide the right accessories and
take care of the ambience as a whole. Although we are a small team (a bigger
one would be more of a hindrance to the models), we are highly professional
and nothing is left to chance. Despite this, sessions are held in a relaxed atmosphere that is often real fun. To make the girls look more natural, I have my
team apply "invisible" make up which is imperceptible and makes them look
very natural. The accessories are designed to enhance the style and look of my
pictures, even if the models are totally naked except for a few scraps of fabric.

Now we come to the distinguished interiors that provide the setting. On the
one hand, they reinforce the fashion and style, and on the other provide a fascinating contrast to the nudity of the models. Not everyone owns such interiors
such as these … ■ I work together with special agencies; they provide me with
this sophisticated architecture. Some houses have been partially furnished for
the shots, while others are already prepared. Of course, we have to ask for
permission from the landlord or owners beforehand. Many find it pretty cool,
and when they see the photos later say "wow, did you create that in my home?
Great!" And they hang up large format prints as art on their walls.

But isn't there a danger that this modern architecture, which is itself a fabulous subject for photography, distracts the viewer from the erotic scenes being
staged in it? ■ Quite the reverse. As the whole environment looks very distinguished, with white walls contrasting strikingly with dark floors, and rooms
often flooded with natural light (I don't often use flash!), my models make a
particularly vivid impression. It's as if the viewer were in their midst.

You talked about the relaxed atmosphere at the photo sessions. Are such
beautiful, glamorous models, some of whom look just like successful businesswomen, really so willing to pose as lasciviously and provocatively as they
do here? Despite the exceptionally relaxing environment? ■ that's just it. The
more beautiful a woman is, the more confident she appears to be. And the
more proud she is of her beauty and perfect body, the more she likes to present
herself openly. Many really beautiful women also have an exhibitionist touch,
with the result that, once in front of the lens, they reveal themselves quite
cheekily and provocatively. During the sessions, many are naturally prepared
to show a little more of themselves, and not with legs closed for every shot.

As a successful erotic photographer, you are certainly not lacking in self-con
fidence yourself, thank goodness! Speaking personally, does this volume of
photos express anything special for you? ■ let me say clearly: come and have
a look at this! My new volume shows I do not only produce erotic photographs
with traditional, romantic settings. The striking combination of unbridled eroticism and masterful architecture shows creative skill, the attraction lies in the
contrast between the familiar and unfamiliar.

Stefan Soell, thank you for the informative interview.
Interview with Stefan Soell by Martin Sigrist.

→ **www.stefansoell.de**

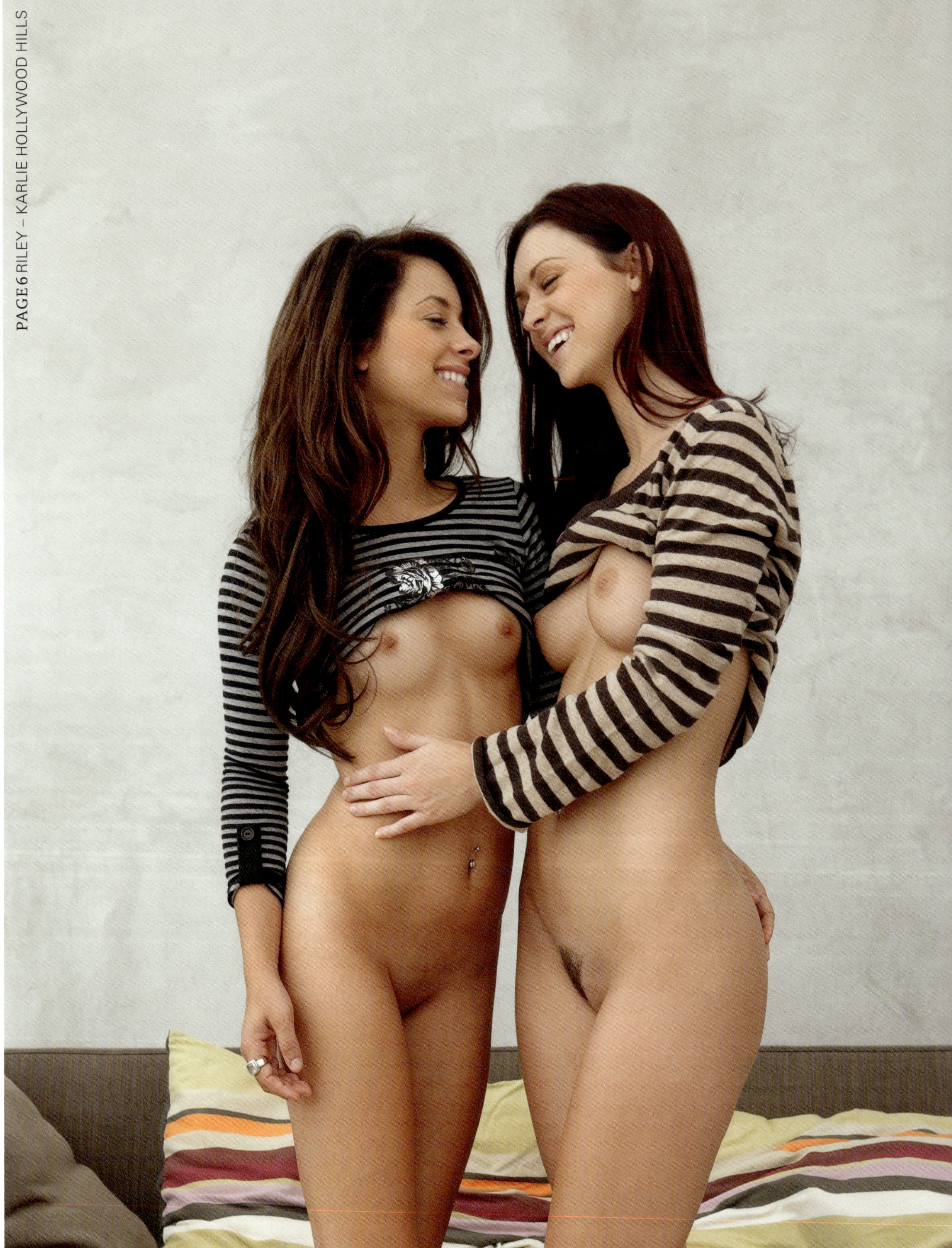

efan Soell, zwei Formensprachen, die kaum unterschiedlicher sein könnten, einigen sich in Ihrem neusten erotischen Bildband zu einer ungewohnten ombination von minimalistischer, kühler Architektur mit heißer Erotik. Wie men Sie auf diese nicht alltägliche, faszinierende Idee? **■ Stefan Soell:** ch meinen beiden ersten Erotikbänden „Alpenglühen" und „Volcanic Girls", denen es bildsprachlich um den nackten Körper in einer romantischen ndschaft ging, sagte ich mir einfach: Jetzt ist erst mal Schluss mit Roman- – und so suchte ich mir neue und ungewohnte Kulissen für diese erotischen zenierungen.

Gegensatz zu den in freier Natur entstandenen bisherigen Erotikaufnahmen d diese weitgehend „indoor" entstanden. Was ist der grundsätzliche Unter- ied bei Aufnahmesessions in Räumen gegenüber solchen in der Land- aft? **■** Es mag seltsam klingen, aber die Erotikfotografie zeigt innerhalb n Räumen eine viel natürlichere Ausstrahlung. Das kommt auch daher, dass Modelle freier und ungehemmter posieren, weil sie sich zu 100 Prozent her vor fremden Blicken fühlen.

ropos Modelle: Solche wundervoll geformten Körper, ja überhaupt so viel hönheit aufs Mal läuft Ihnen vermutlich nicht jeden Tag vor die Kamera – nnen Sie sich vorstellen, was sicher die meistgestellte heimliche Frage der trachter dieser Bilder ist? **■** Hmm, ganz leicht kann ich mir das vorstellen, r fragen Sie doch konkret …

n, die Frage lautet natürlich: Wie kommen Sie zu all diesen prachtvollen s, und wie bringen Sie sie dann noch dazu, sich vor der Kamera splitter- ckt auszuziehen und teils recht freizügig zu posieren? **■** Ich habe für diesen liegenden Band tatsächlich volle drei Jahre lang nach den perfektesten delen gesucht. Von den über 30 verschiedenen Modellen, die hier zu se- sind, sind übrigens 16 echte Neuentdeckungen, die noch nie vor meiner era gestanden sind. Zudem achte ich darauf, nur mit Modellen zu arbei- , die für den späteren Betrachter auch wirklich neu sind. Manchmal ist die- Aufwand wie die berühmte Suche nach der Stecknadel im Heuhaufen …

ür sind Sie auch ganz schön in der Welt umhergereist, wie Sie mir erzähl- . Doch nochmals konkret: Wo sind Sie denn fündig geworden? **■** Etwa die fte der Girls sind Amerikanerinnen, dort ist das Modelbusiness – bei aller hgesagten Prüderie der Amerikaner – viel offener und kommunikativer als uns. Aber auch in Osteuropa sind immer wieder Scouts, wie man diese zielle Art von Pfadfindern nennt, auf der Suche nach ganz bestimmten arakteren.

nn Sie von Charakteren sprechen: Müssen die Modelle denn nicht in erster e einen prachtvollen Körper und ein hübsches Gesicht und vielleicht noch e Haare aufweisen? **■** So einfach ist das nicht, denn ich suche nach dem nschen insgesamt, und dazu gehört für mich auch eine starke Ausstrah- g und selbstsicherer Blick, der den Betrachter später zu fesseln und gerade- ns Bild hineinzuziehen vermag.

iben wir kurz bei Gesicht und Haaren (um später auf den Körper zu kom- n) Ihre Fotos sehen bei aller Erotik aus wie anspruchsvollste moderne deaufnahmen in teuren Hochglanzmagazinen. Wie erreichen Sie diesen ekt, abgesehen von der Wahl der Modelle? **■** Ich arbeite natürlich unter olut professionellen Bedingungen, und das heisst auch, dass Haar- und

Make-up-Spezialisten für das perfekte Aussehen und Stylisten für die passenden Accessoires und das ganze Ambiente sorgen. Wir sind zwar nur ein kleines Team – mehr wäre für die Modelle auch hinderlich – aber wir arbeiten hochprofessionell und nichts wird dem Zufall überlassen. Trotzdem finden die Aufnahmen in einer entspannten, oft richtig fröhlichen Atmosphäre statt. Damit die Girls noch natürlicher wirken, lasse ich ein sogenanntes „No Make-up Make-up" machen, das heißt, ein Make-up, das nicht als solches wahrgenommen wird und deshalb besonders natürlich wirkt. Die modischen Accessoires schließlich sollen den Fashion-Style meiner Bilder untermalen, auch wenn die Modelle schlussendlich bis auf wenige Textilfetzen nackt sind.

Kommen wir nun zu den überaus edlen Räumen, die einerseits diesen Fashion-Style untermalen und andererseits diesen faszinierenden Kontrast zur Nacktheit der Modelle bilden. Nicht jeder besitzt ja solche Räume…? **■** Ich arbeite mit spezialisierten Agenturen zusammen, welche für mich diese anspruchsvolle Architektur vermitteln. Die Häuser werden dann teilweise eigens möbliert, teils sind sie es bereits. Die Vermieter, aber auch die eigentlichen Besitzer müssen wir natürlich vorgängig um Erlaubnis fragen. Viele finden das übrigens ziemlich cool und sagen sich später beim Betrachten der Fotos: „Wow, das ist bei mir zu Hause entstanden? Toll!" Und hängen sich dann sogar grossformatige Prints als Kunst an die Wände.

Aber besteht denn nicht die Gefahr, dass gerade diese moderne Architektur, die ja an sich schon fantastische Fotomotive ergibt, von den darin inszenierten erotischen Szenerien ablenkt? **■** Im Gegenteil, weil das ganze Umfeld so edel wirkt, weil viel Weiß an den Wänden in Kombination mit dunklen Böden vorherrscht und die Räume meist von natürlichem Licht durchflutet sind – geblitzt wird bei mir ganz selten! –, wirken die darin inszenierten Körper besonders lebendig. Als stünde der Betrachter mitten drin.

Sie sprachen von der entspannten Atmosphäre bei den Aufnahmesessions. Sind solch wunderschöne, an glamouröse Fashion-Starmodels oder erfolgreiche Businesswomen erinnernde Frauen trotz aller Entspannung ohne Weiteres bereit, so lasziv und freizügig zu posieren, wie sie es hier tun? **■** Das ist es ja gerade: Je schöner eine Frau ist, desto selbstbewusster gibt sie sich auch. Und je stolzer sie auf ihre Schönheit und ihren formvollendeten Körper ist, desto eher mag sie es auch, sich ungeniert zu präsentieren. Vielen wirklich wunderschönen Frauen ist auch ein Hauch von Exhibitionismus eigen, und das führt dazu, dass sie sich frech und durchaus provokativ vor der Kamera zeigen. Viele sind dann wie selbstverständlich bereit, während der Aufnahmen auch mal etwas mehr zu zeigen und die Beine nicht nur geschlossen zu halten …

An Selbstbewusstsein fehlt es auch Ihnen, dem erfolgreichen Erotikfotografen, zum Glück nicht. Was möchten Sie mit diesem Bildband ganz persönlich ausdrücken? **■** Ich sage damit schlicht allen: Schaut her, der Stefan Soell fotografiert Erotik nicht nur im gewohnten Umfeld von Romantik und Natur, sondern er zeigt, wie vielfältig und kontrastreich er sich in der ungewohnten und deshalb besonders reizvollen Kombination von unbändiger Erotik und beherrschter Architektur ausdrücken kann.

Stefan Soell, wir danken herzlich für das informative Gespräch.
Das Interview mit Stefan Soell führte Martin Sigrist.

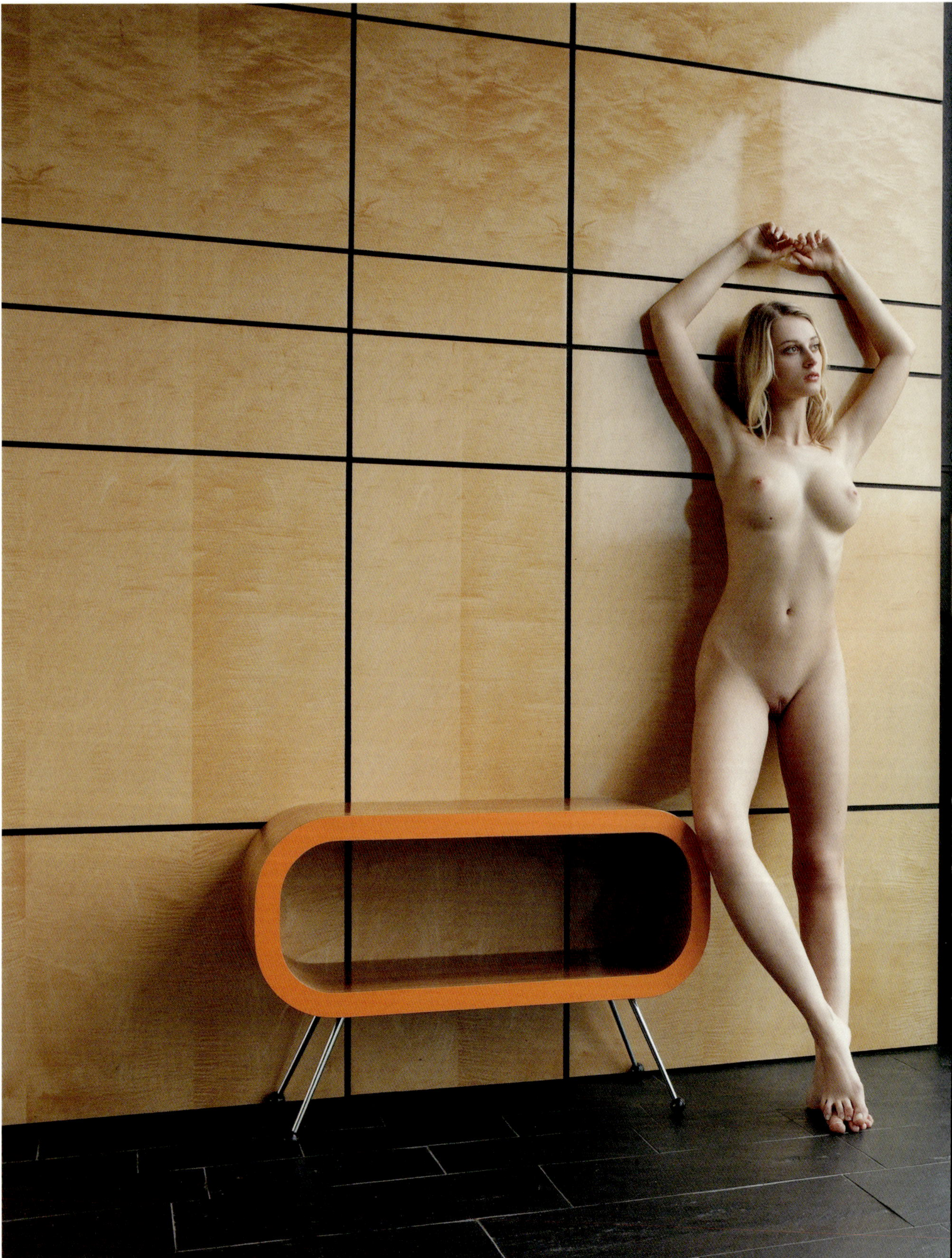

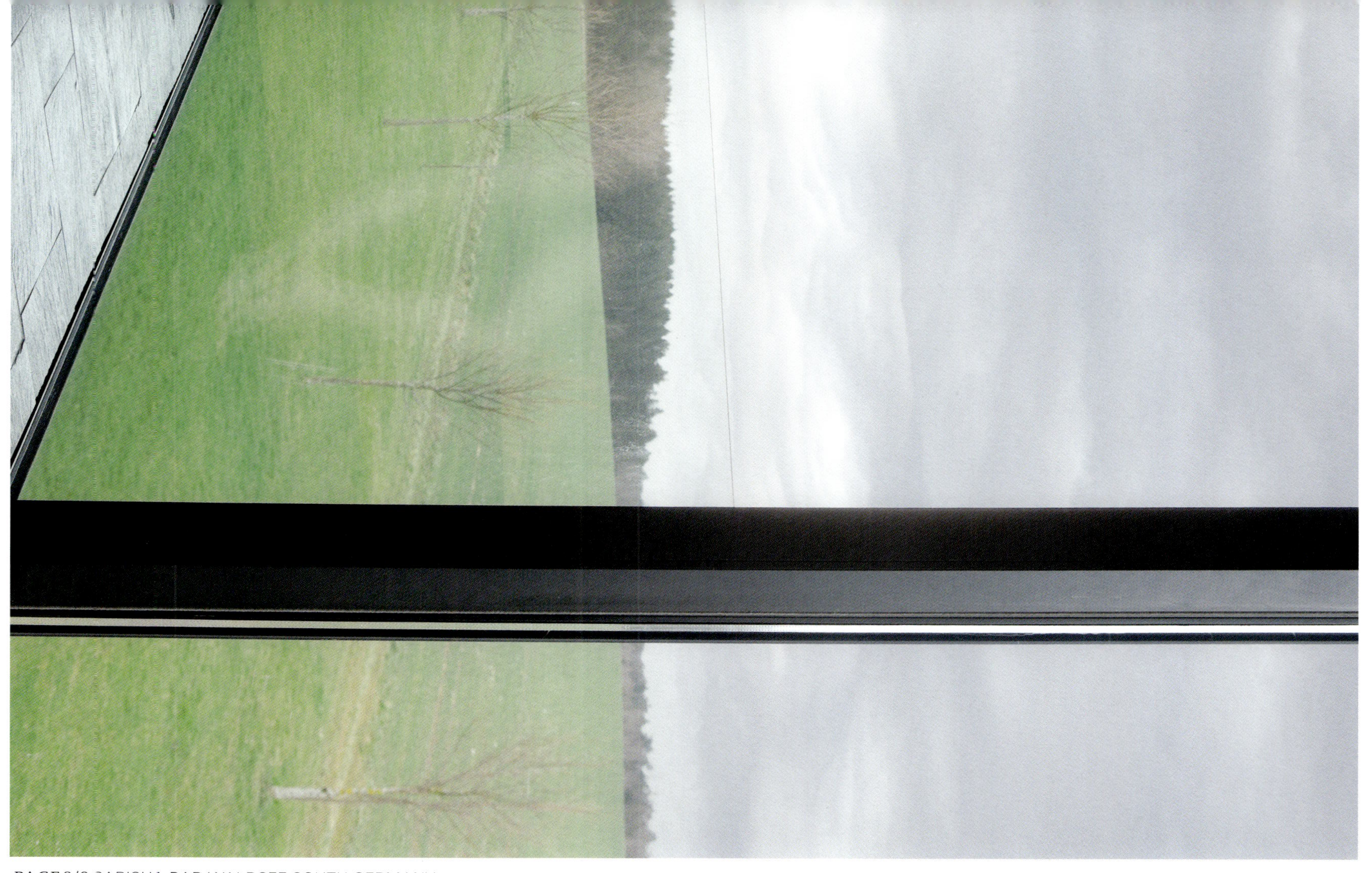

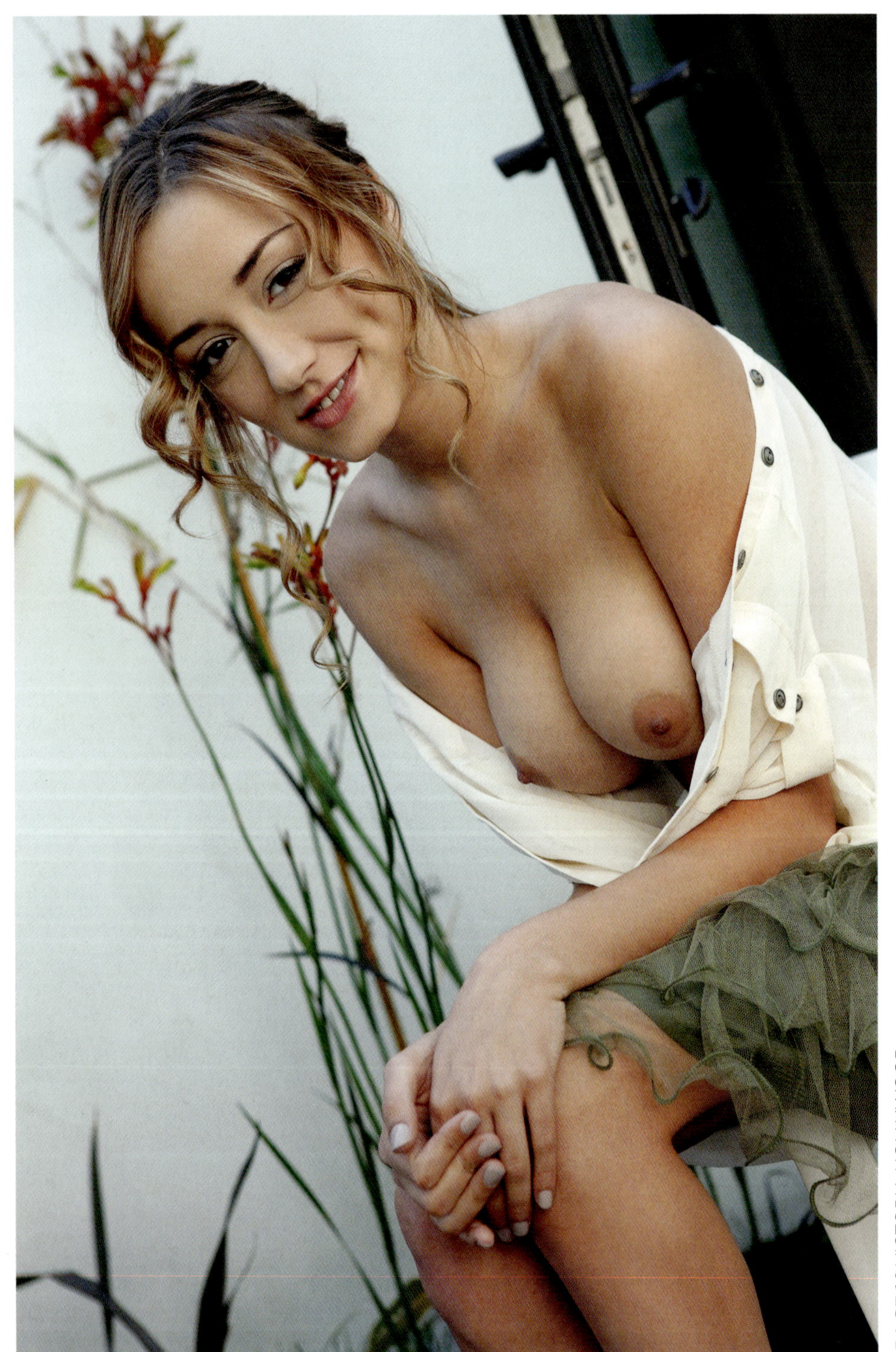

PAGE 10 VICTORIA HOLLYWOOD

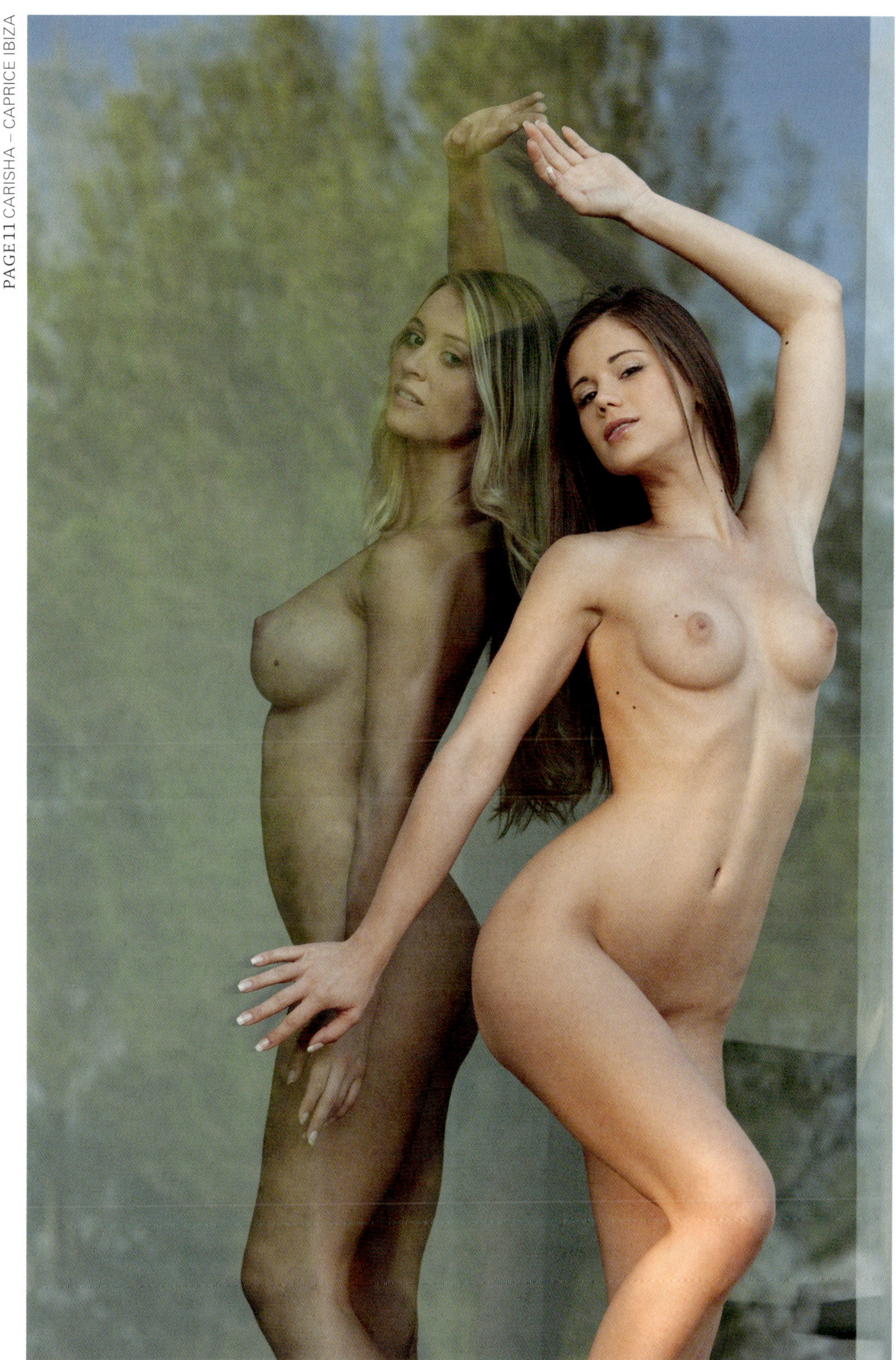

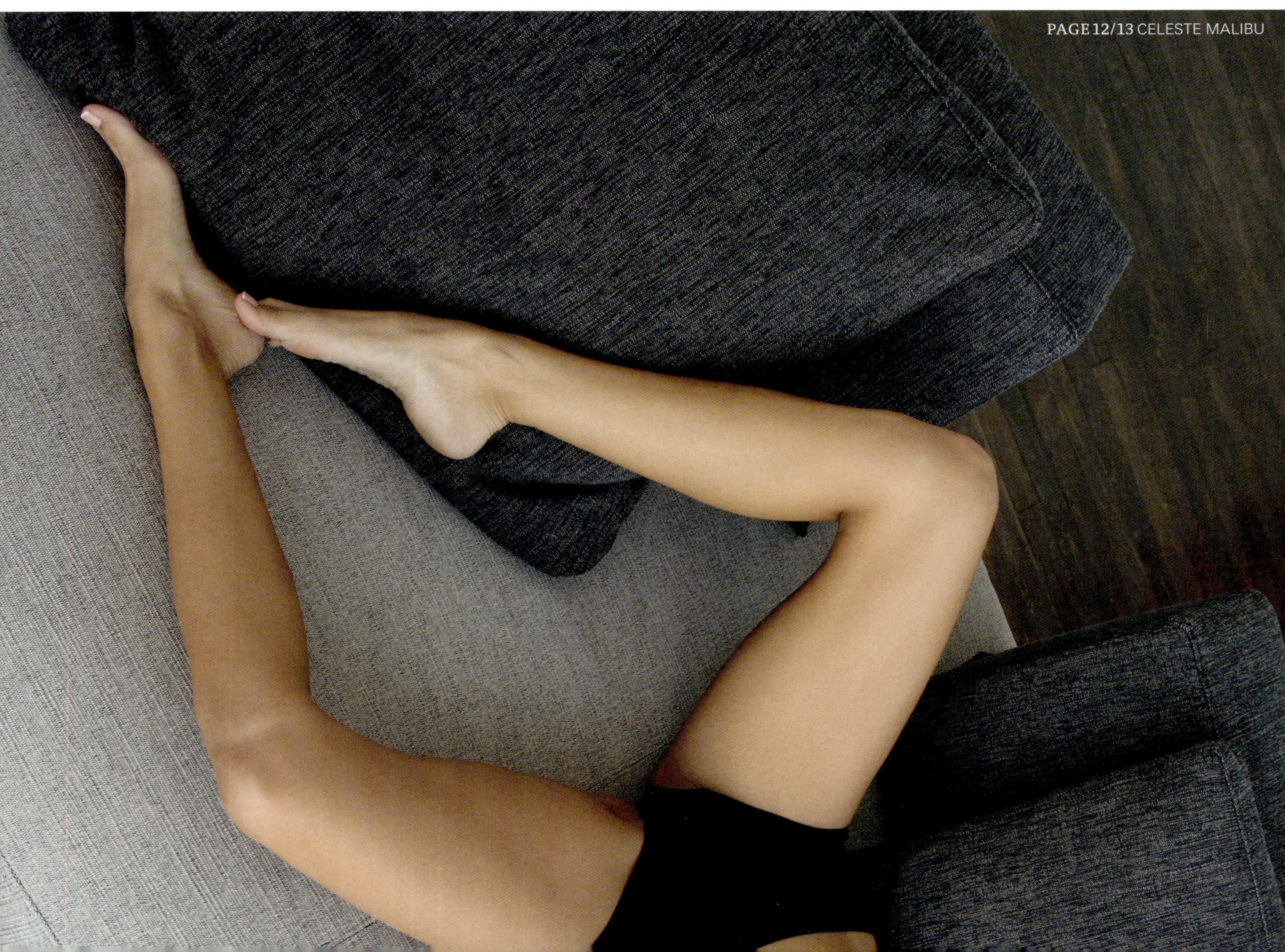

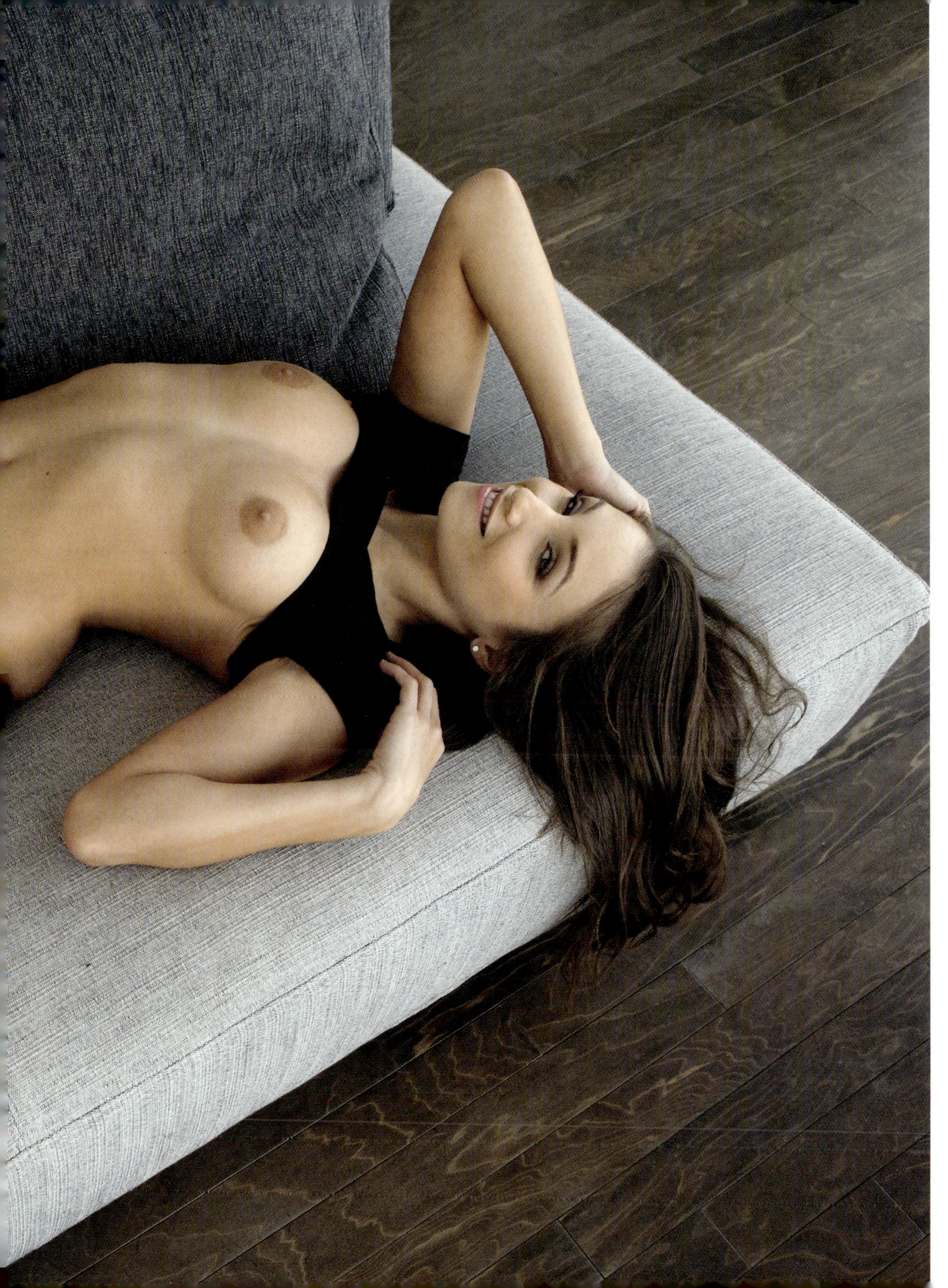

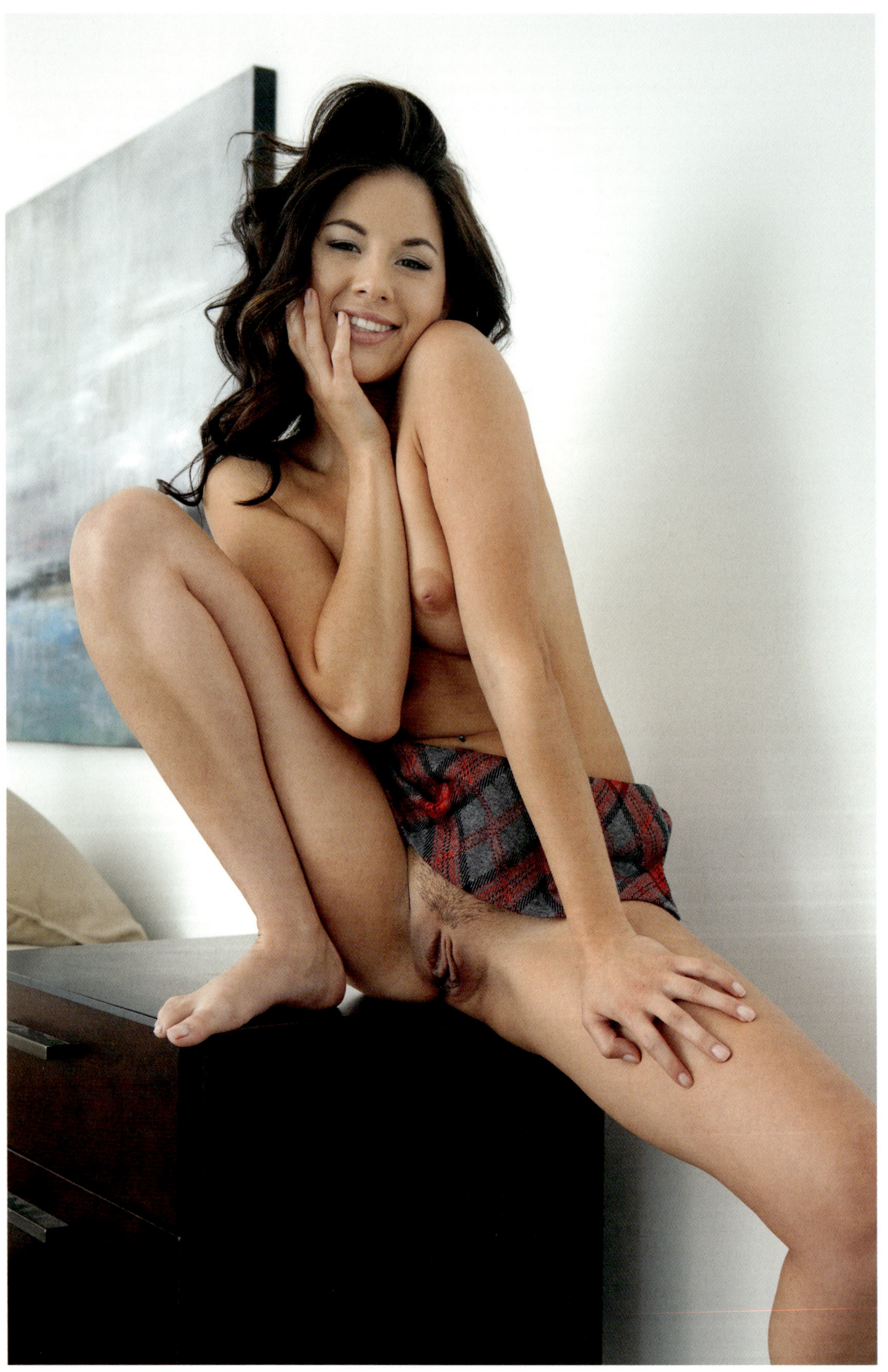

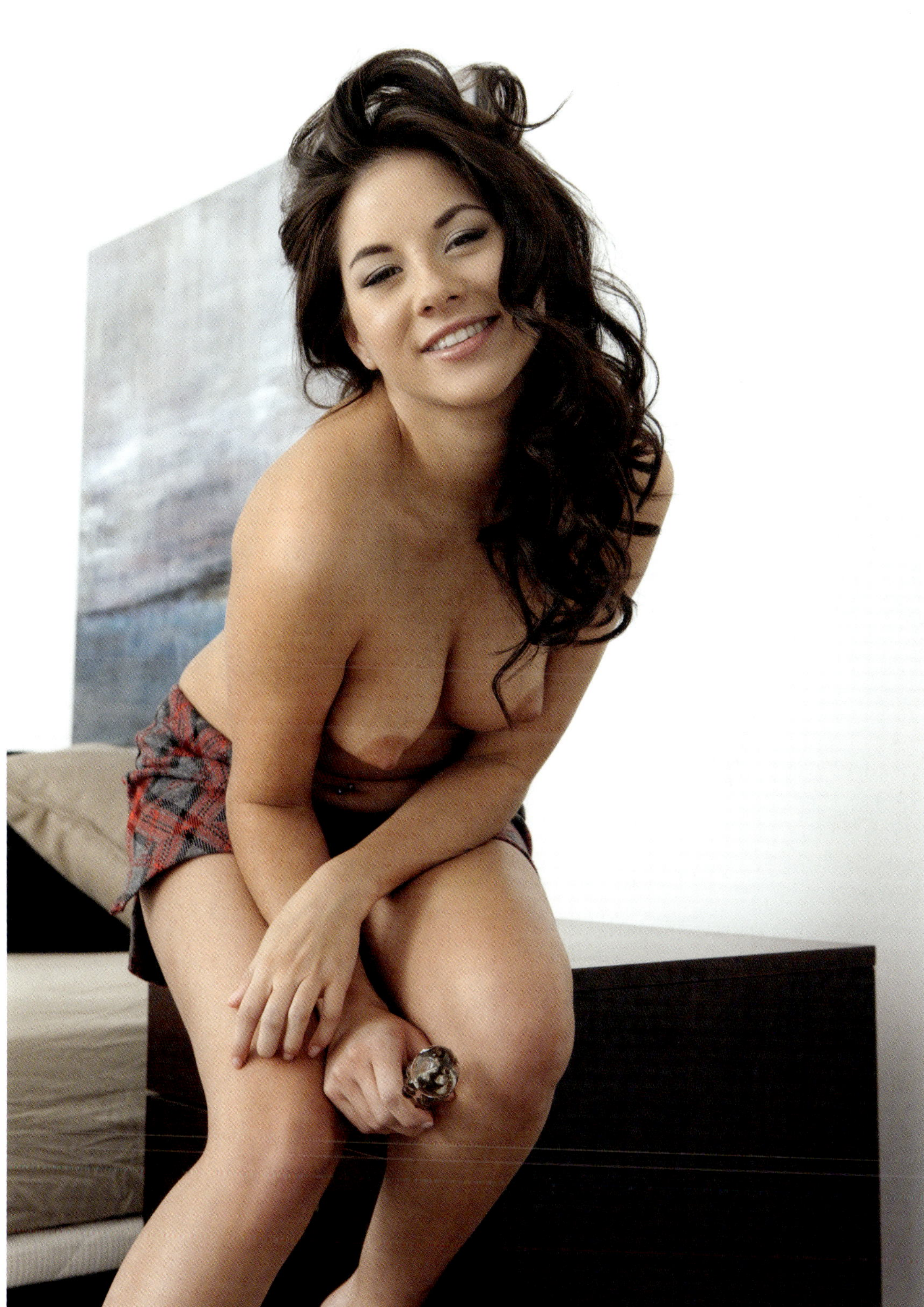

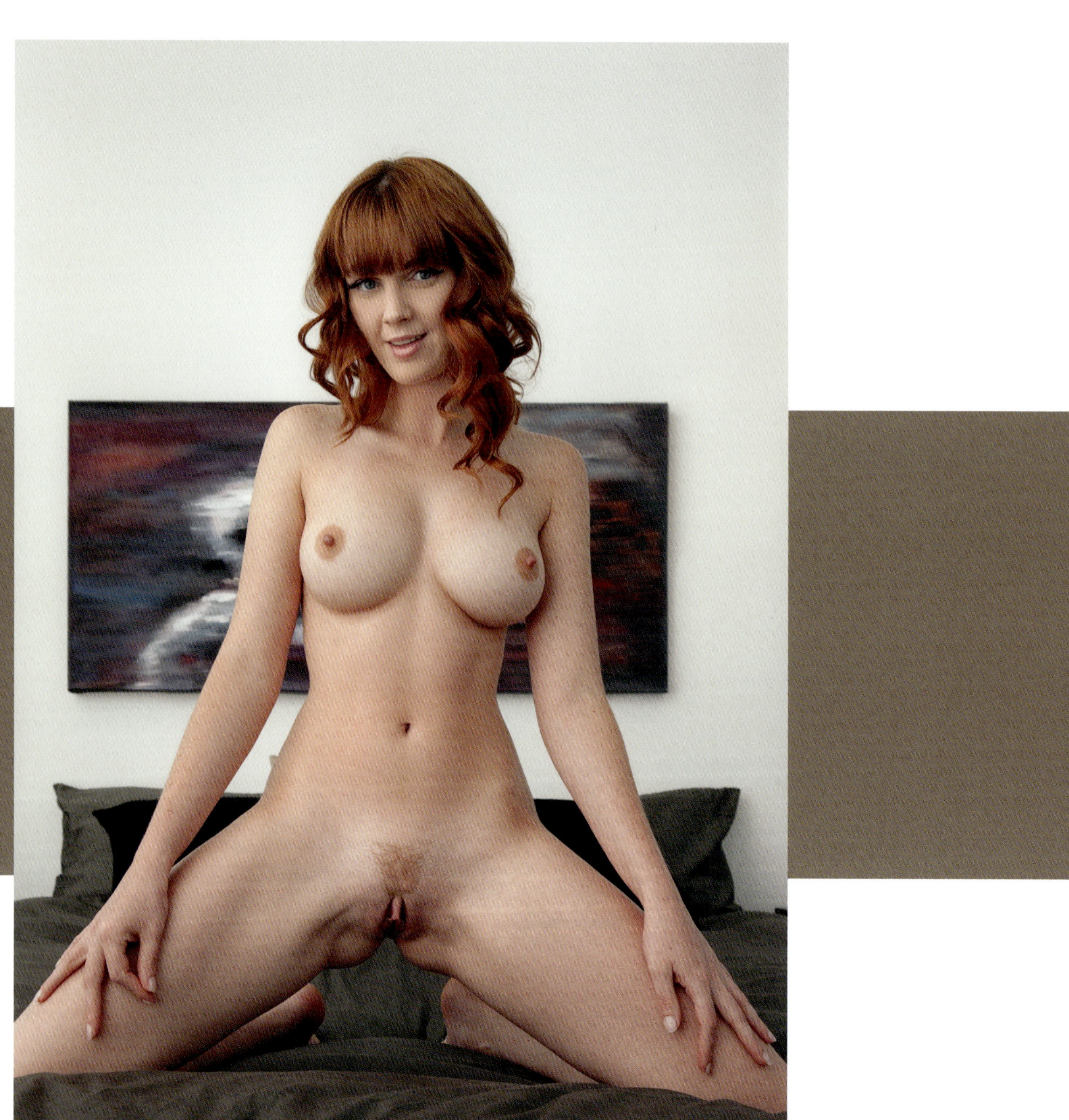

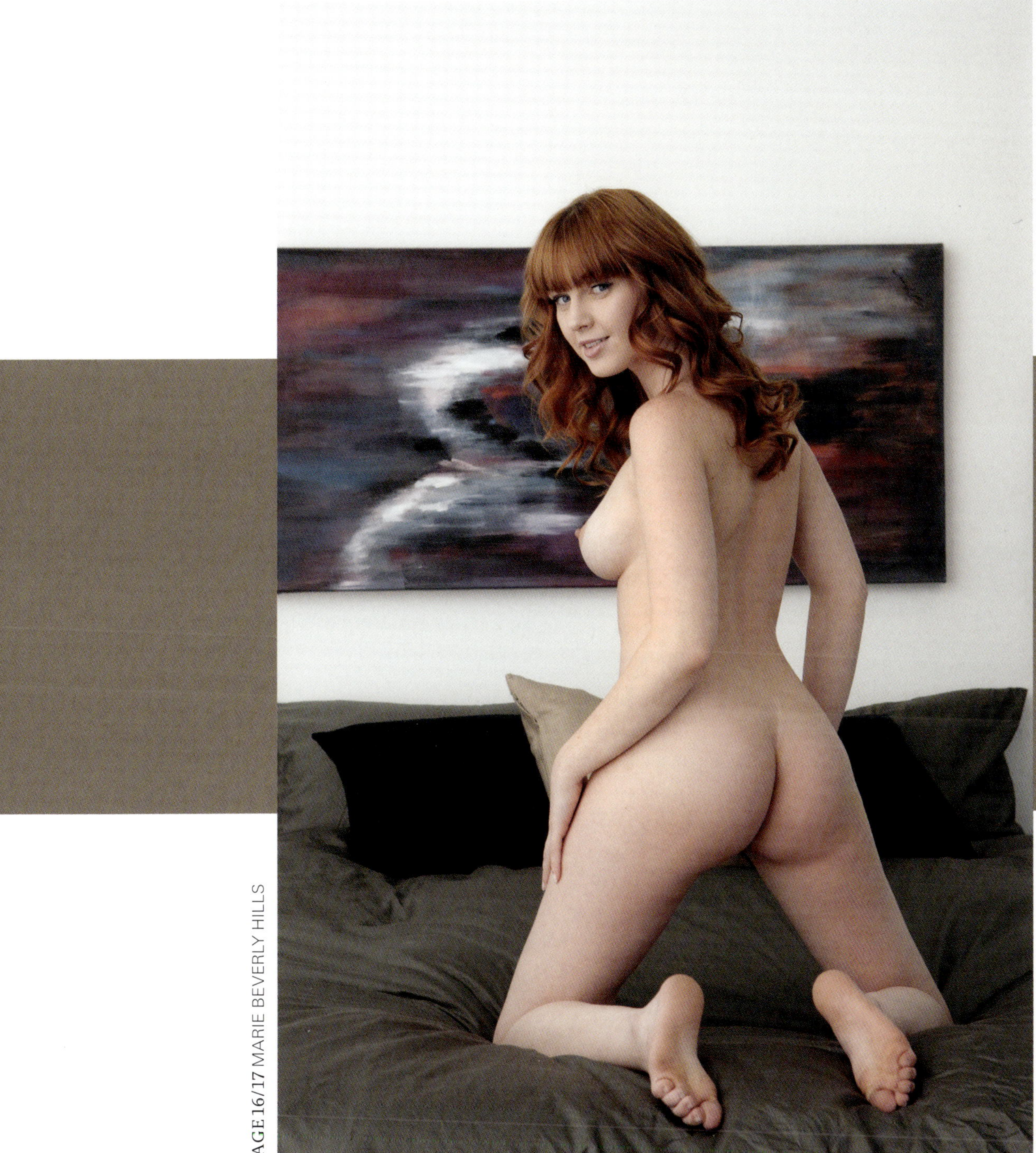

PAGE 16/17 MARIE BEVERLY HILLS

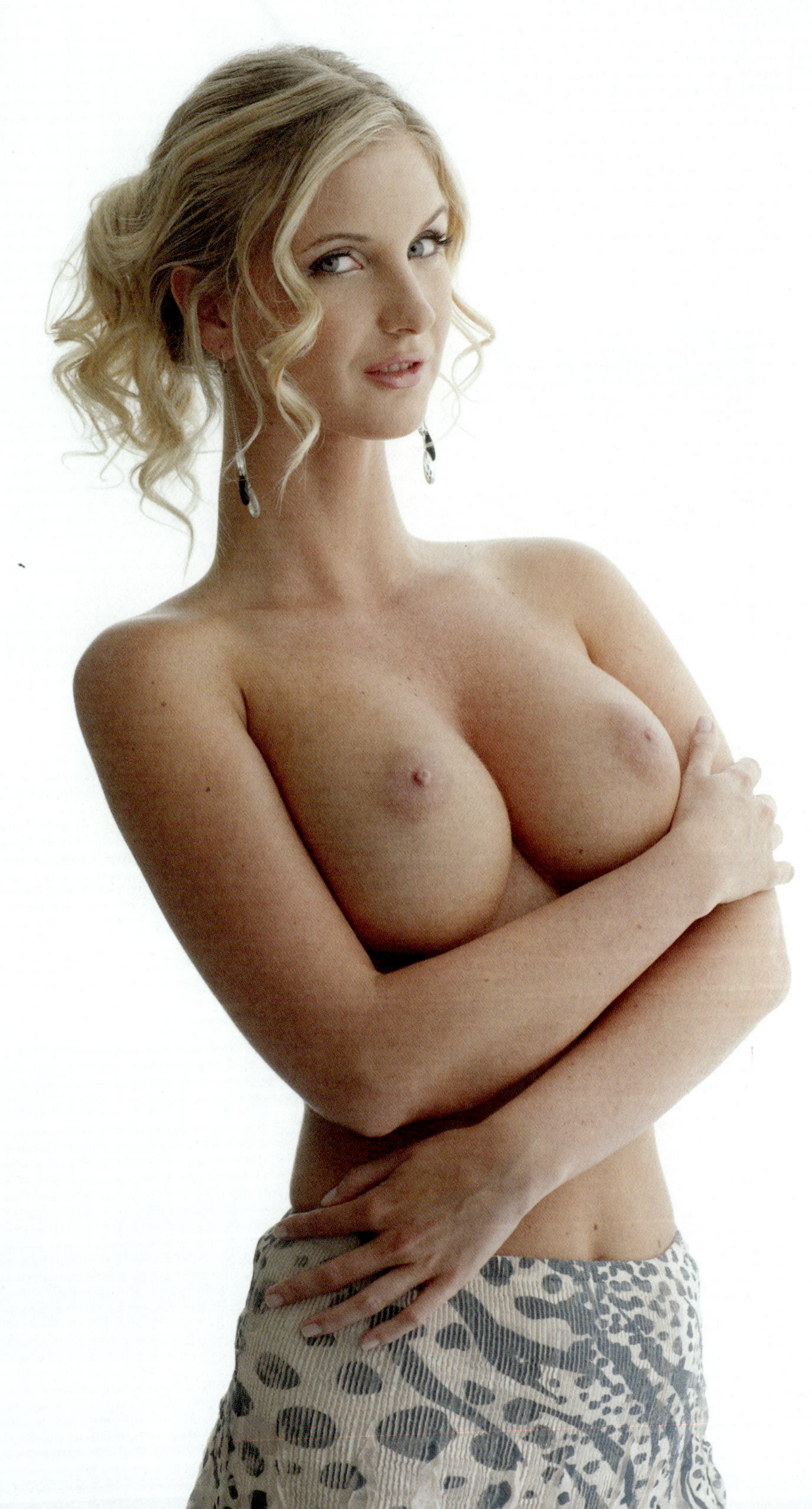

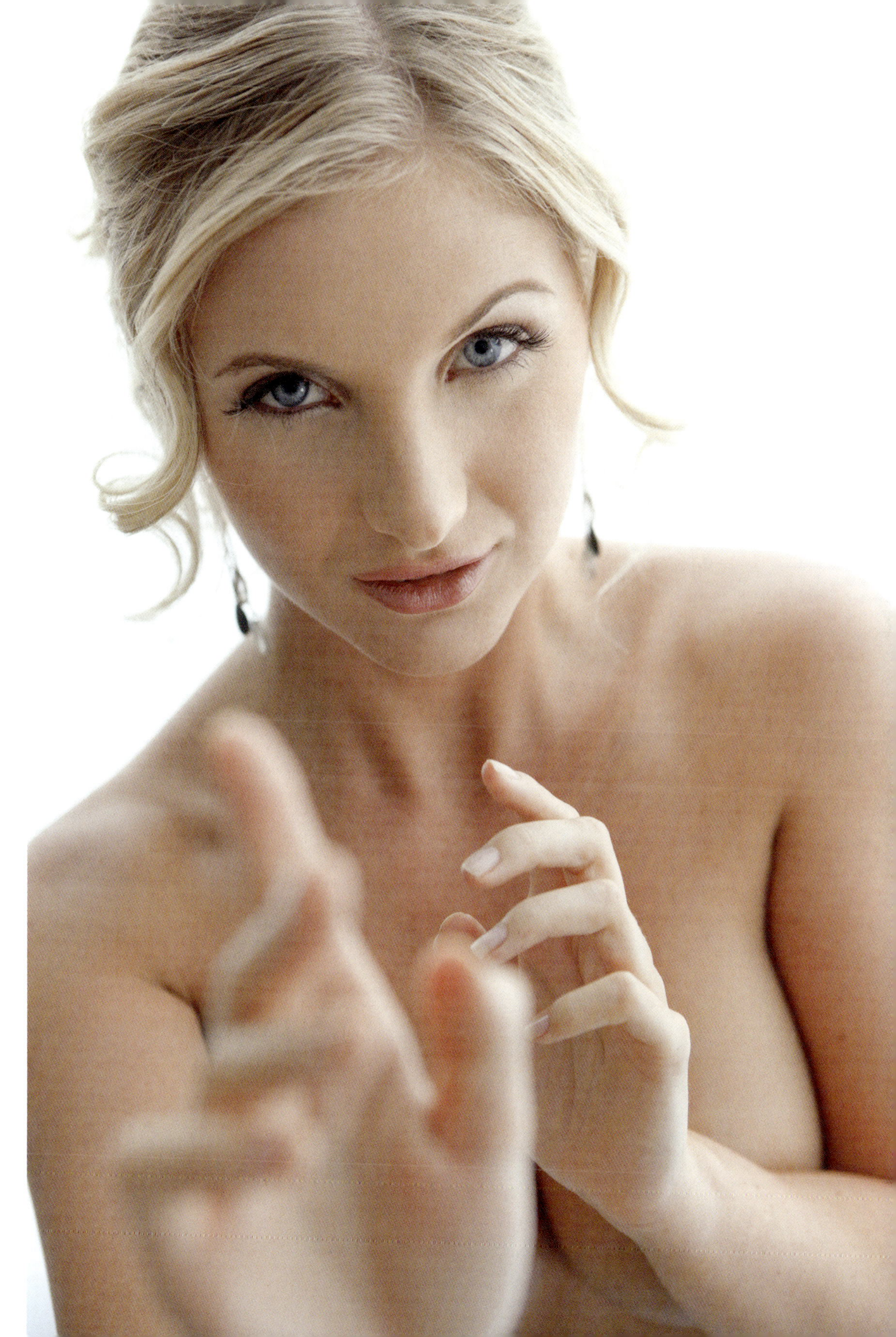

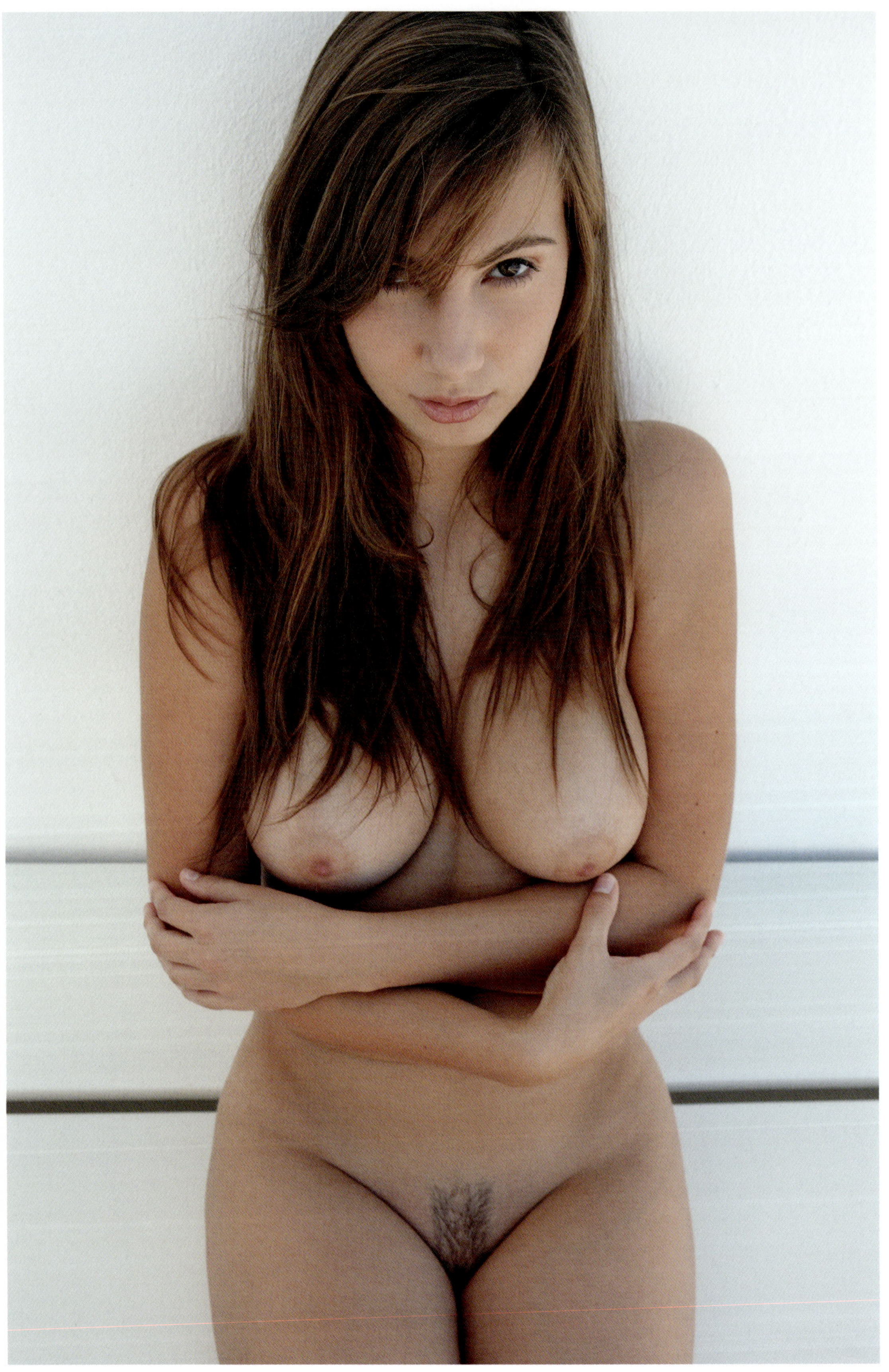

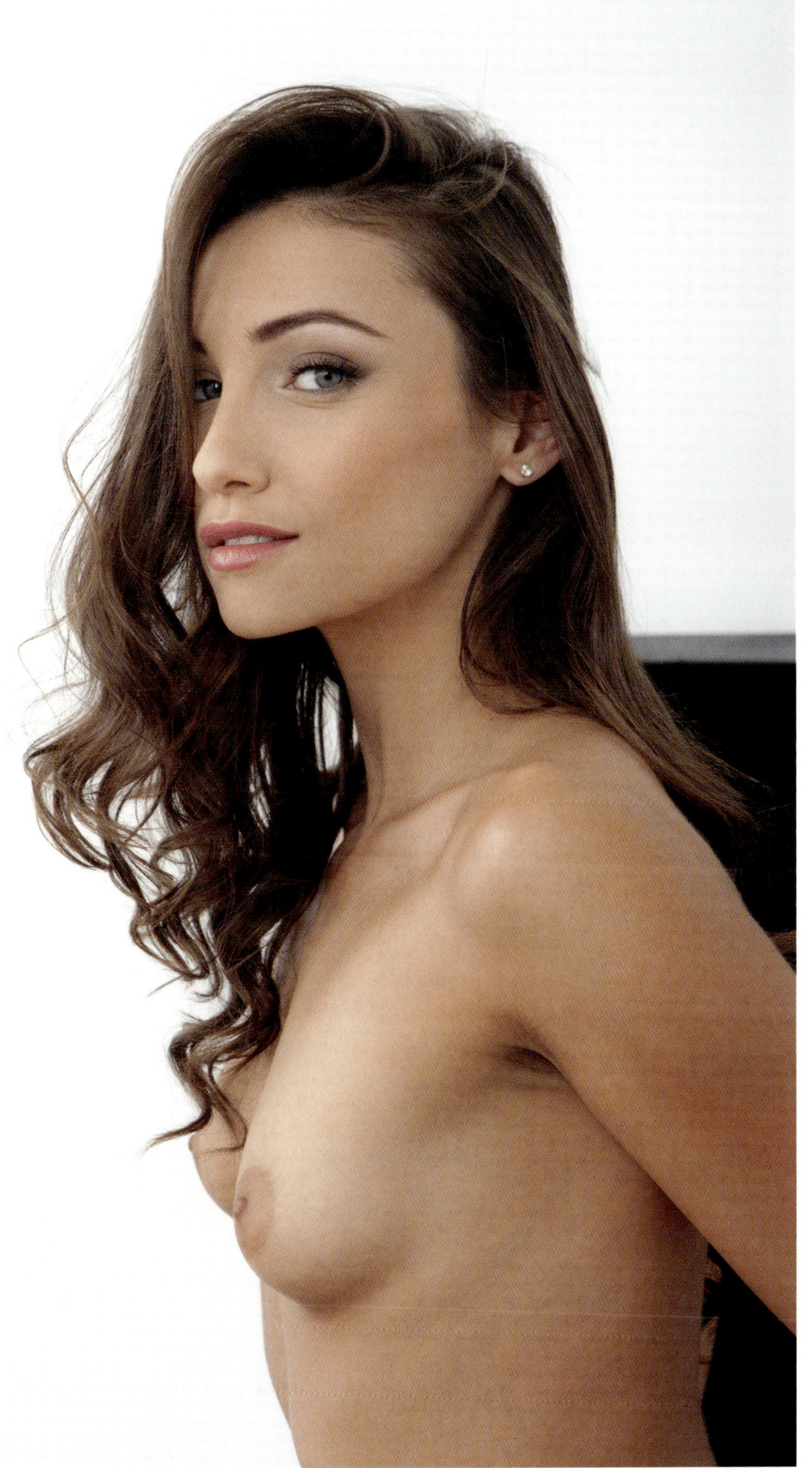

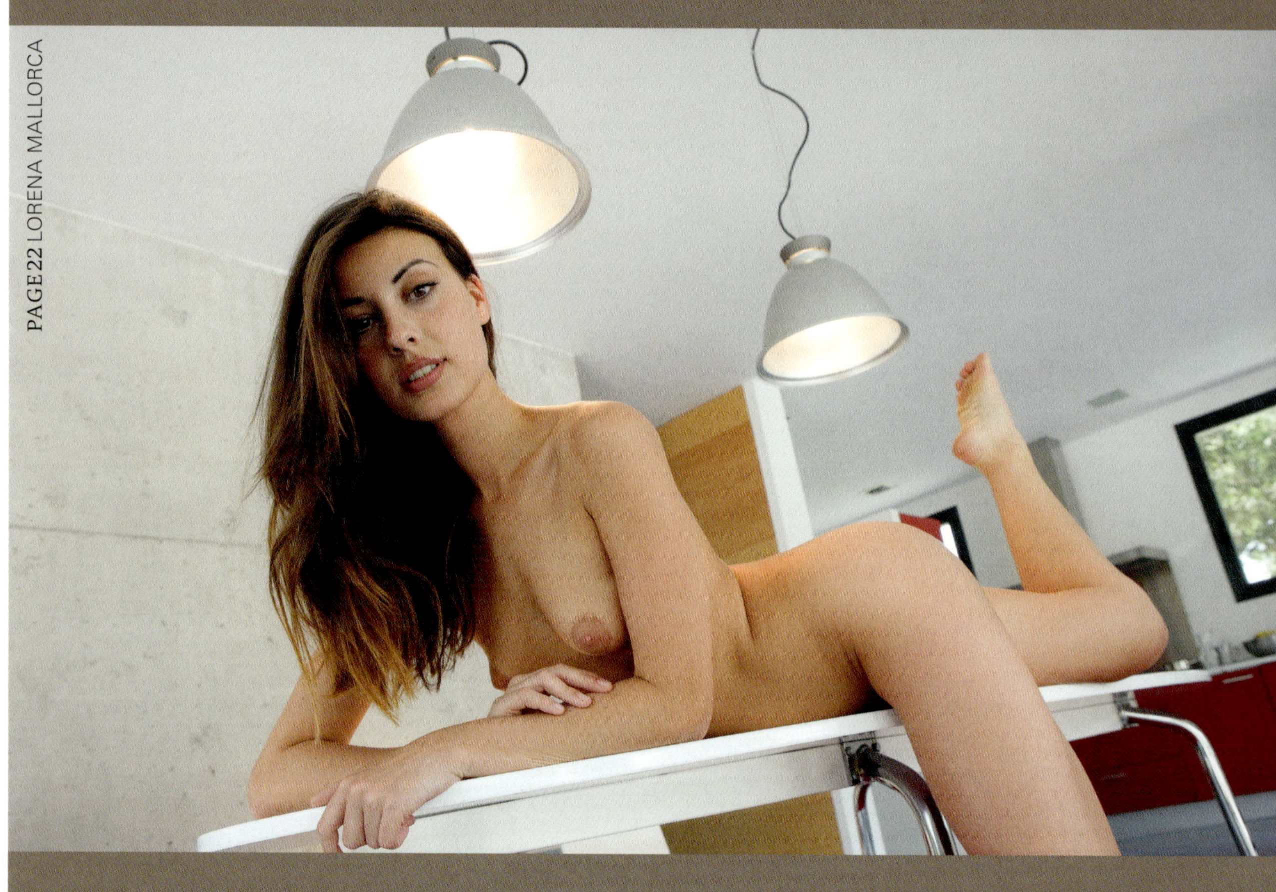

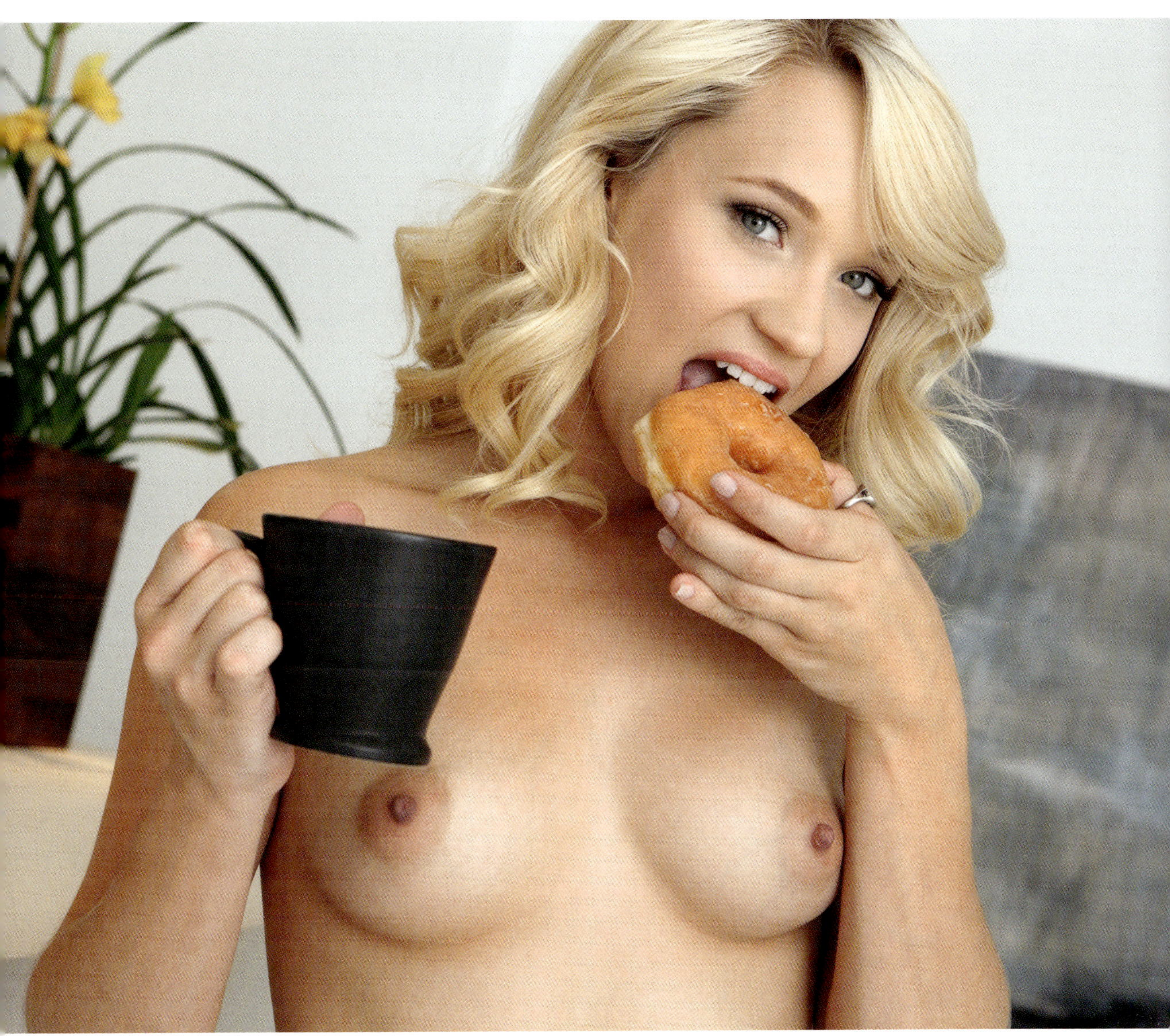

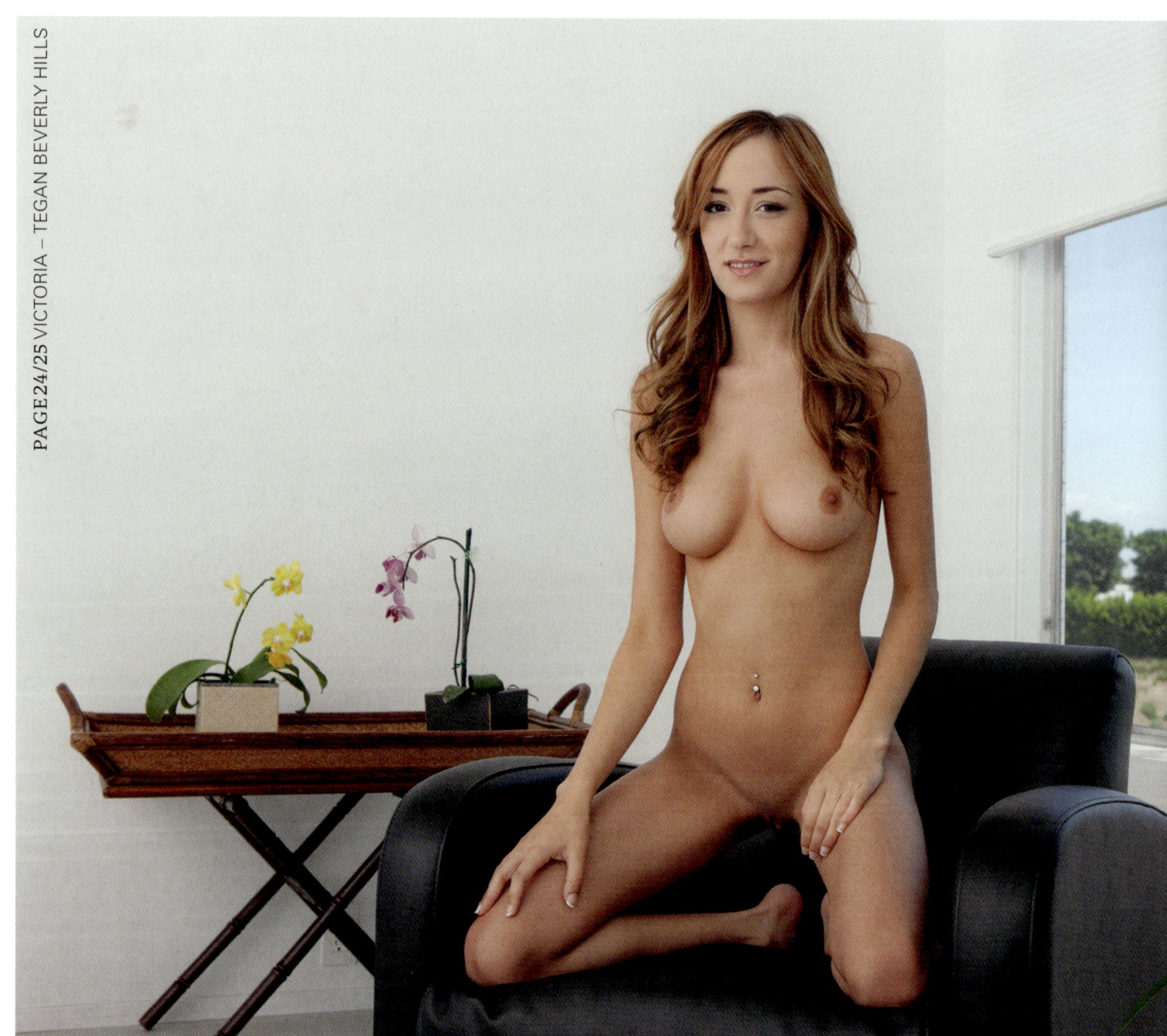

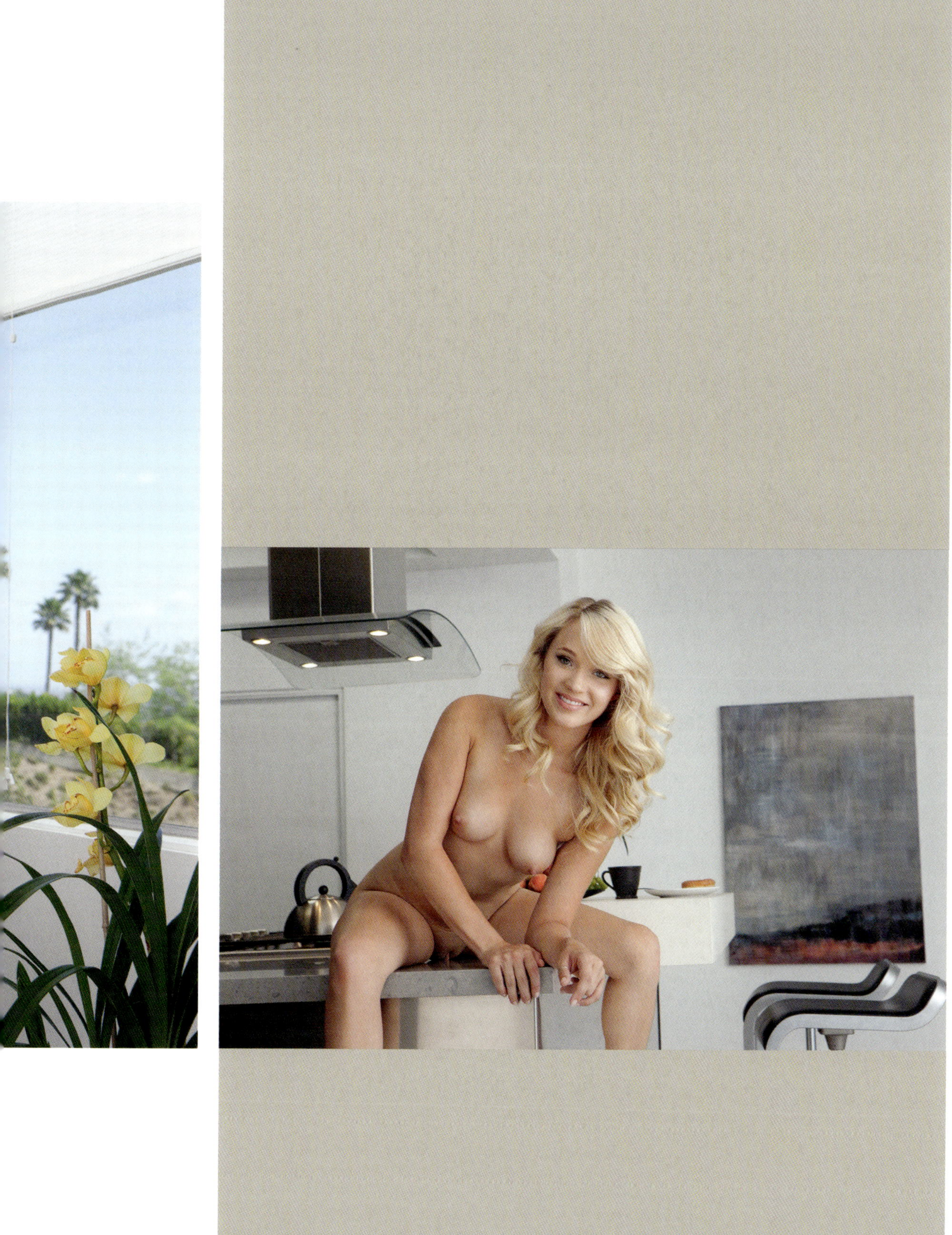

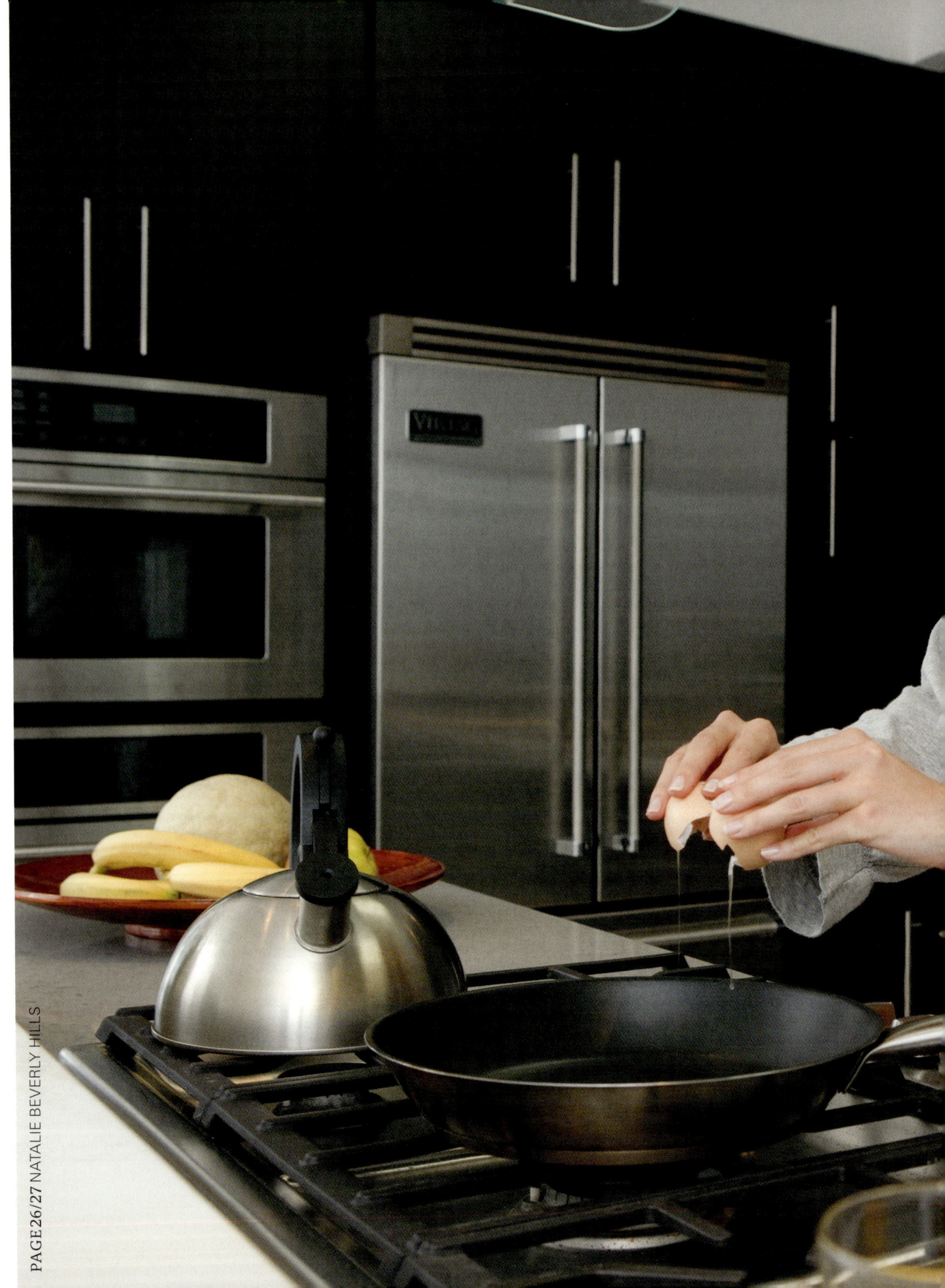

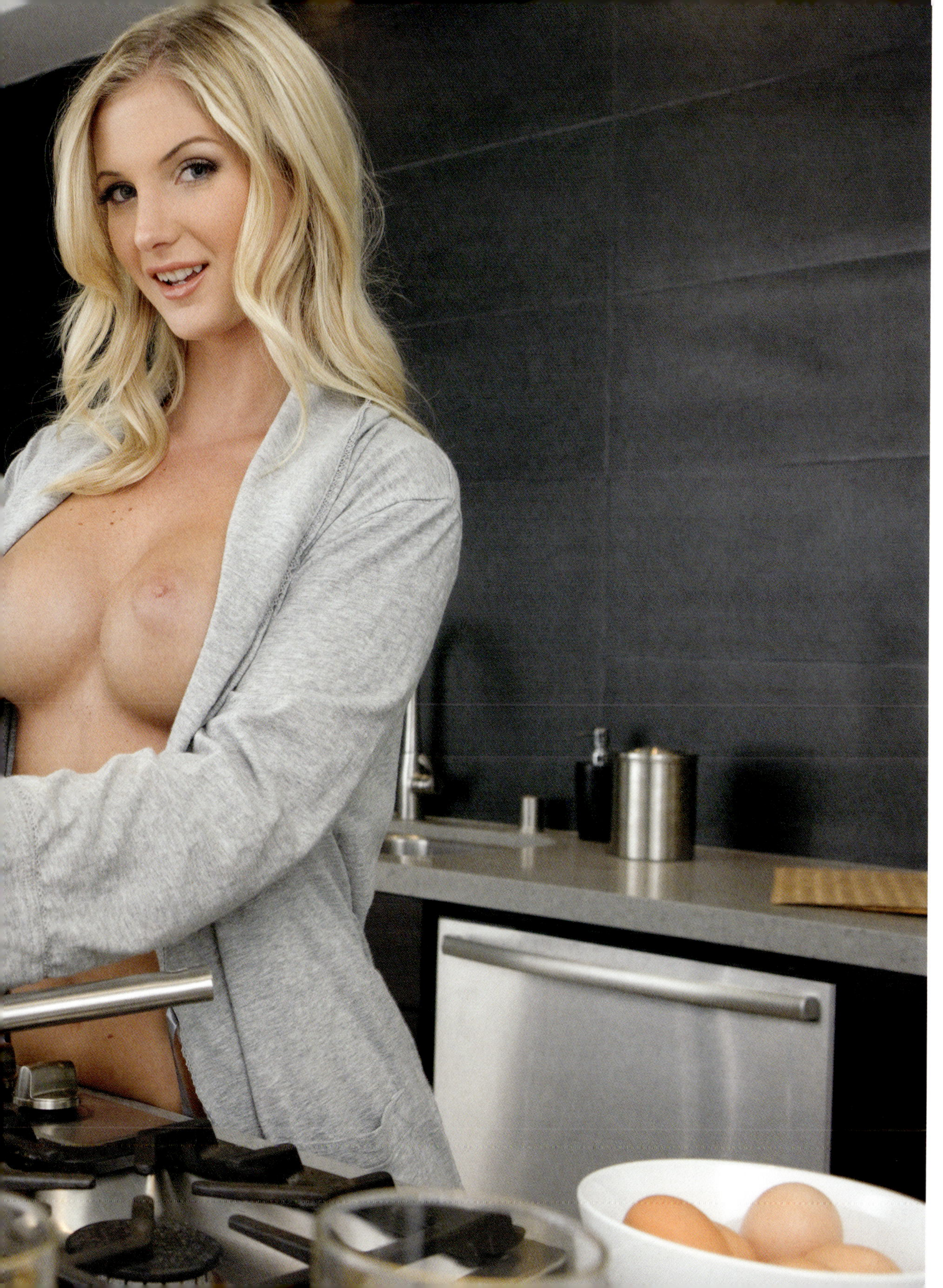

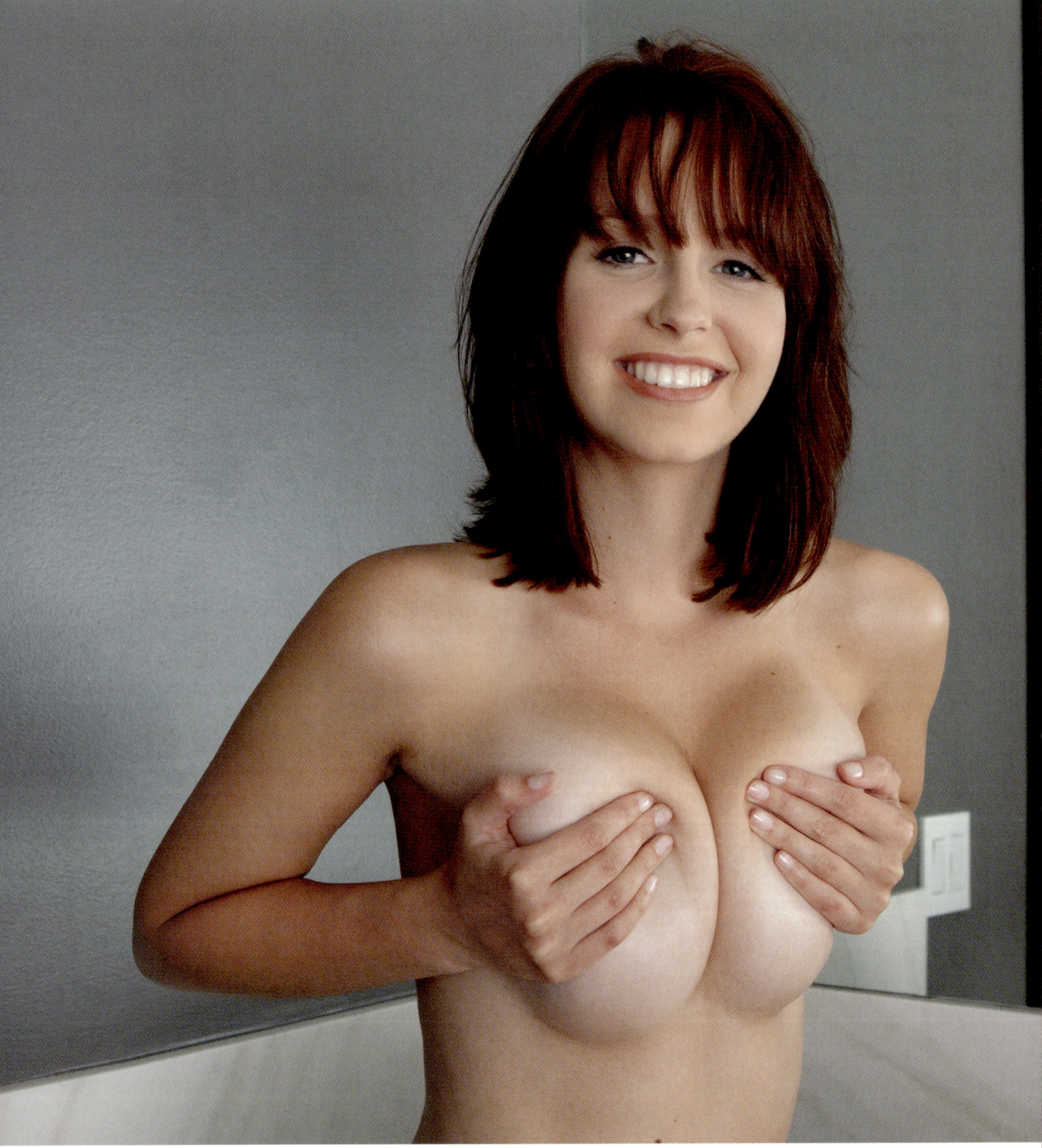

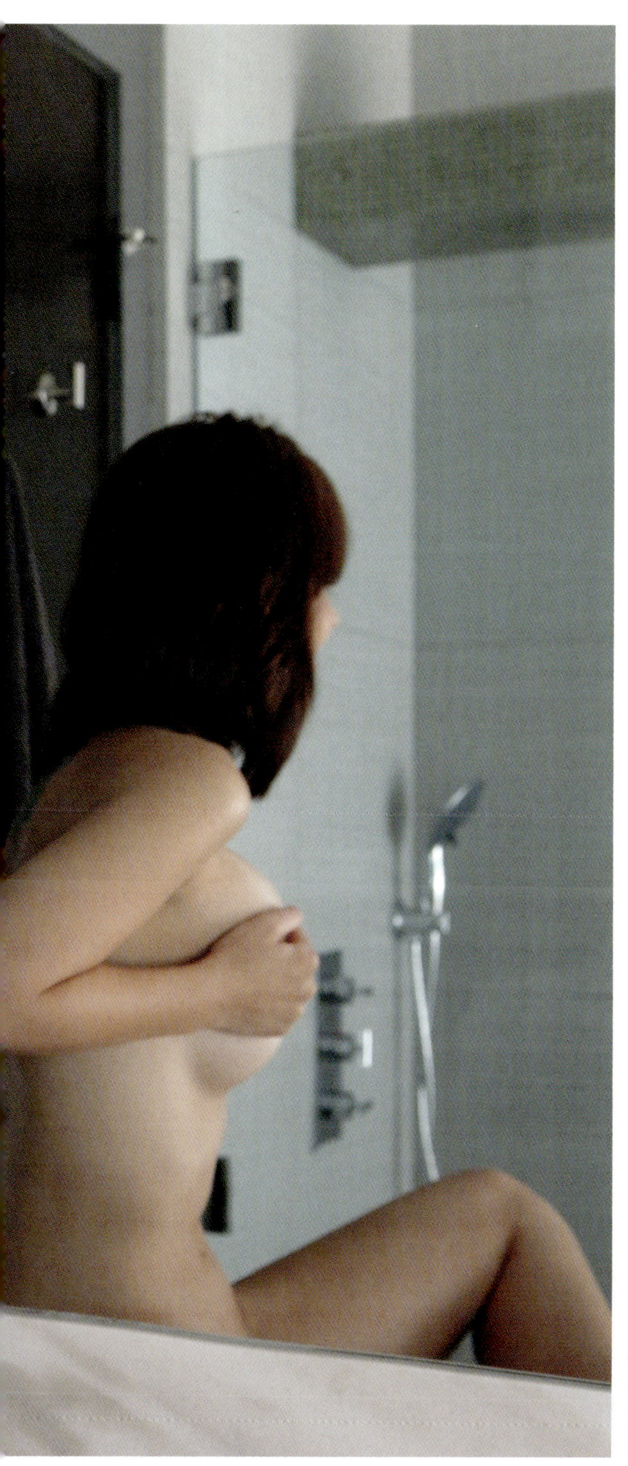

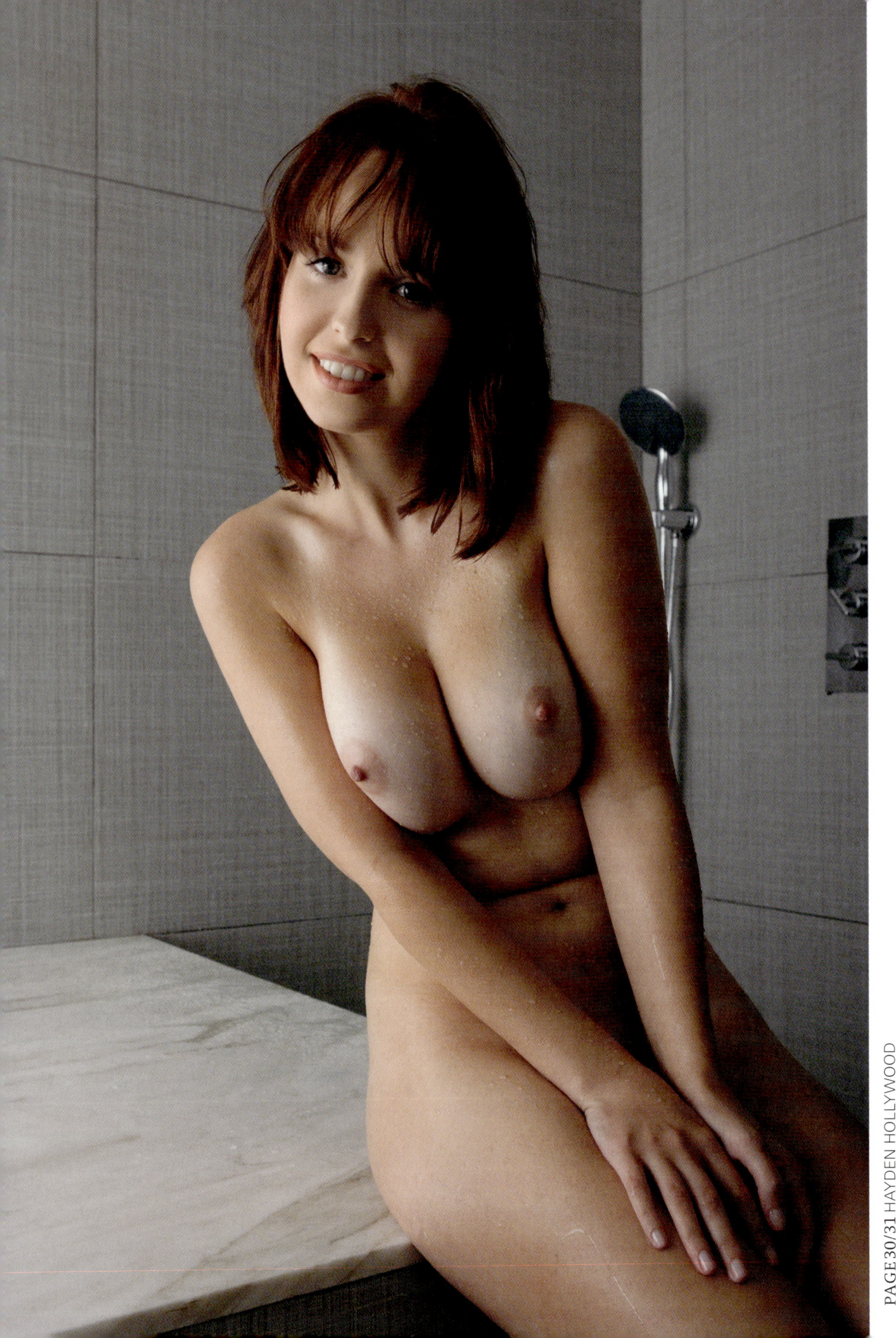

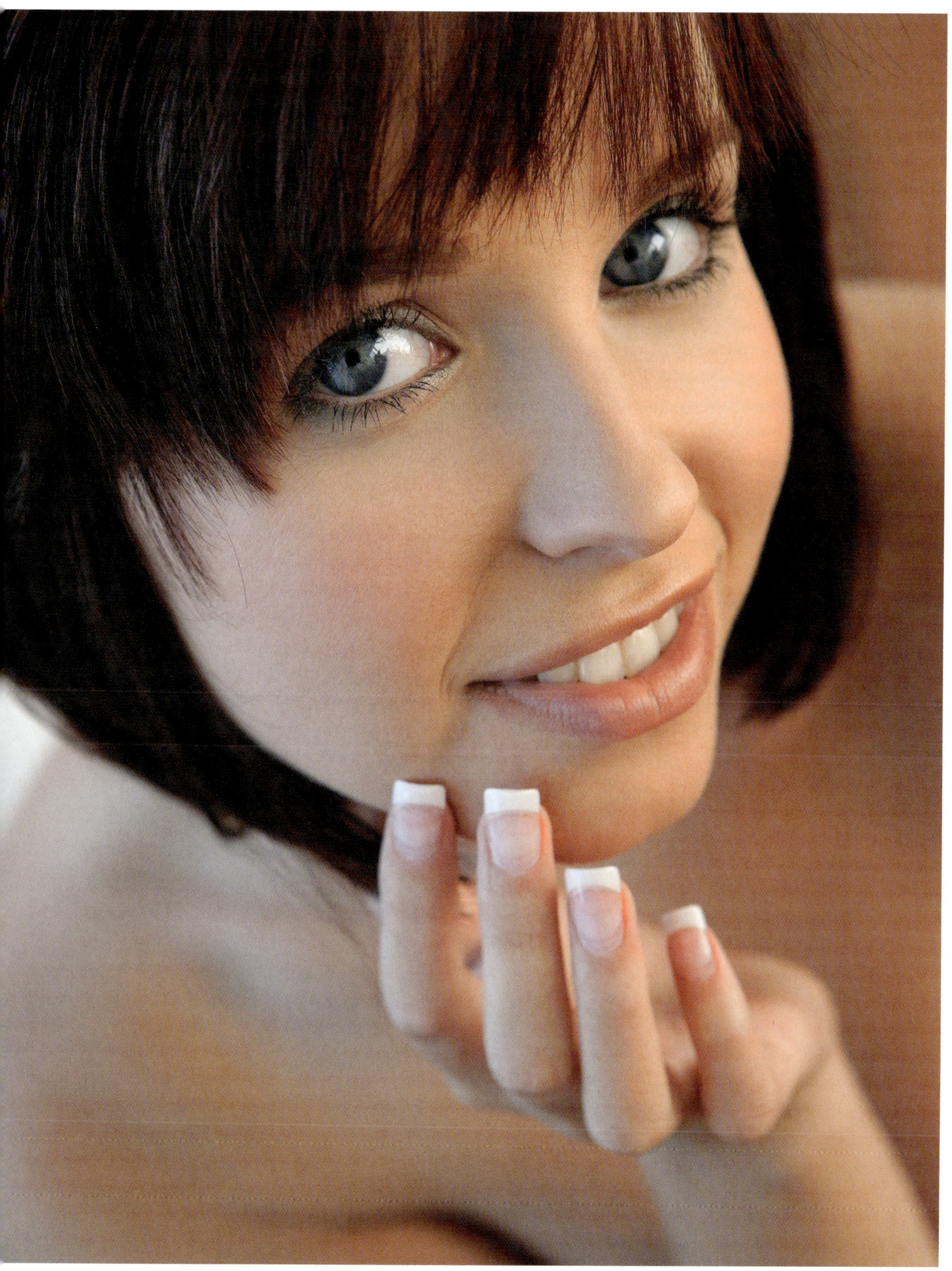

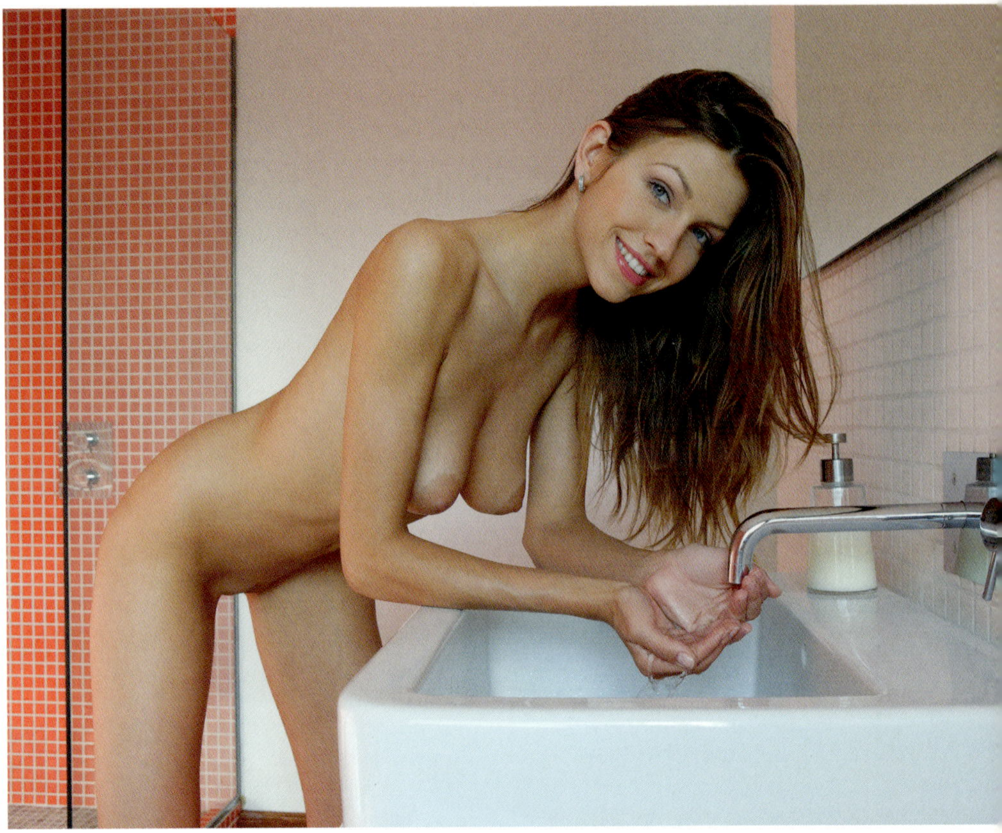

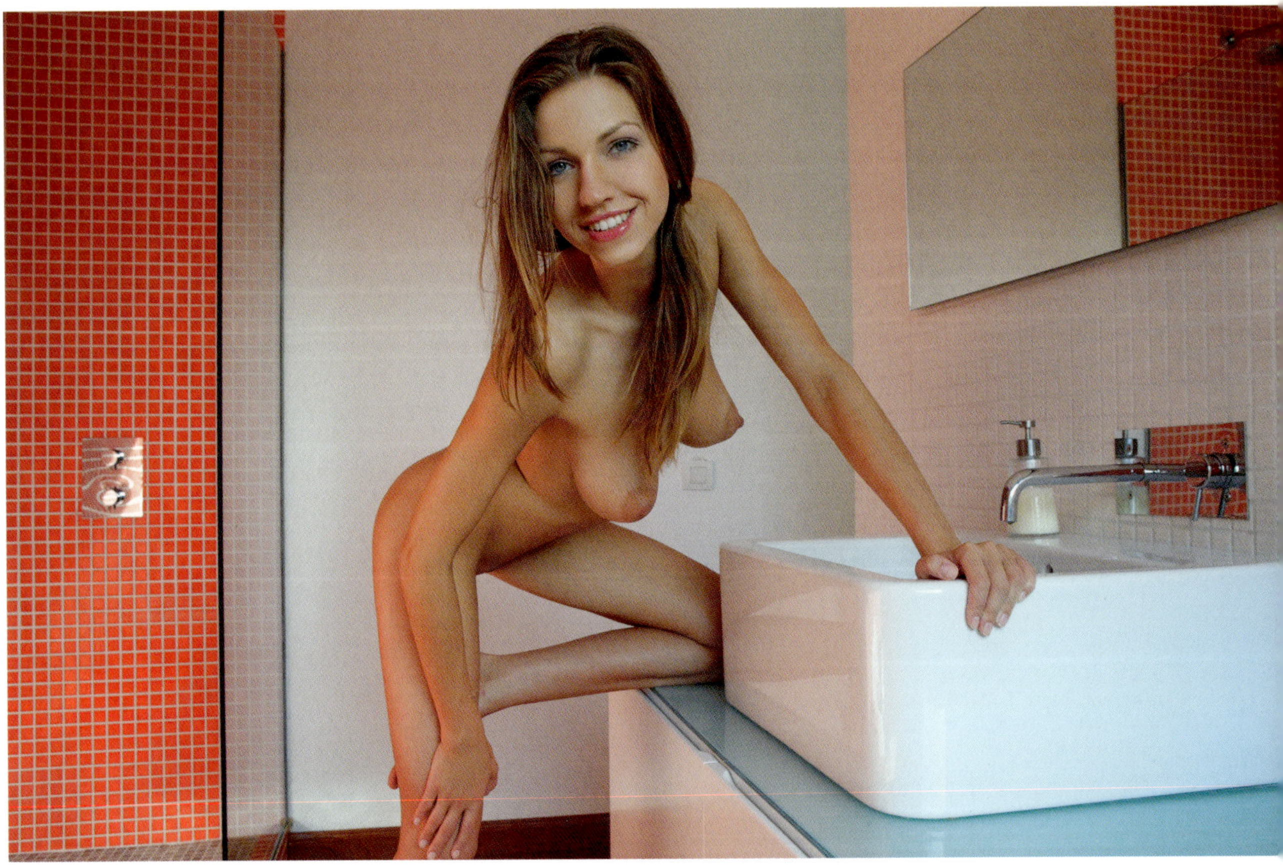

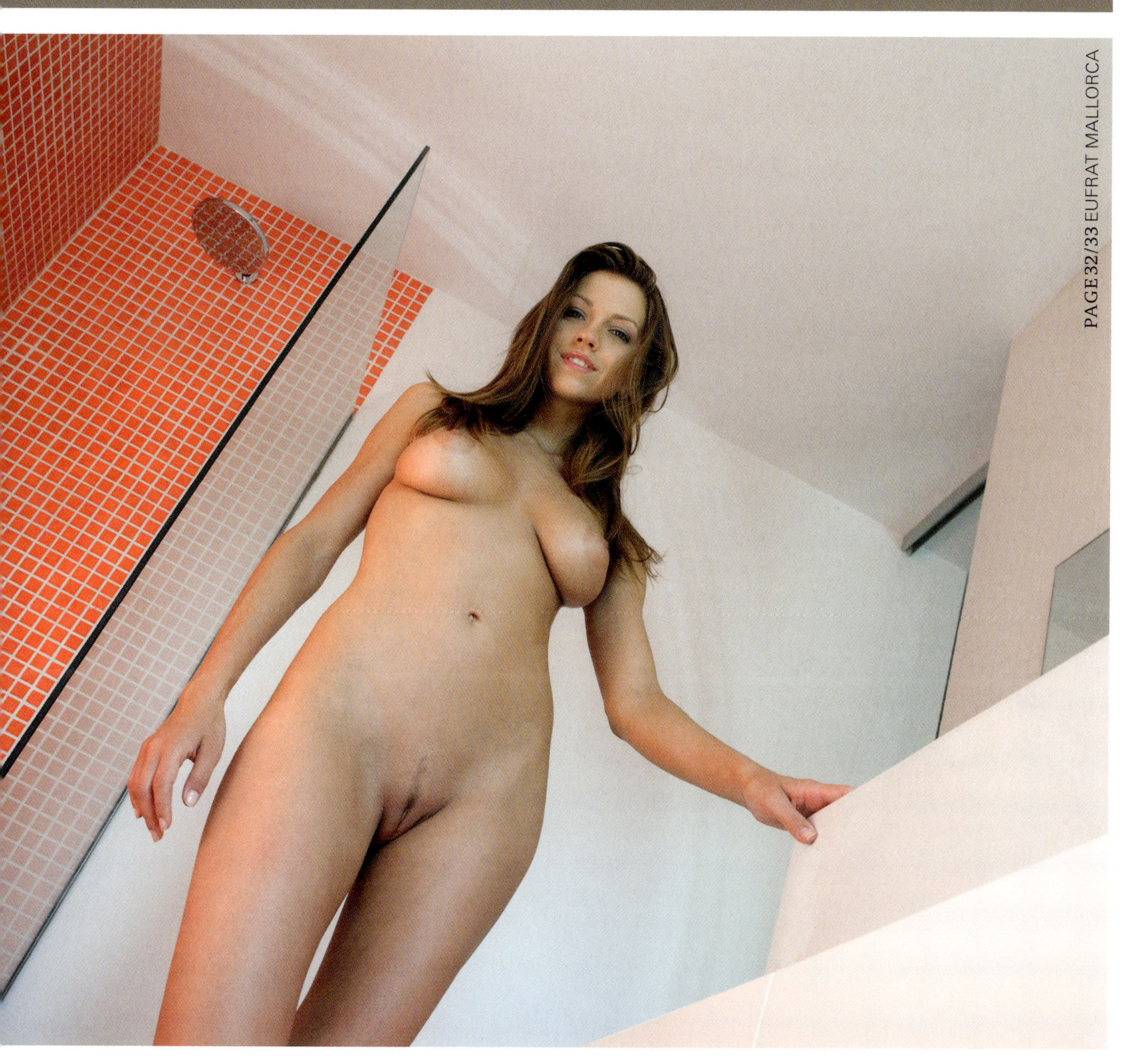

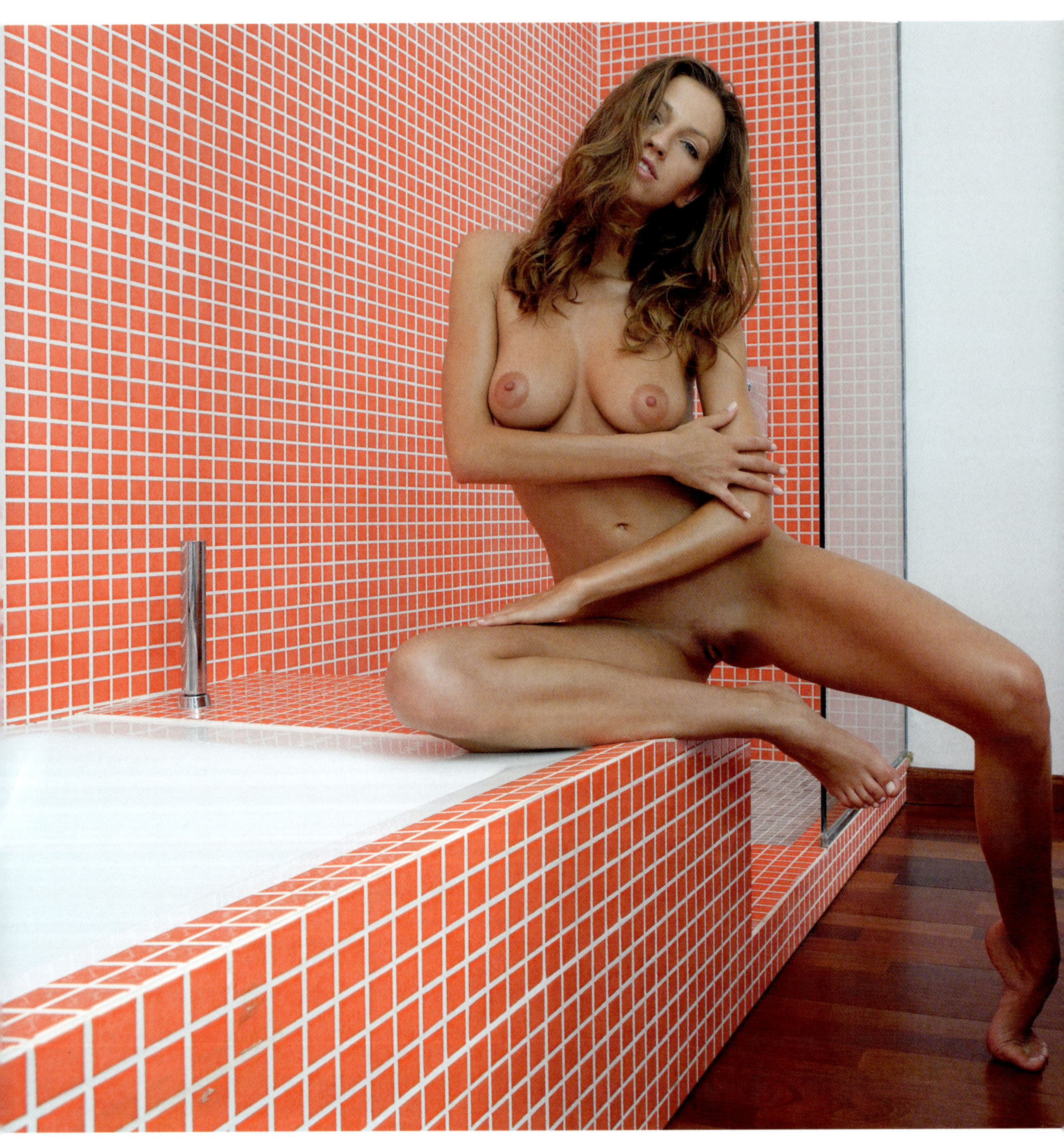

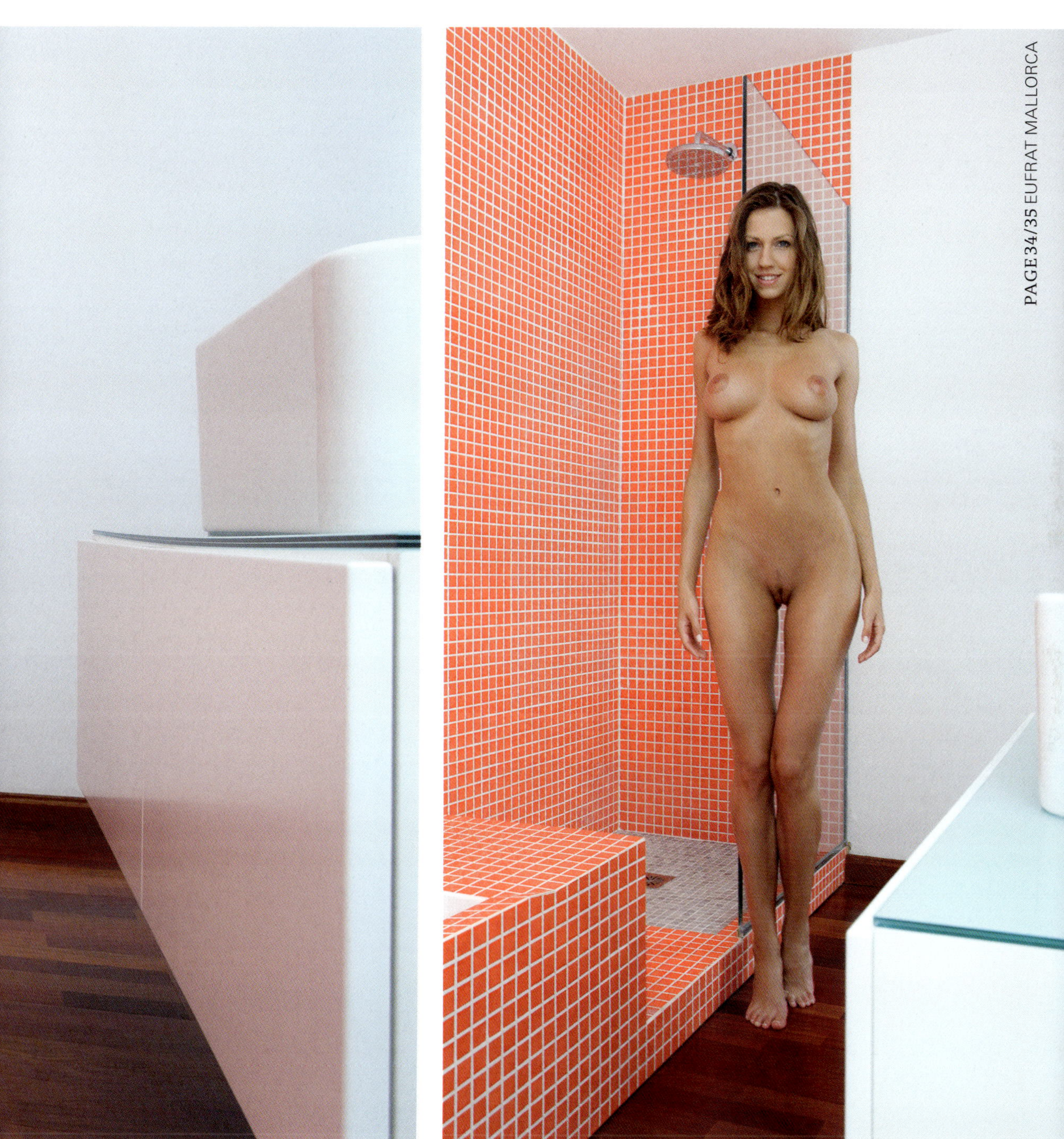

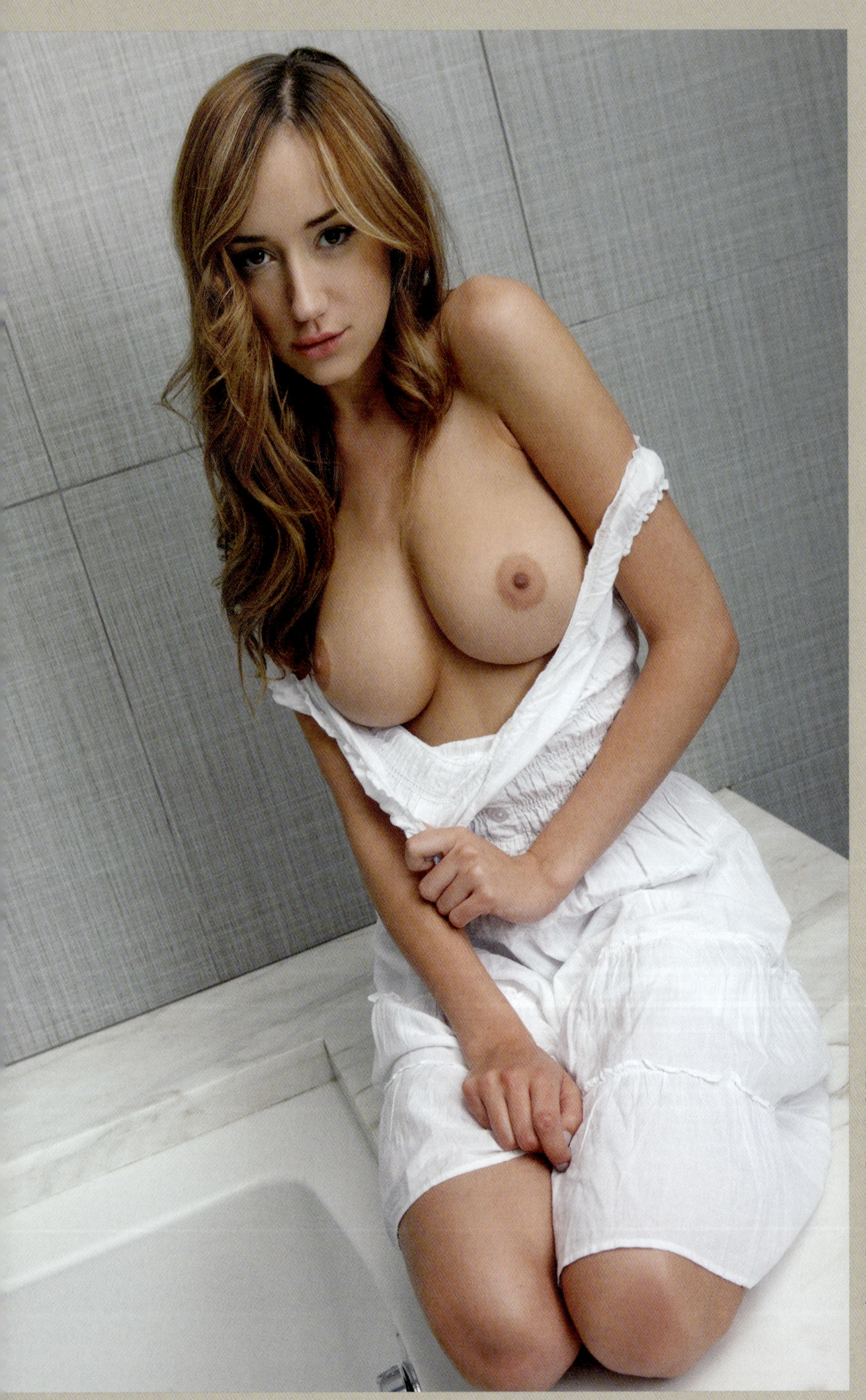

PAGE 36/37 VICTORIA HOLLYWOOD

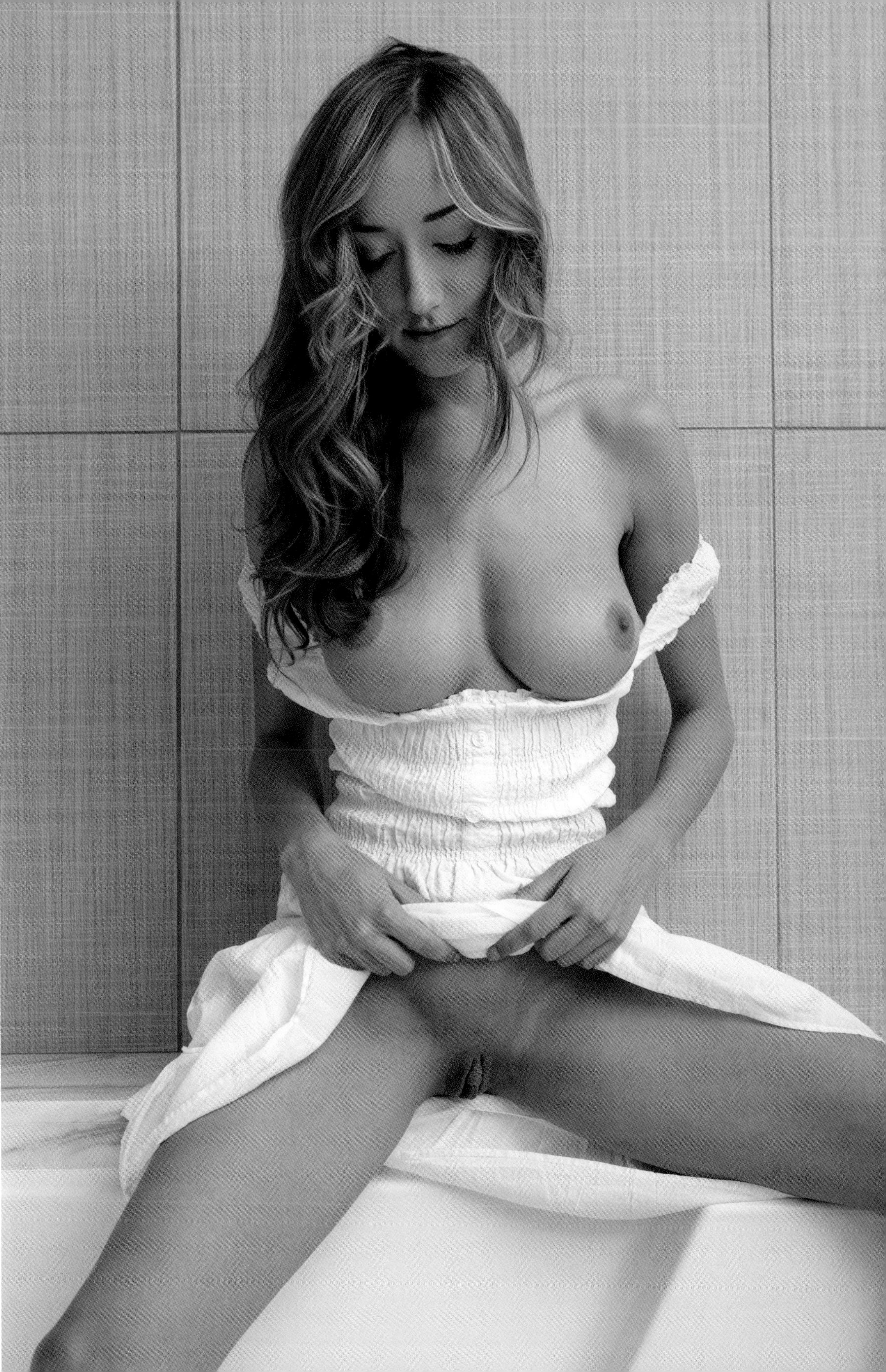

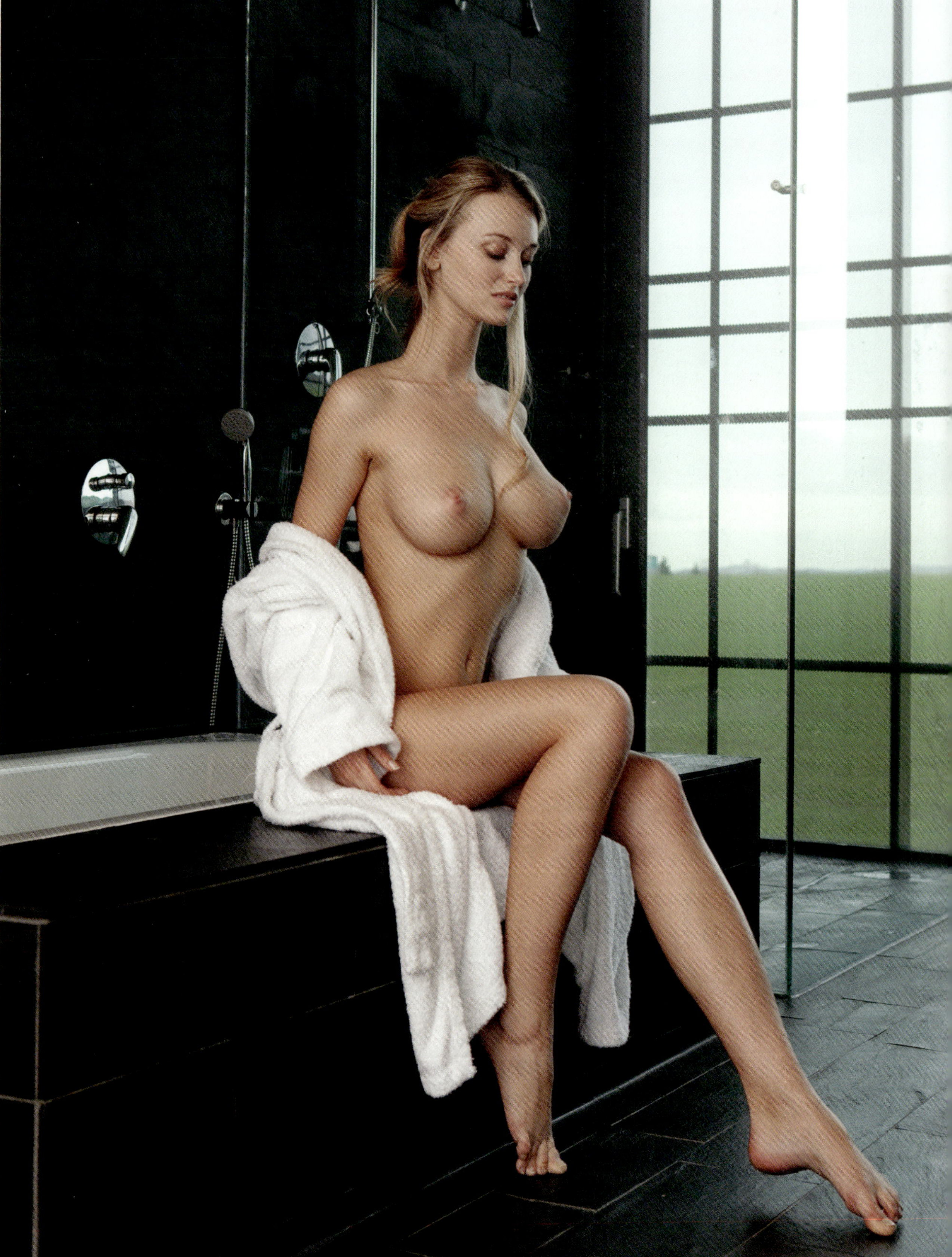

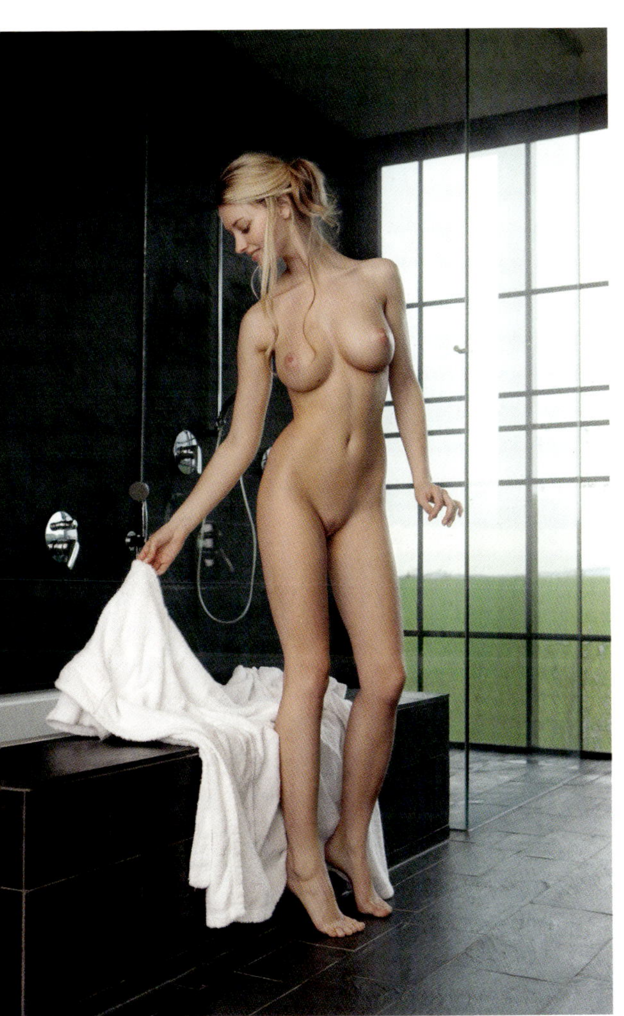
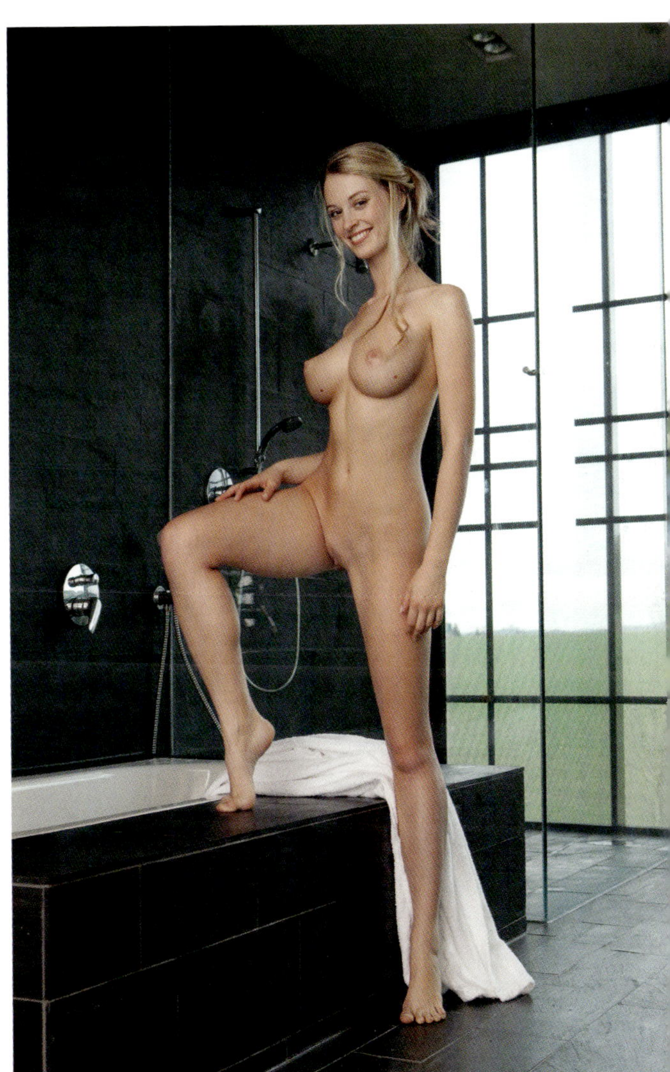

PAGE 38/39 CARISHA BAD WALDSEE SOUTH GERMANY

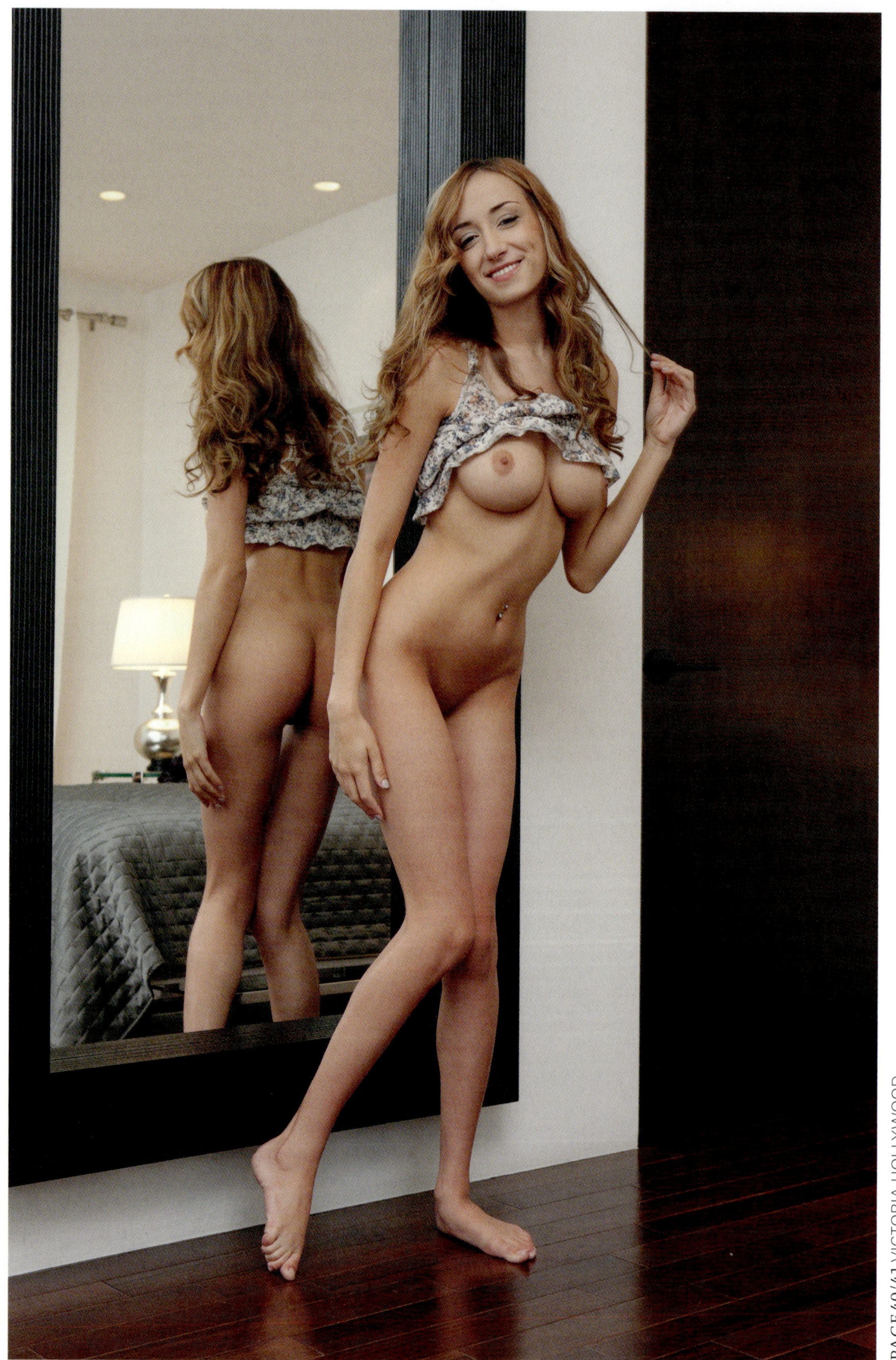

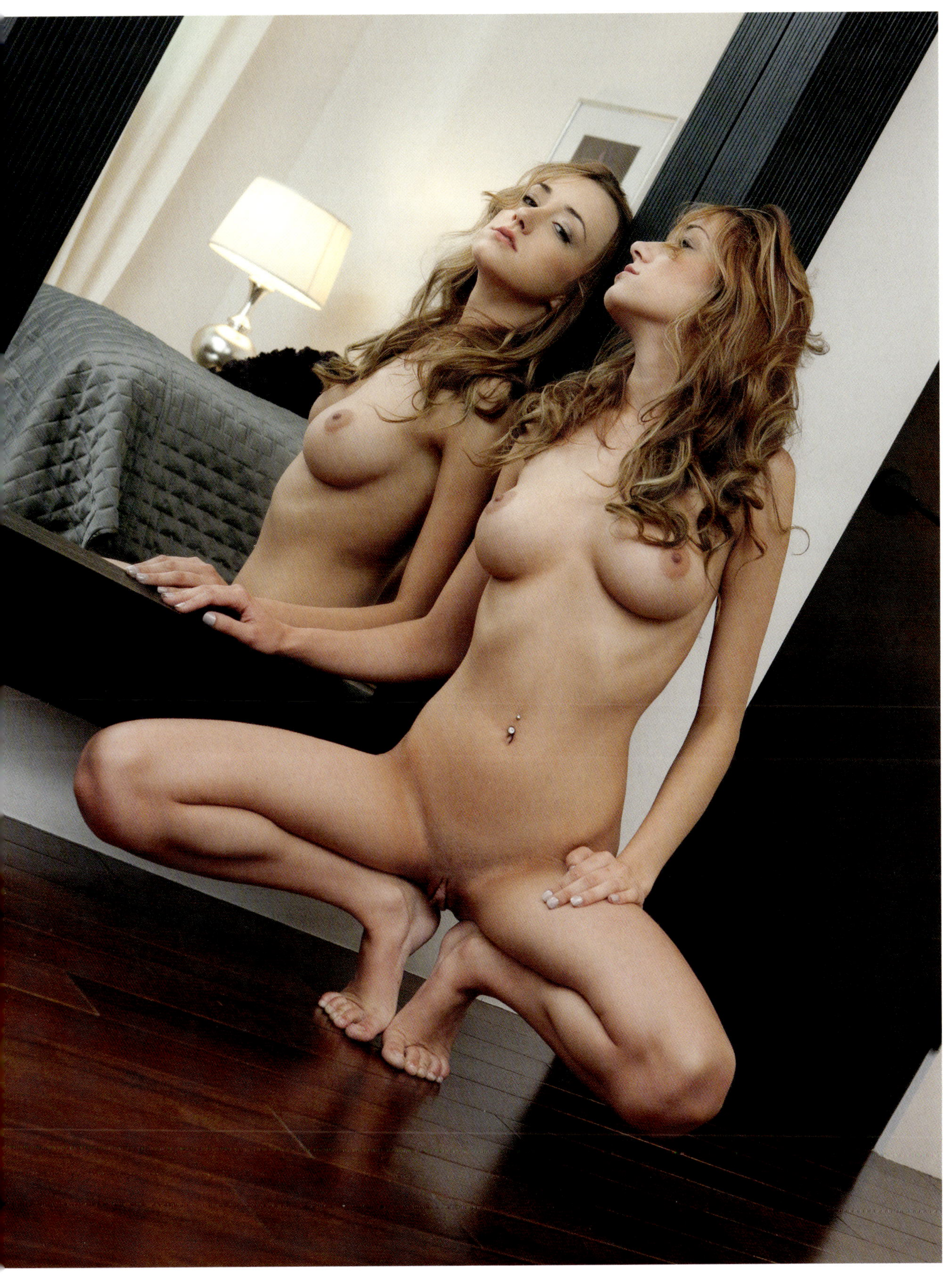

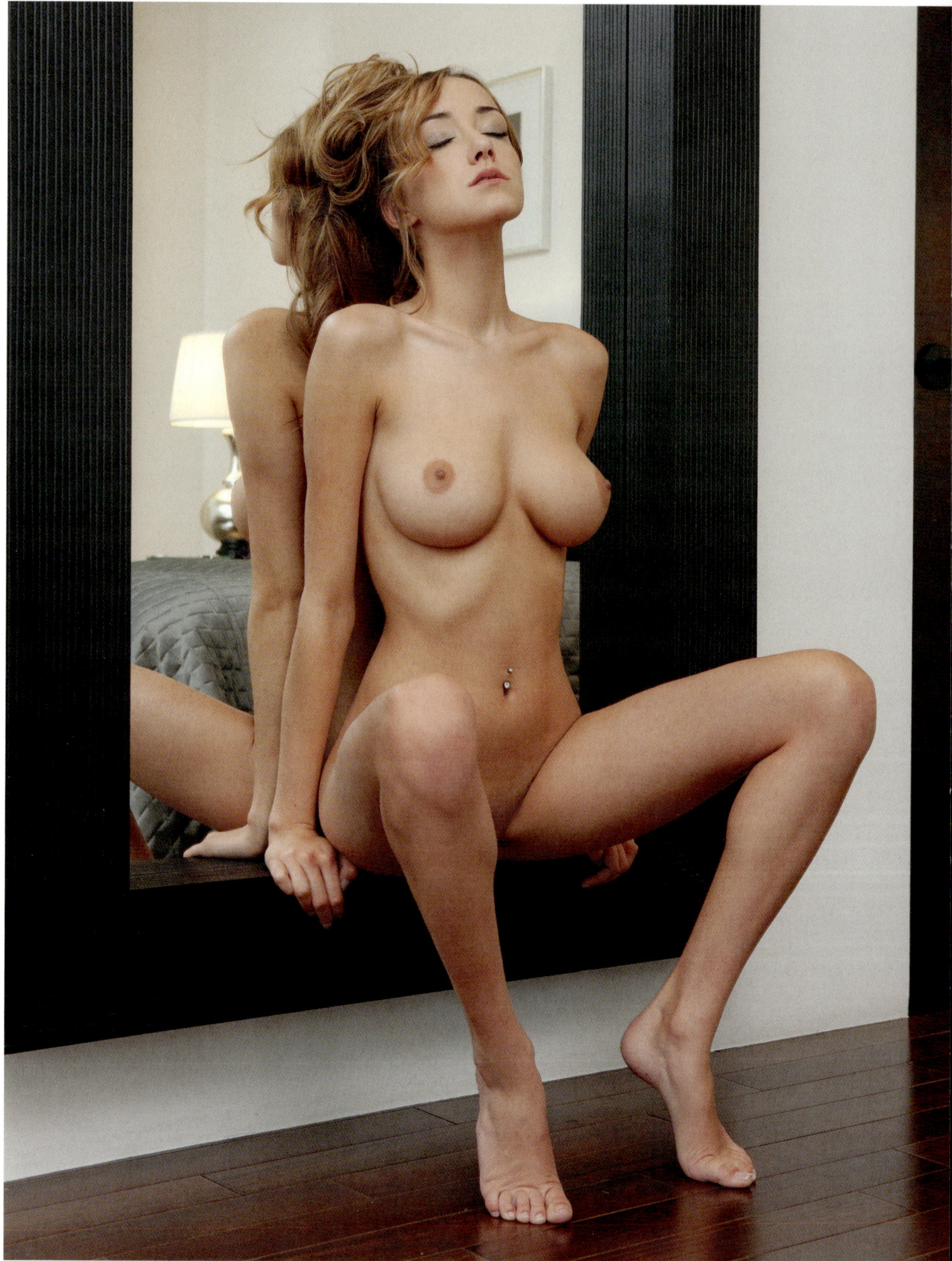

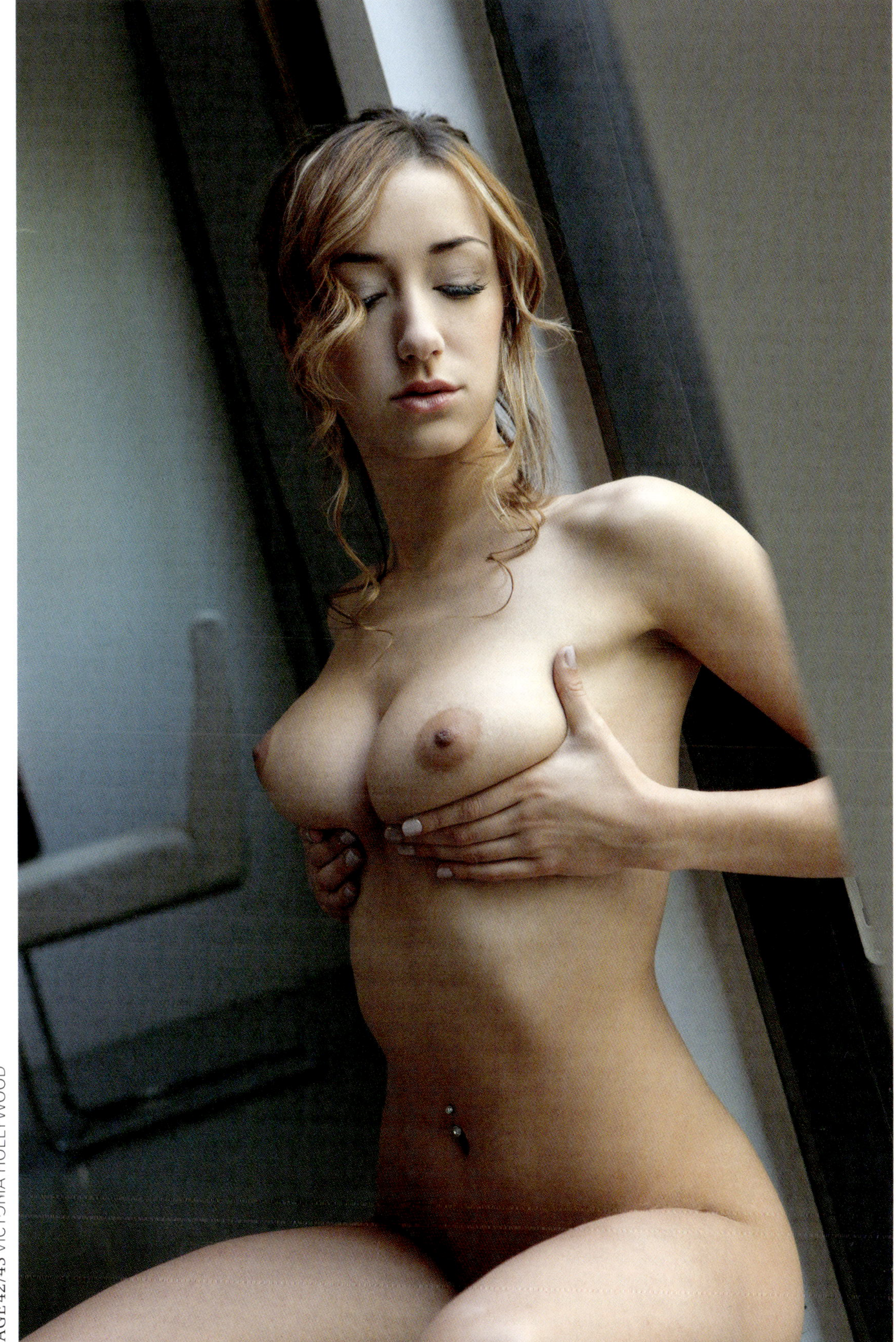

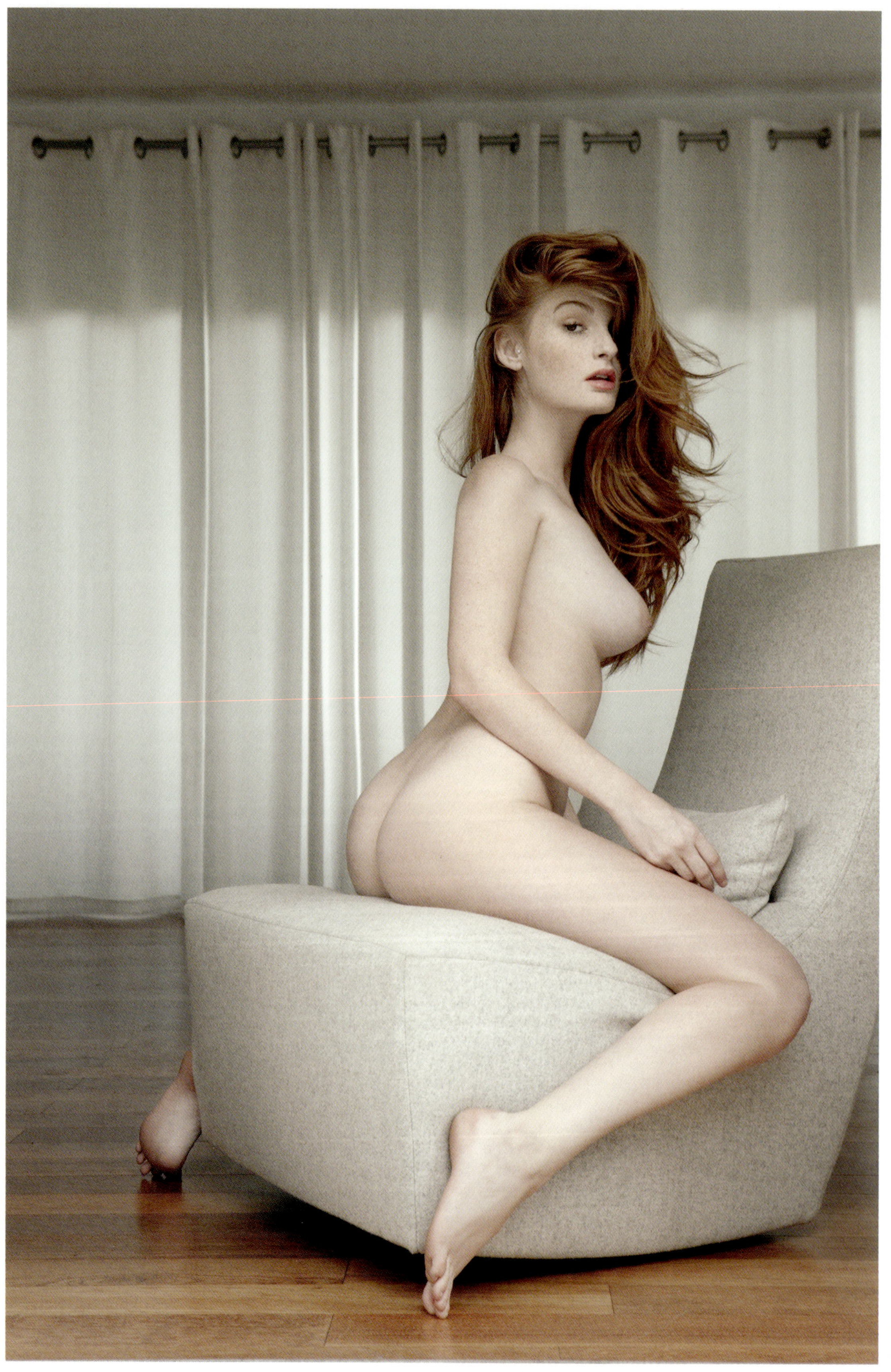

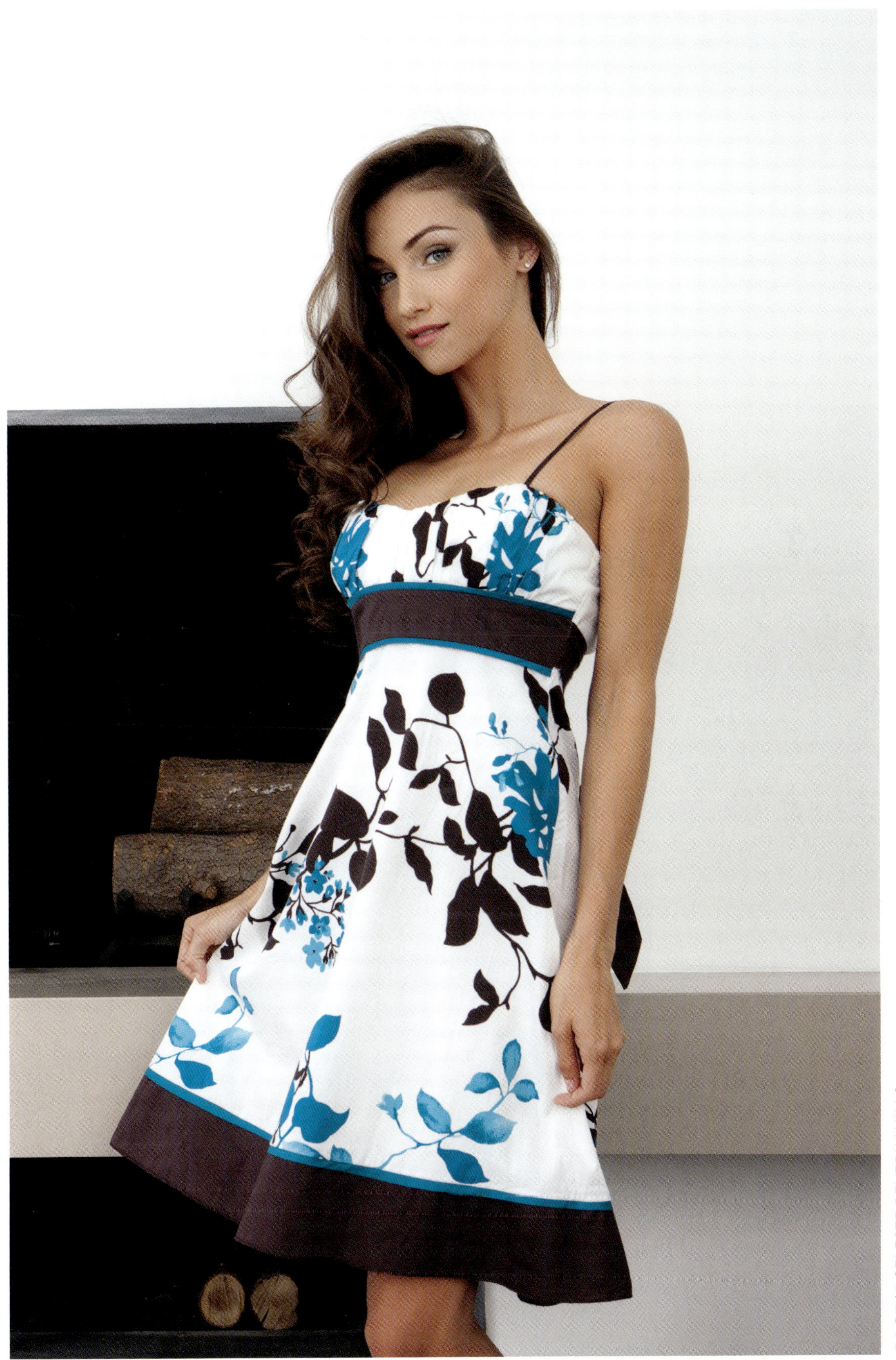

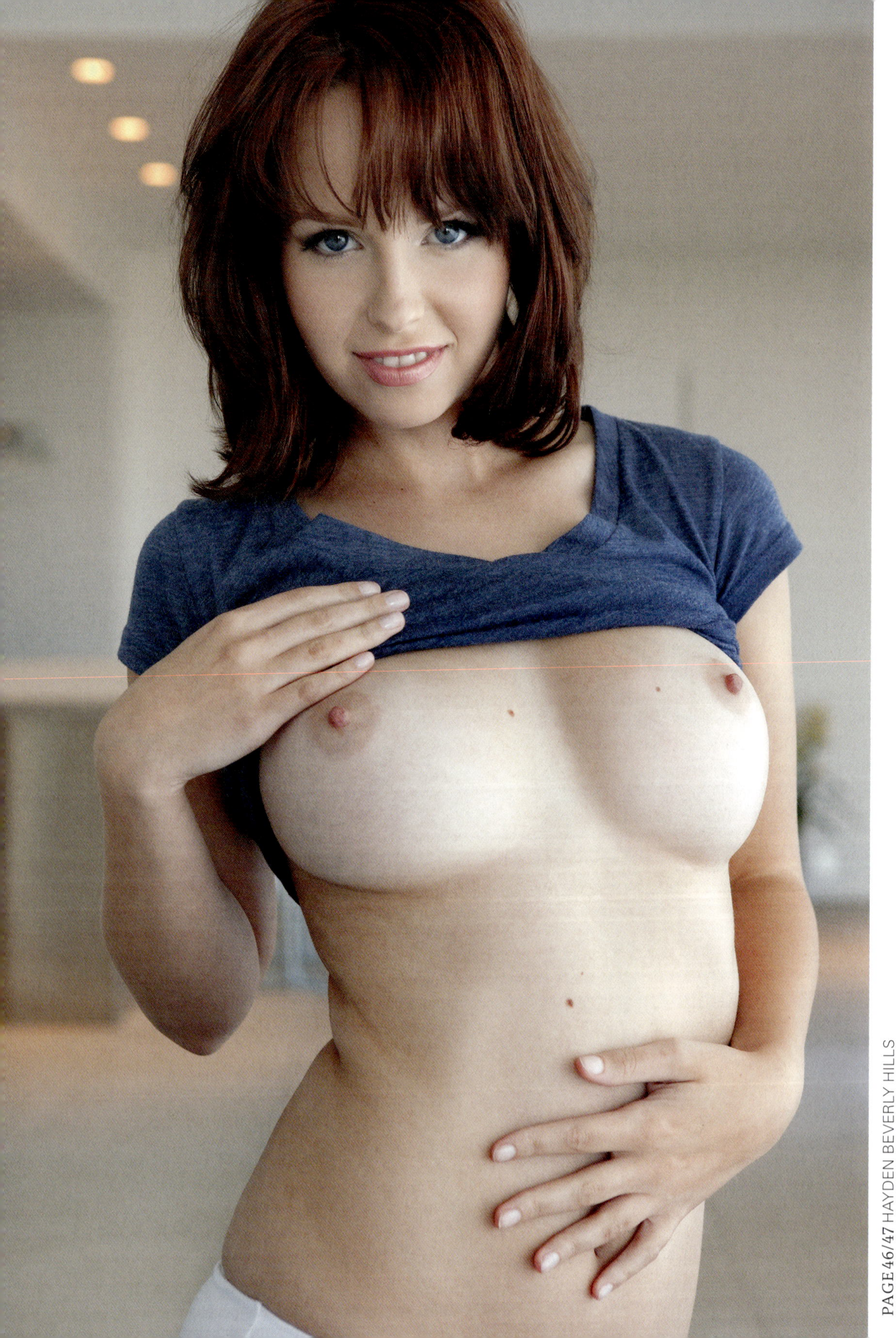

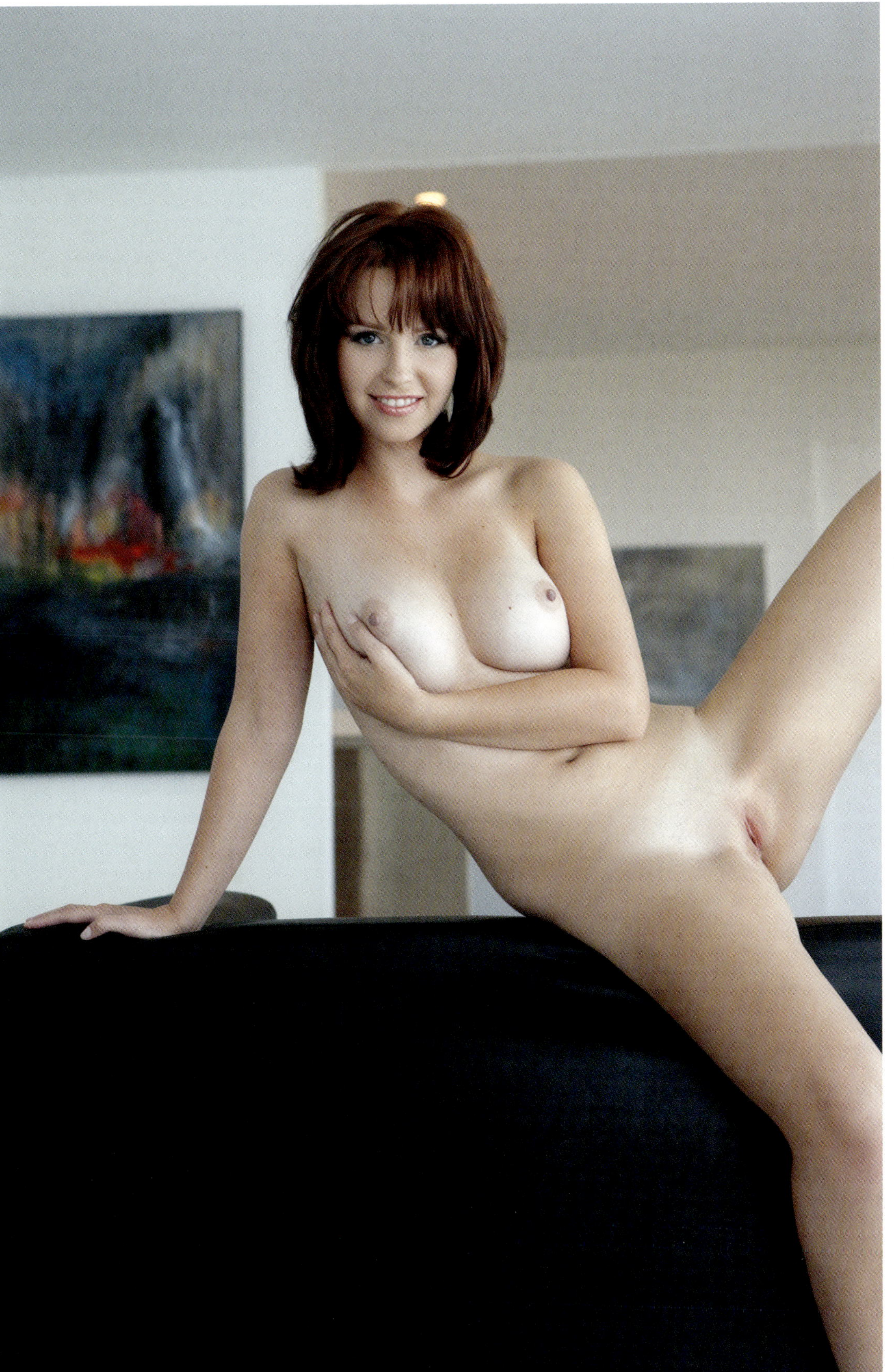

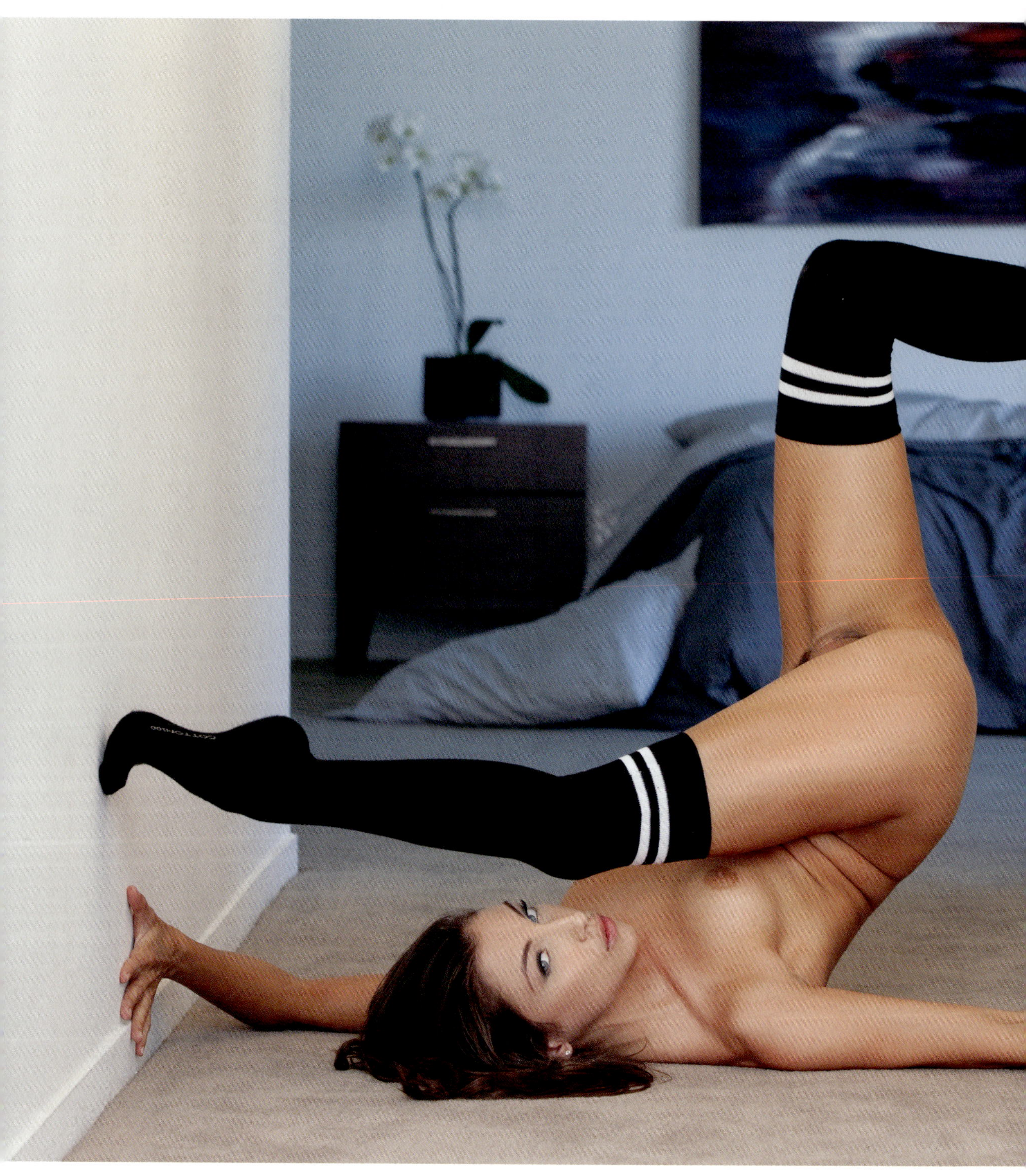

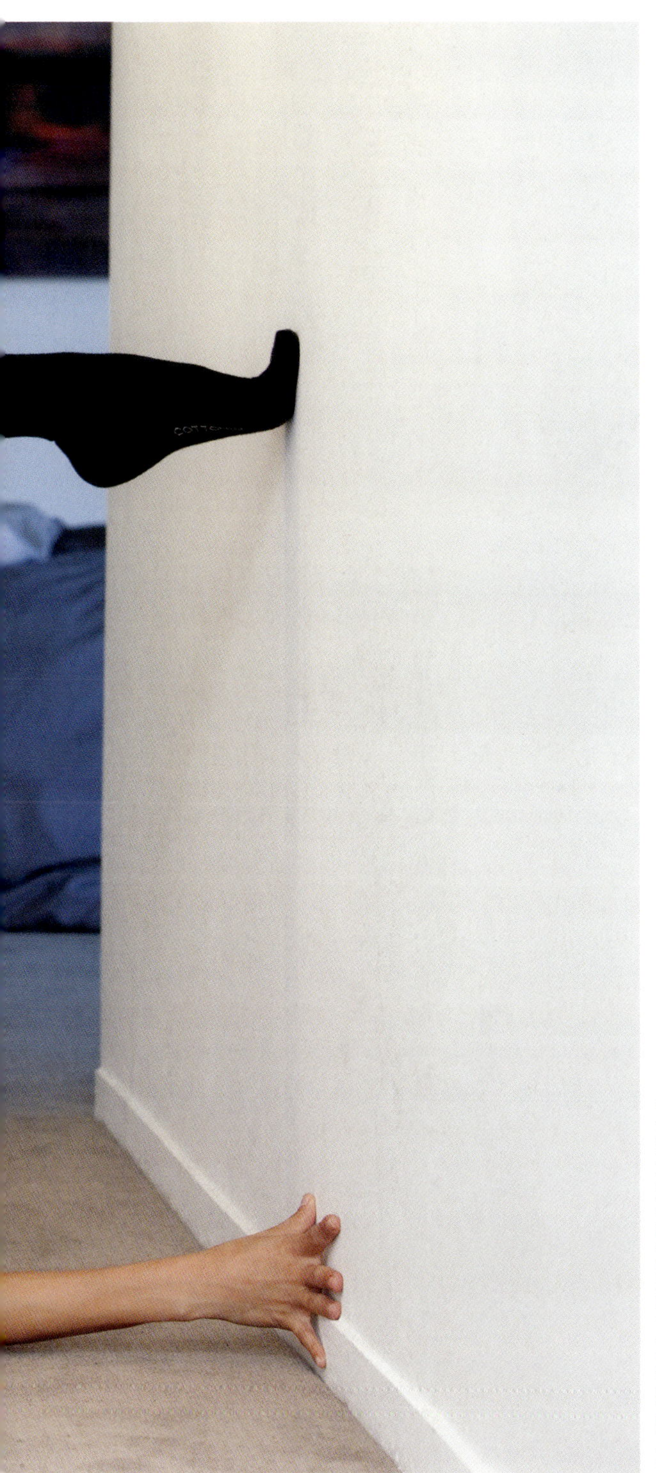

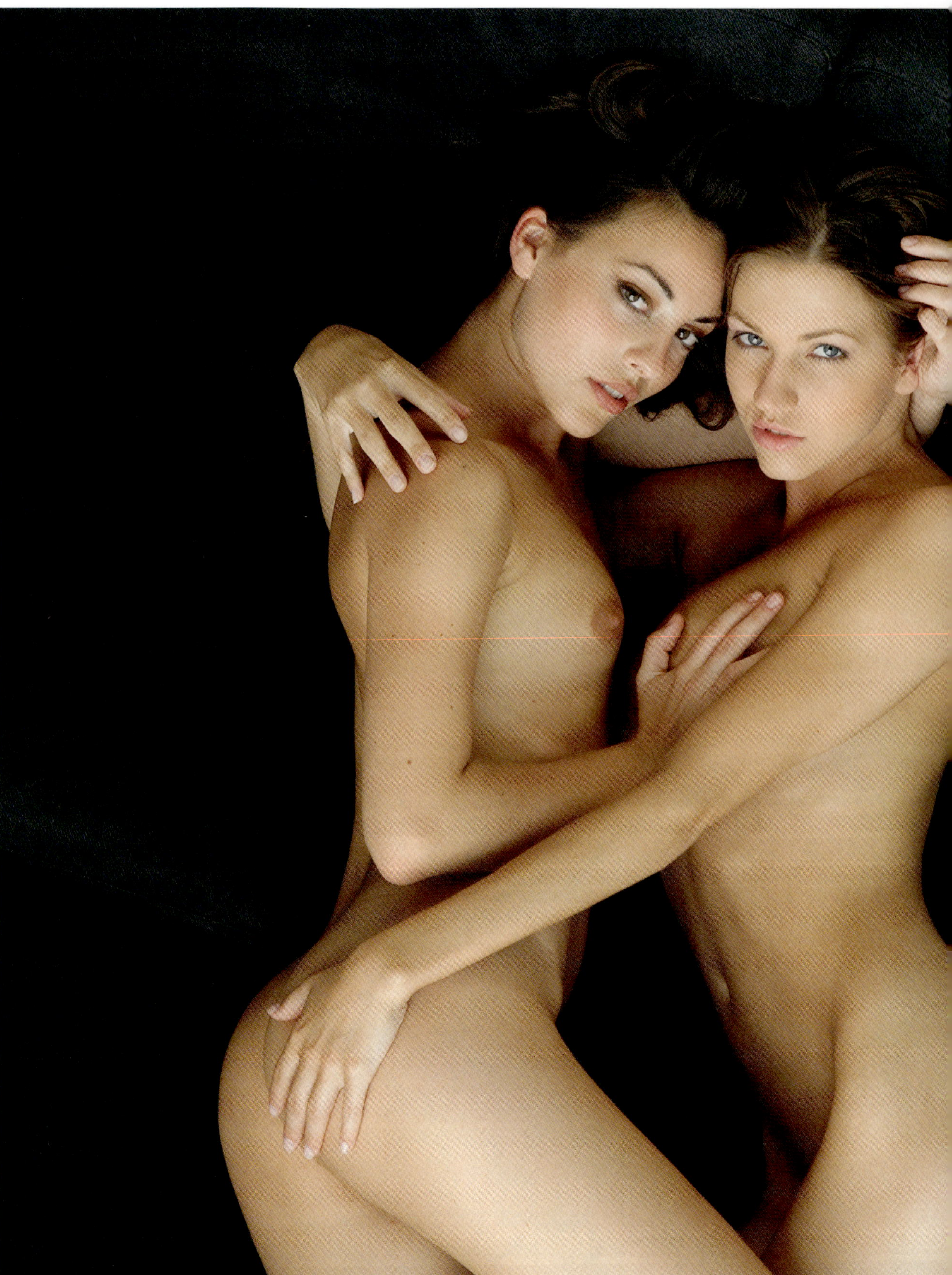

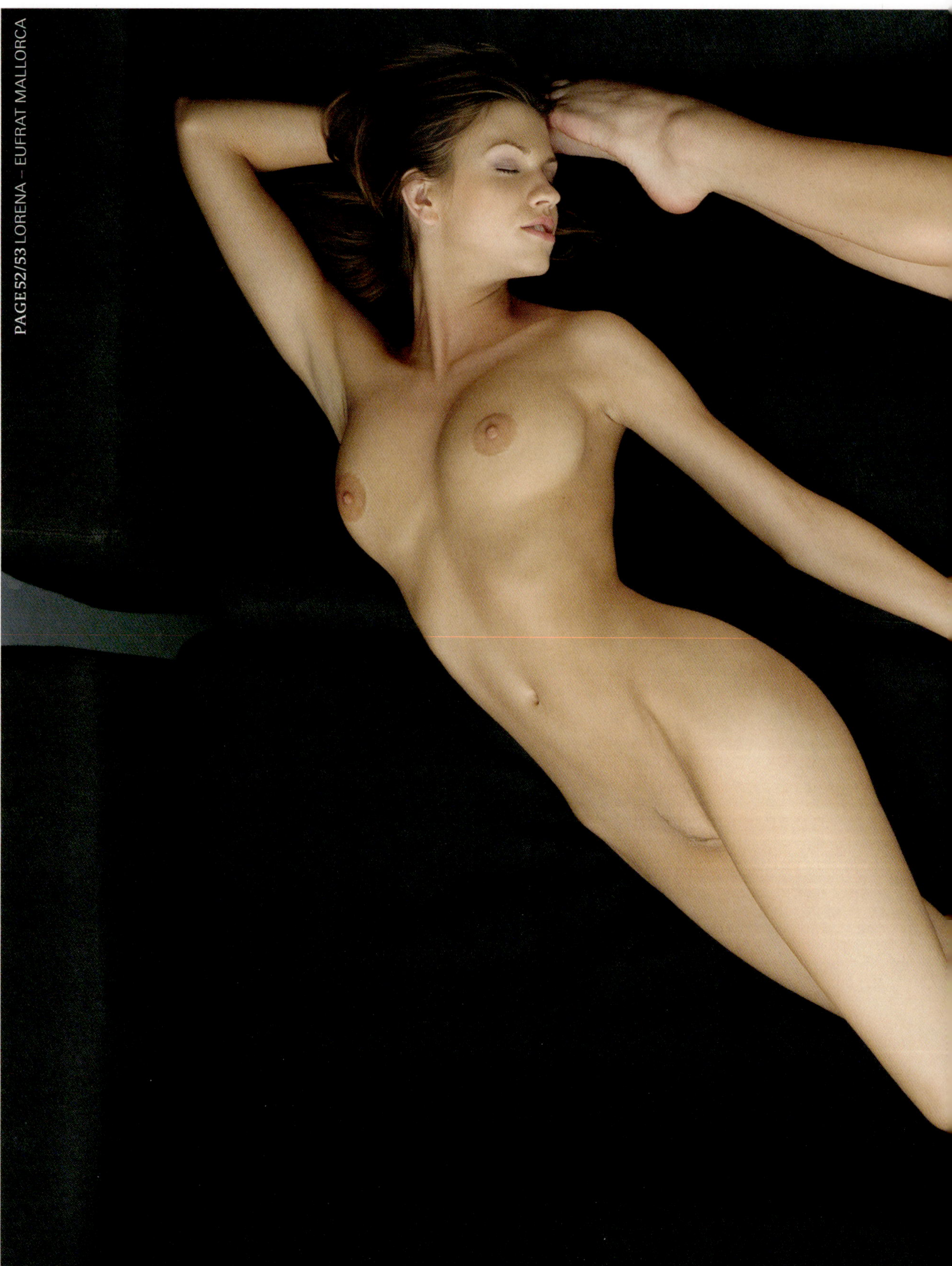

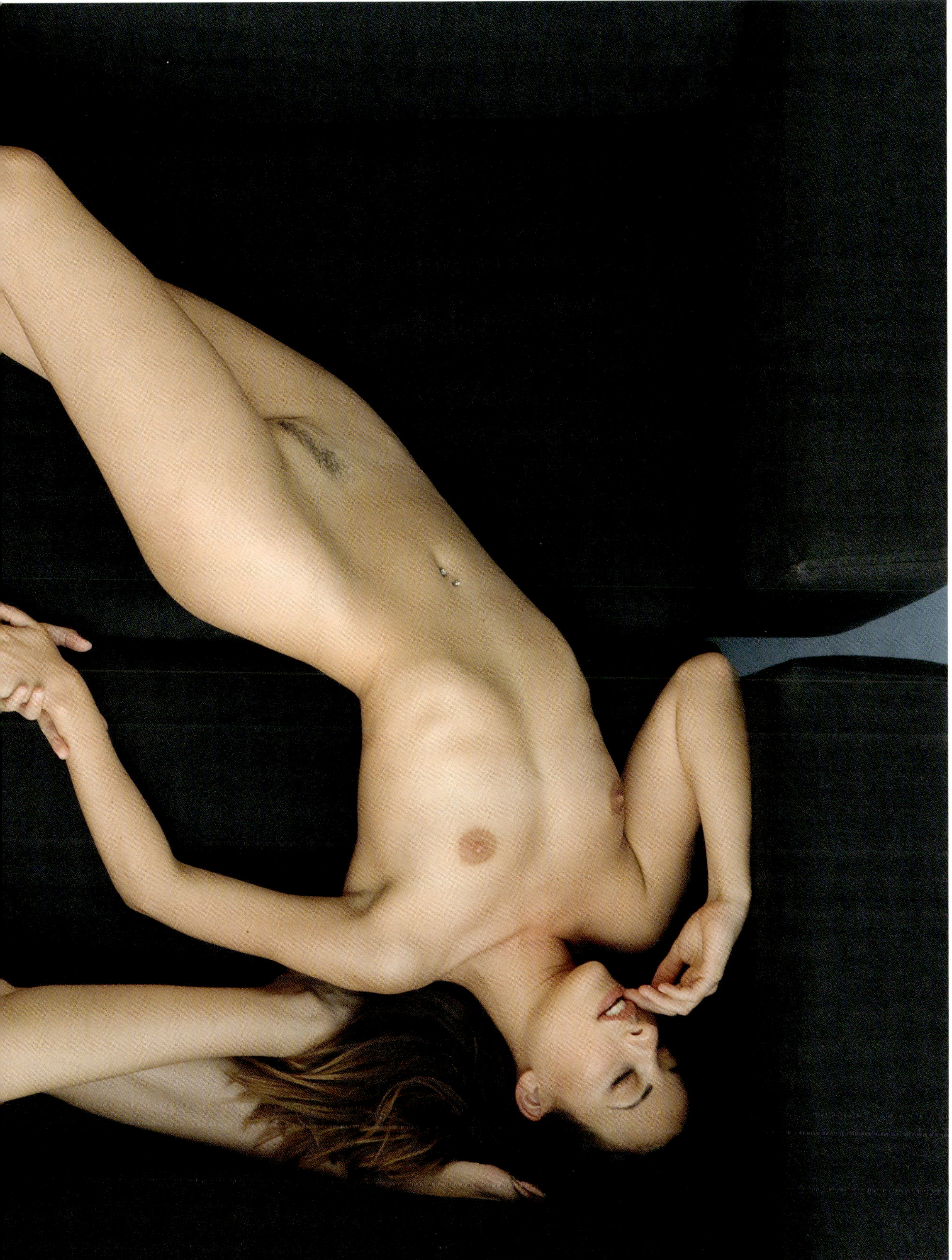

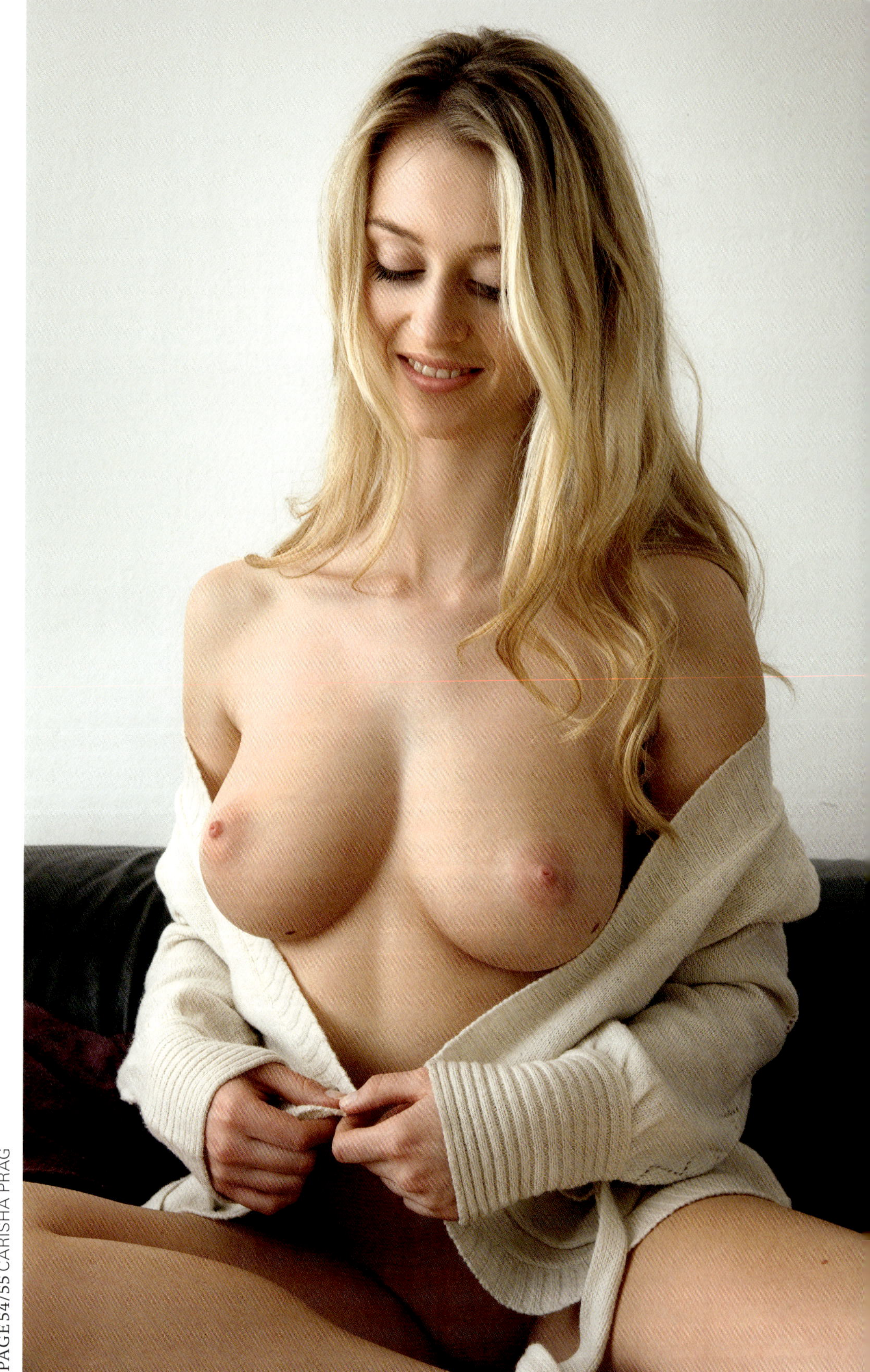

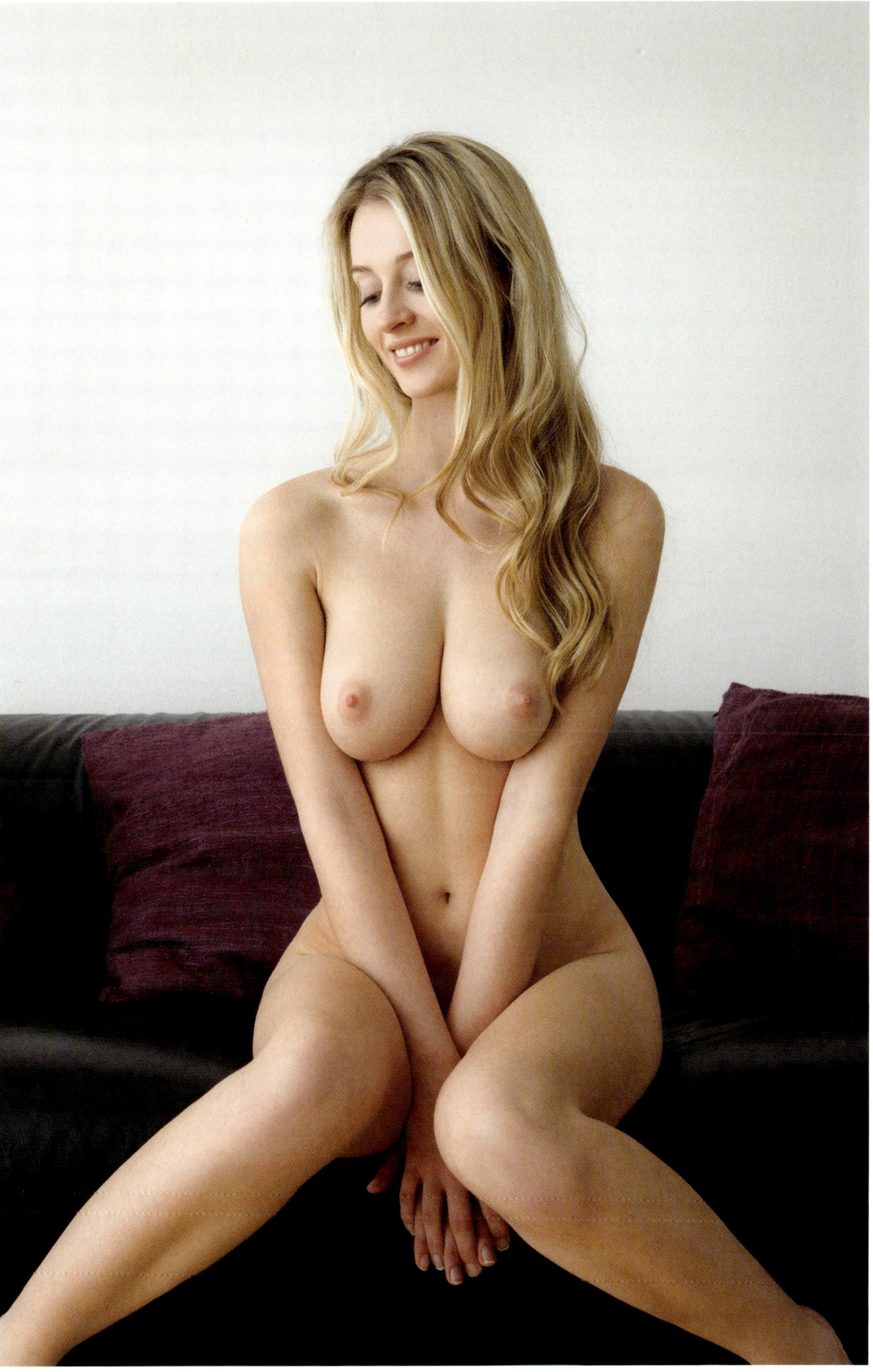

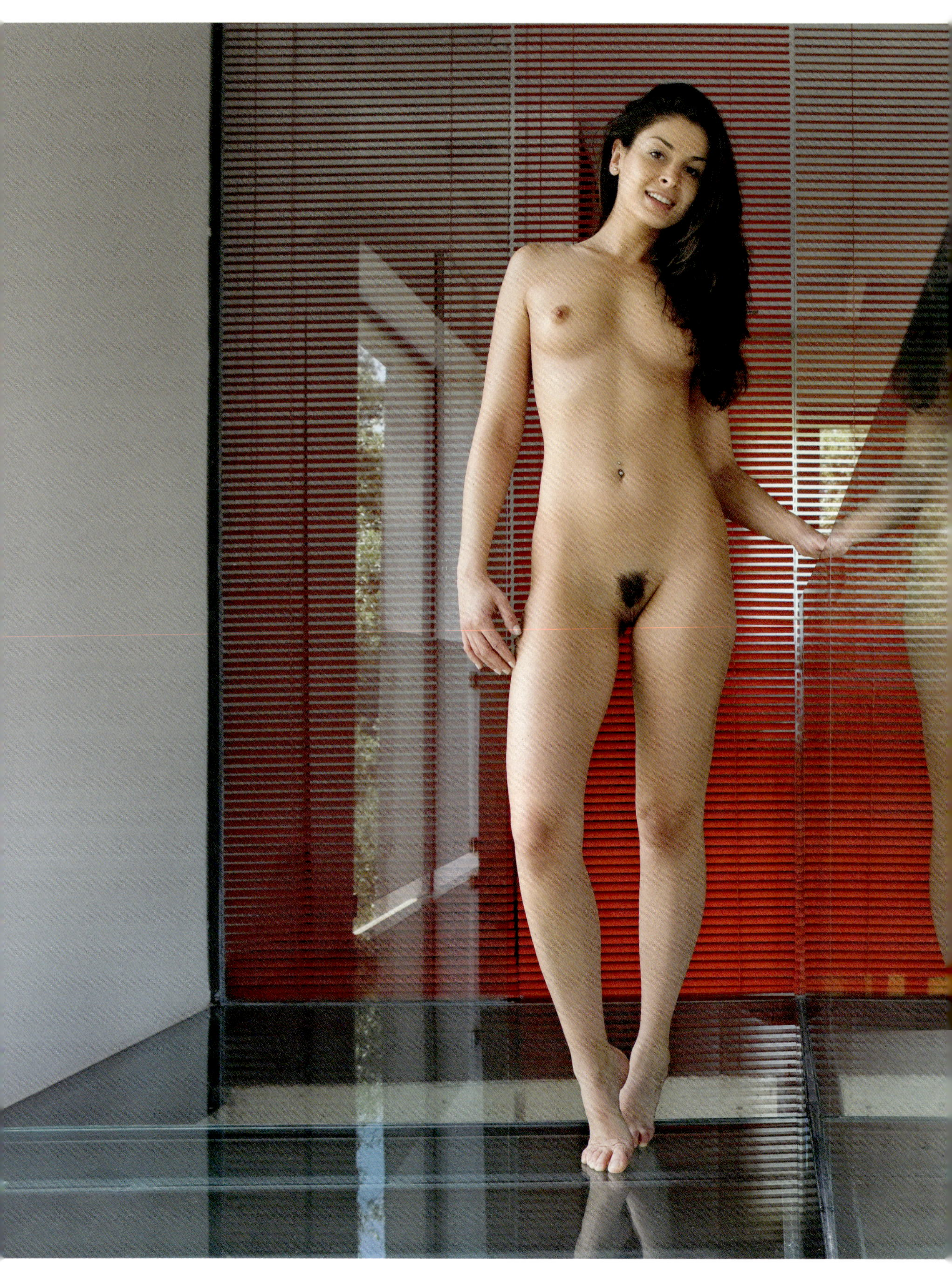

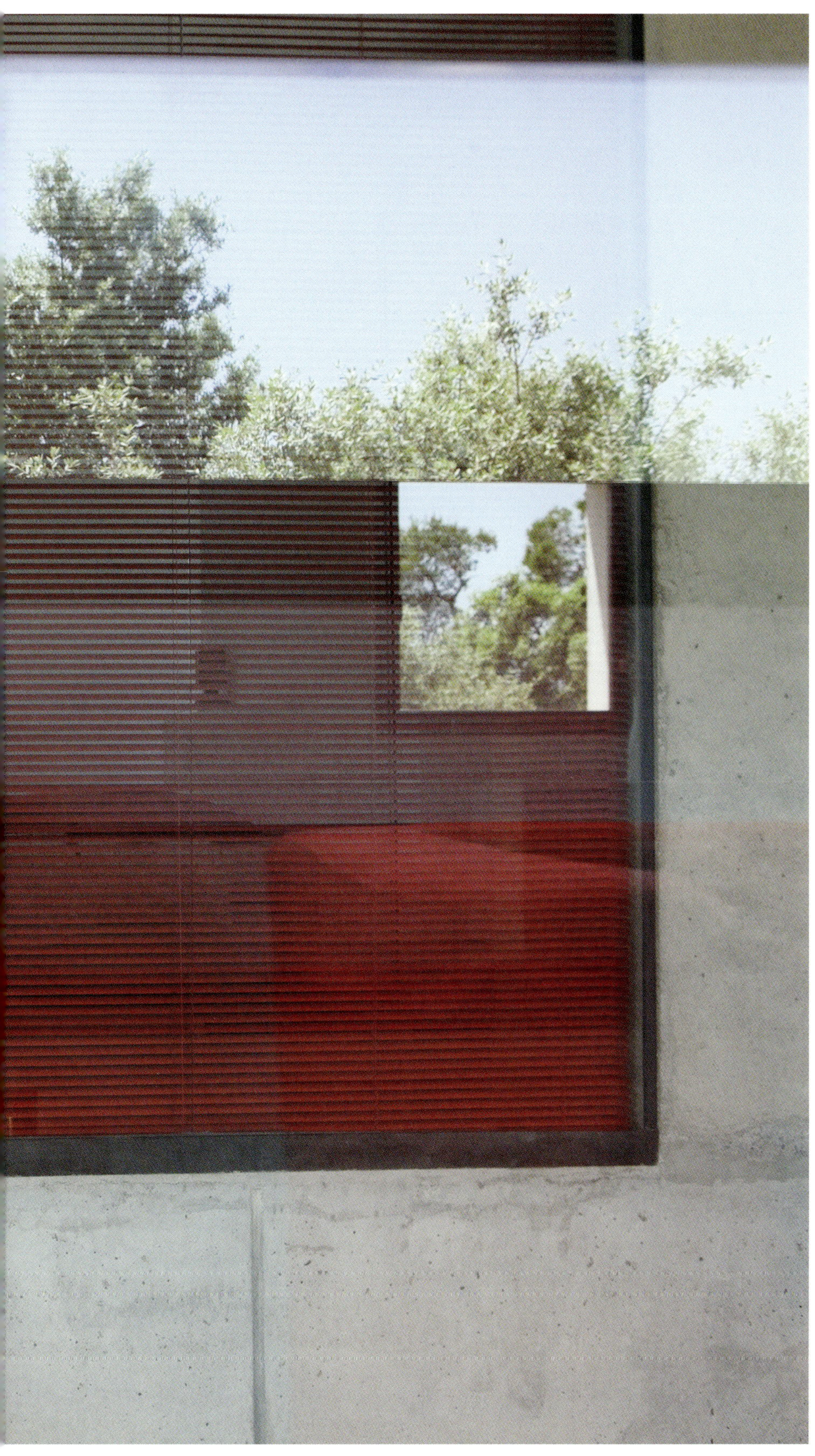

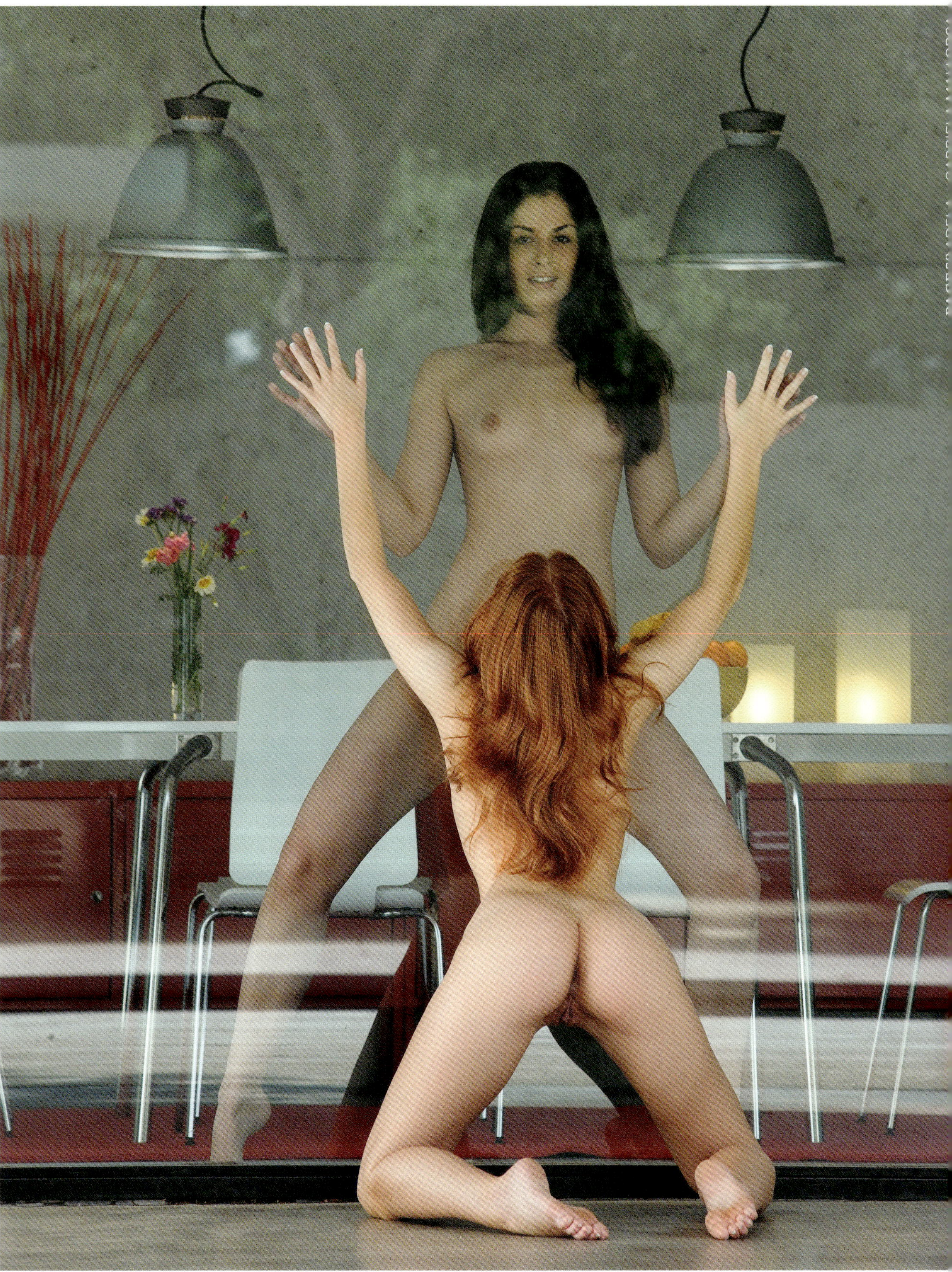
RAFFAELLA GABRIELA

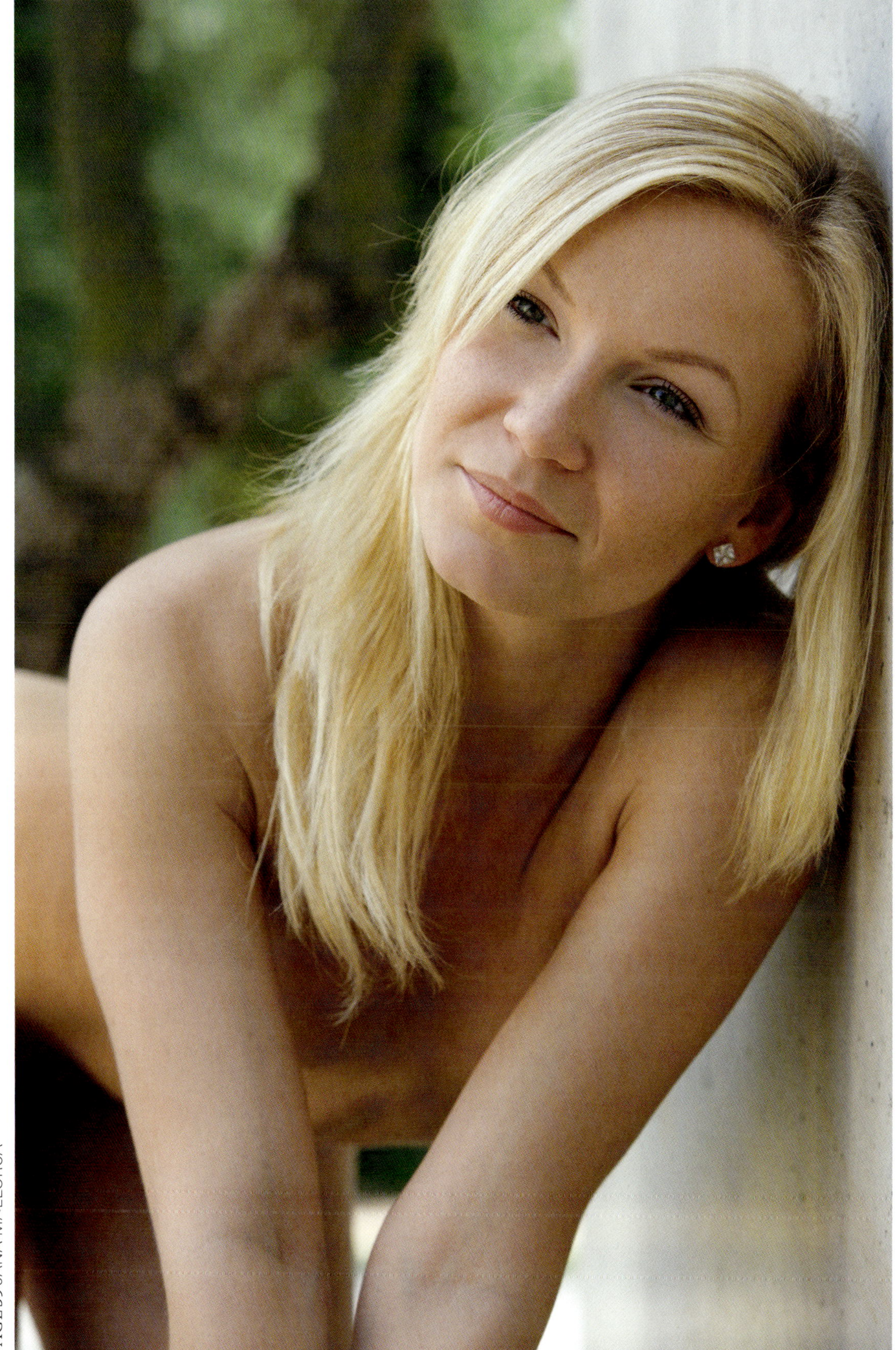

PAGE 59 JANA MALLORCA

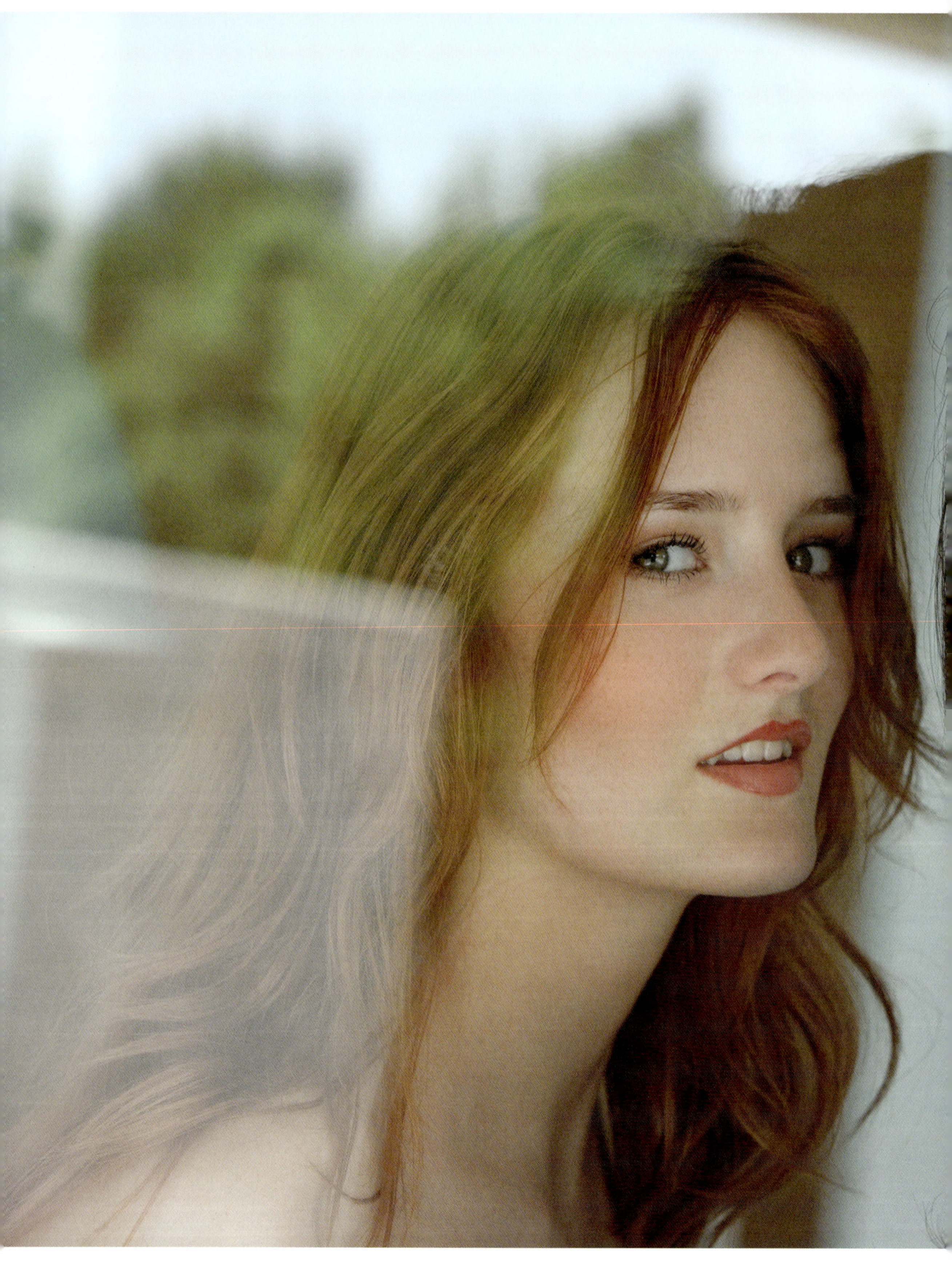

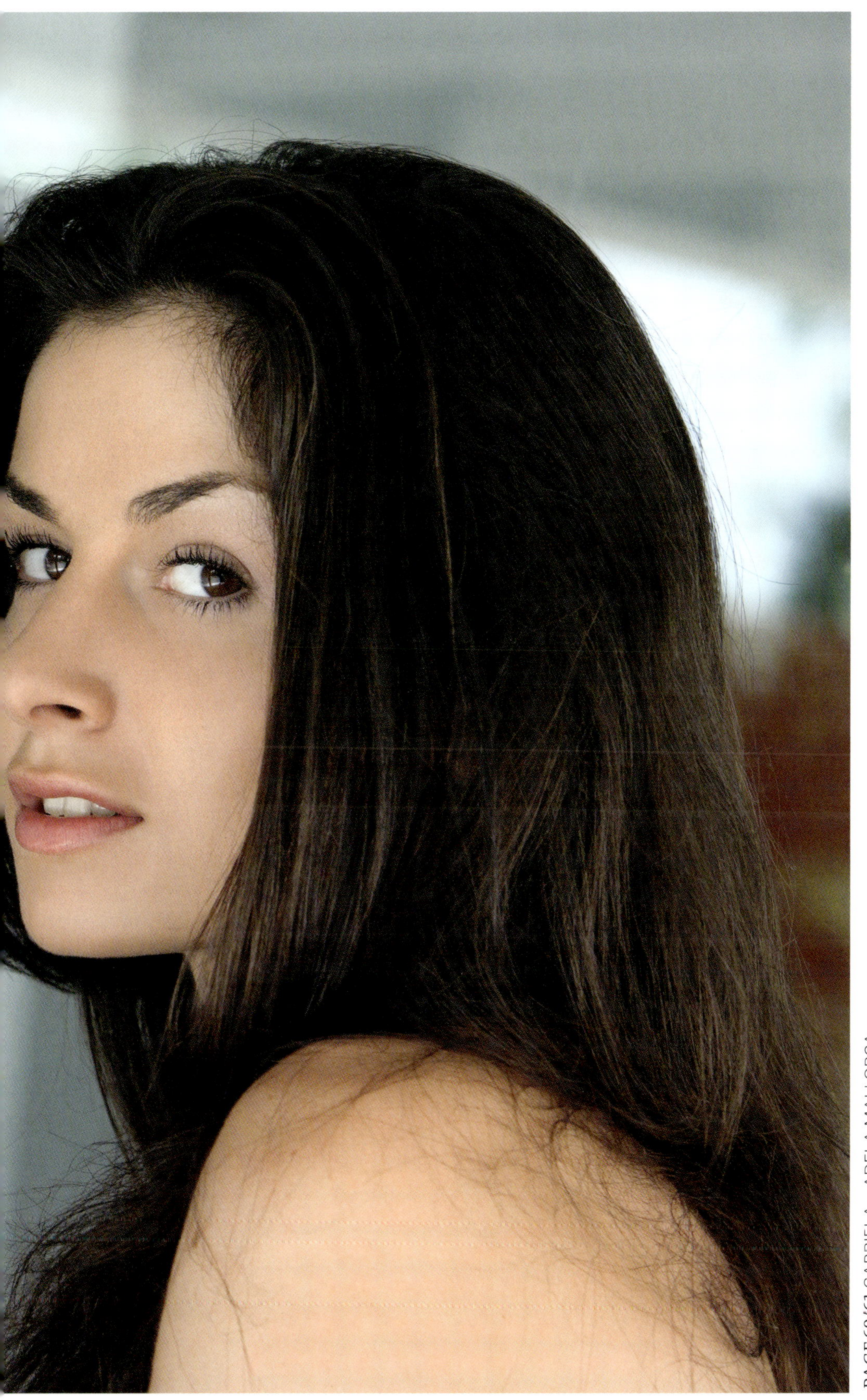

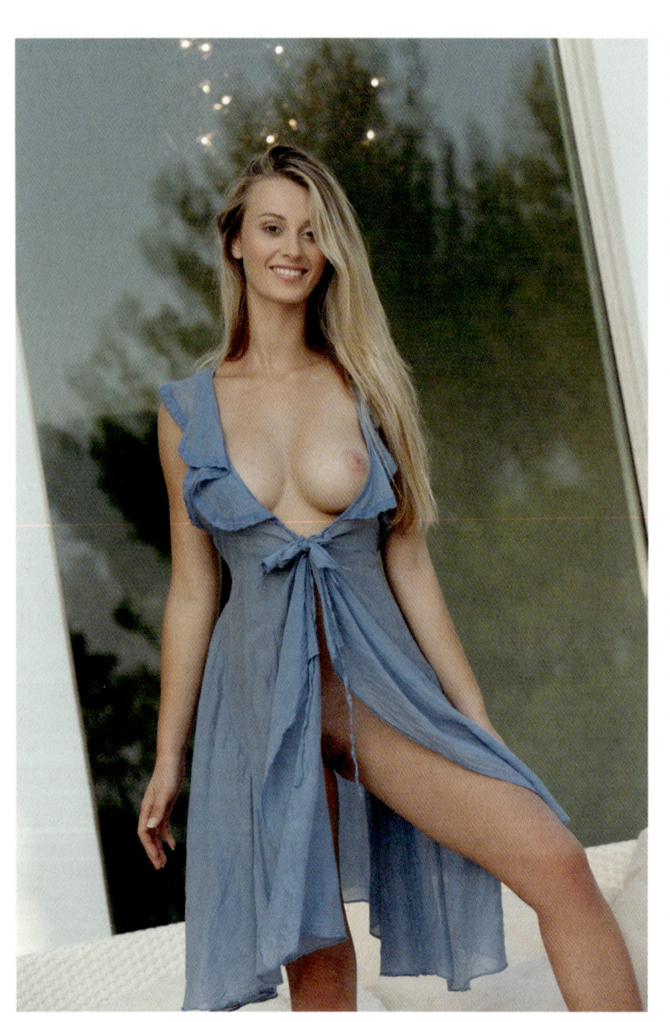
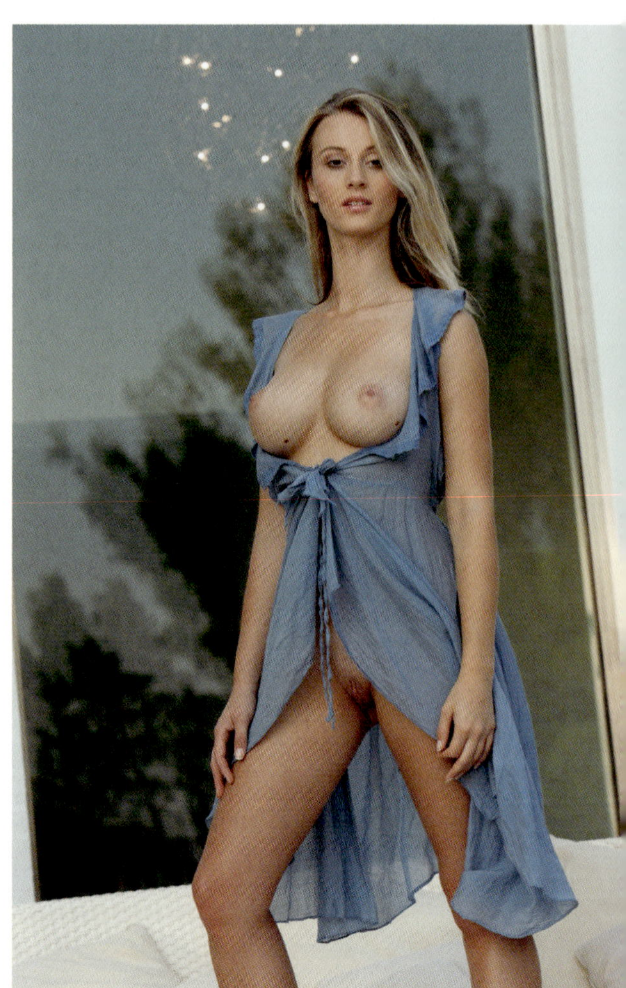

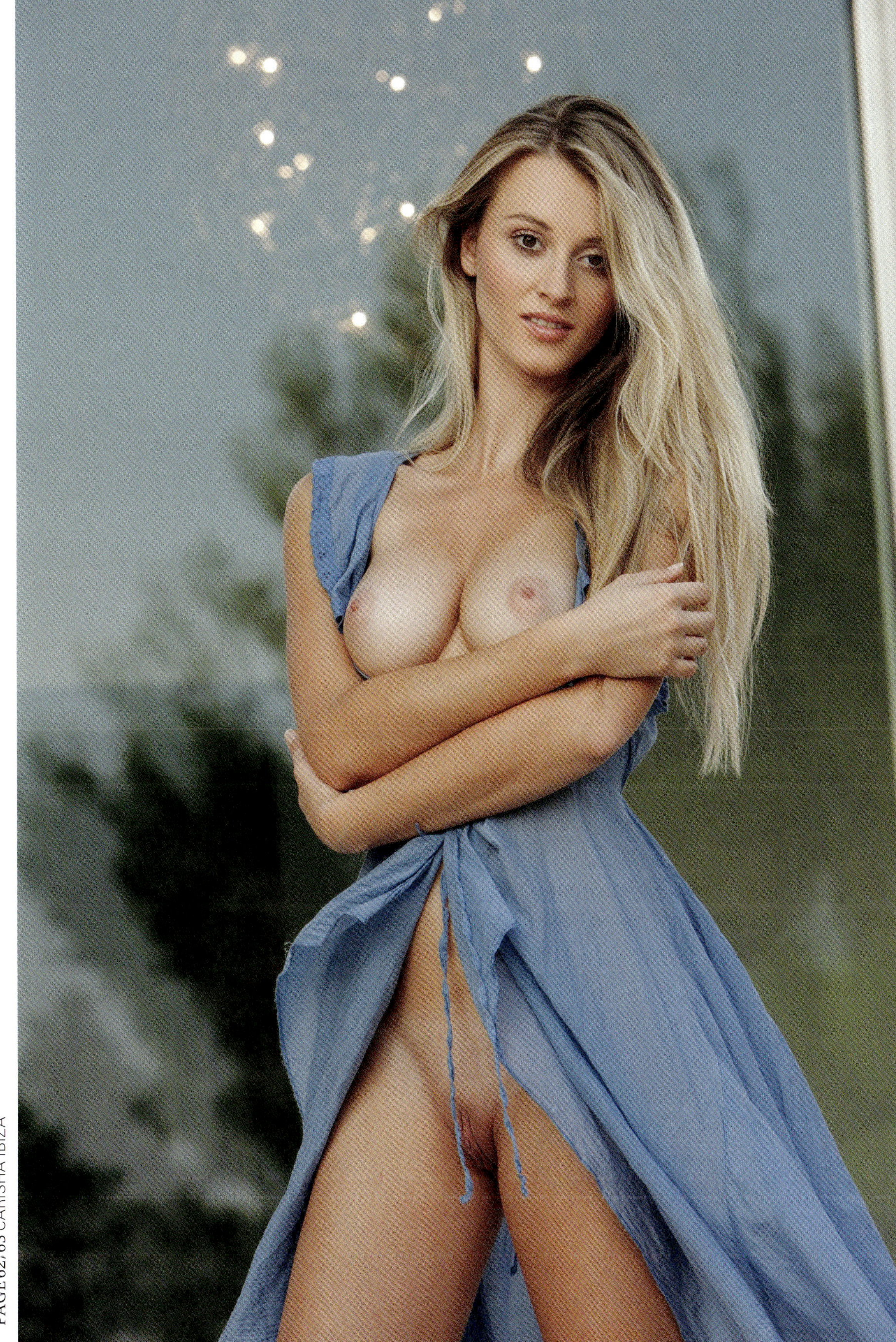

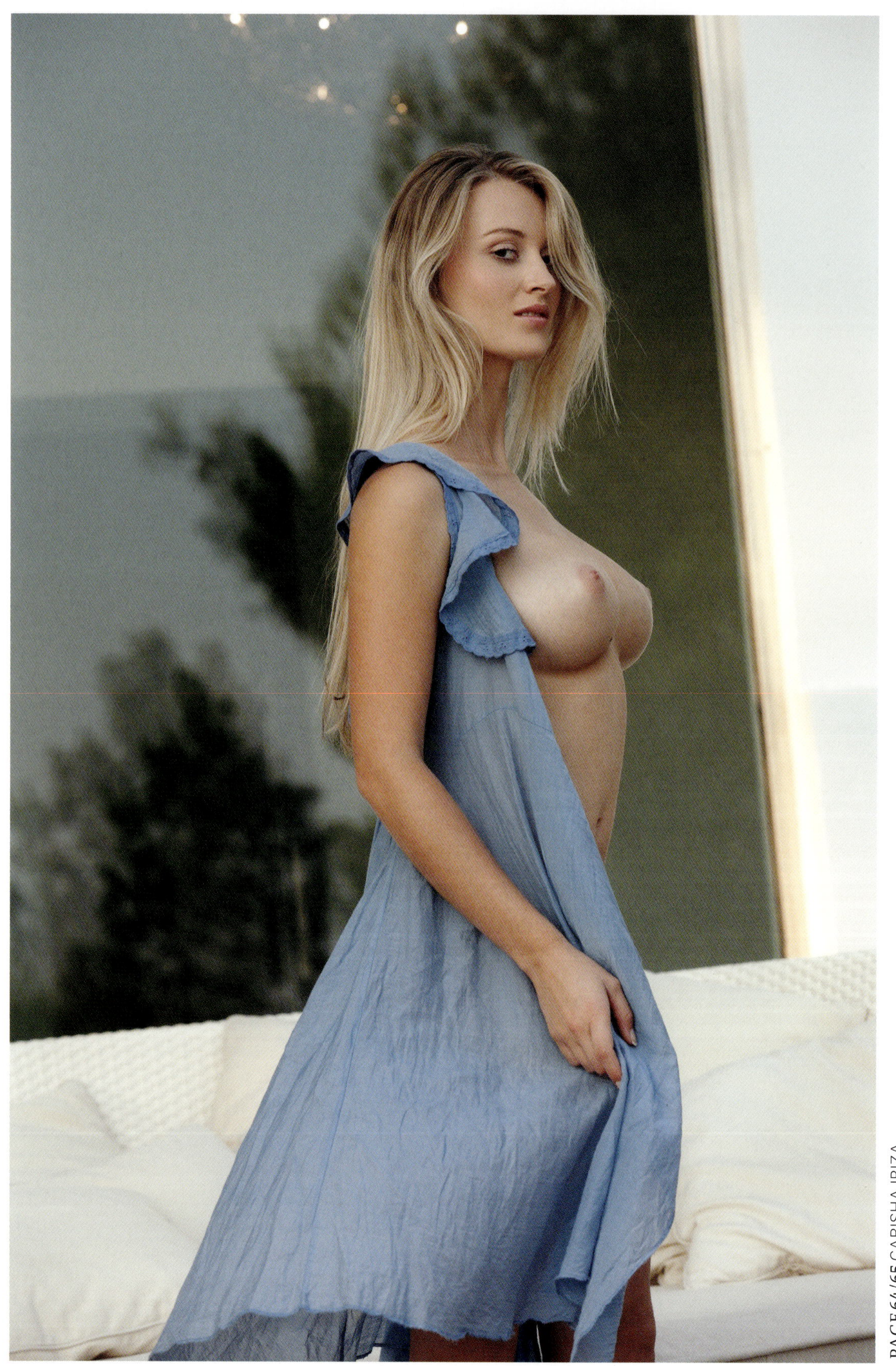

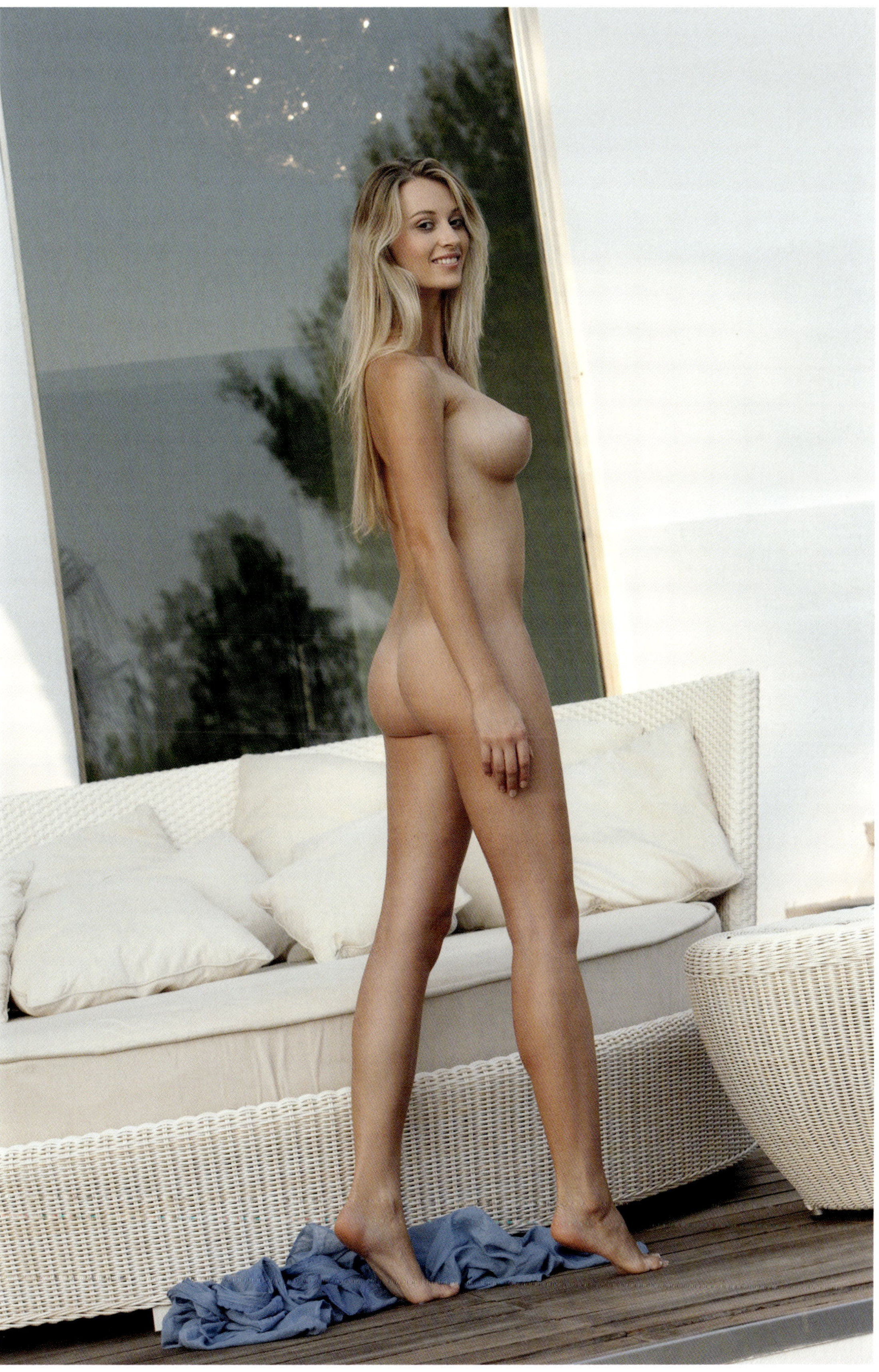

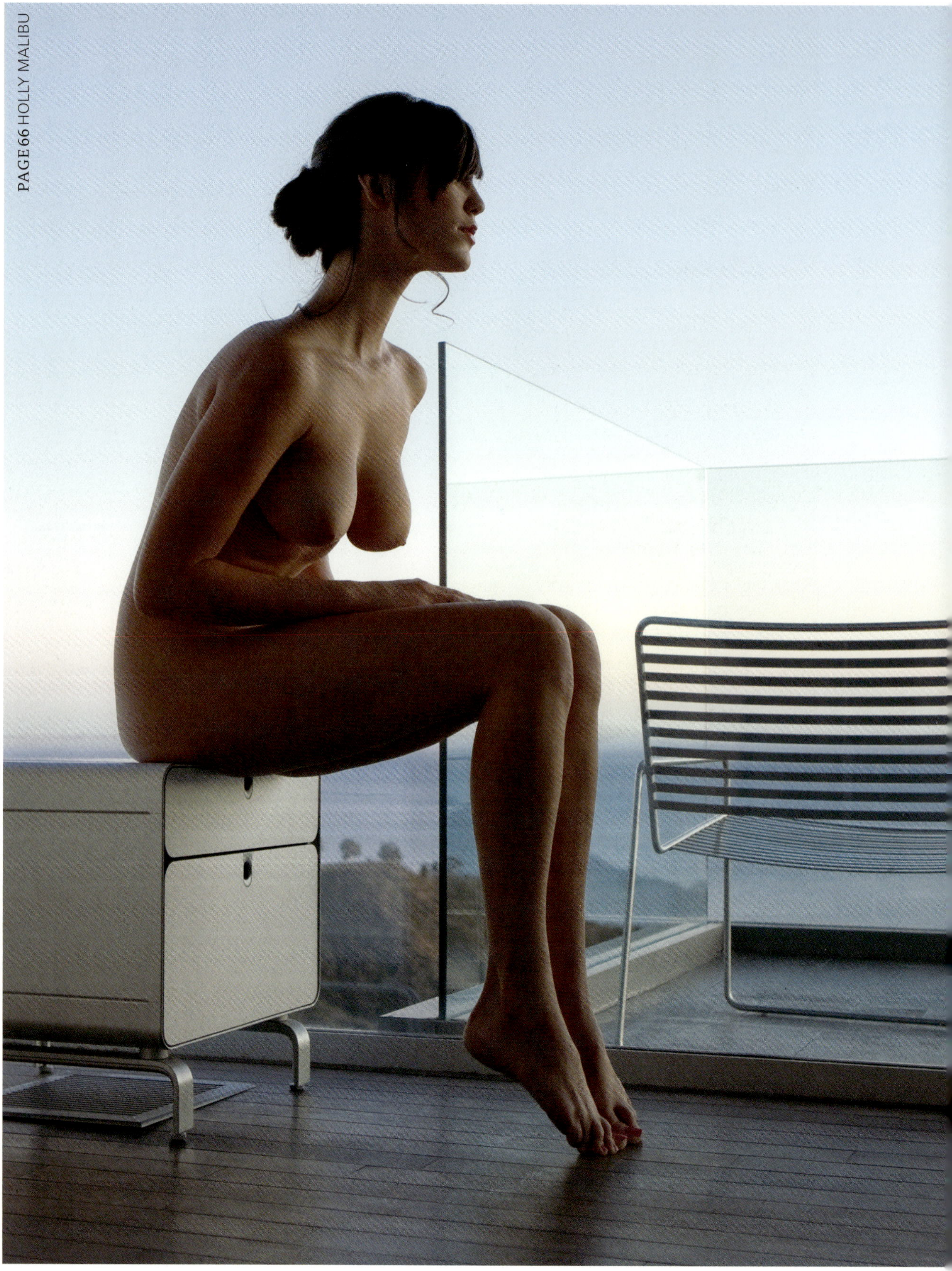

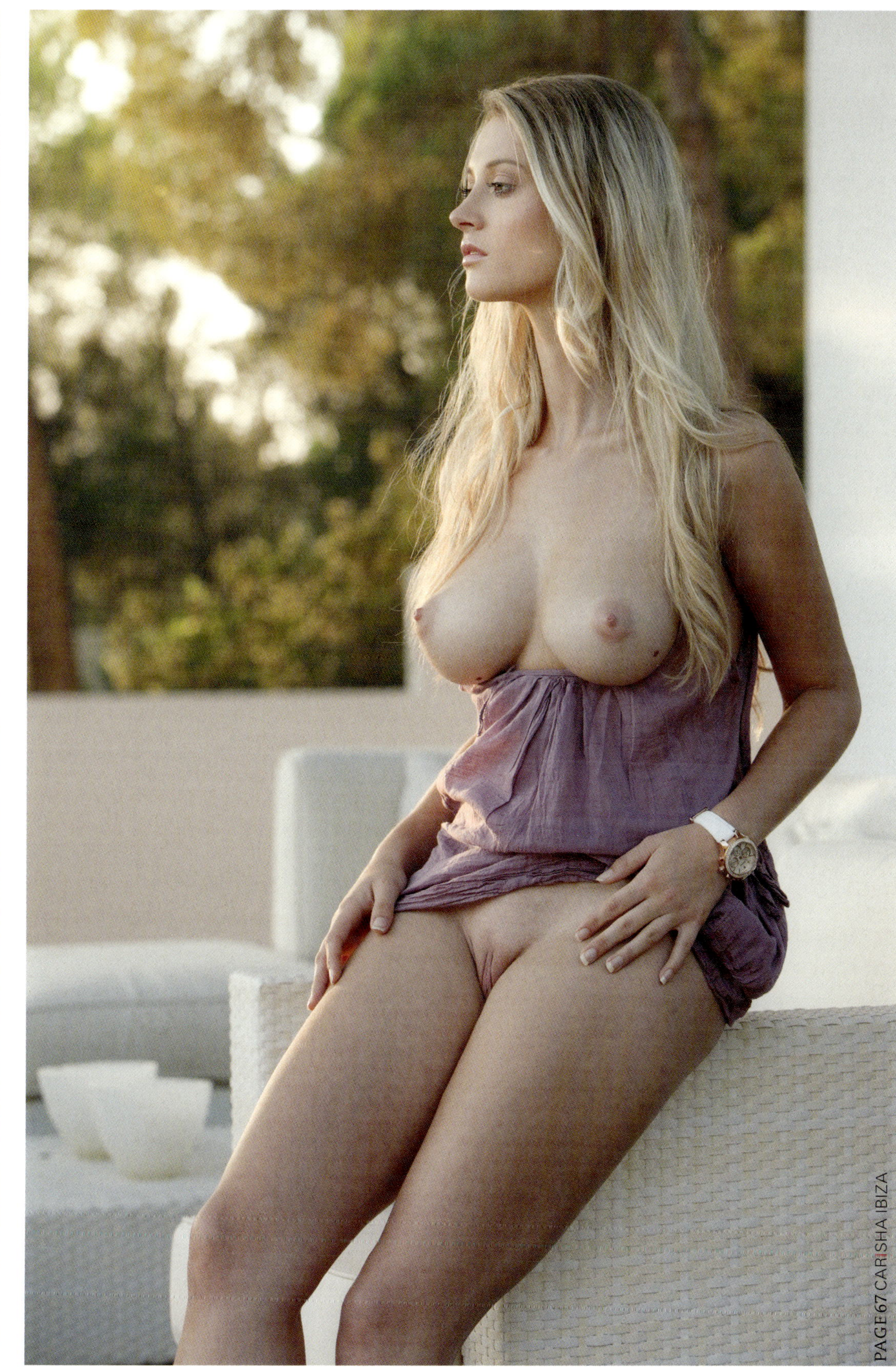

PAGE 67 CARISHA IBIZA

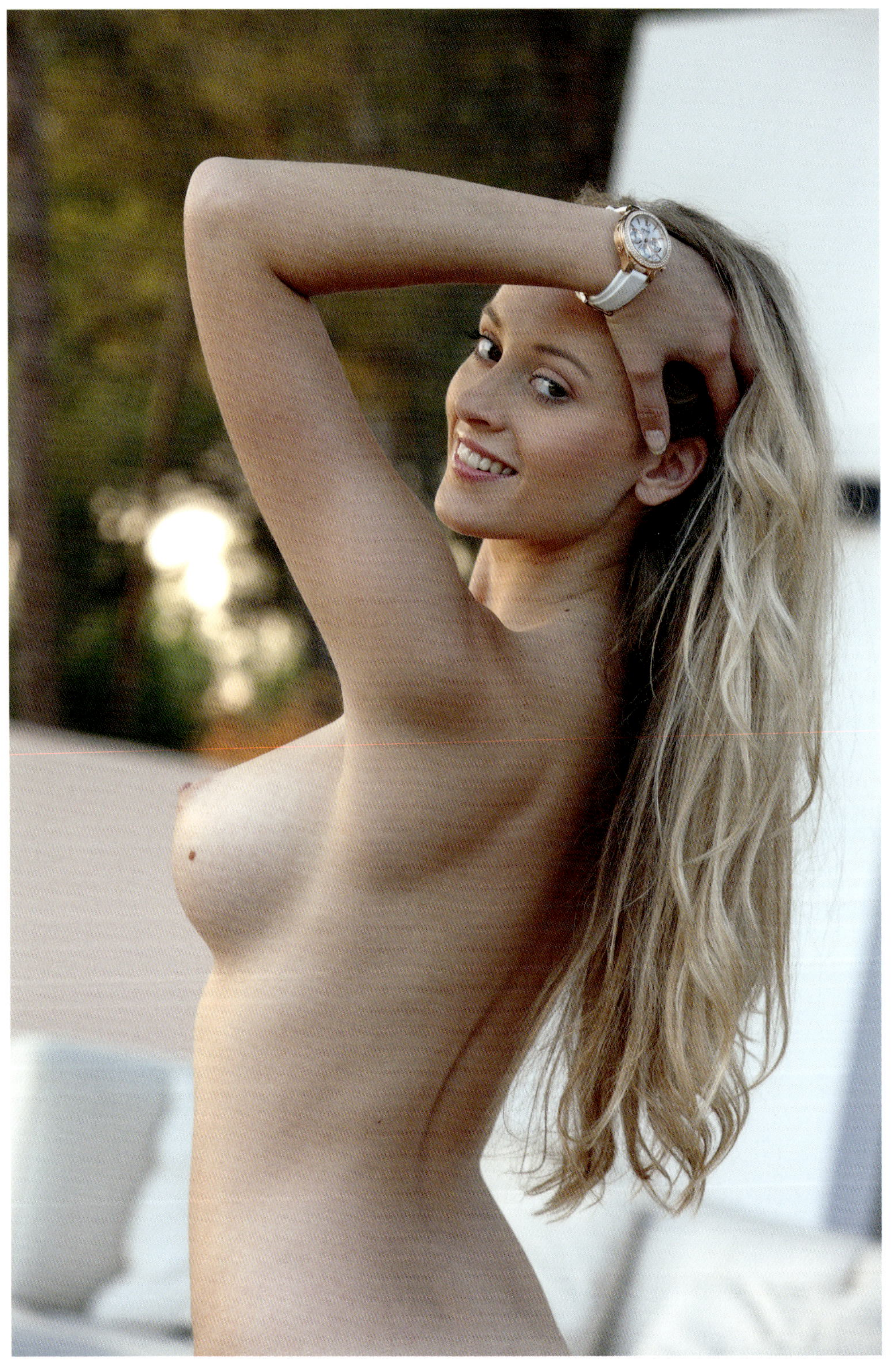

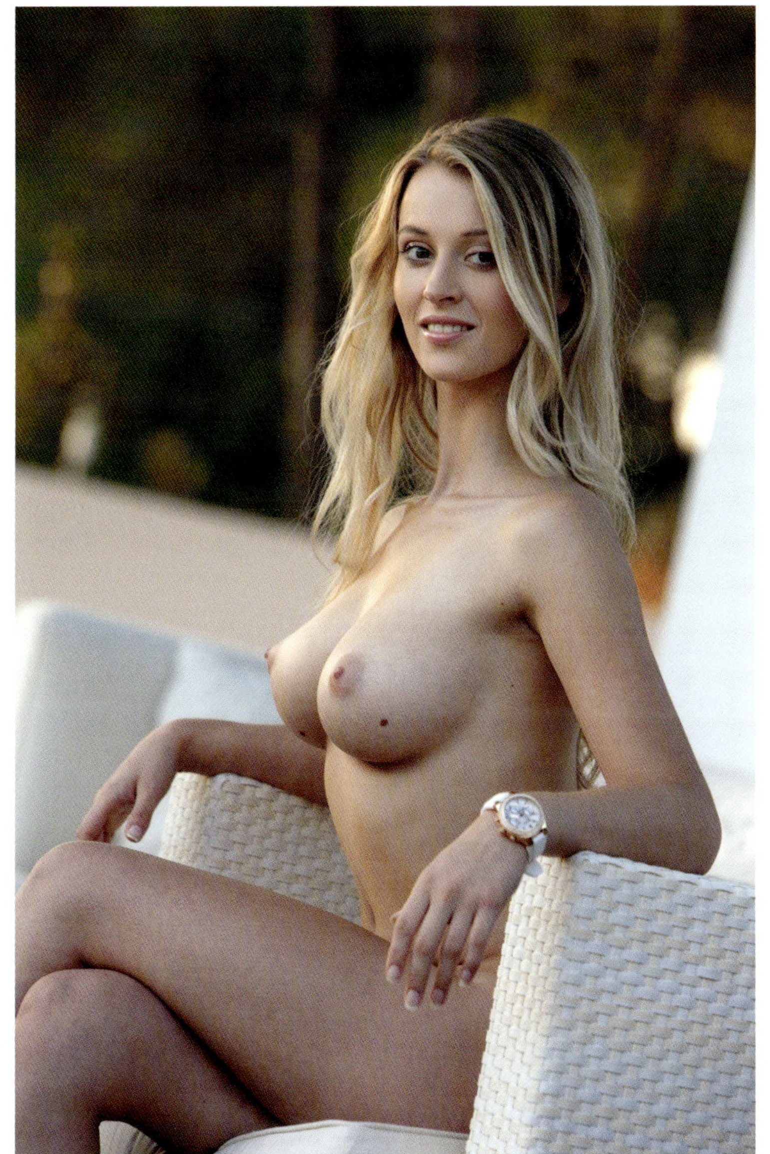

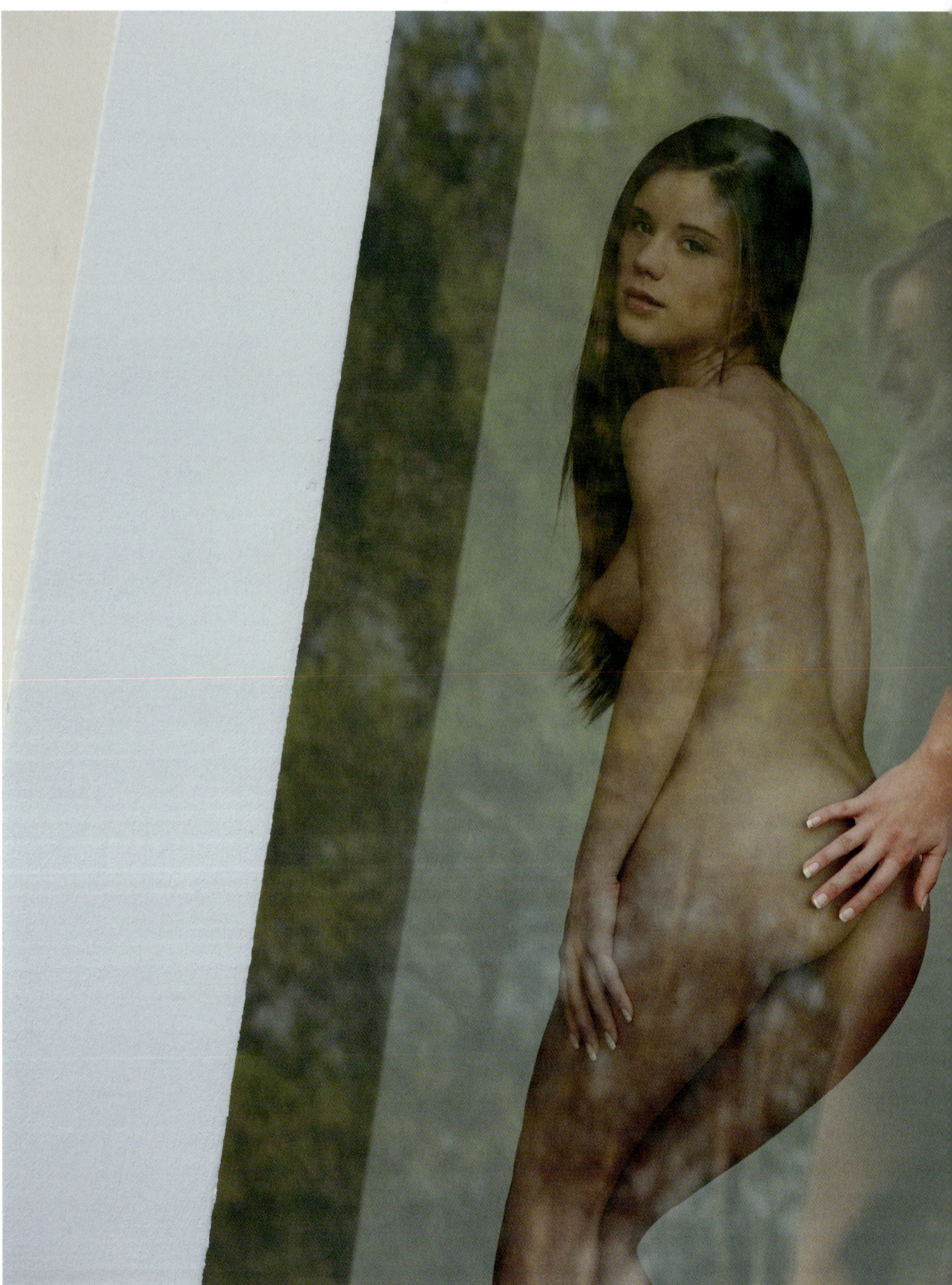

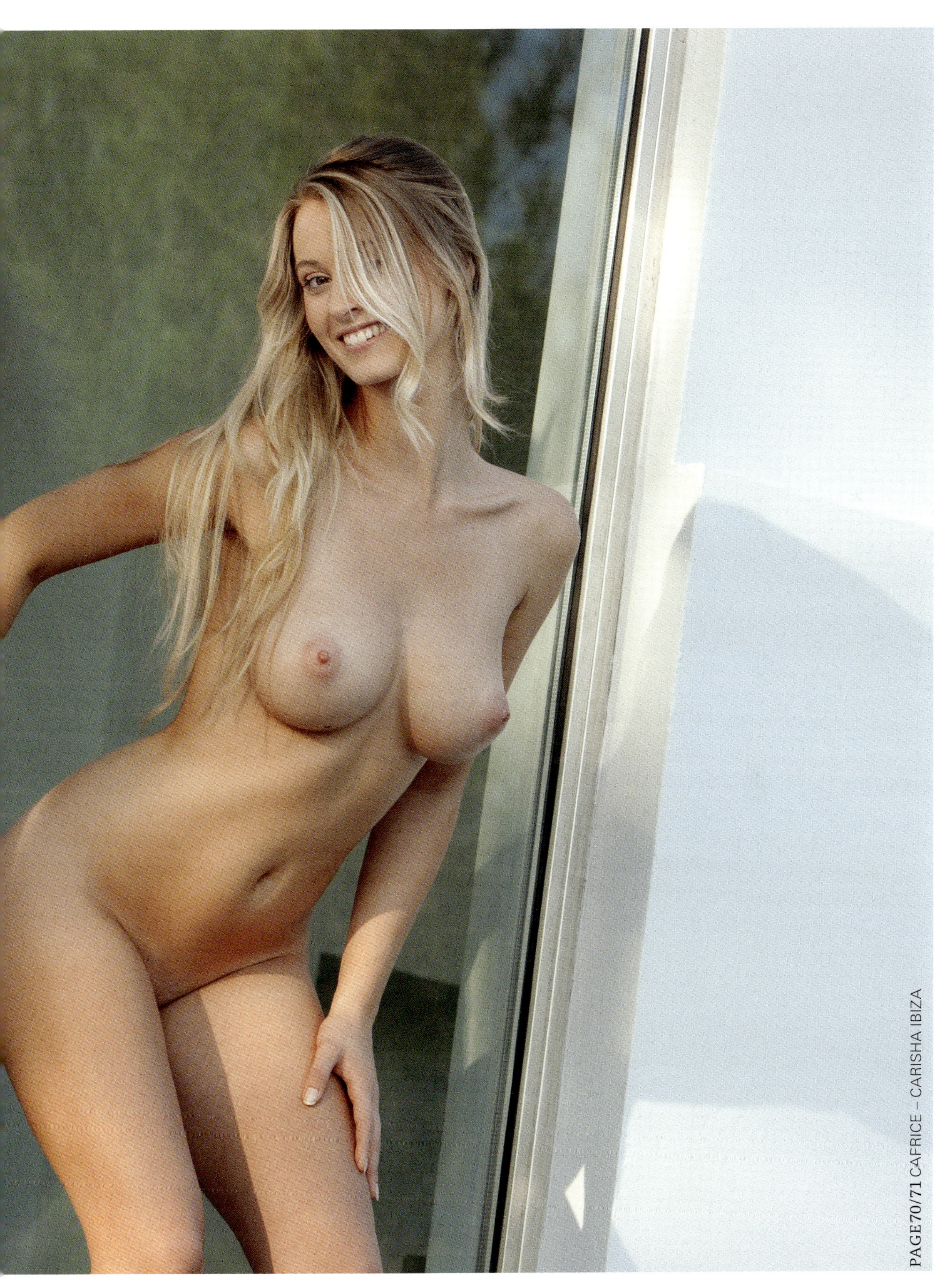

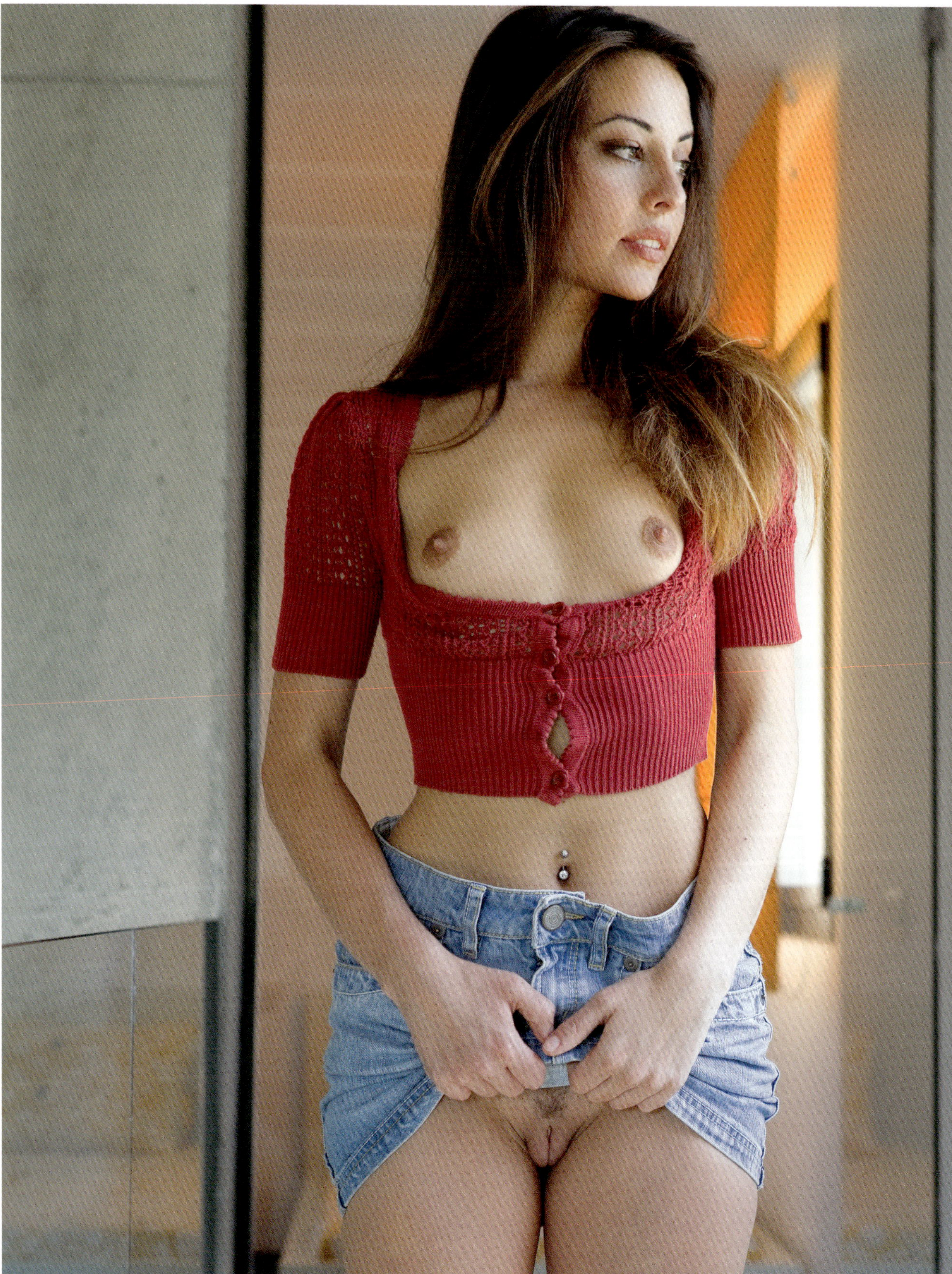

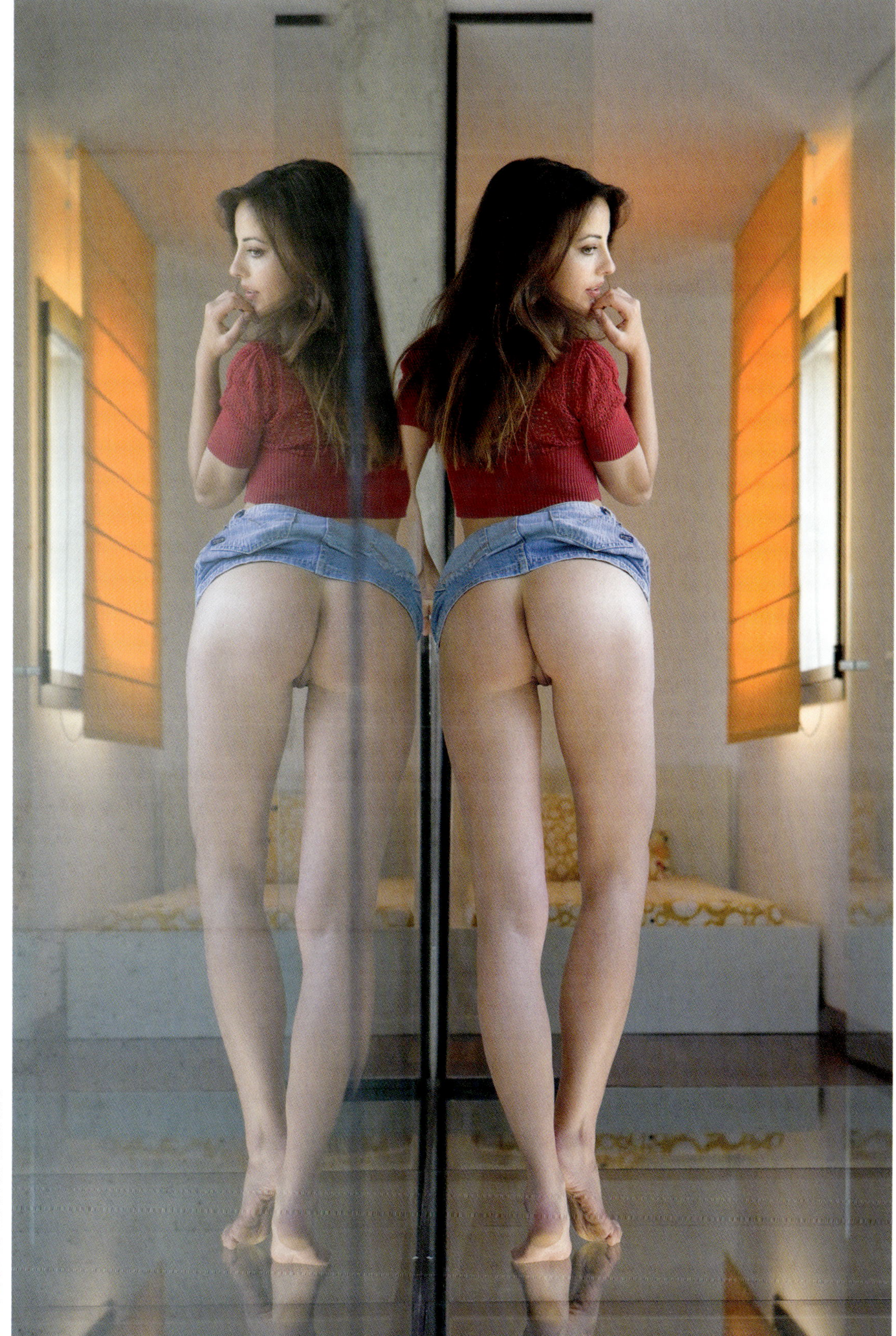

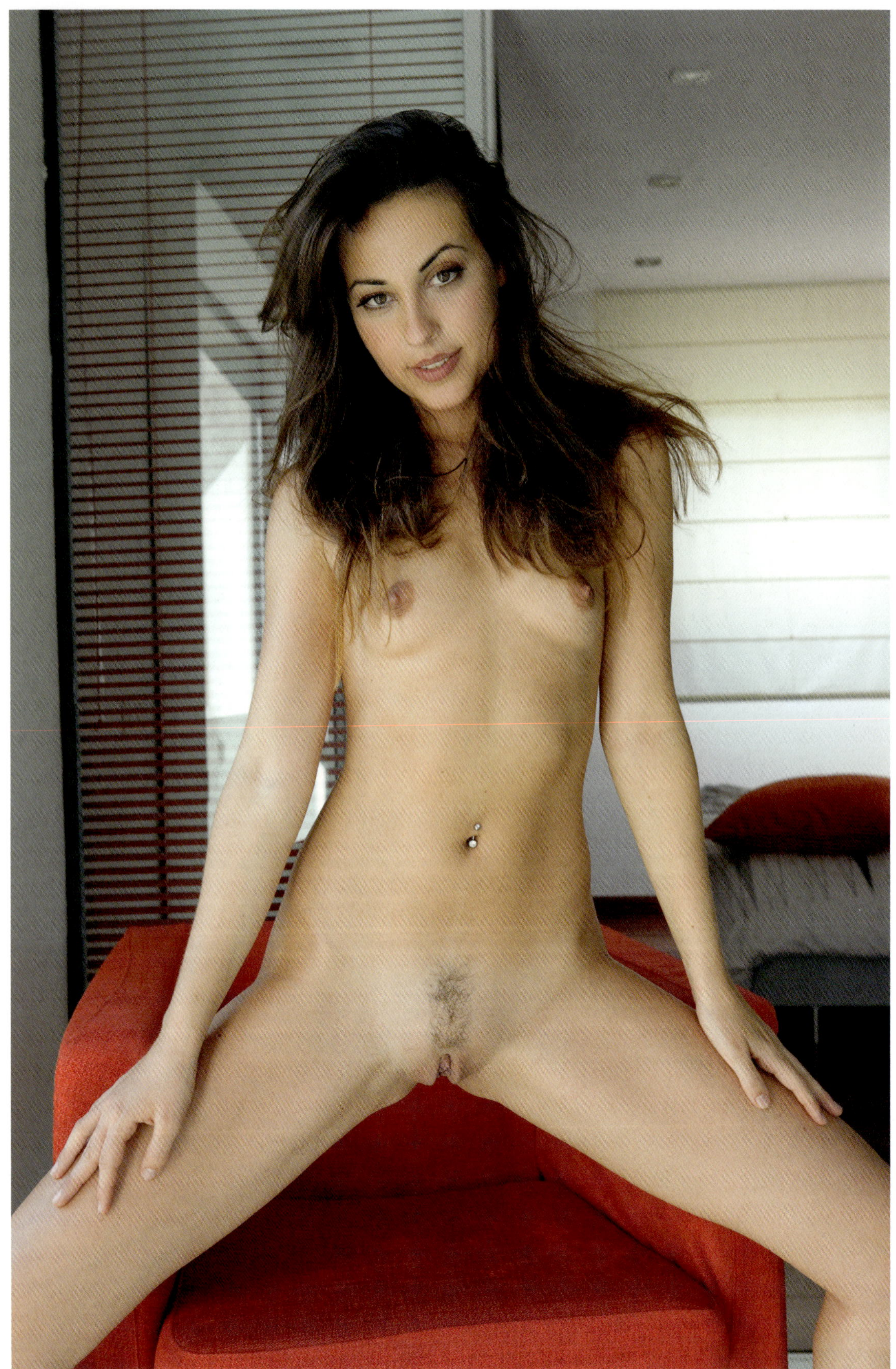

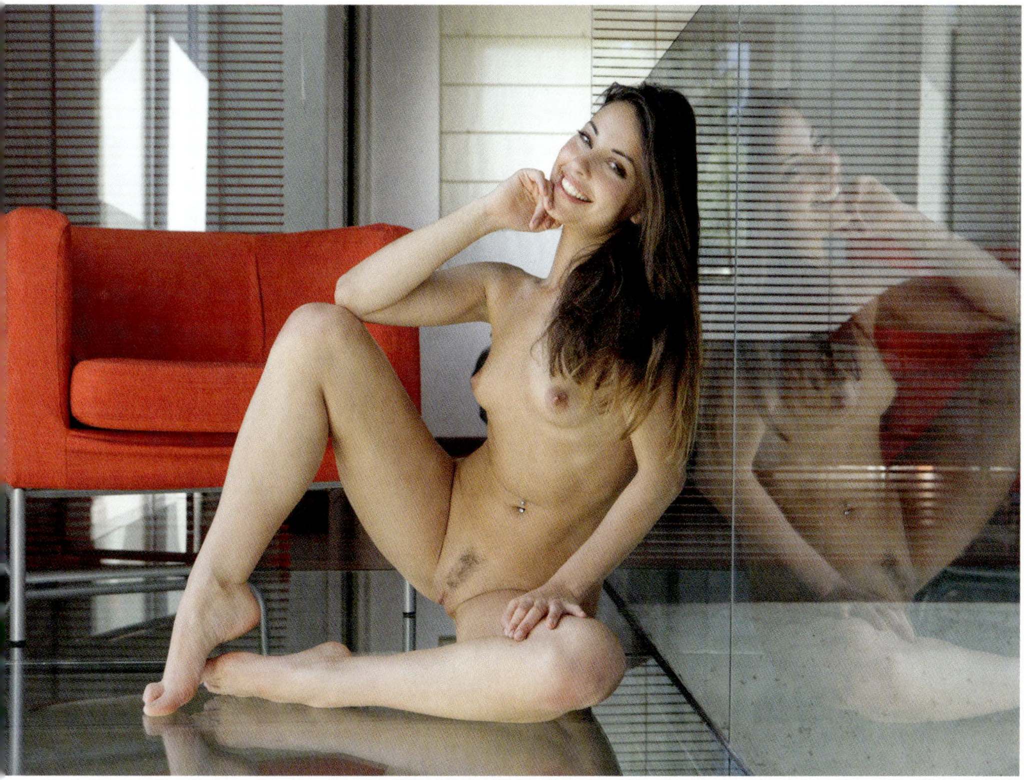

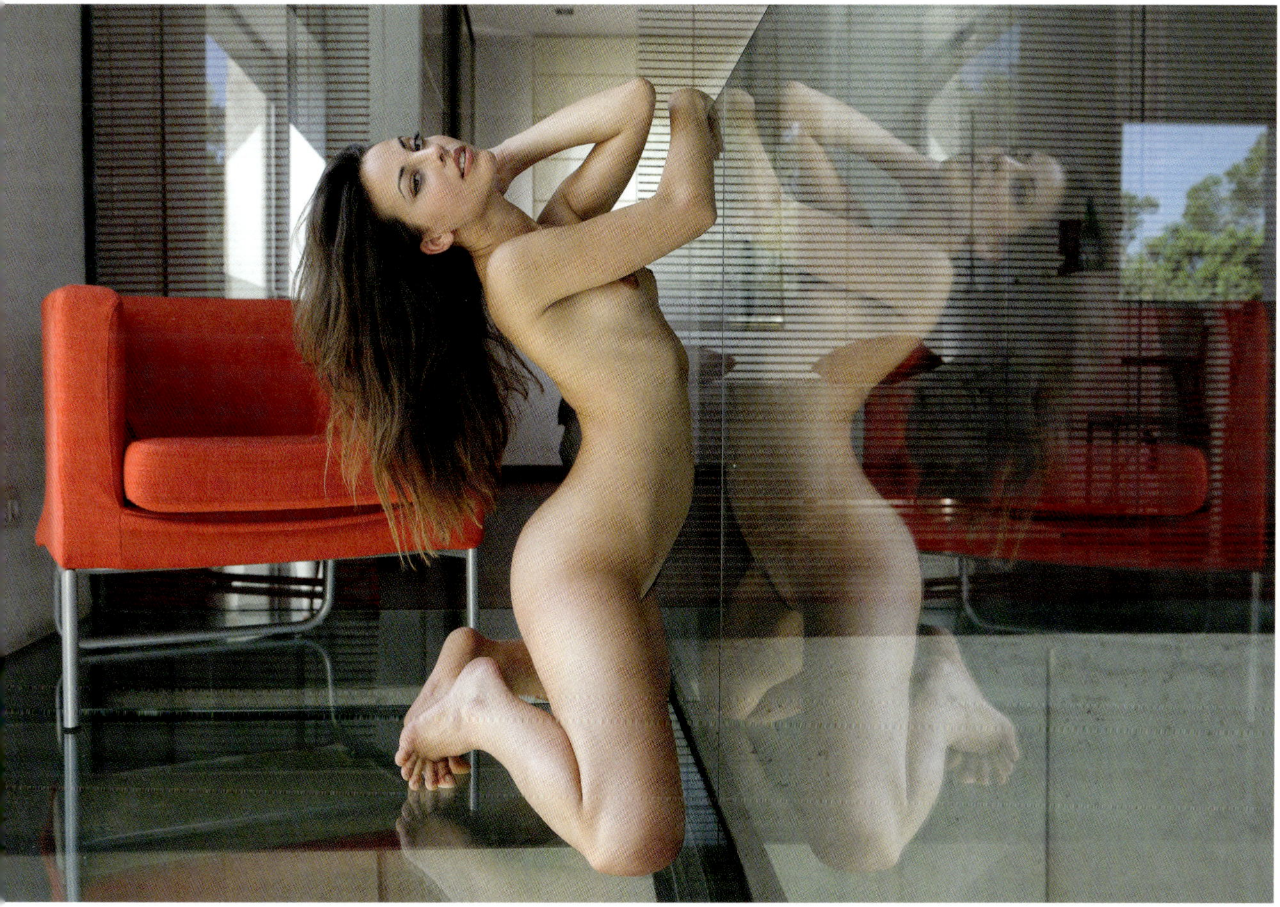

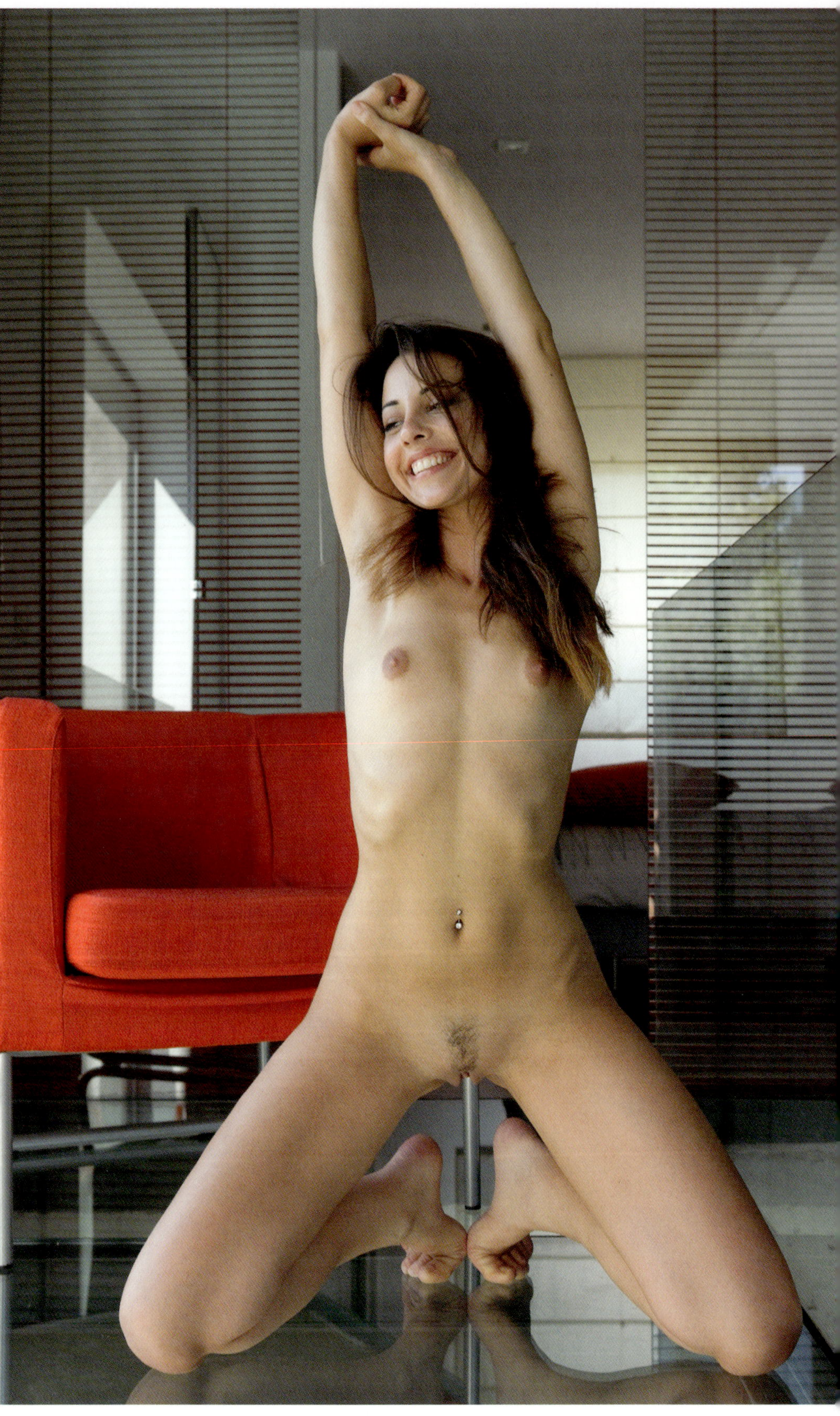

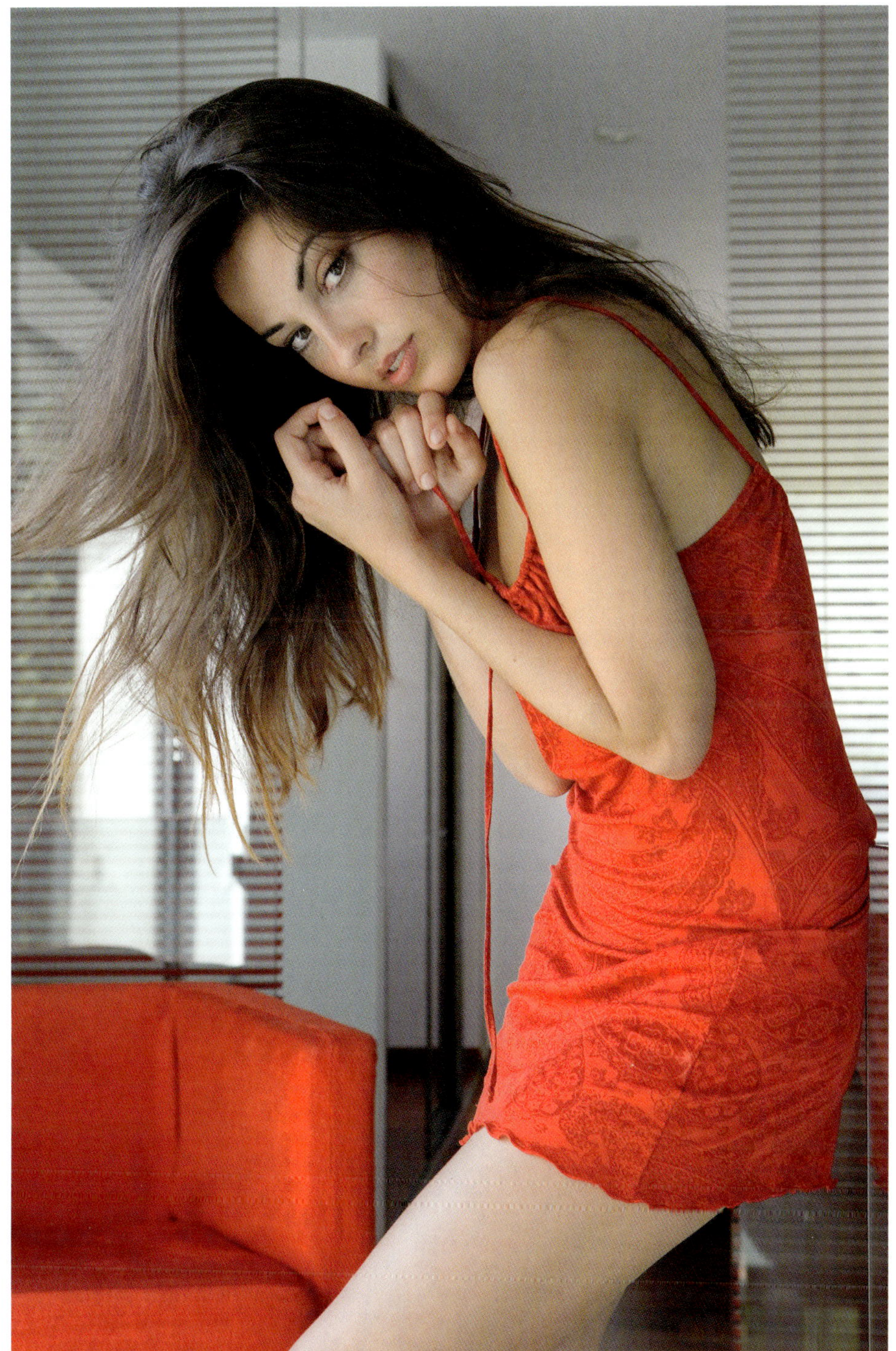

PAGE 76/77 LORENA MALLORCA

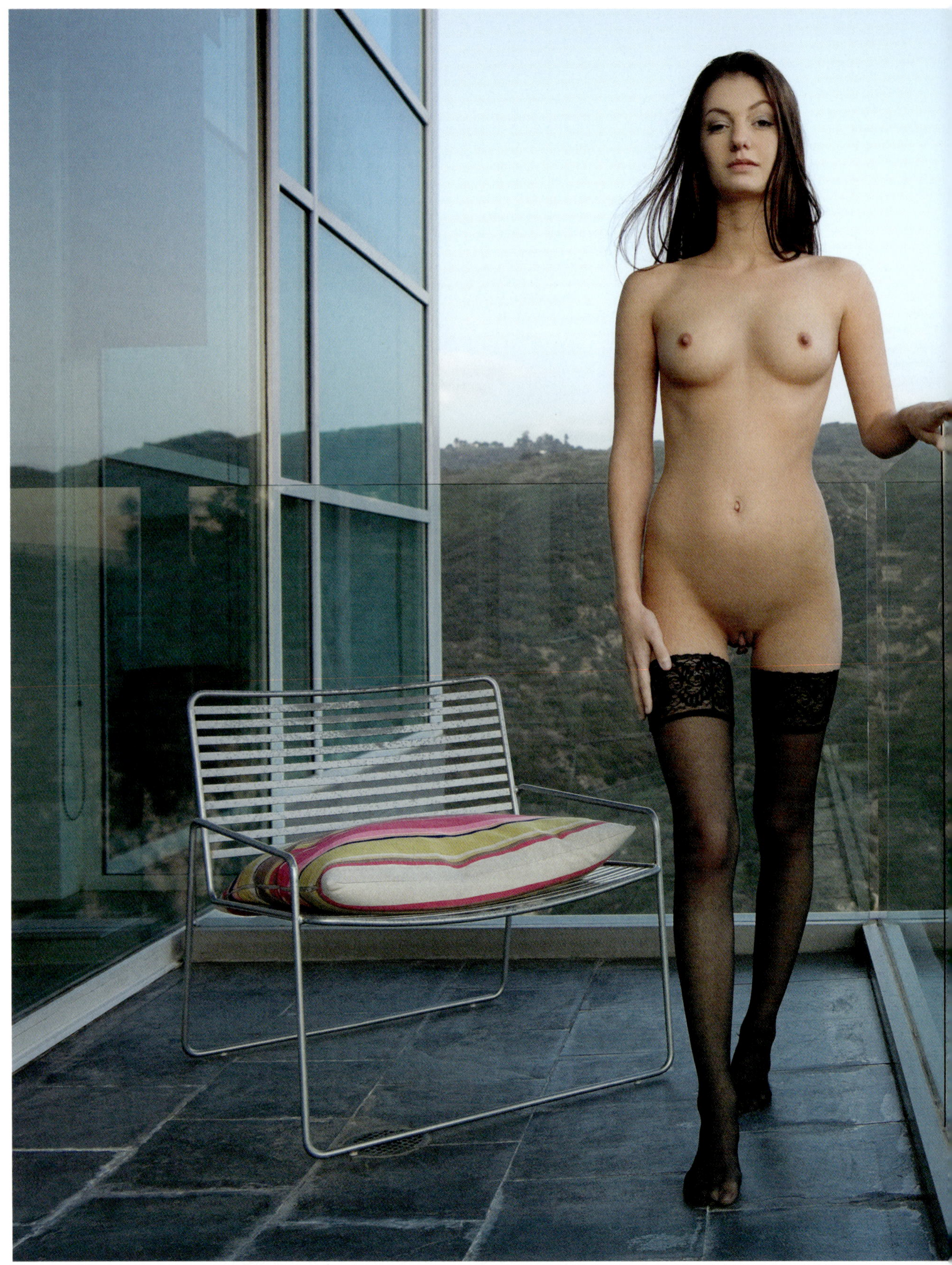

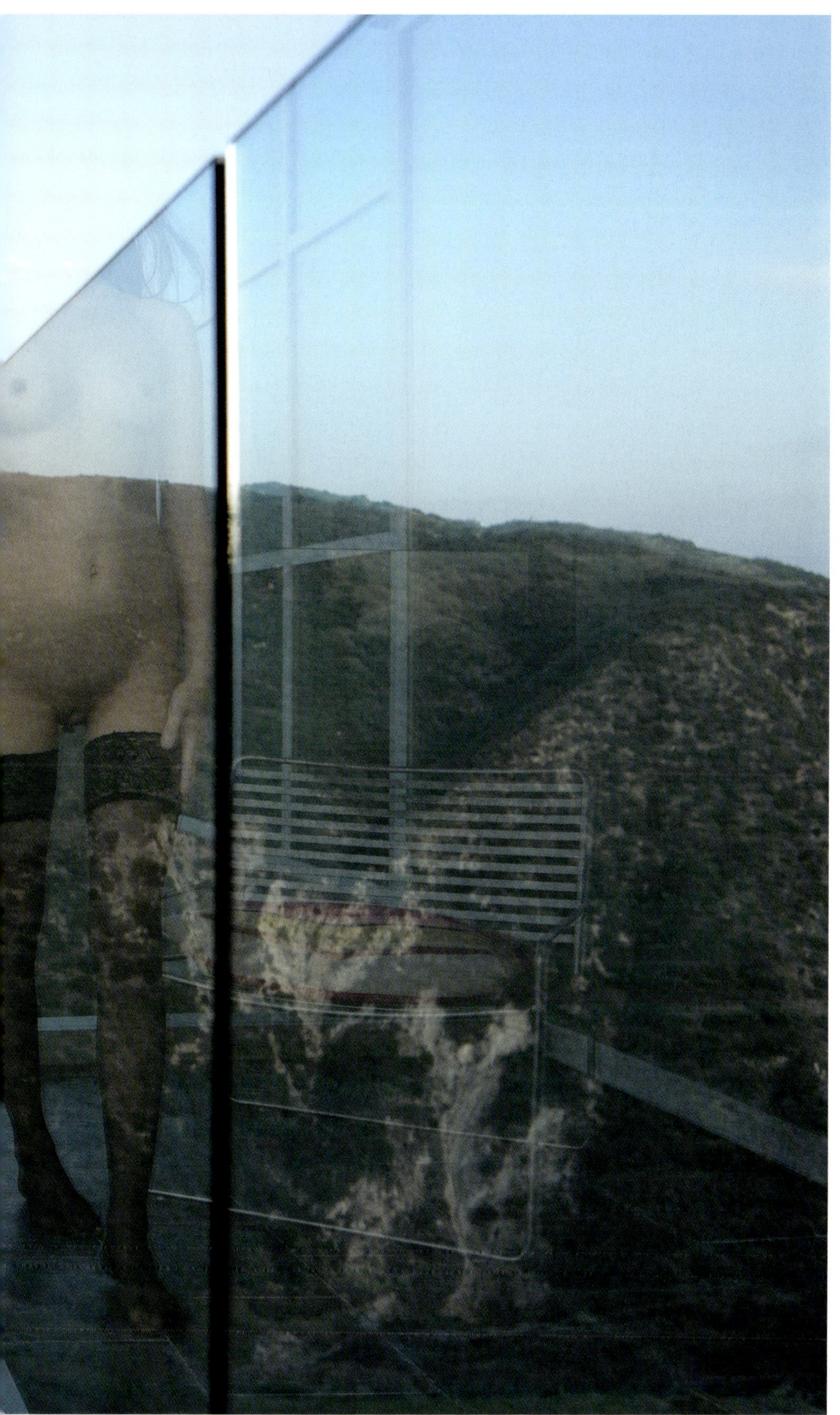

PAGE 78/79 ALEXIS MALIBU

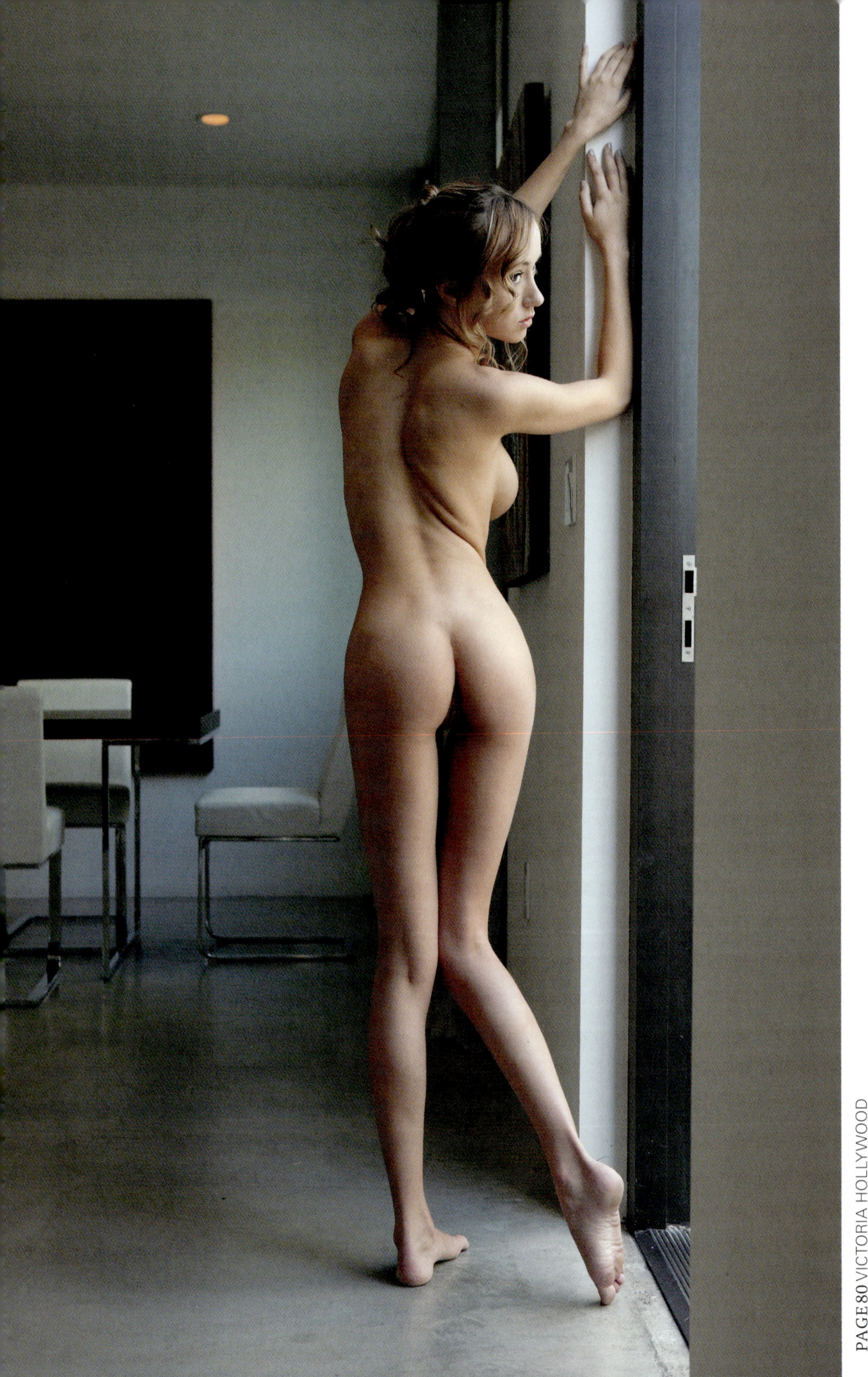

PAGE 80 VICTORIA HOLLYWOOD

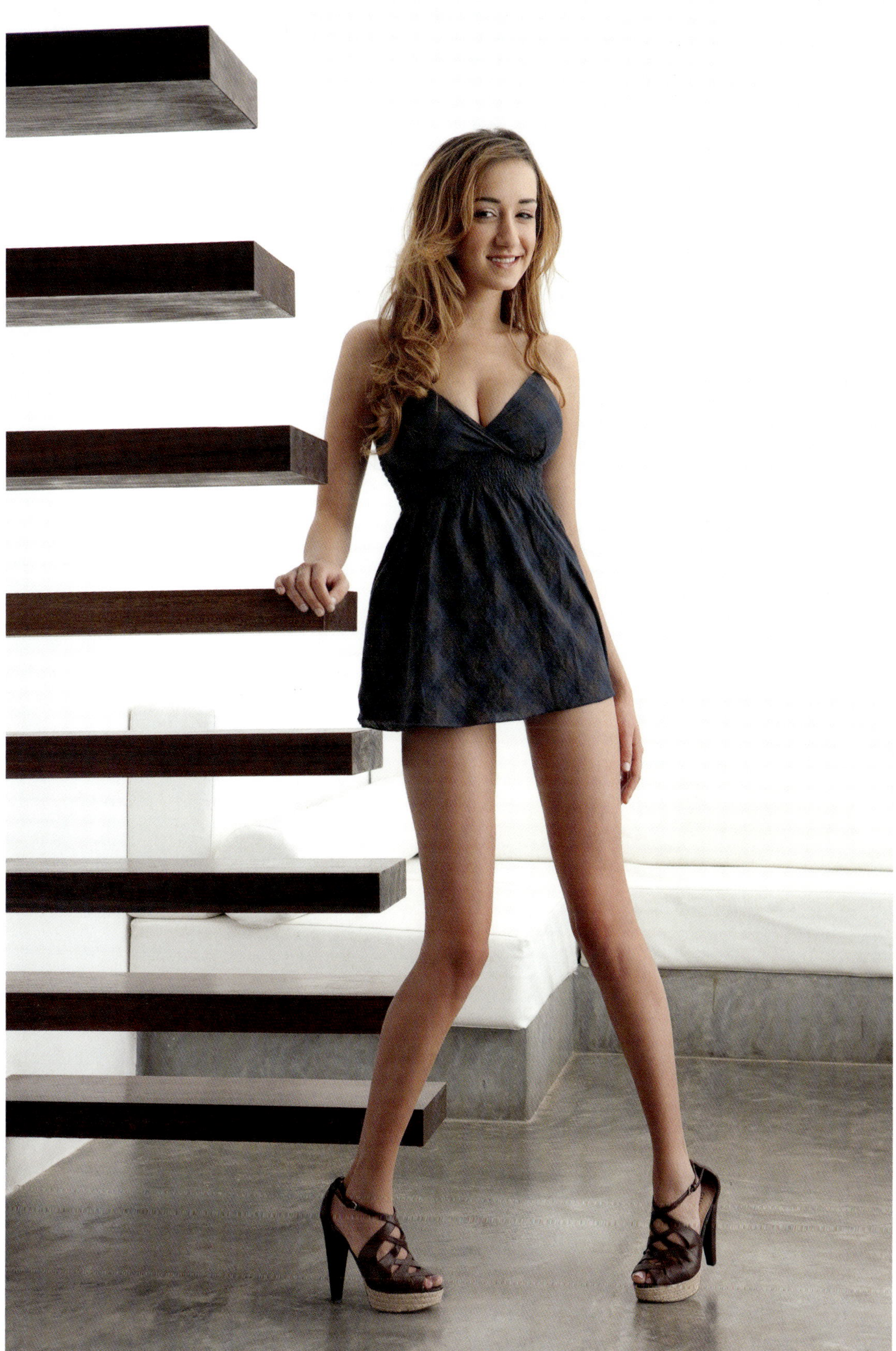

PAGE 81 VICTORIA IBIZA

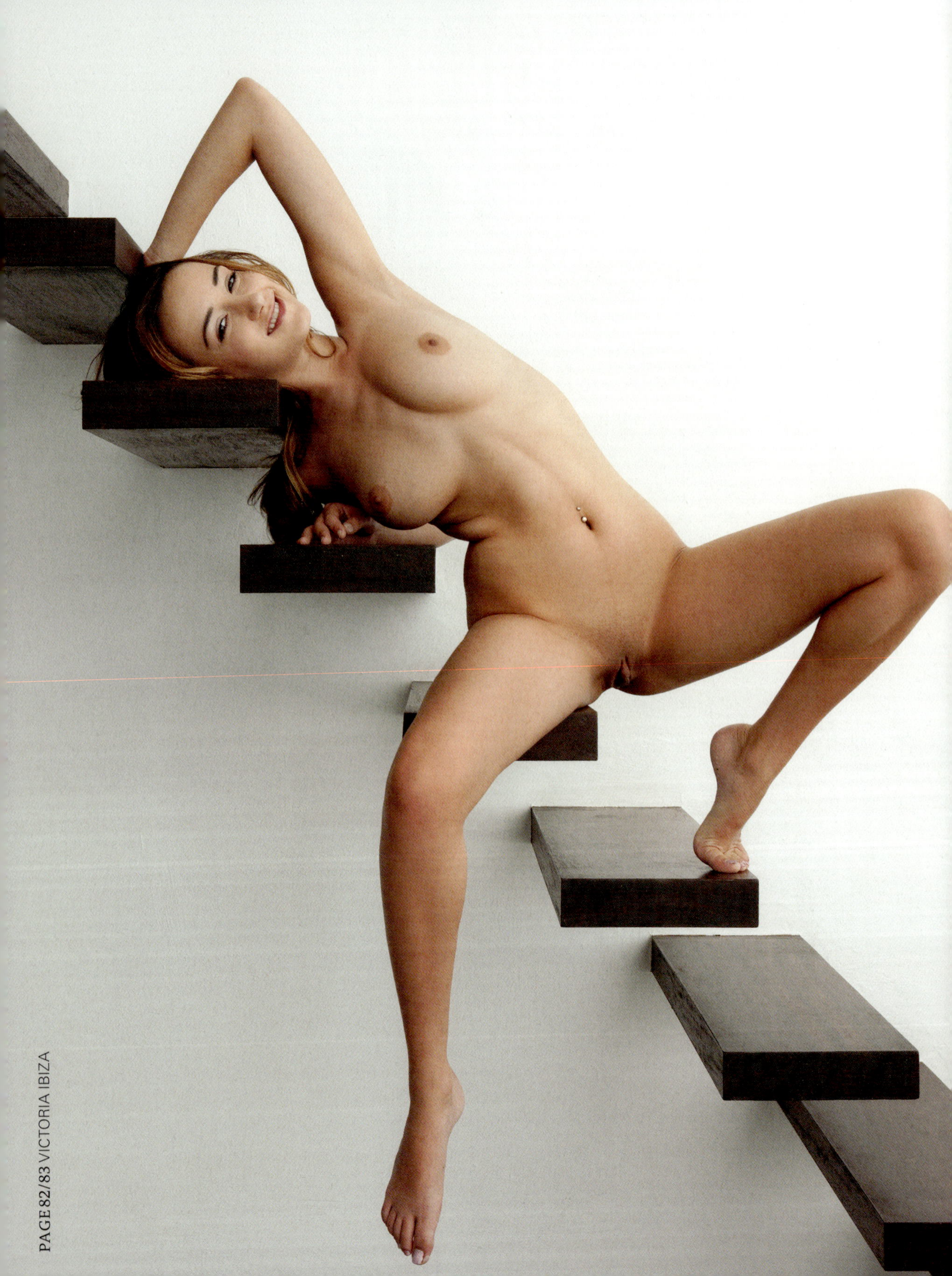
PAGE 82/83 VICTORIA IBIZA

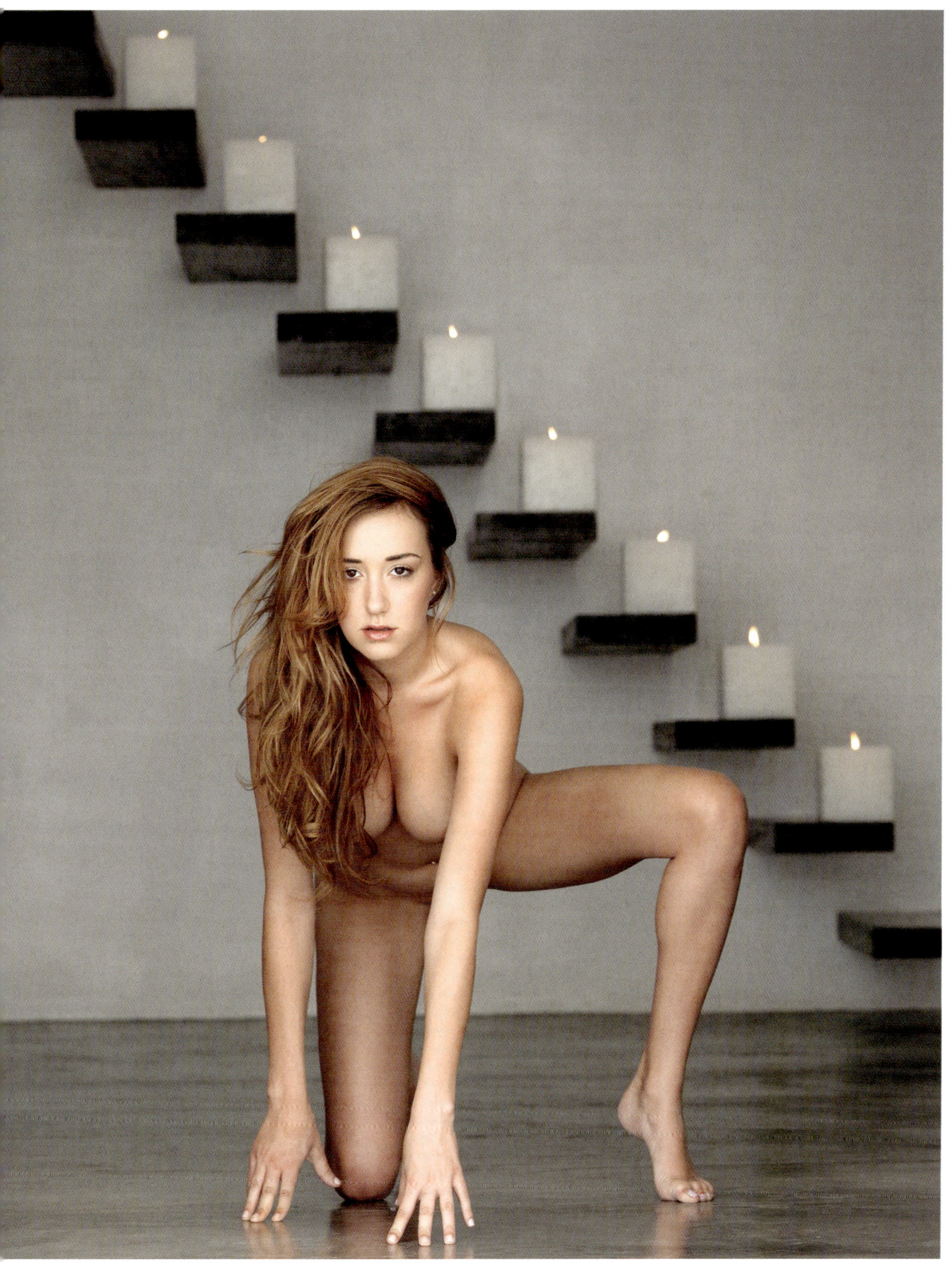

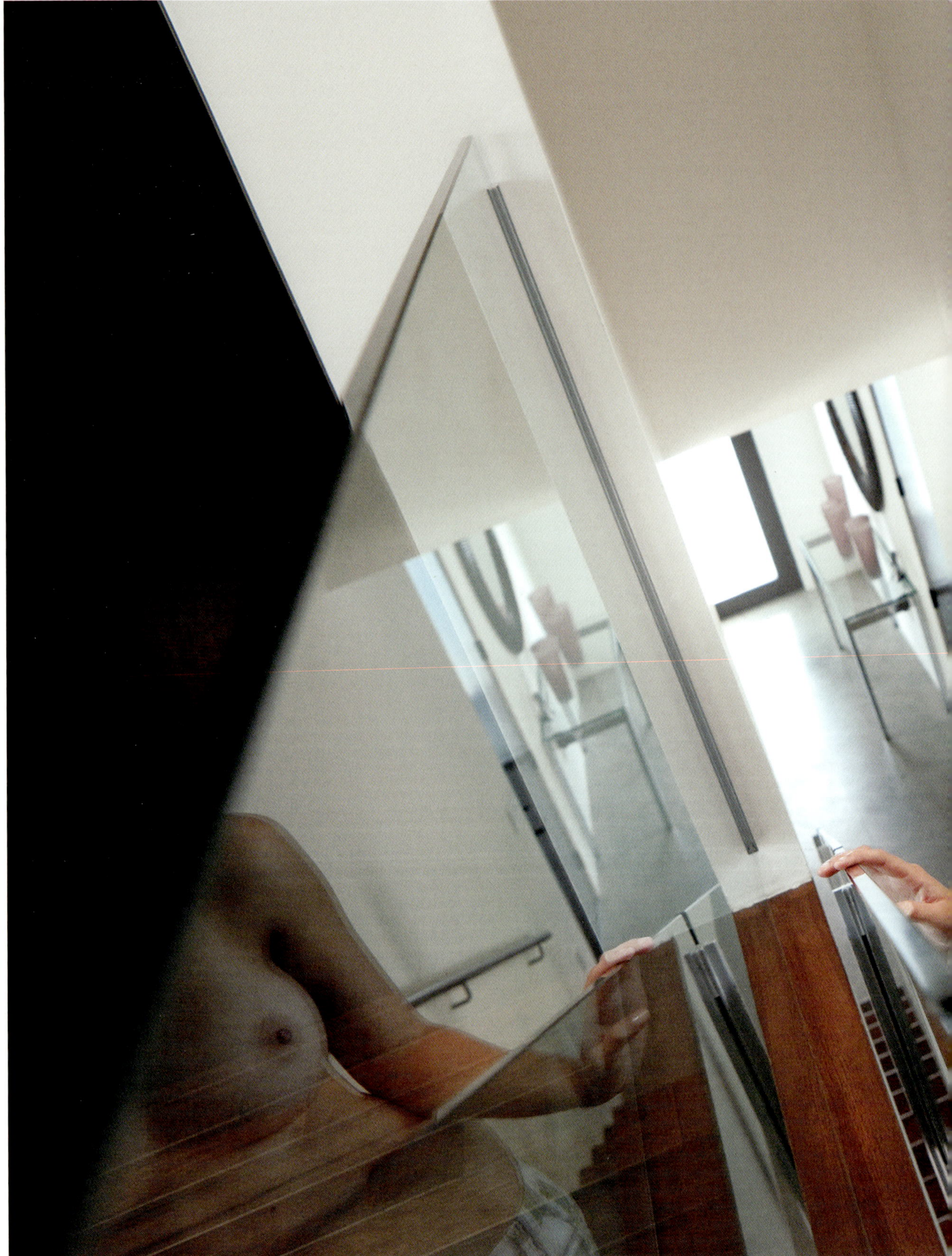

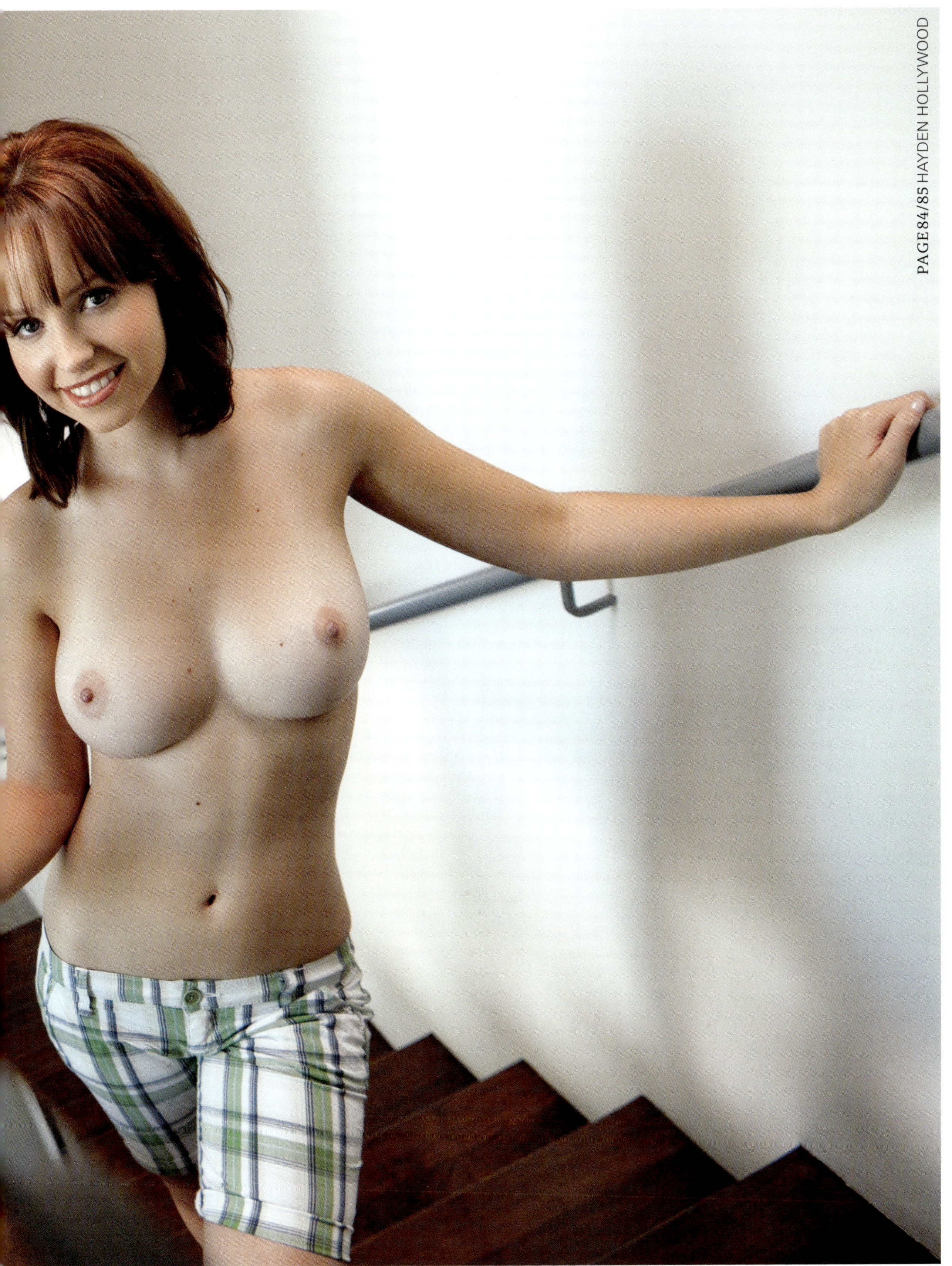

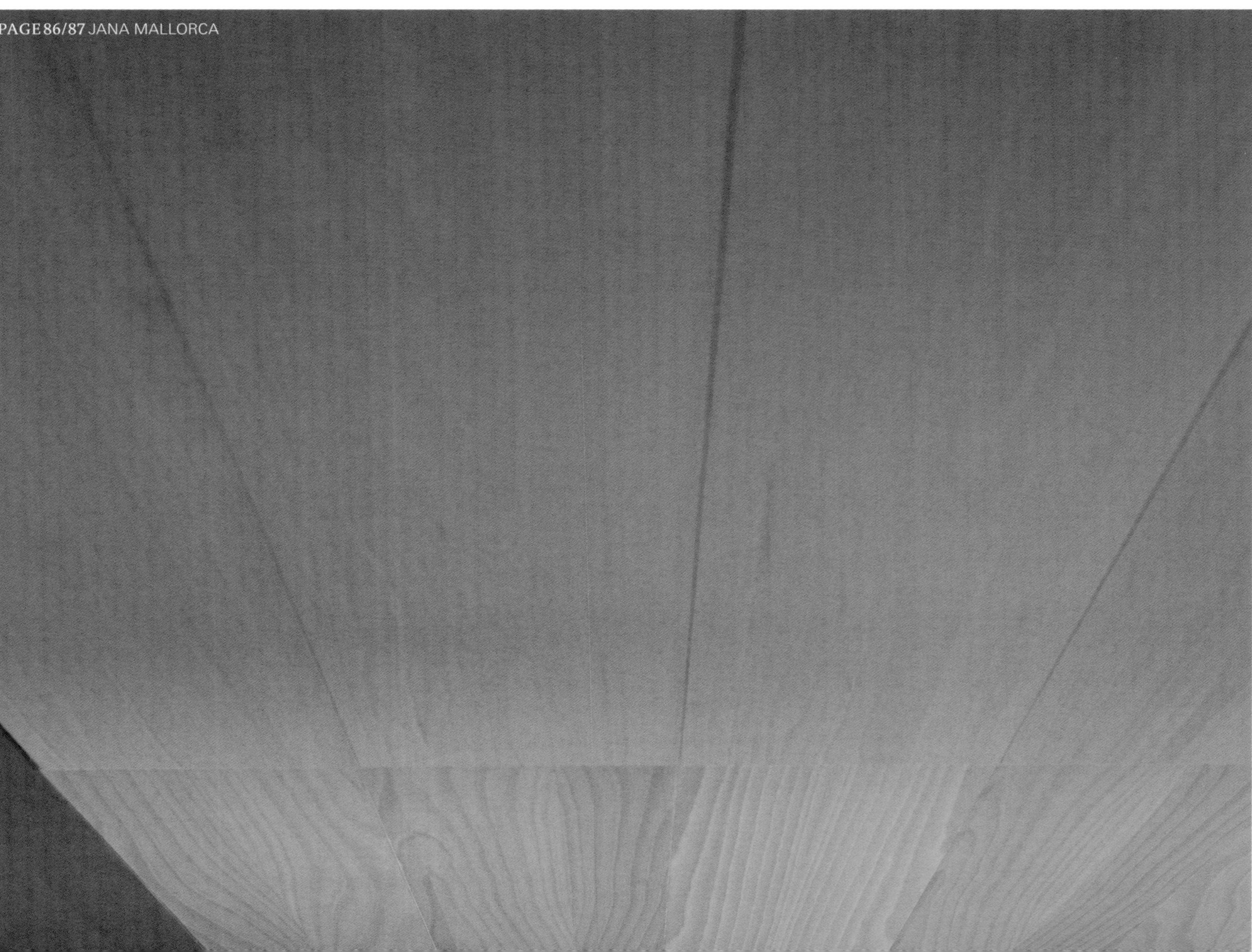

PAGE 86/87 JANA MALLORCA

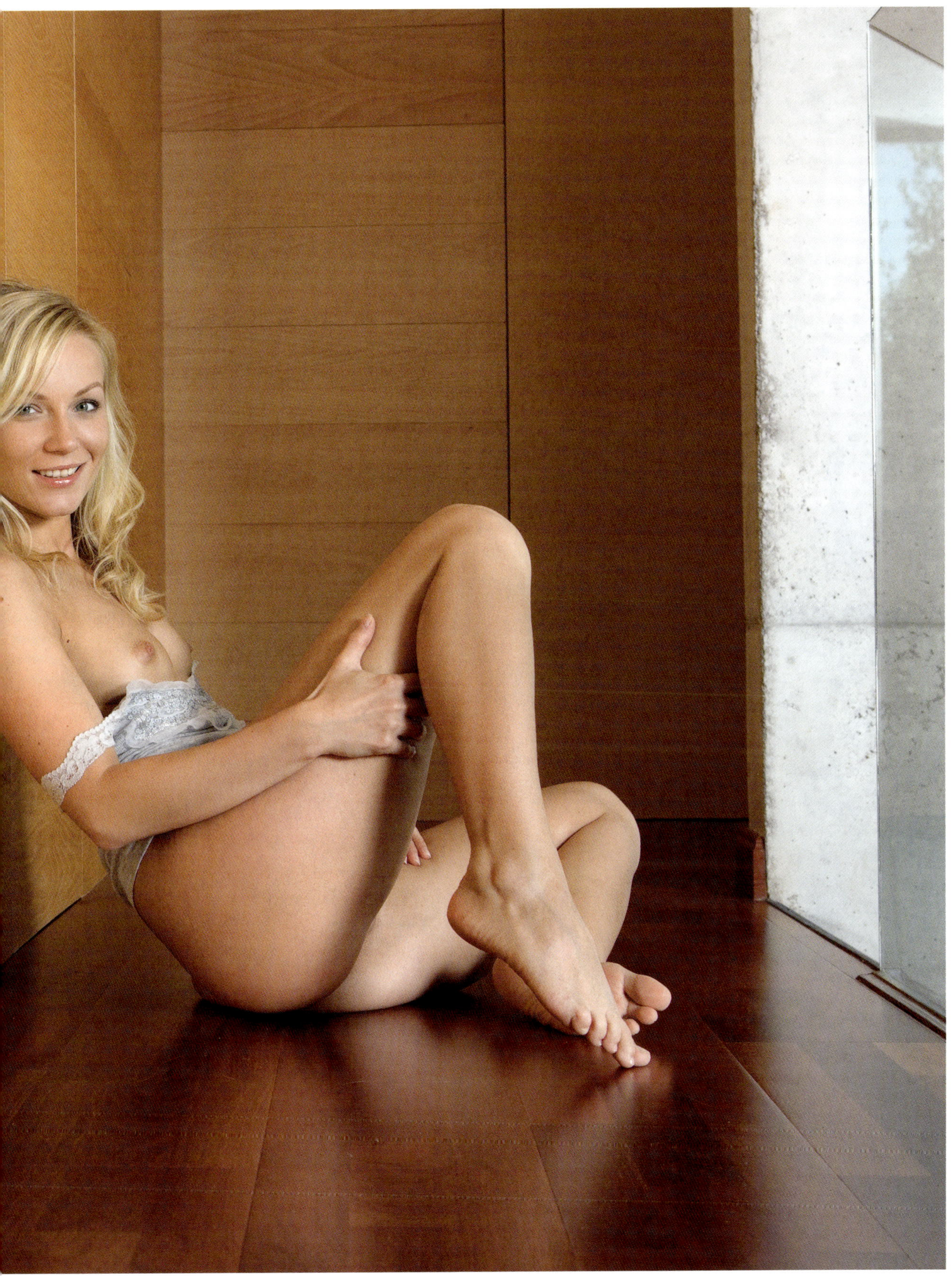

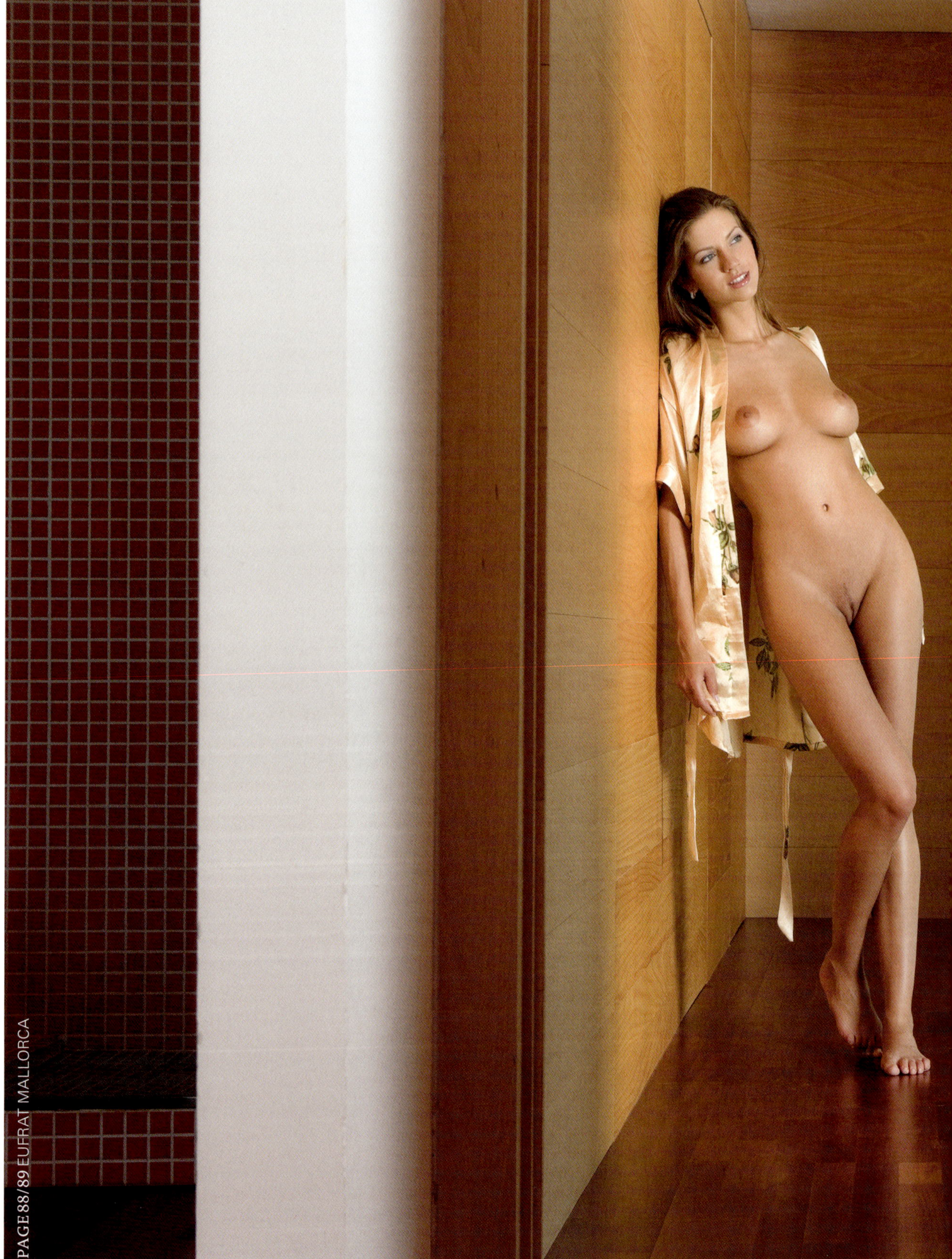
PAGE 88/89 EUFRAT MALLORCA

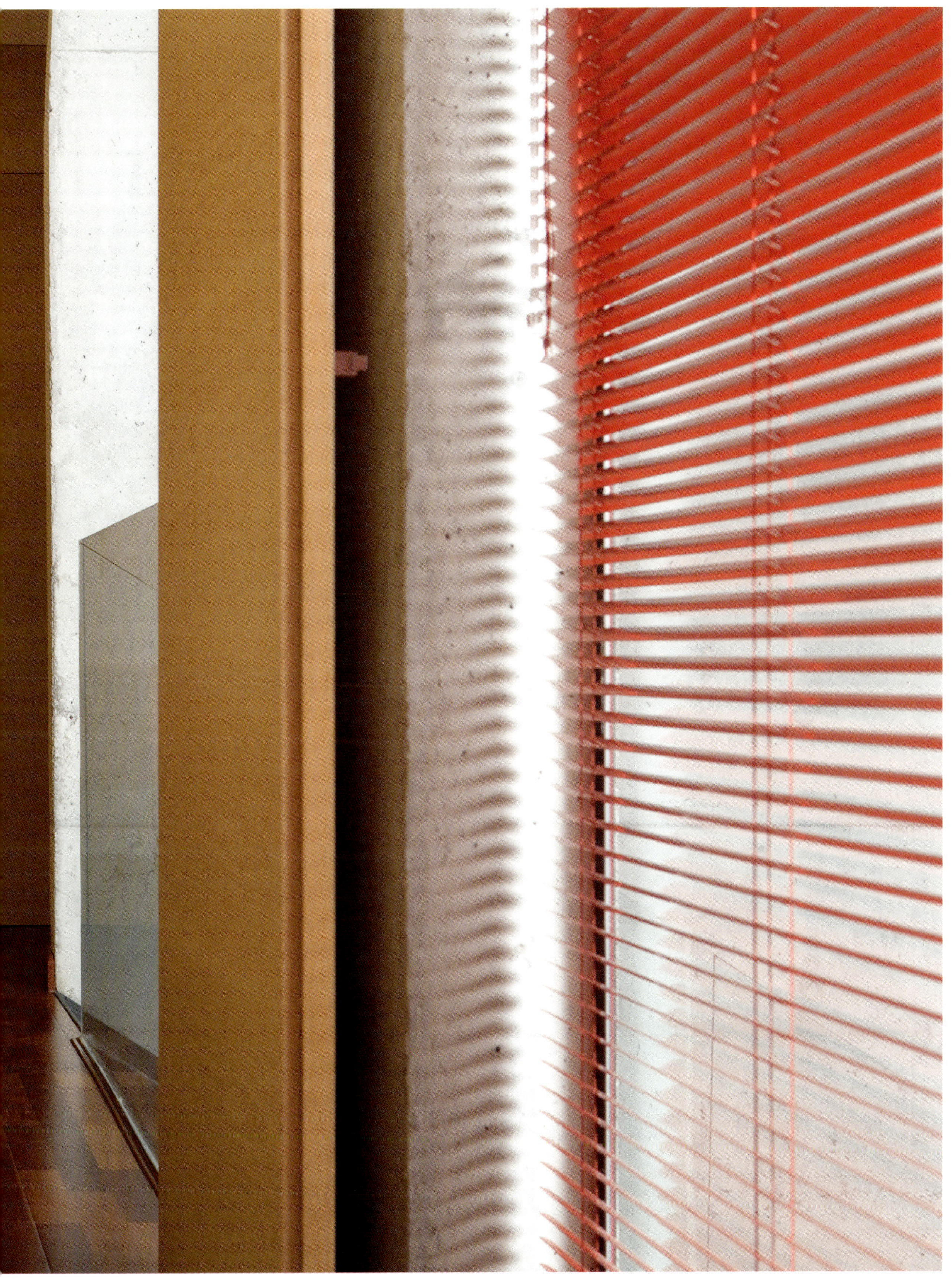

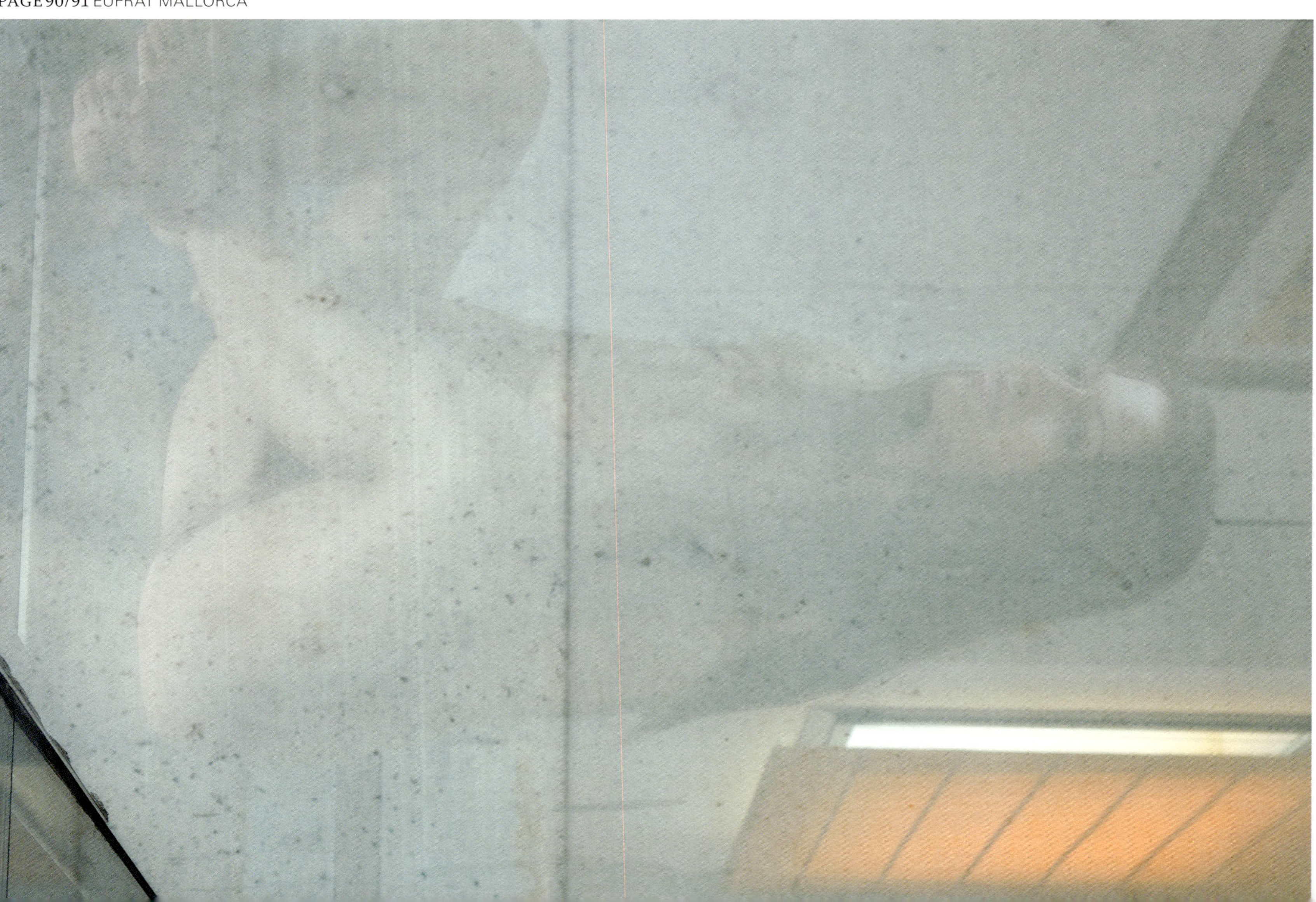

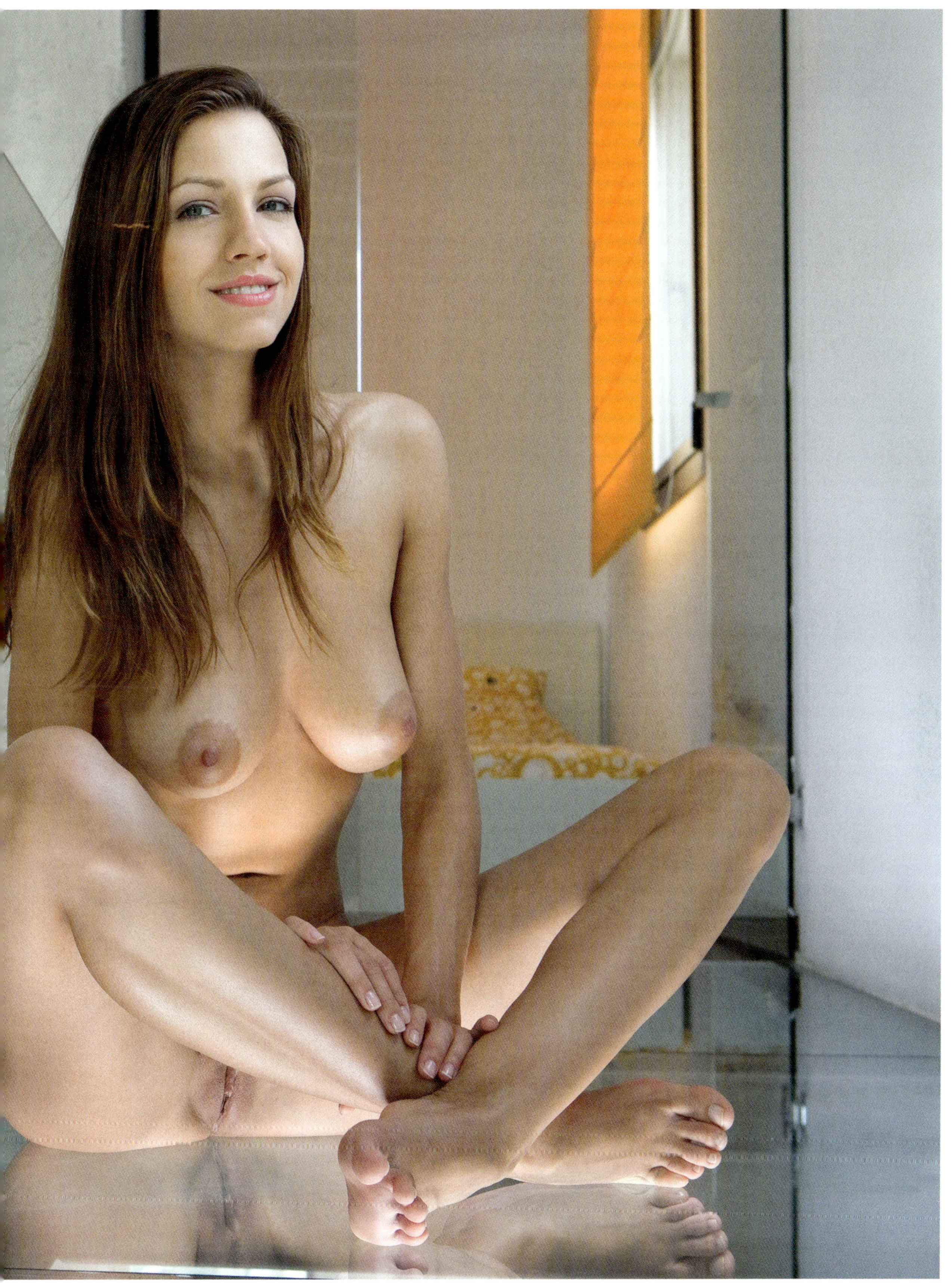

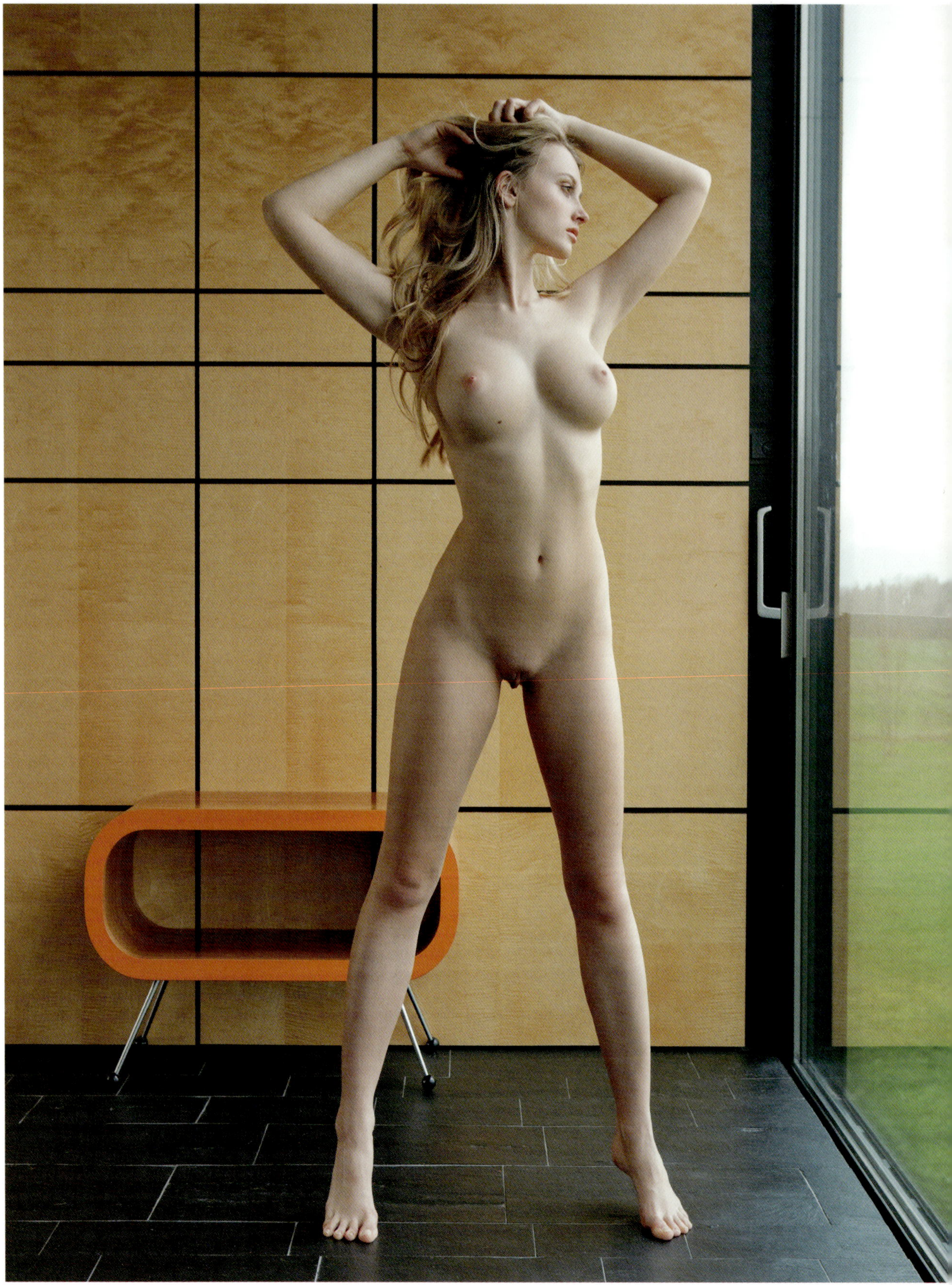

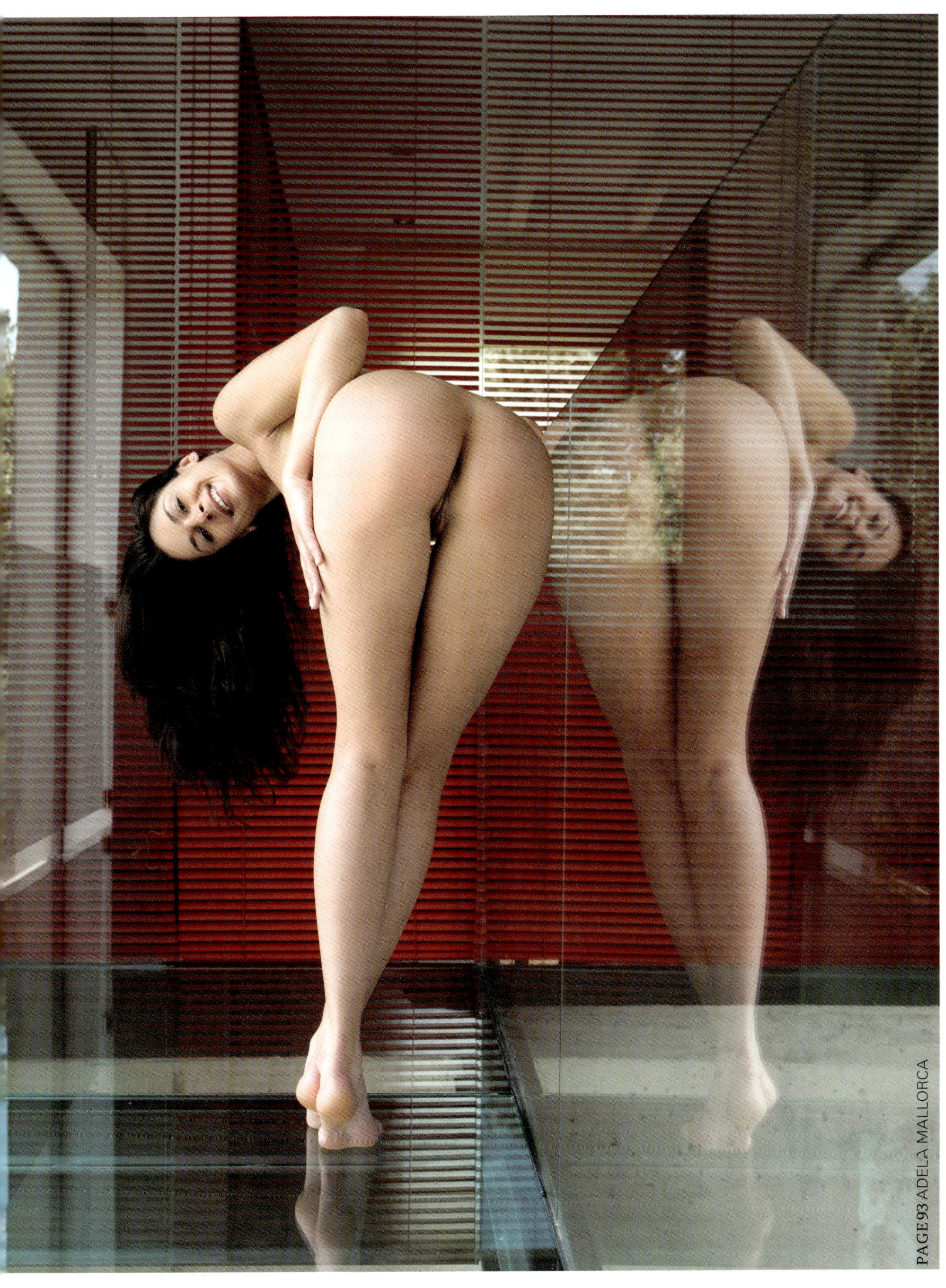
PAGE 93 ADELA MALLORCA

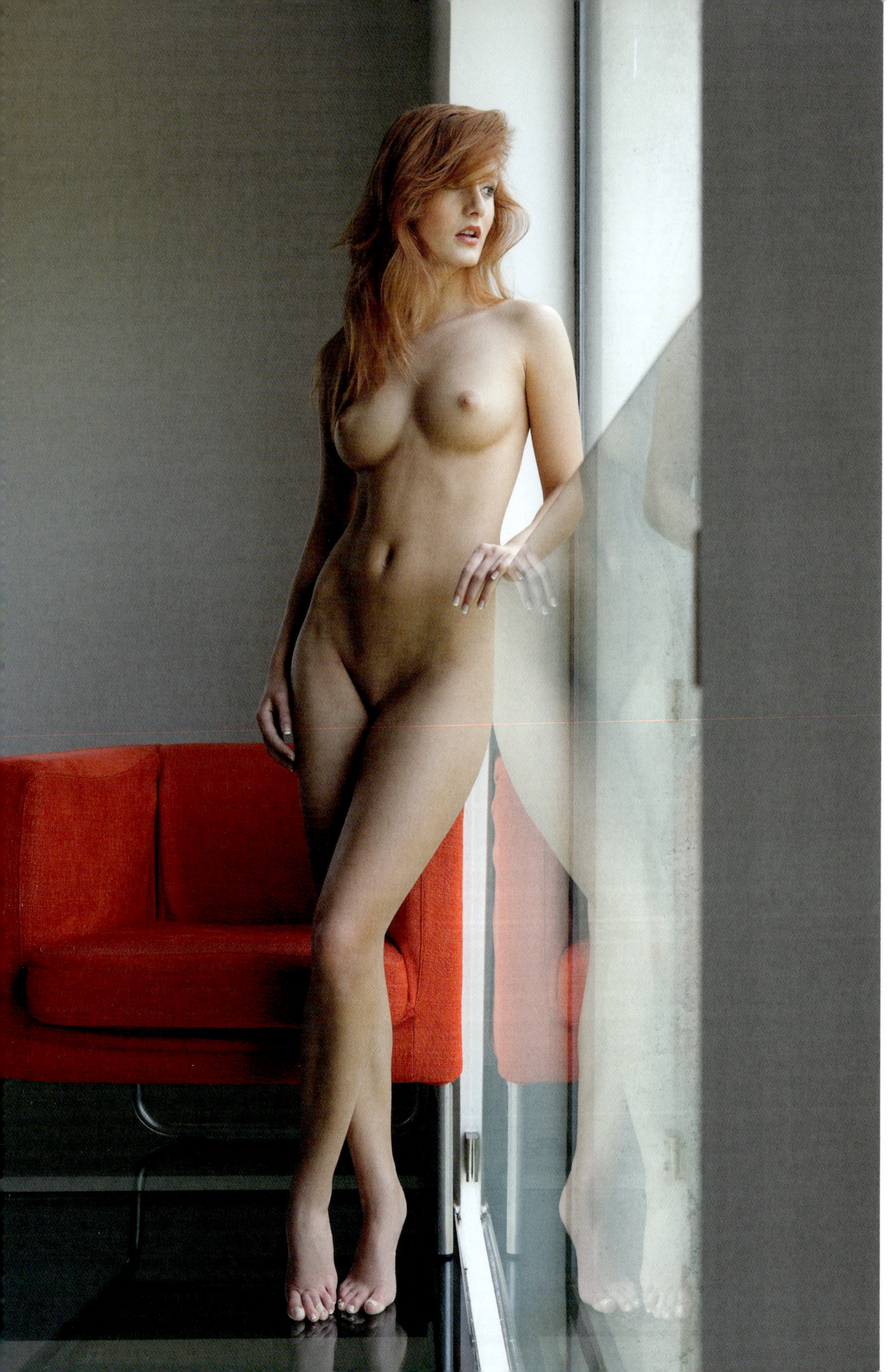

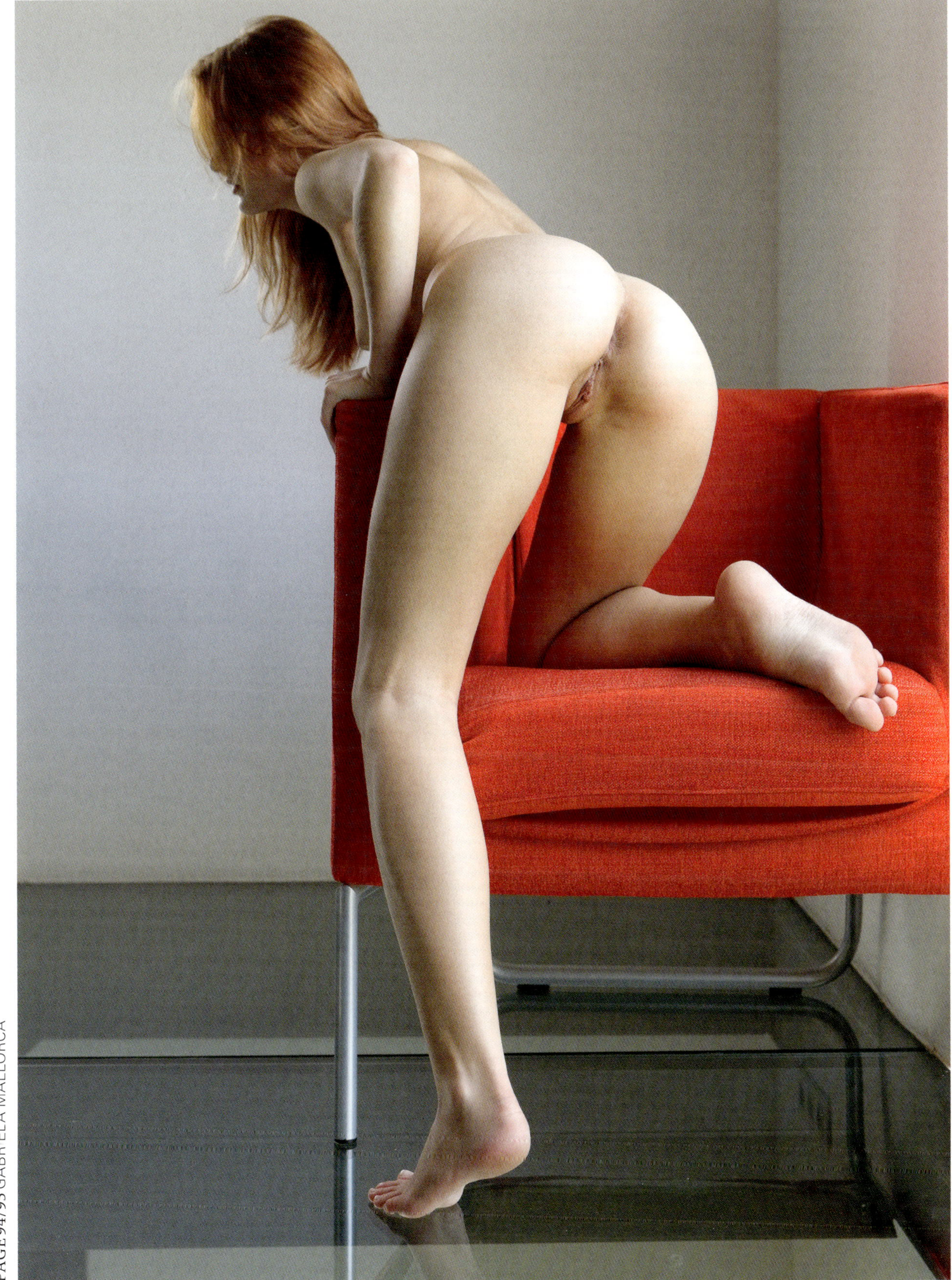

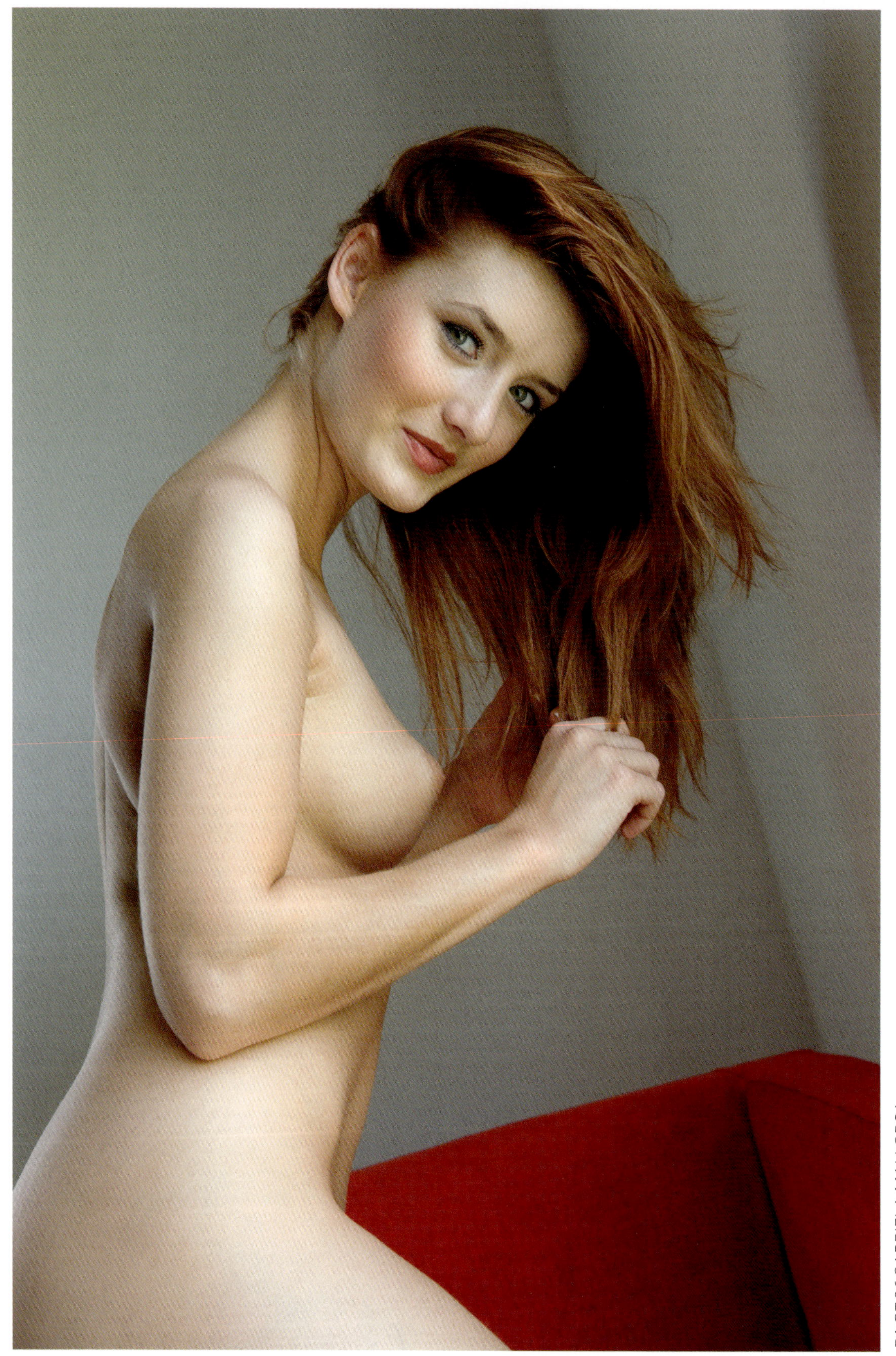

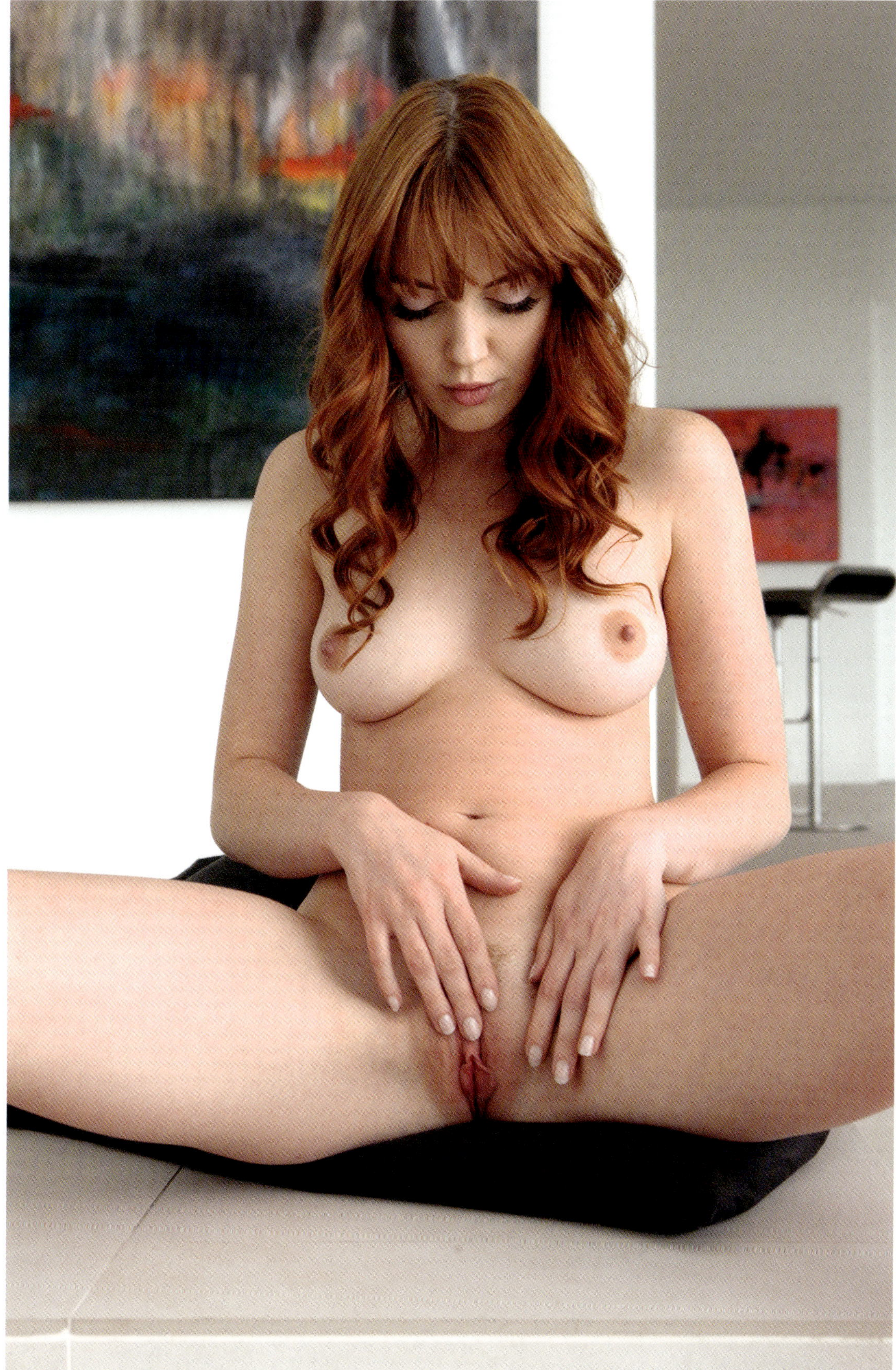

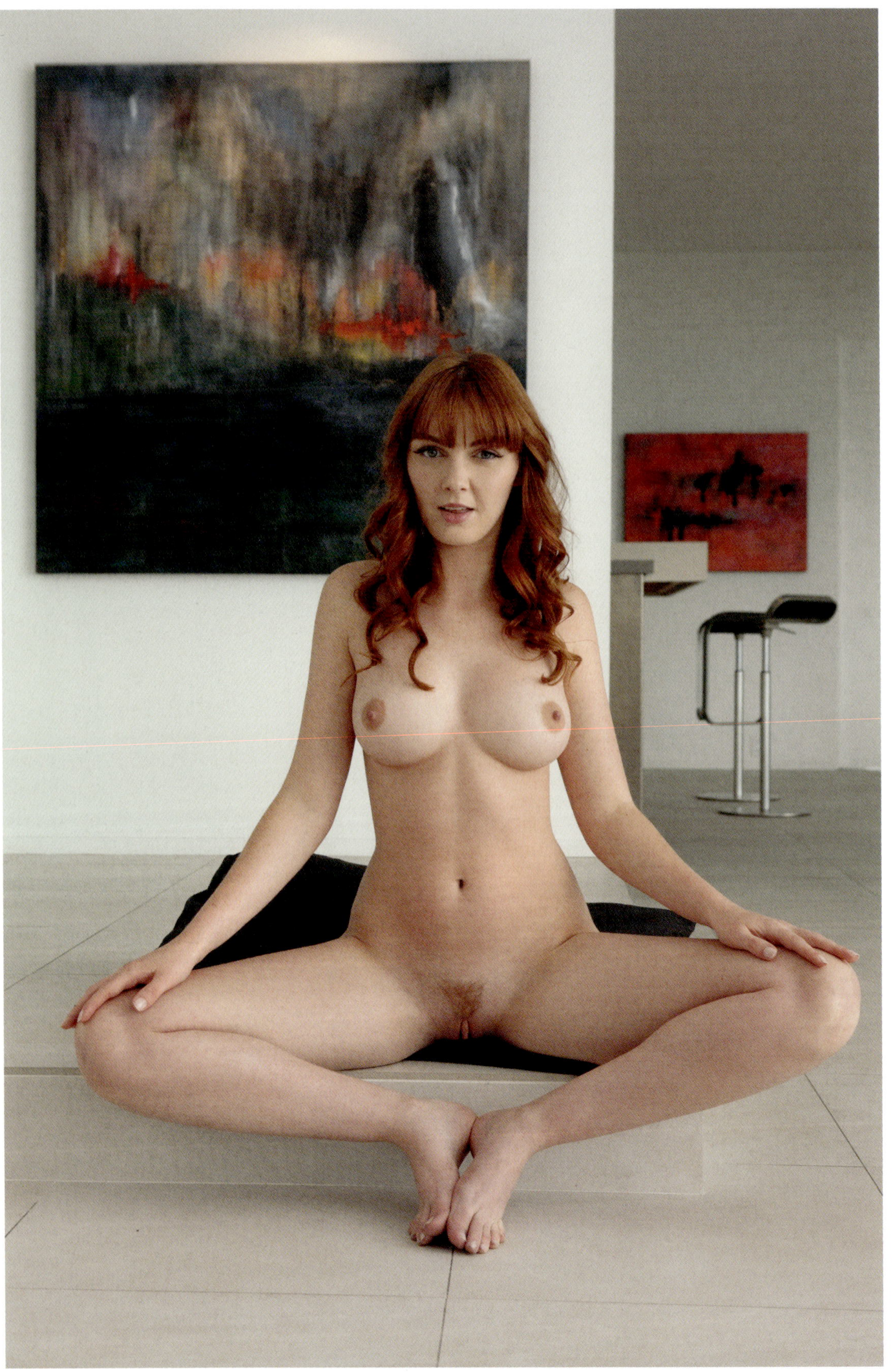

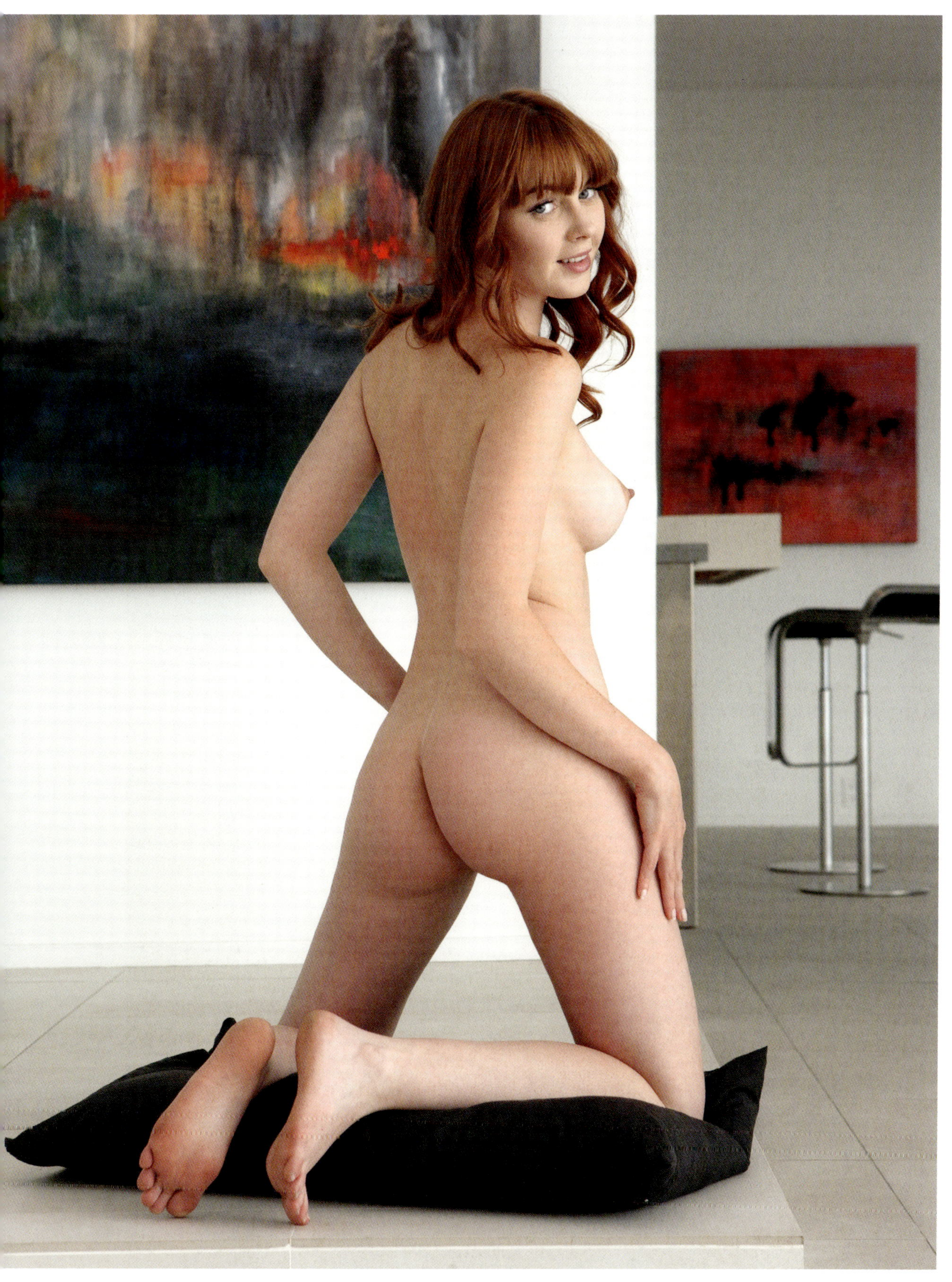

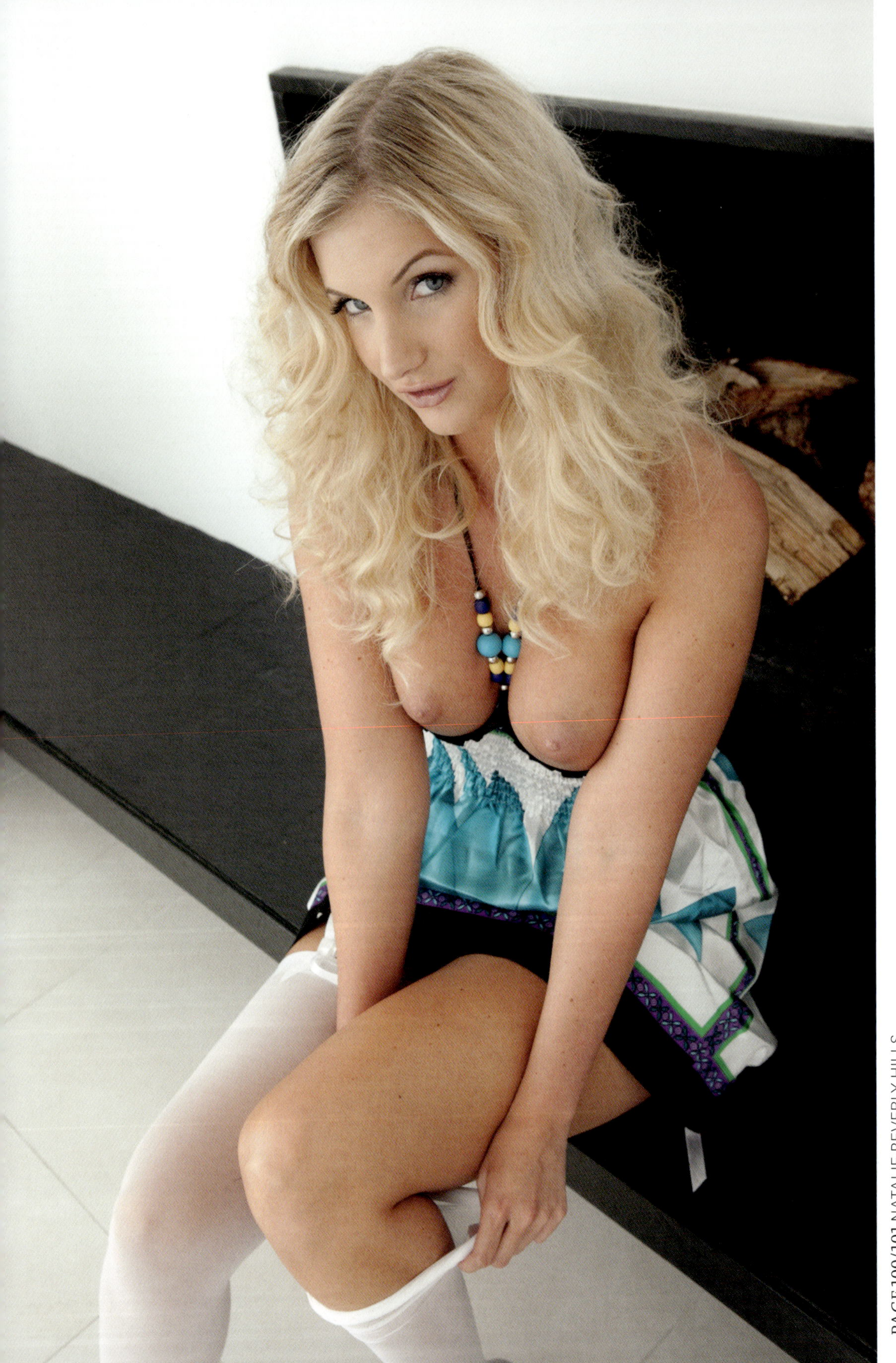

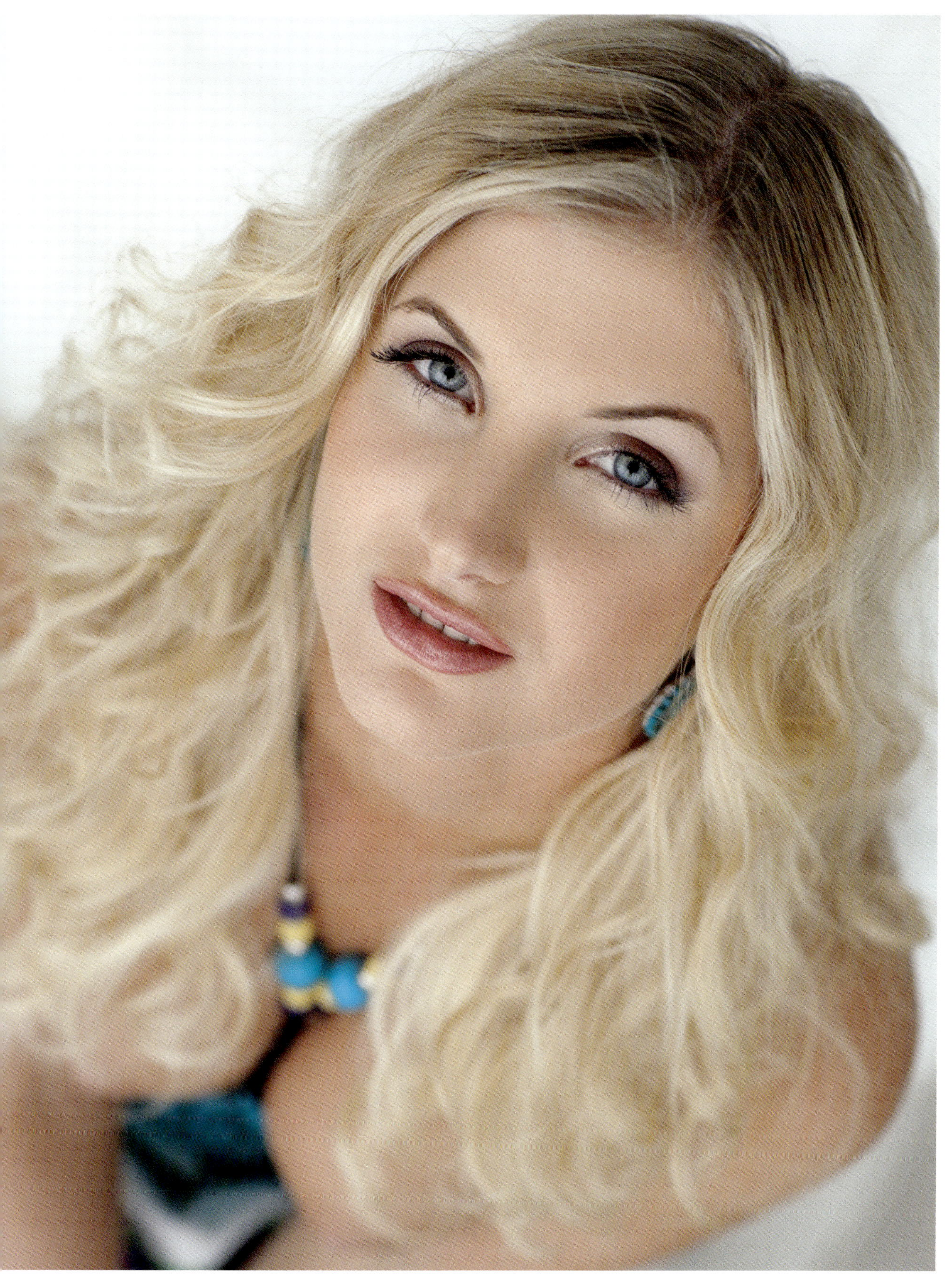

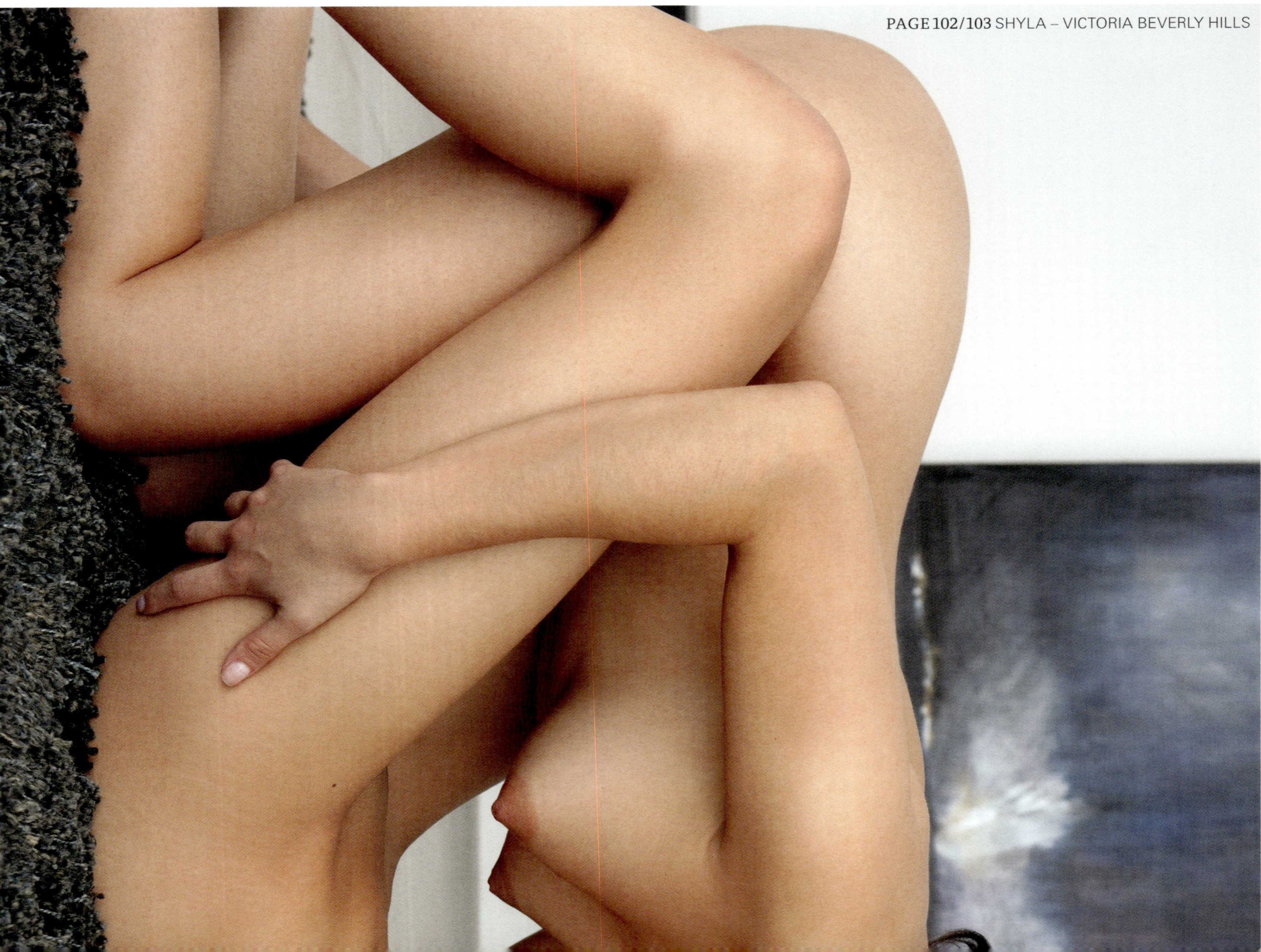

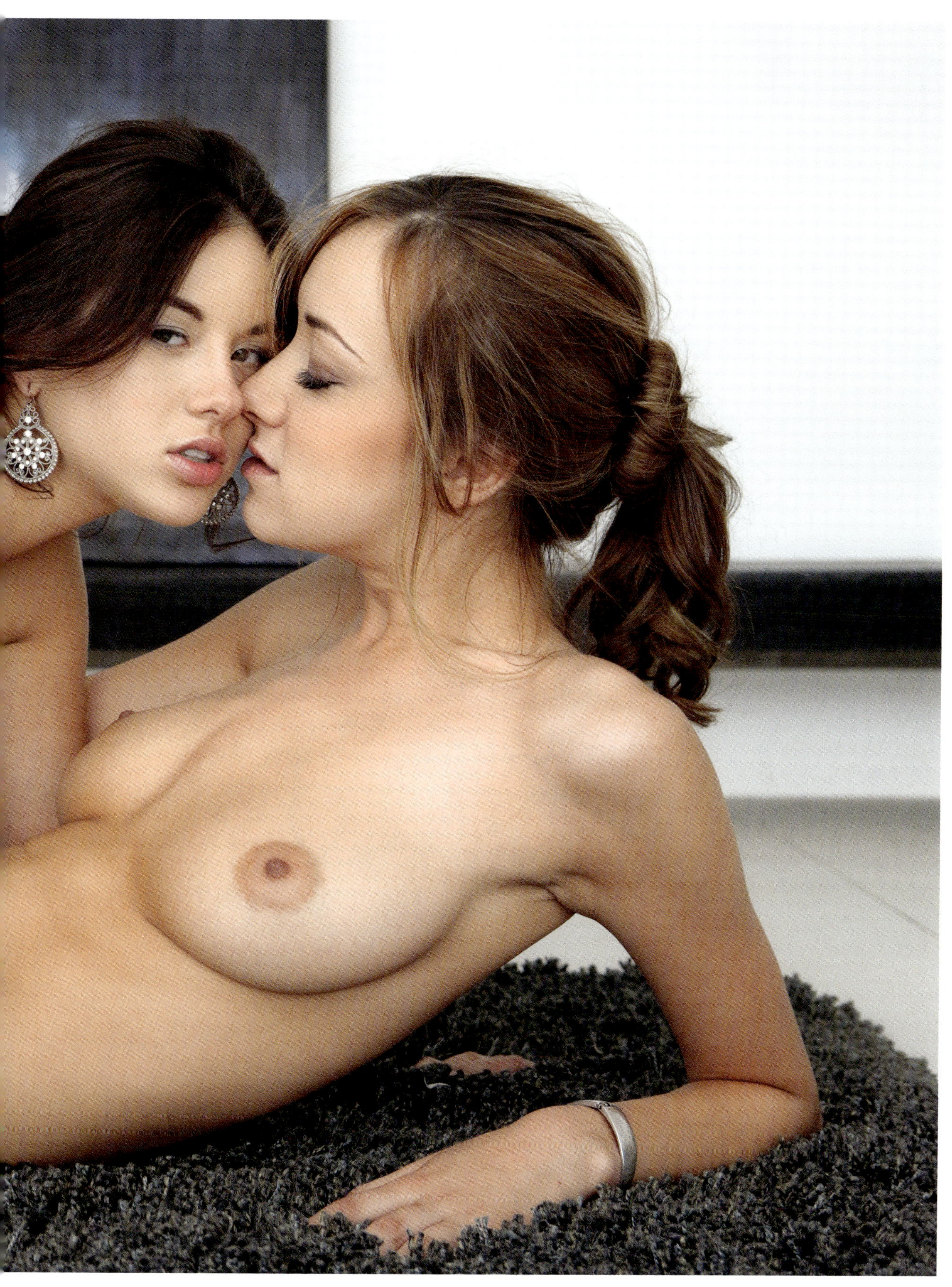

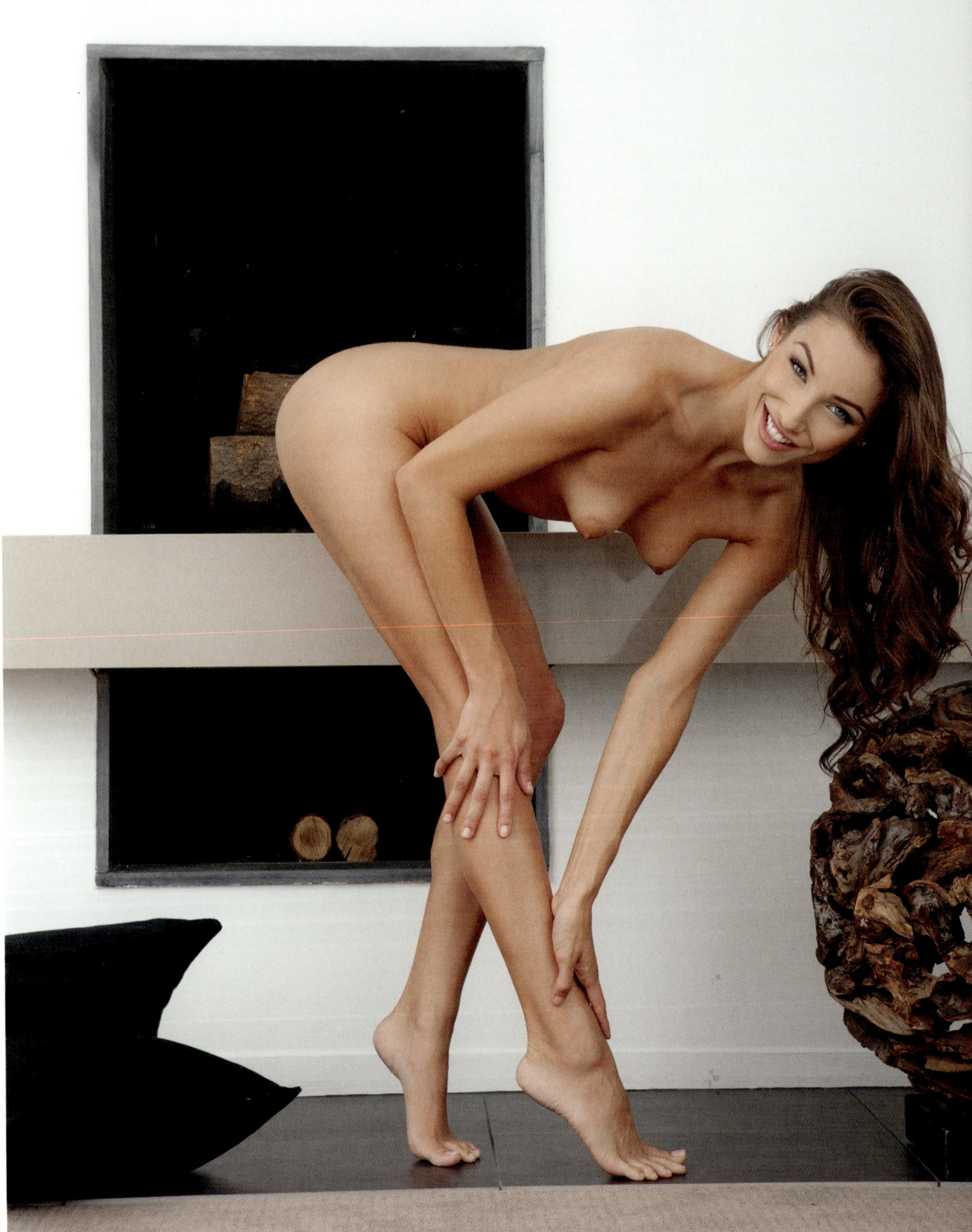

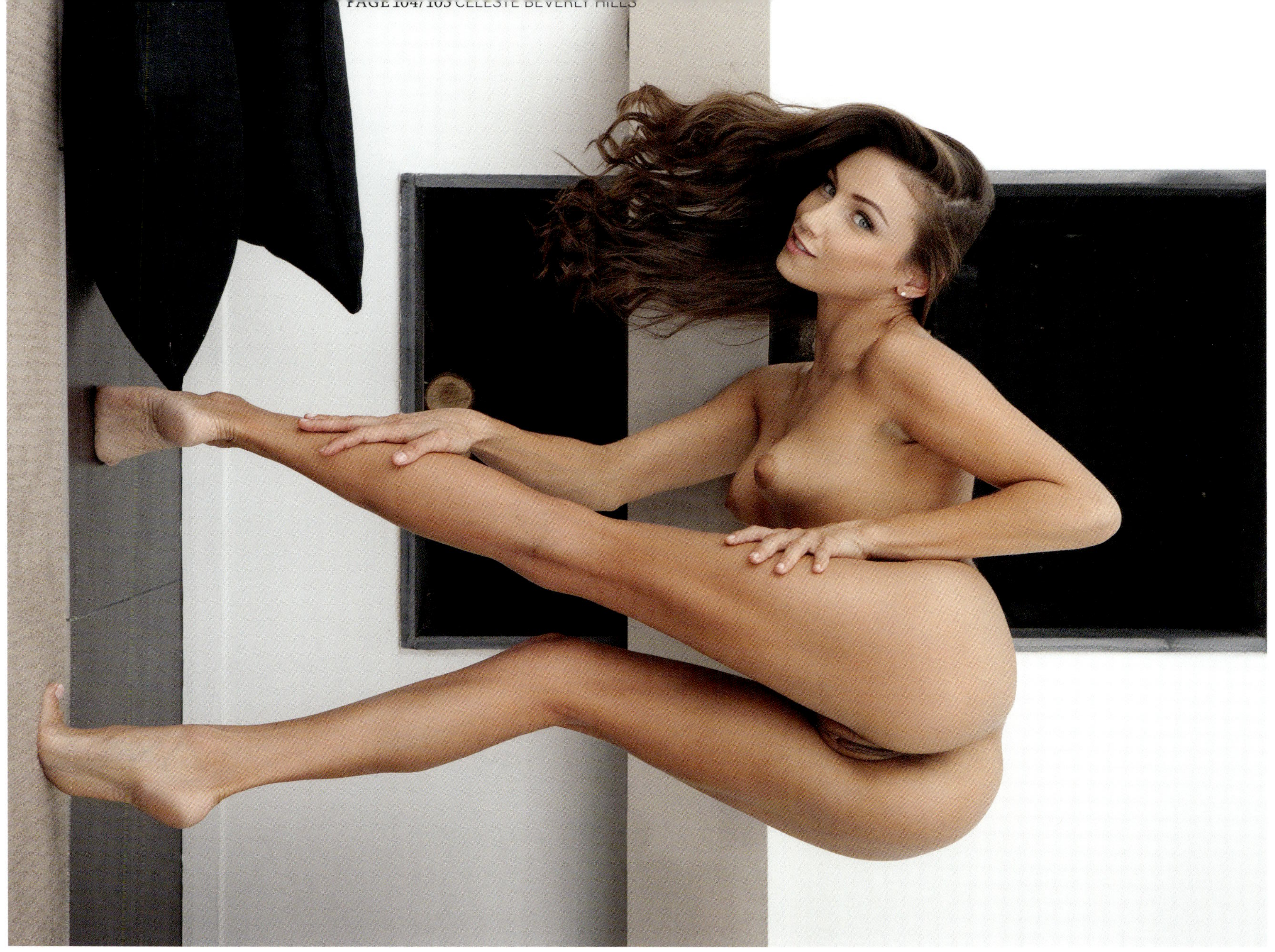

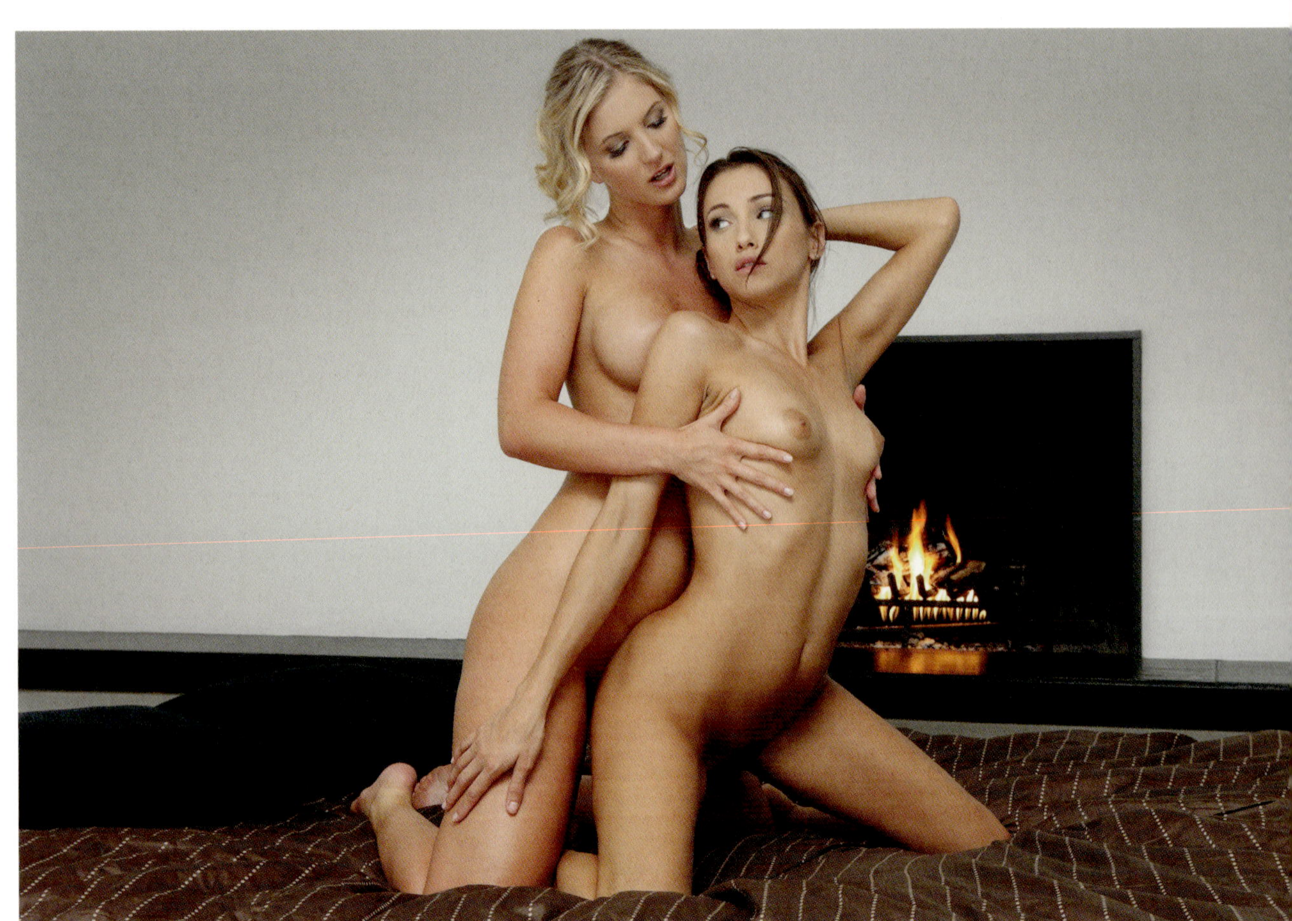

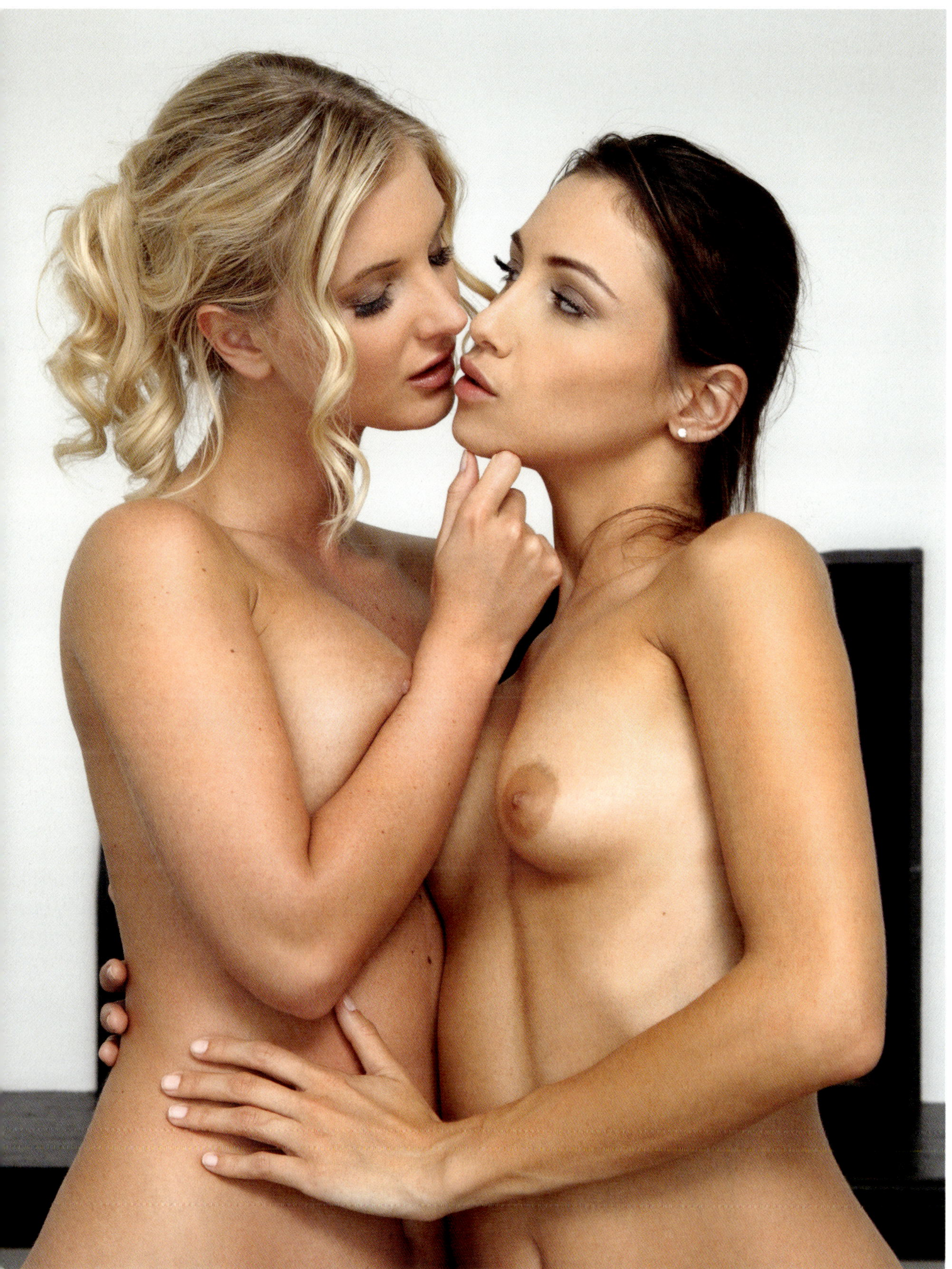

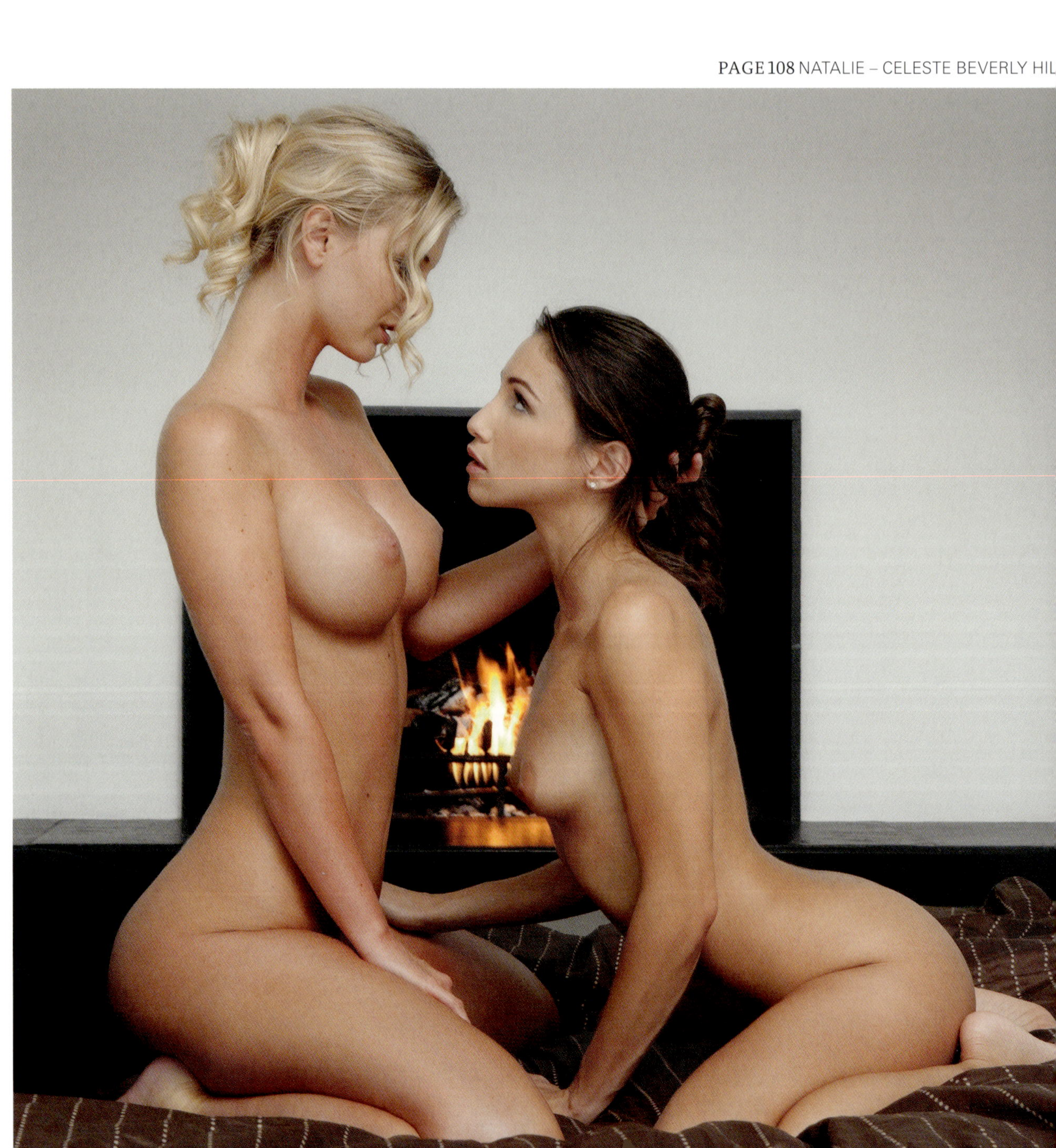

PAGE 109 VICTORIA – SHYLA BEVERLY HILLS

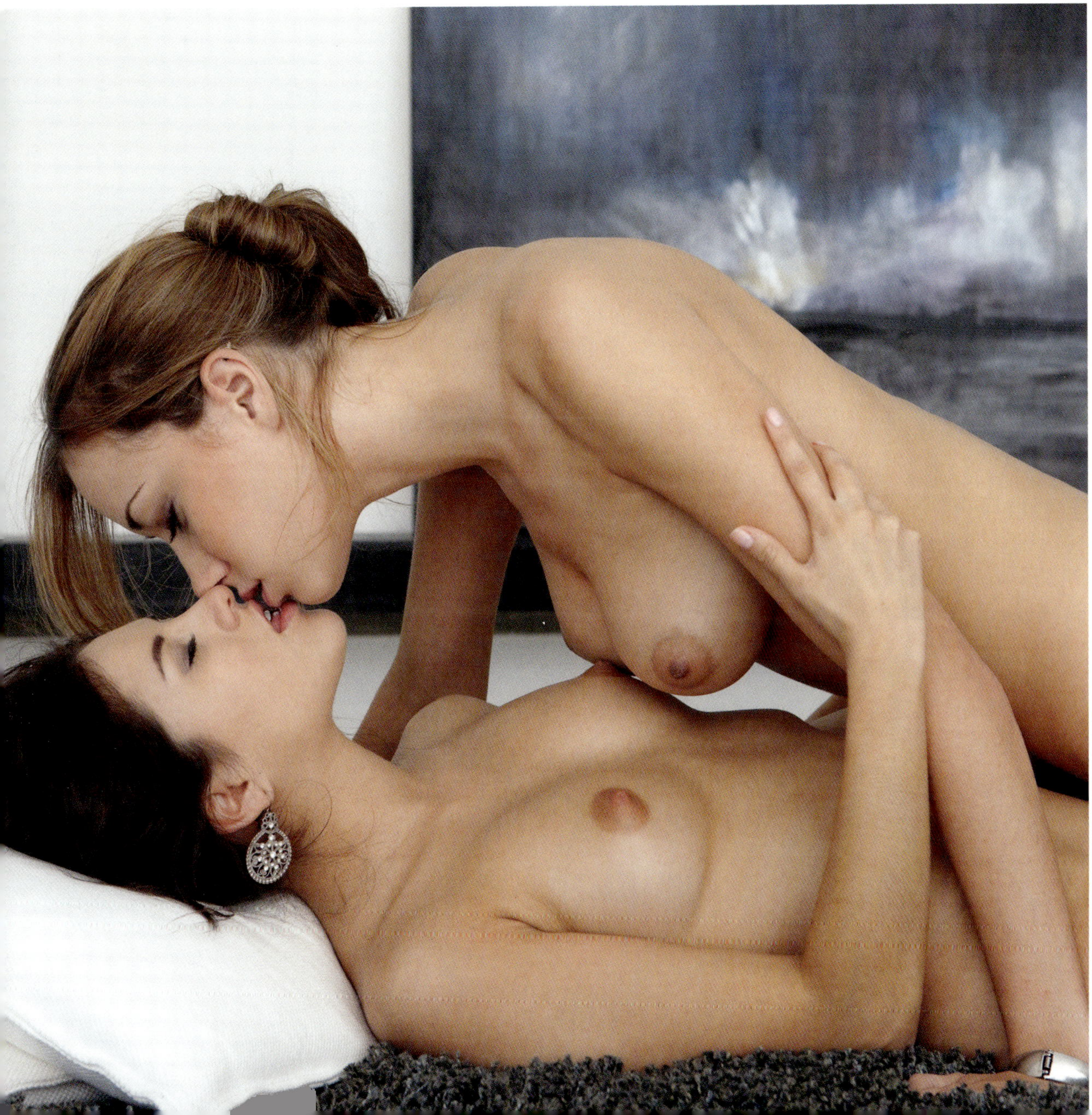

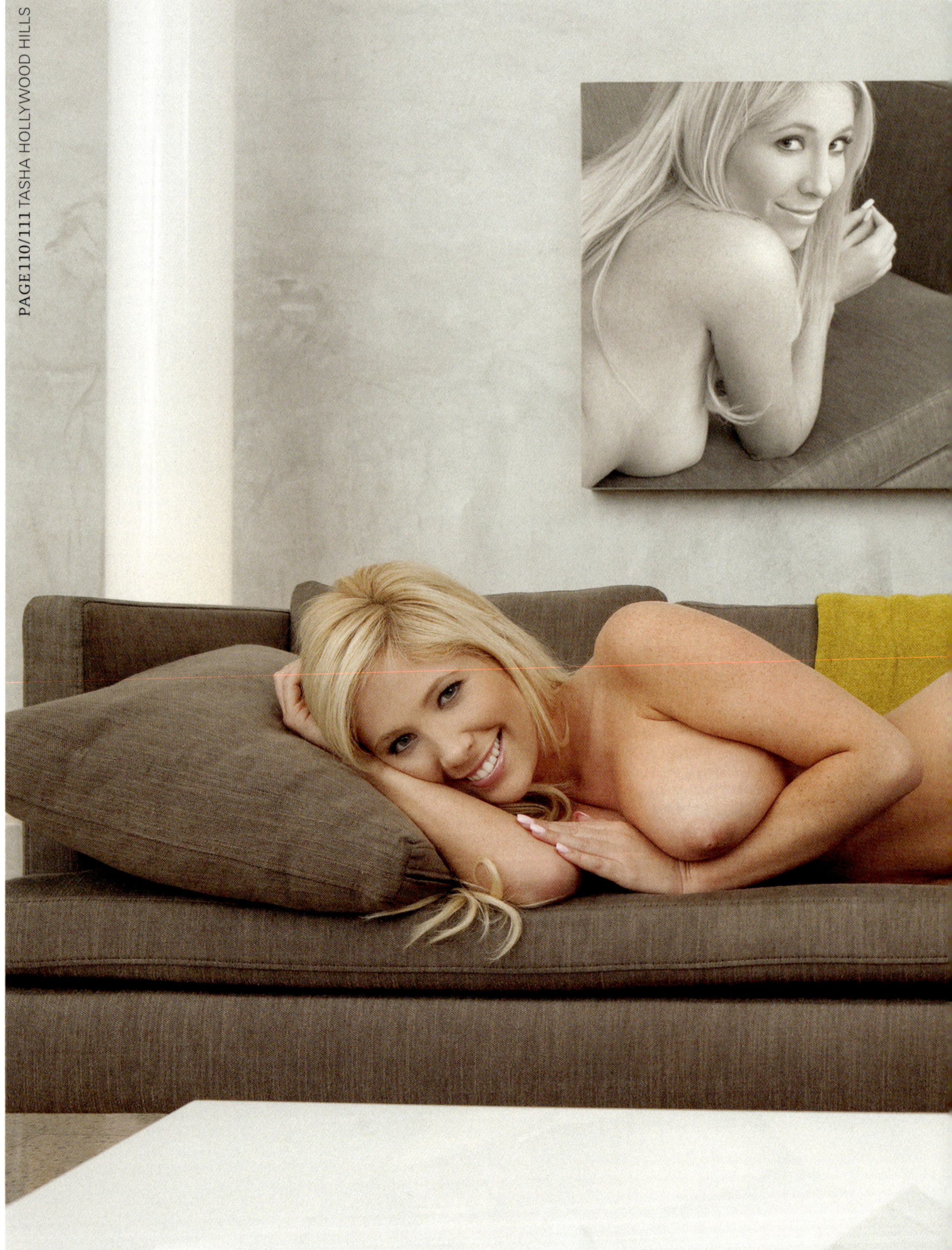

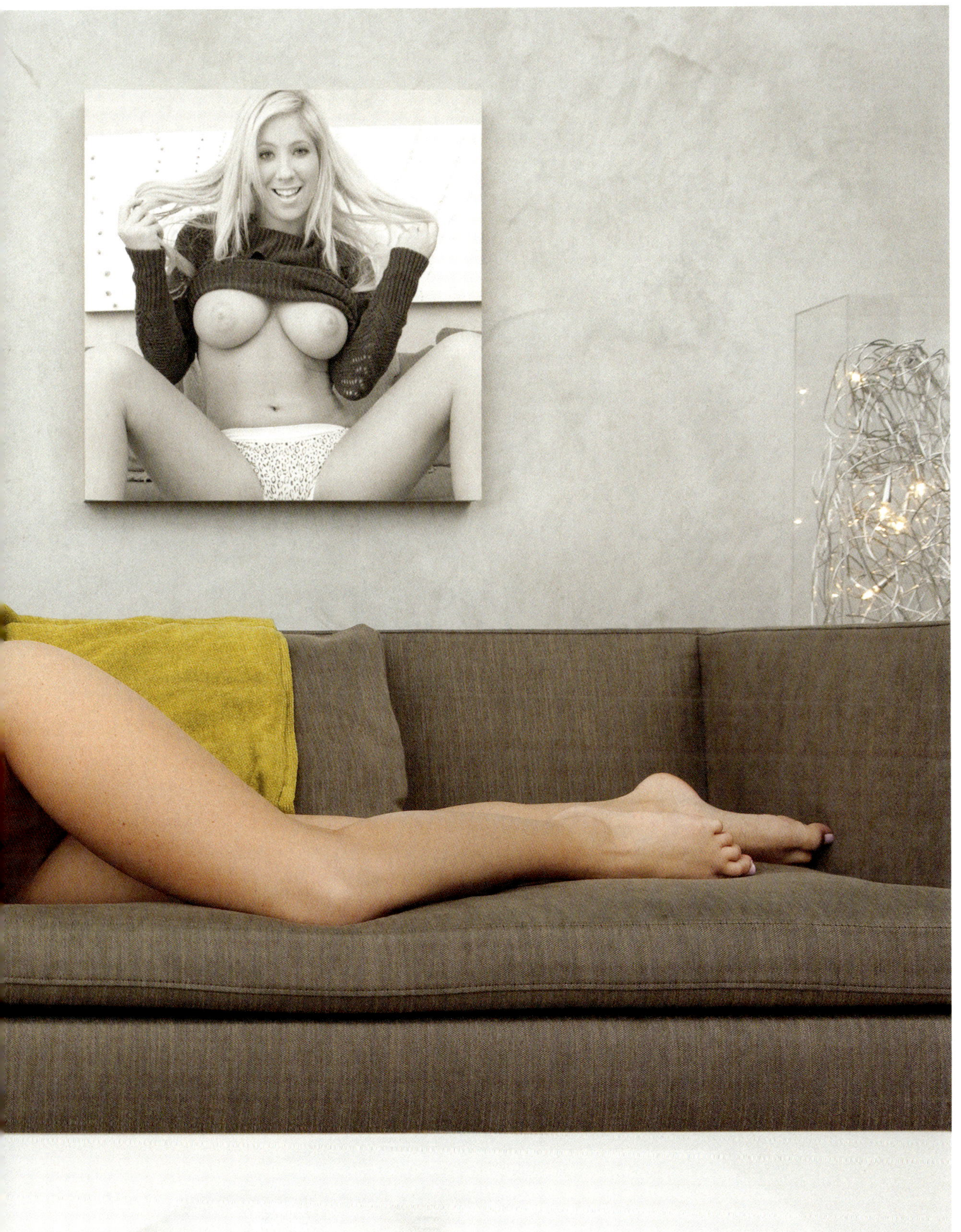

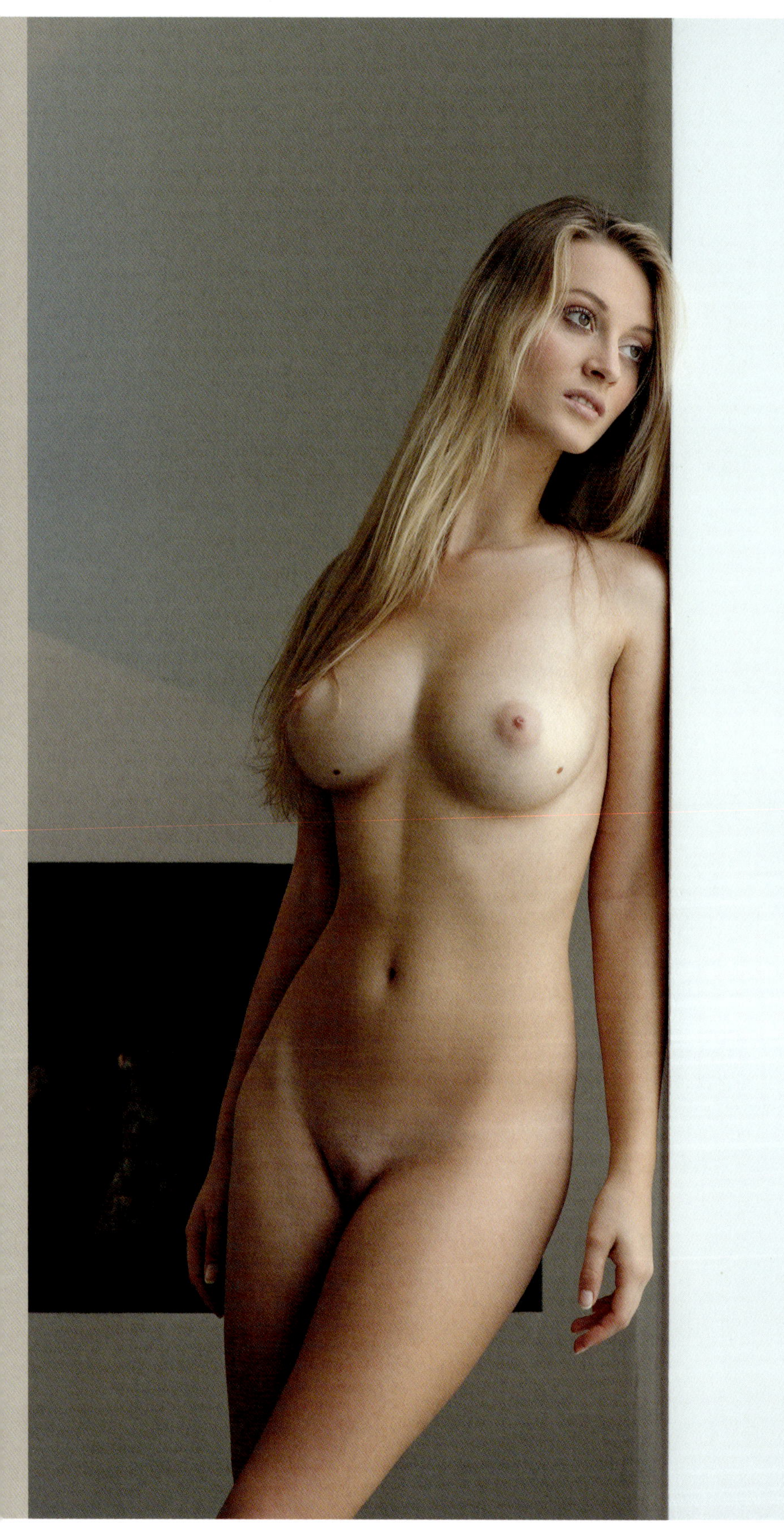

PAGE 112 CARISHA IBIZA

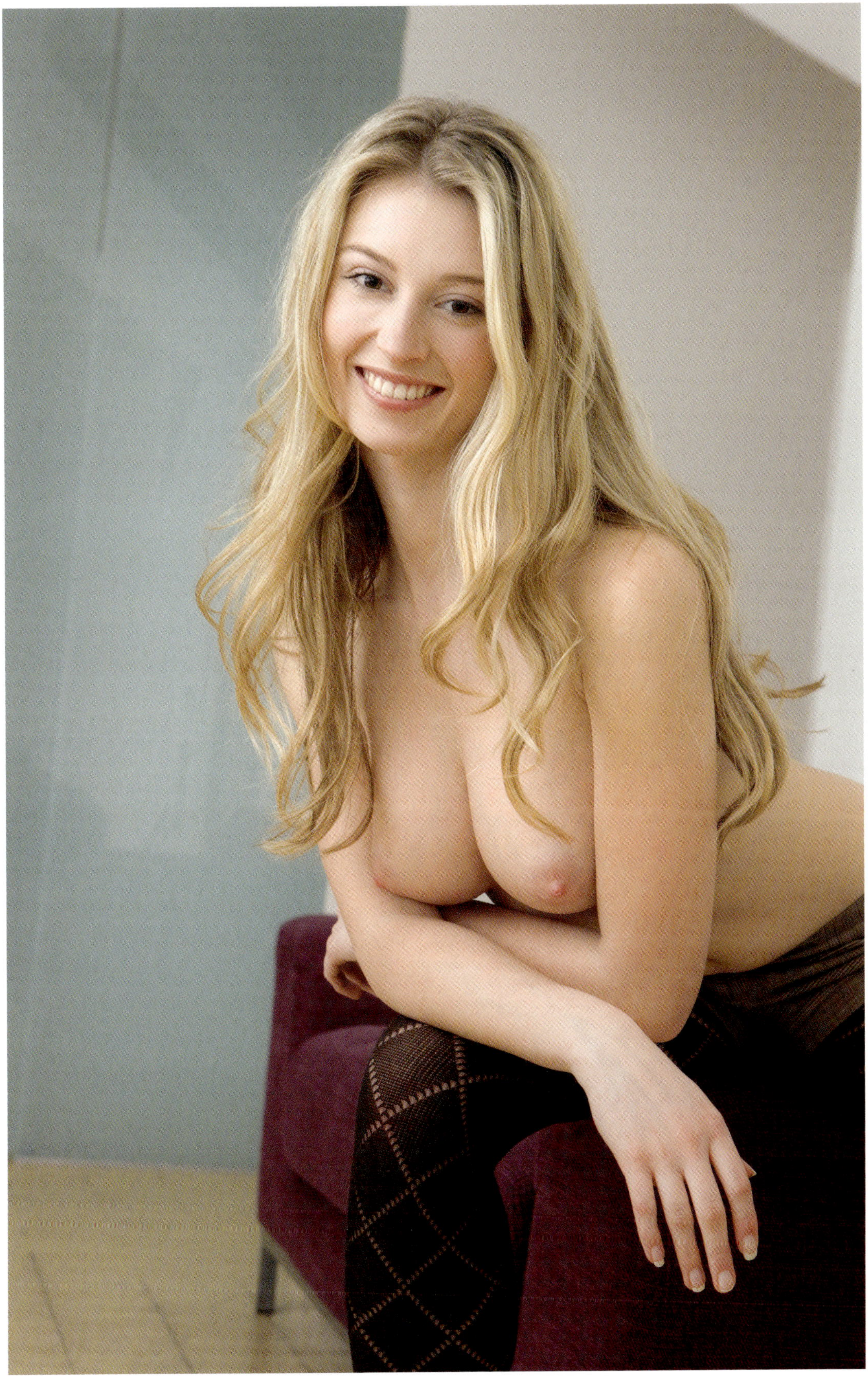

PAGE113 CARISHA PRAG

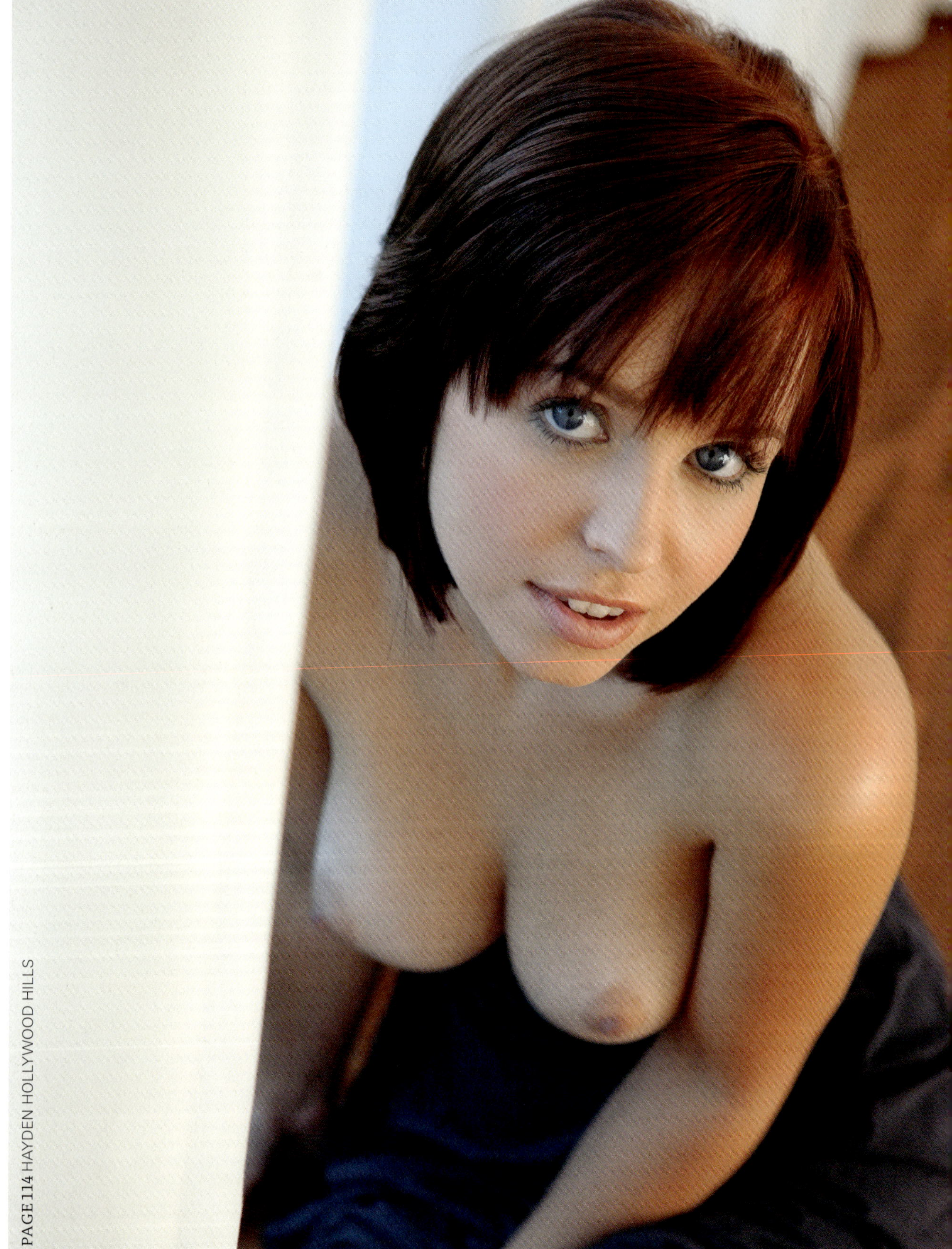

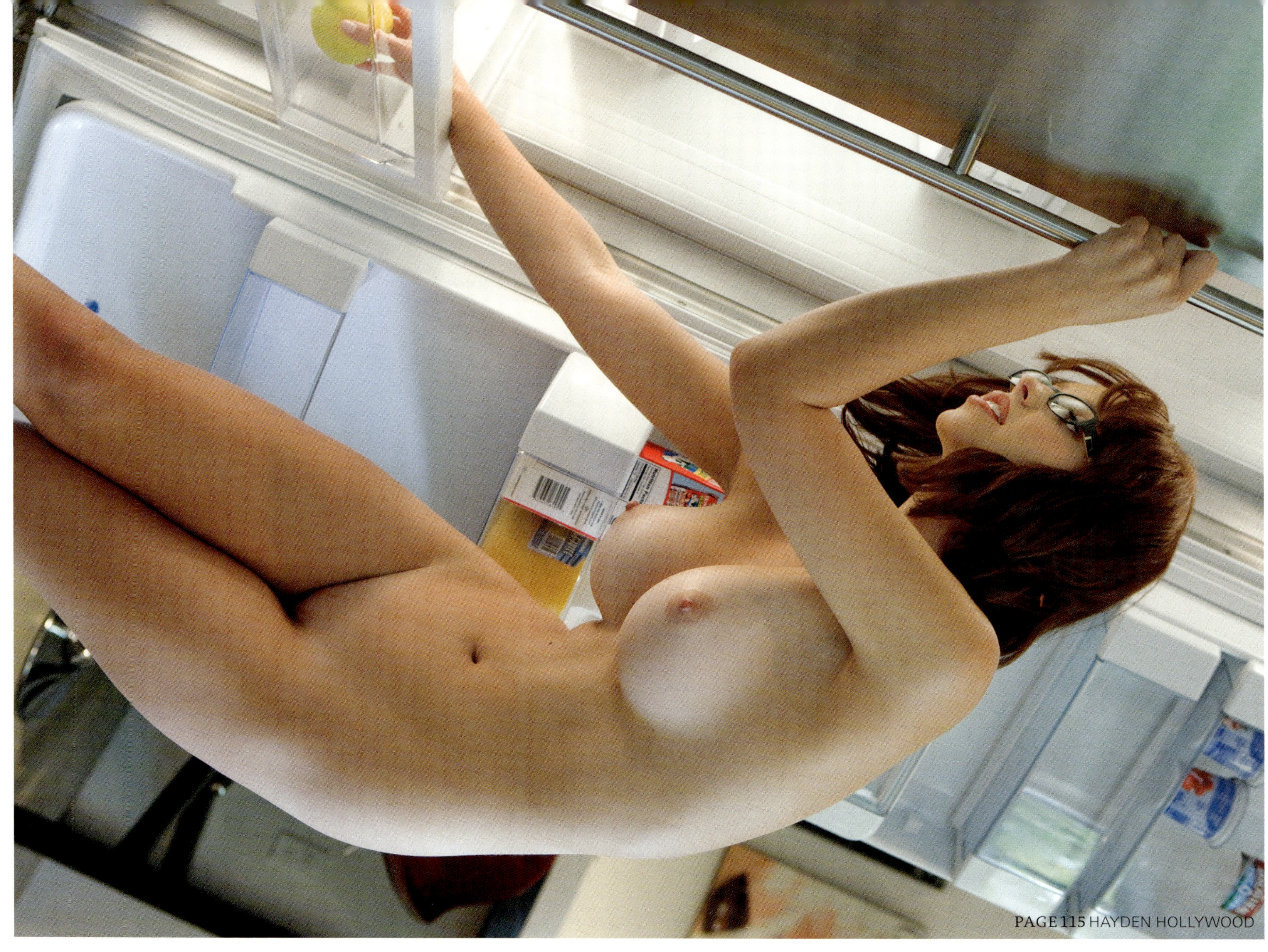
PAGE 115 HAYDEN HOLLYWOOD

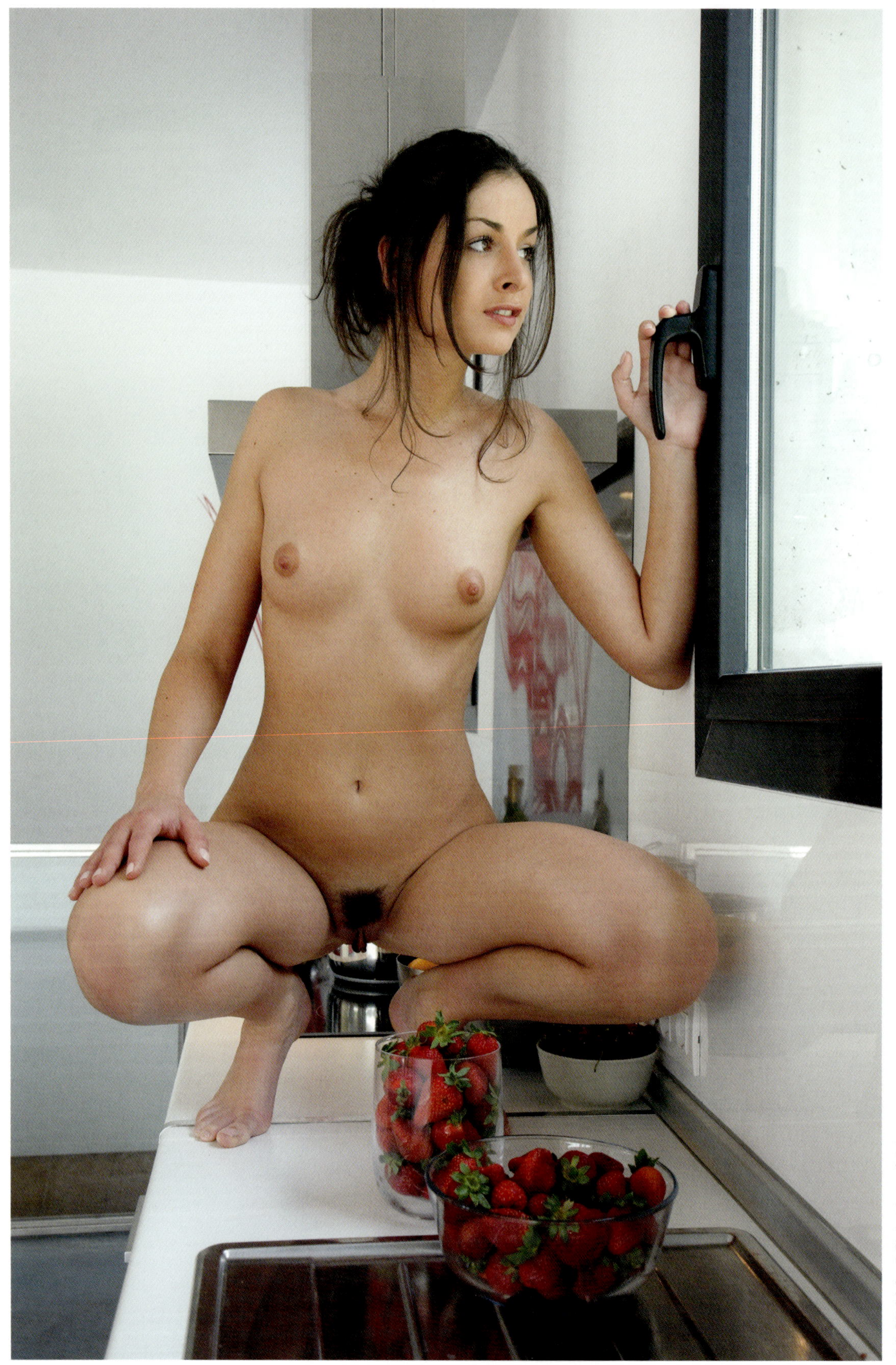

PAGE 116 ADELA MALLORCA

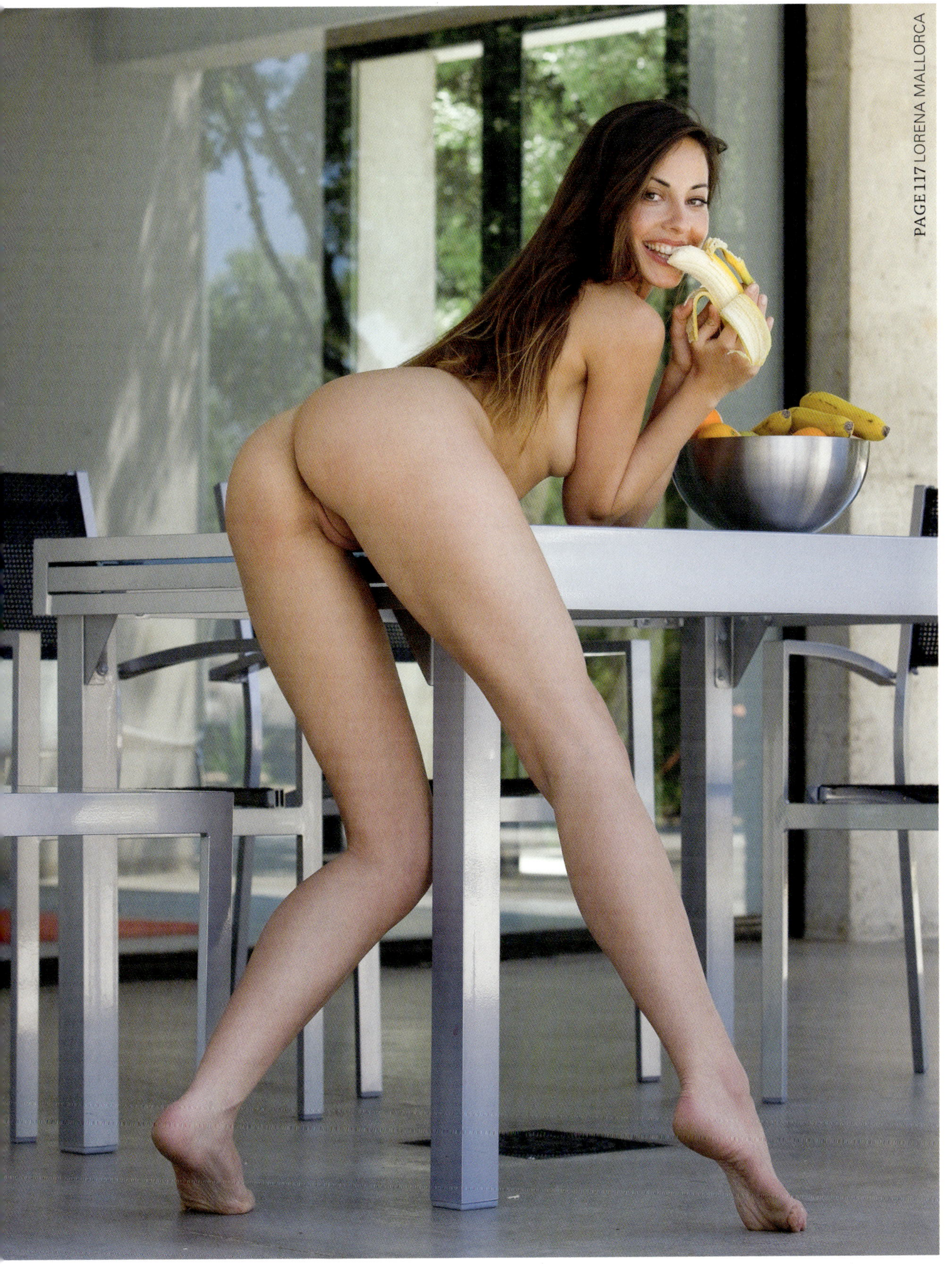
PAGE 117 LORENA MALLORCA

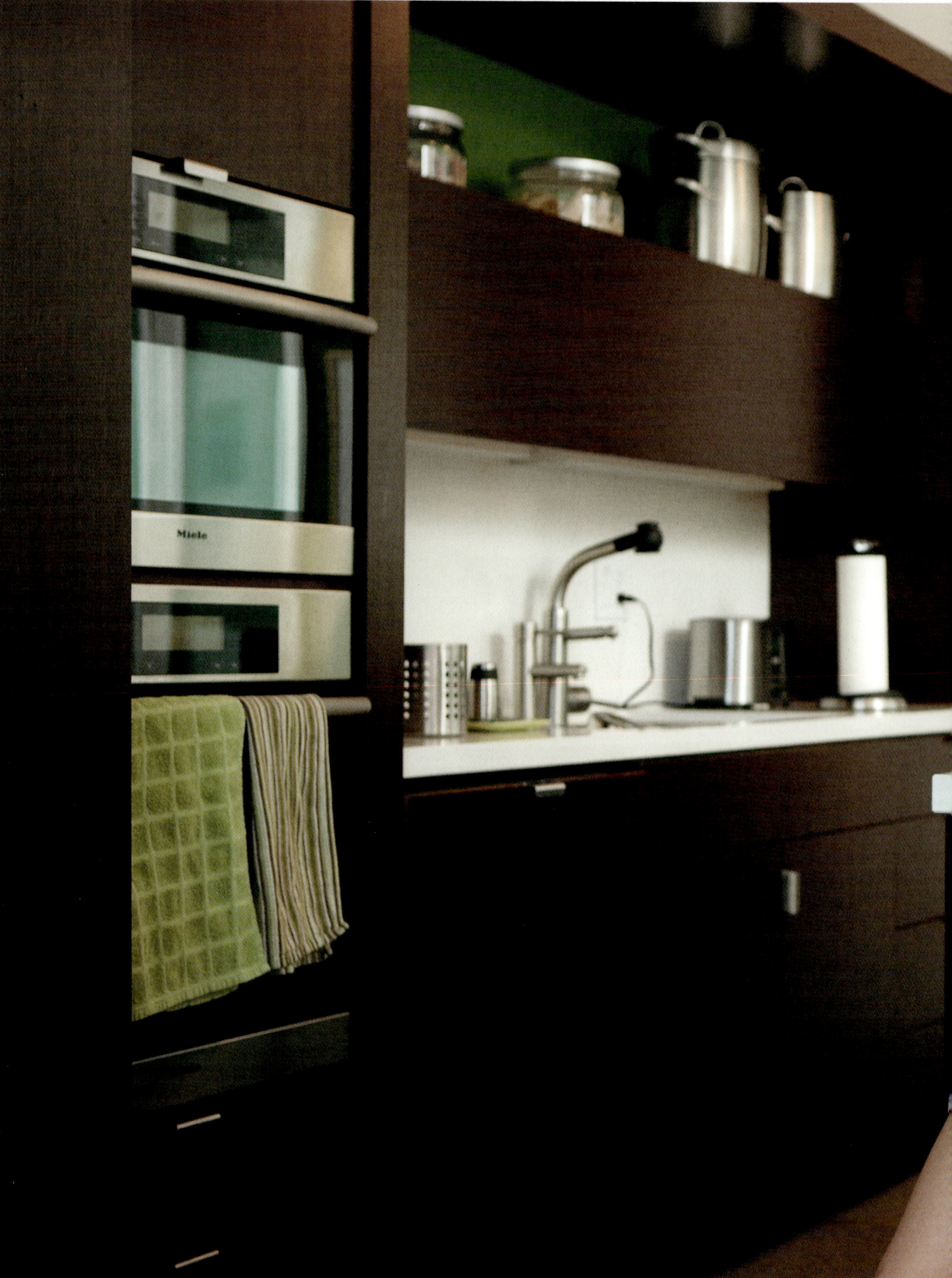

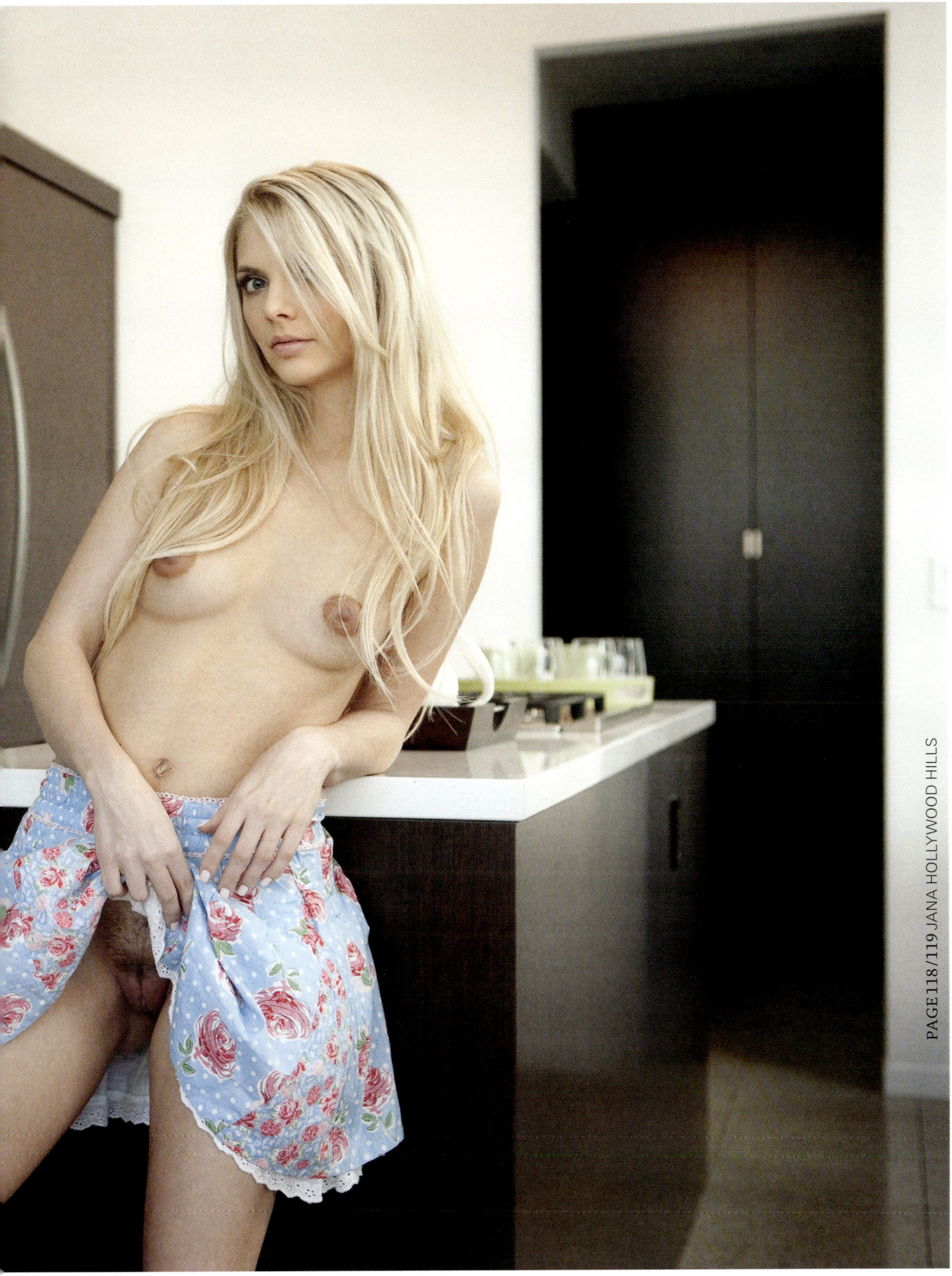

PAGE 118/119 JANA HOLLYWOOD HILLS

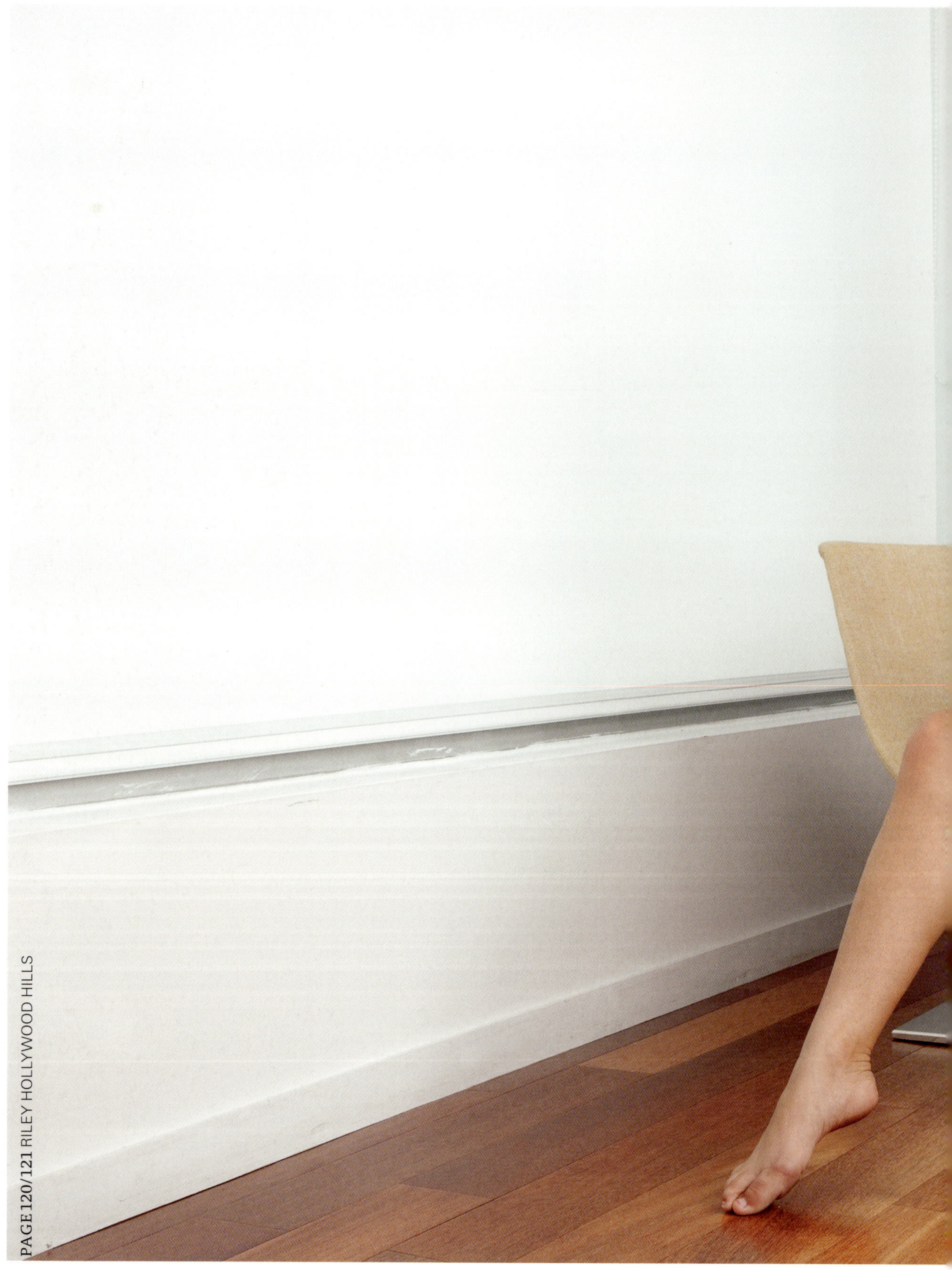

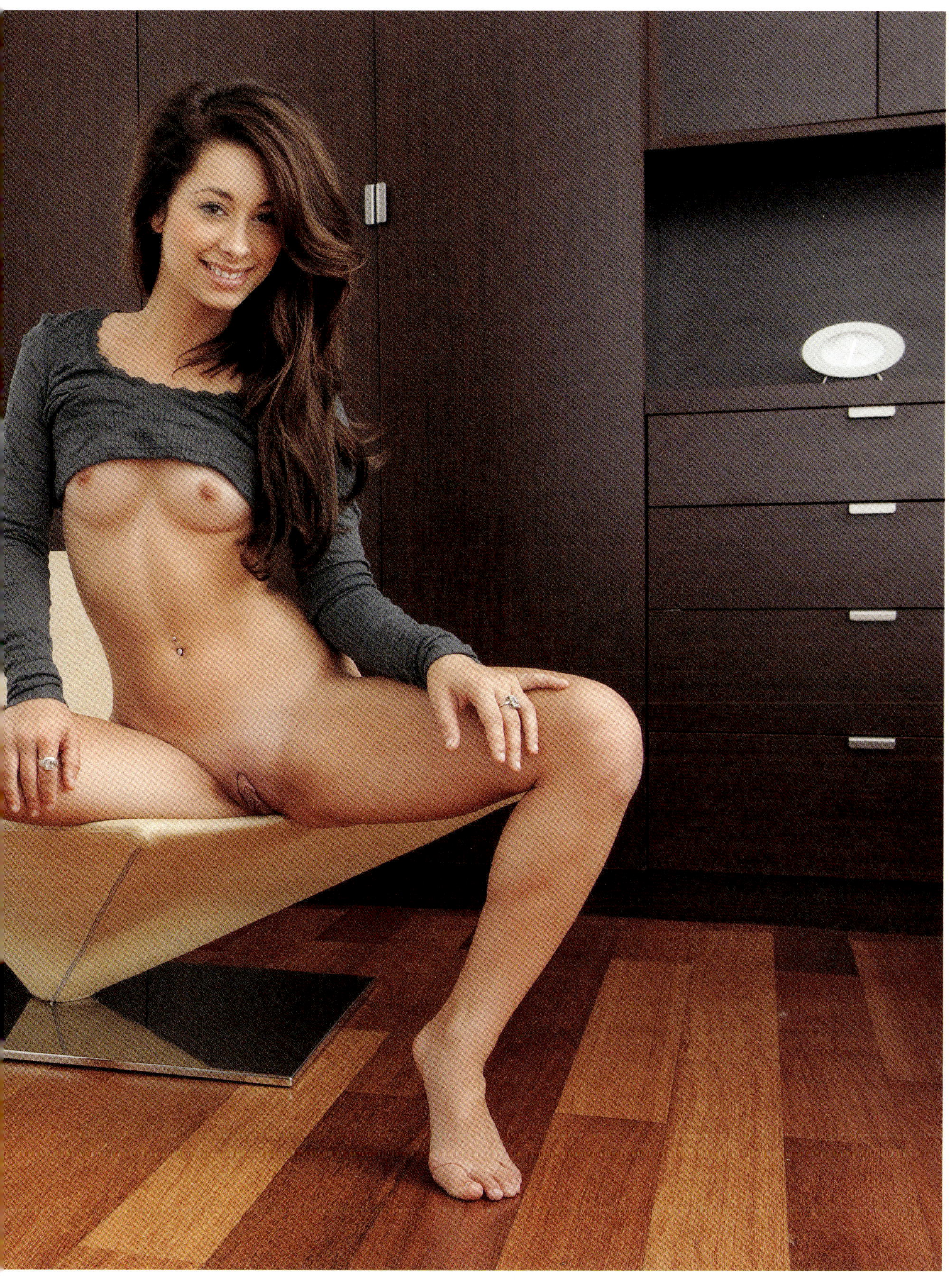

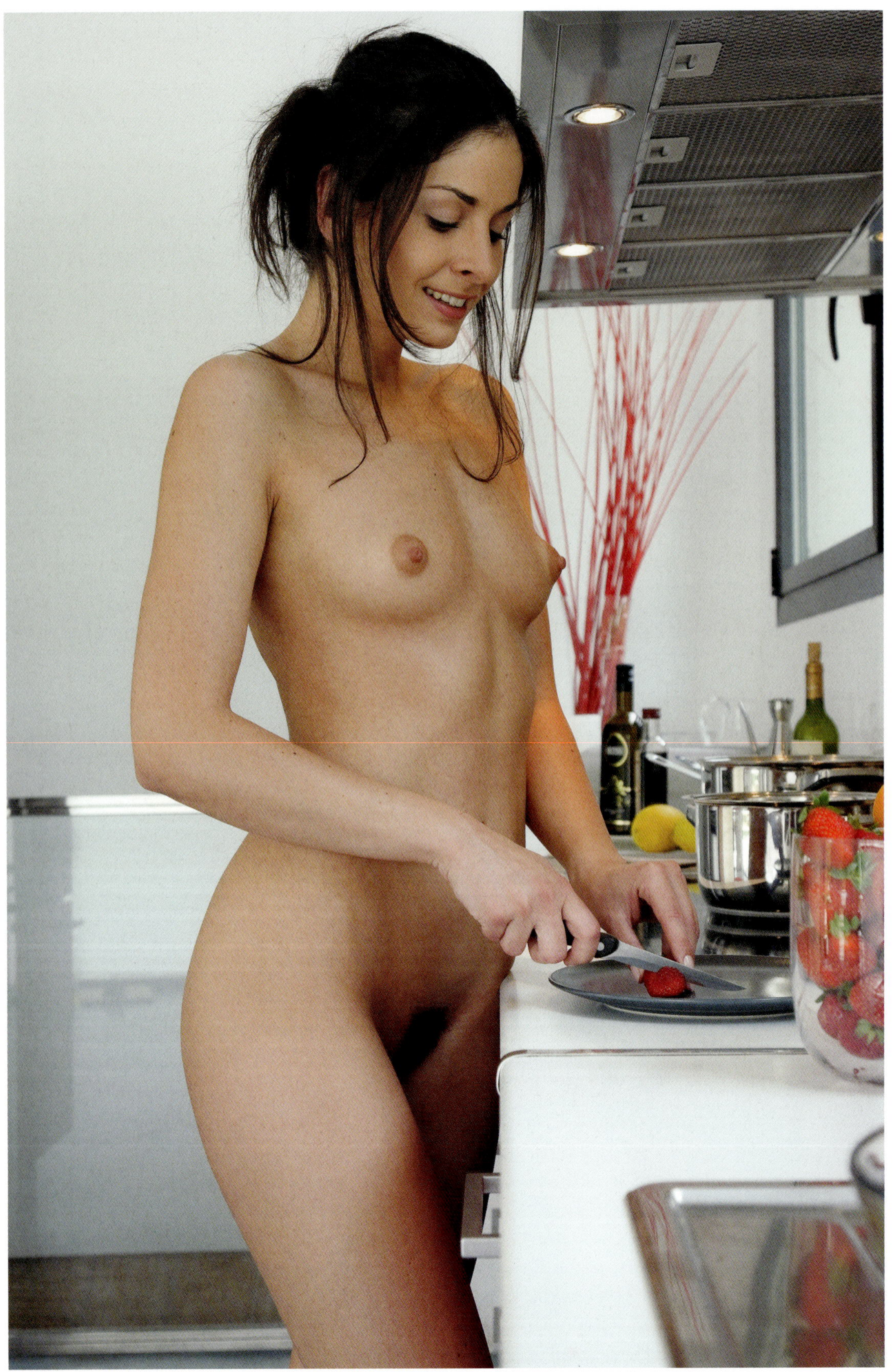

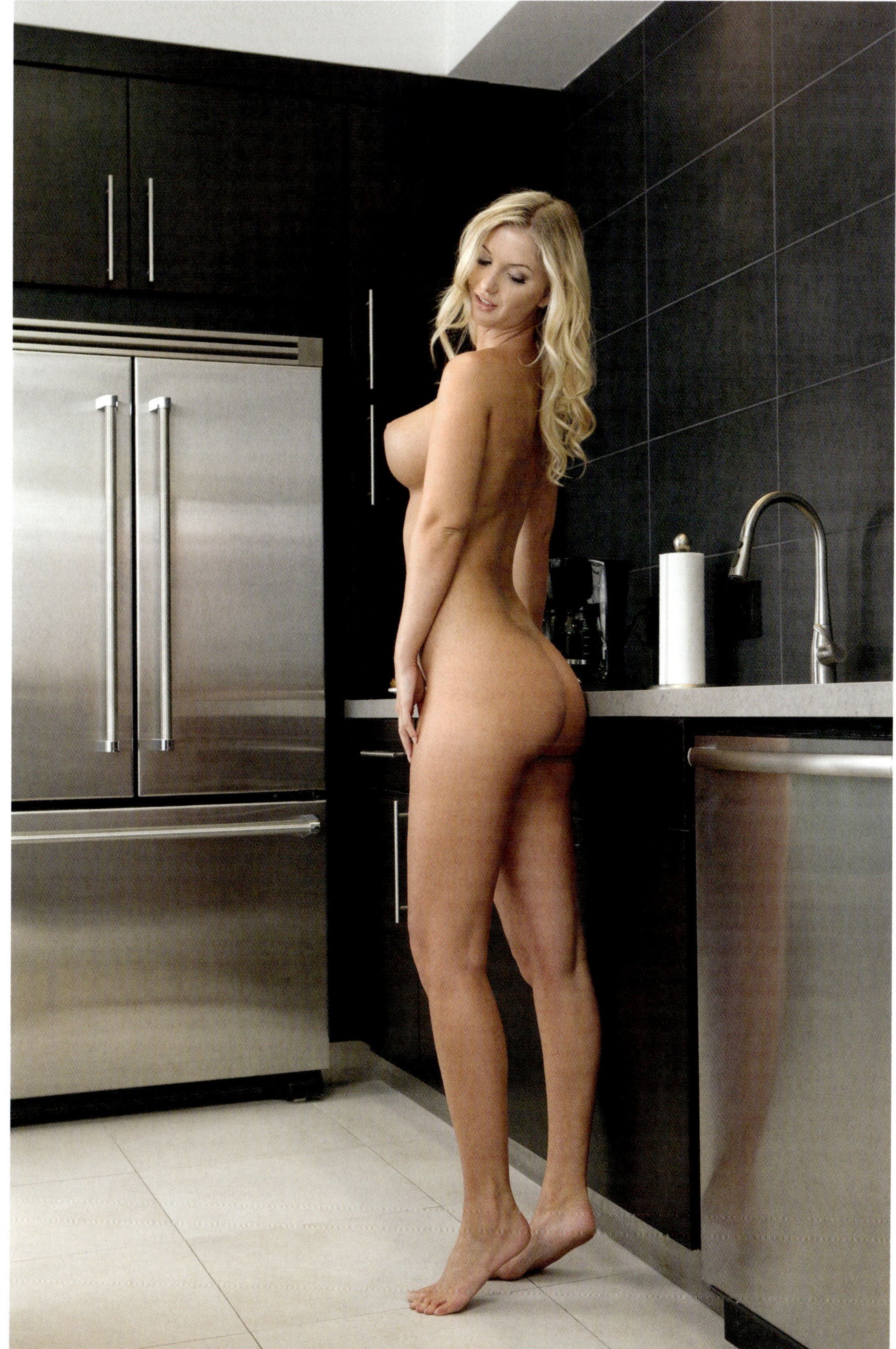

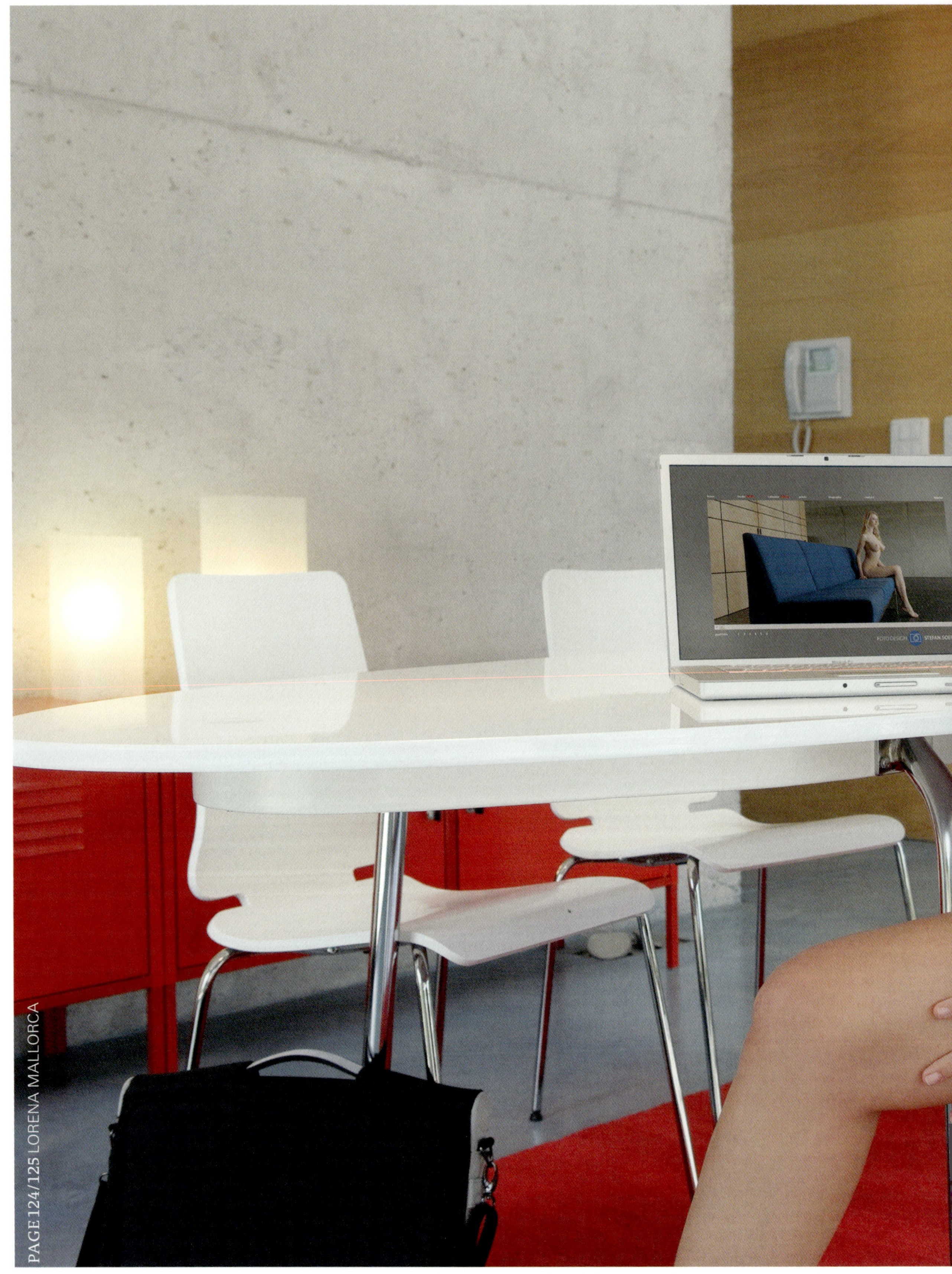

FOTO-DESIGN STEFAN.SOELL

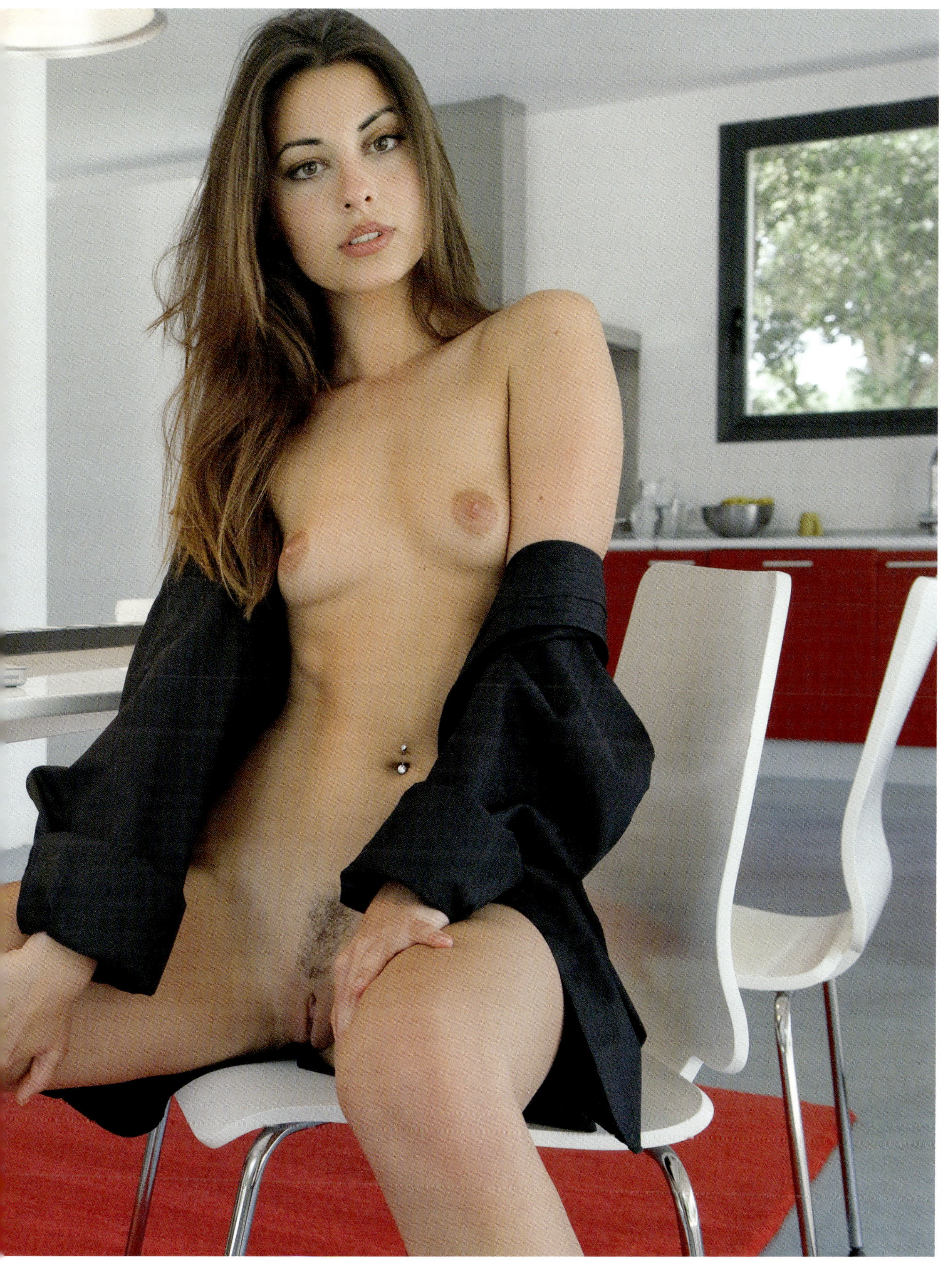

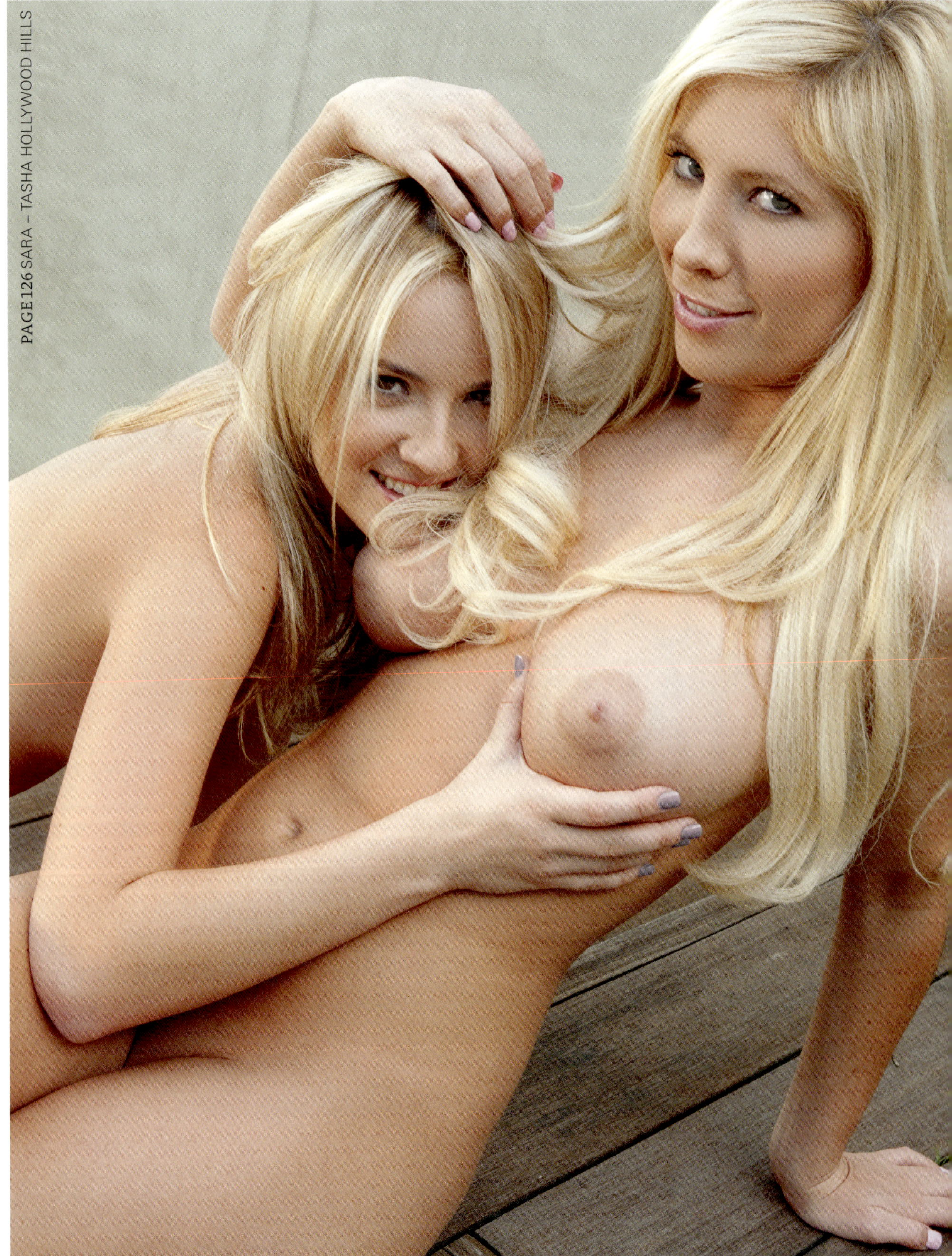

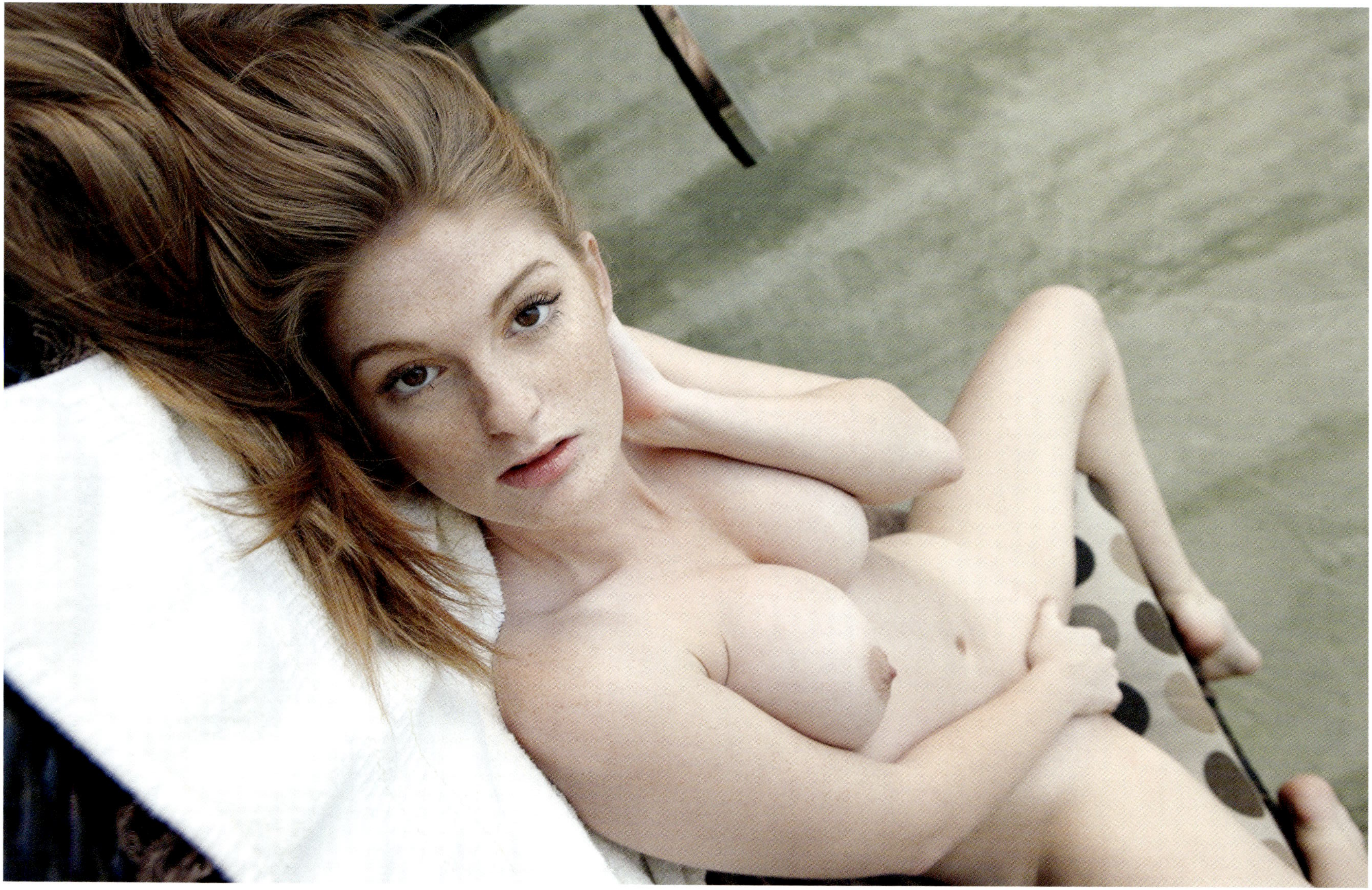

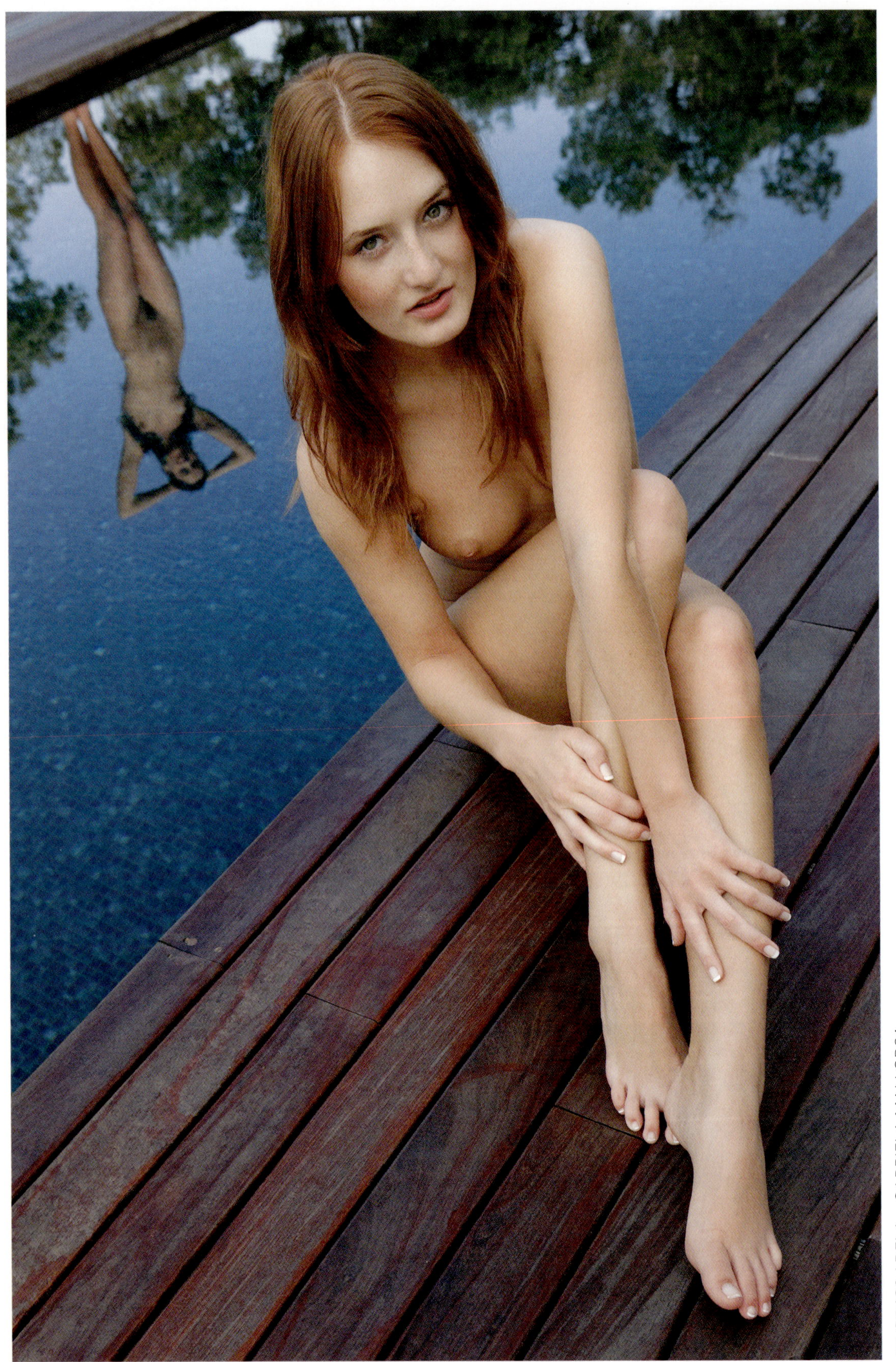

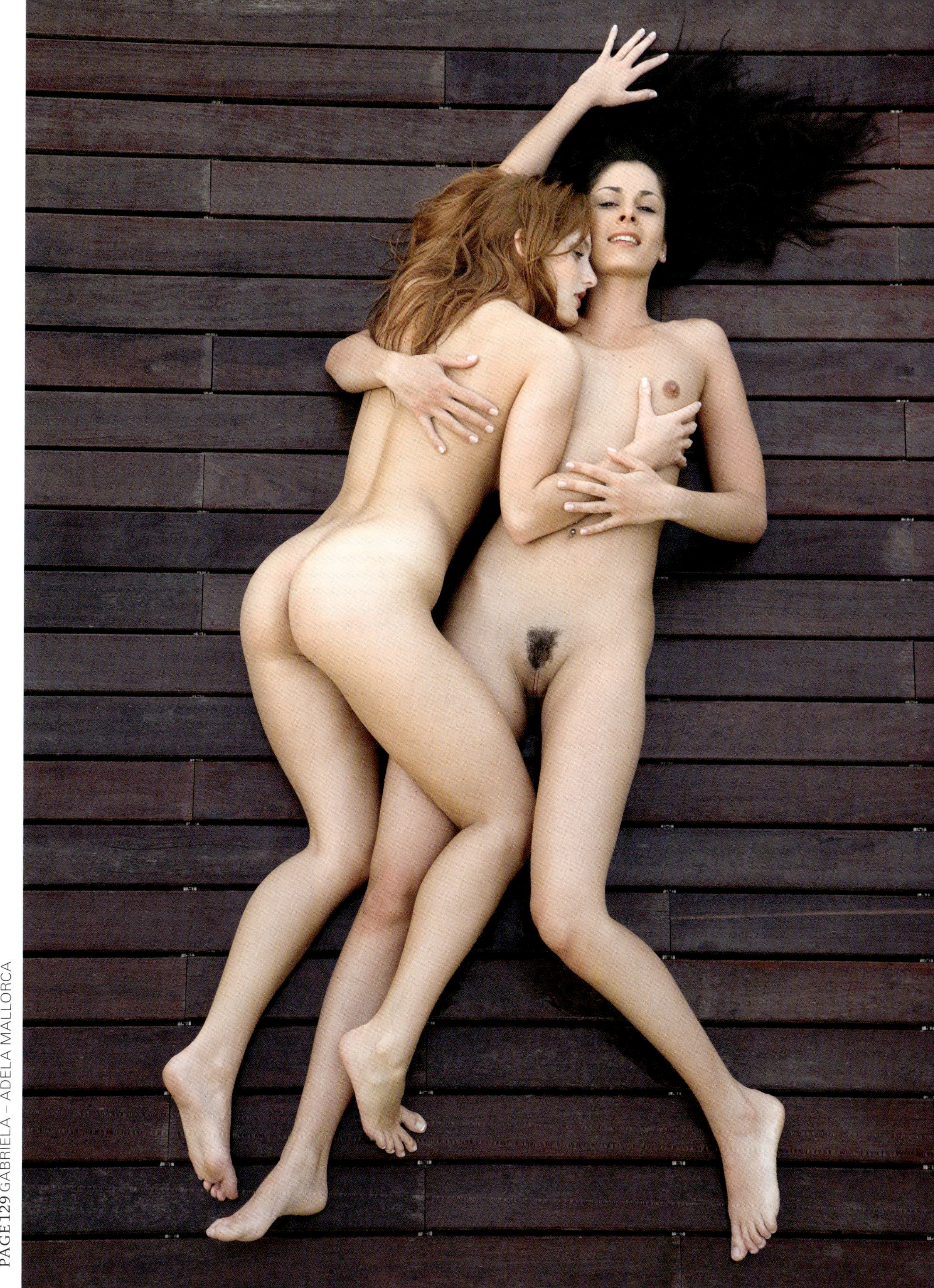

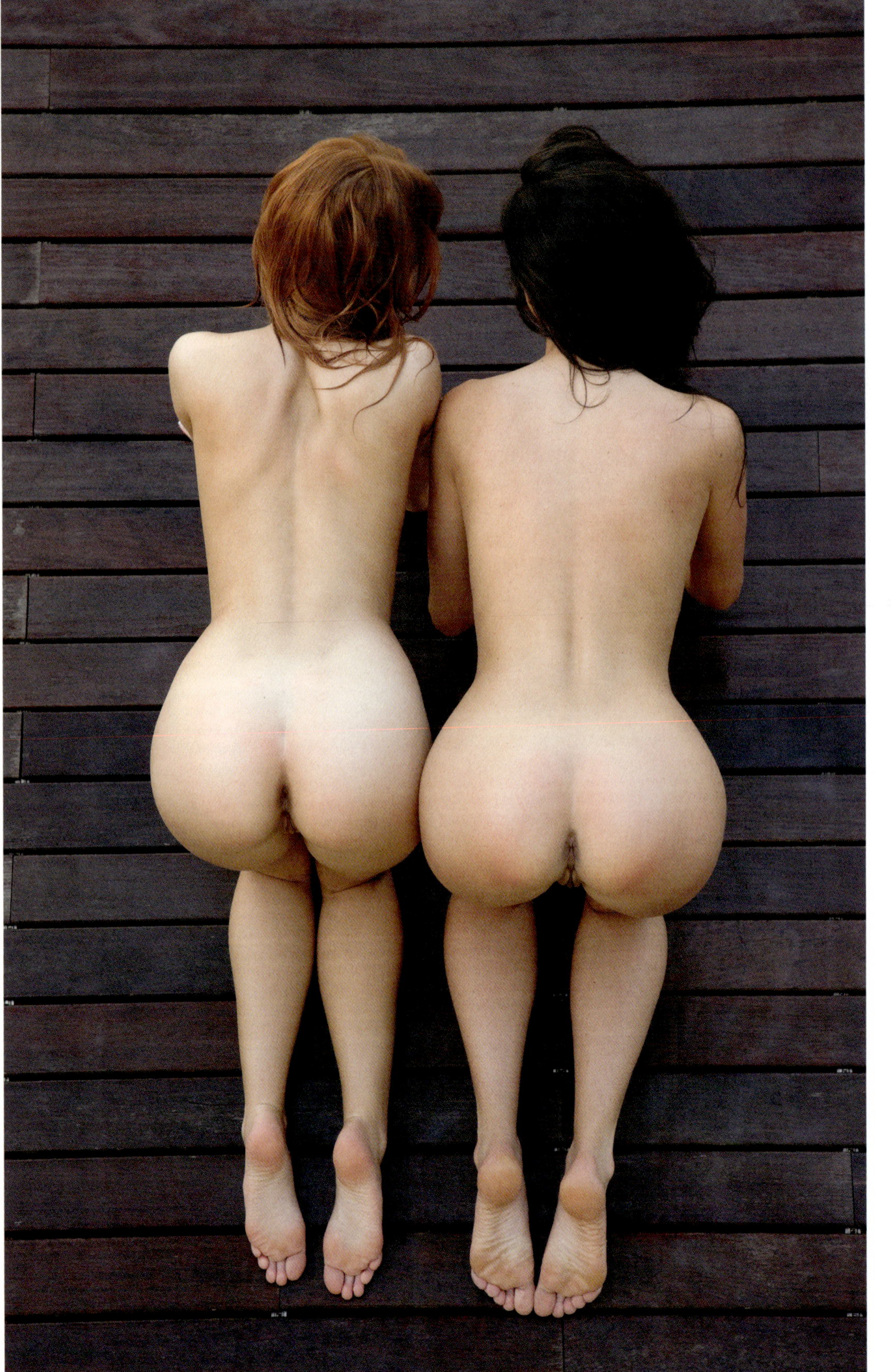

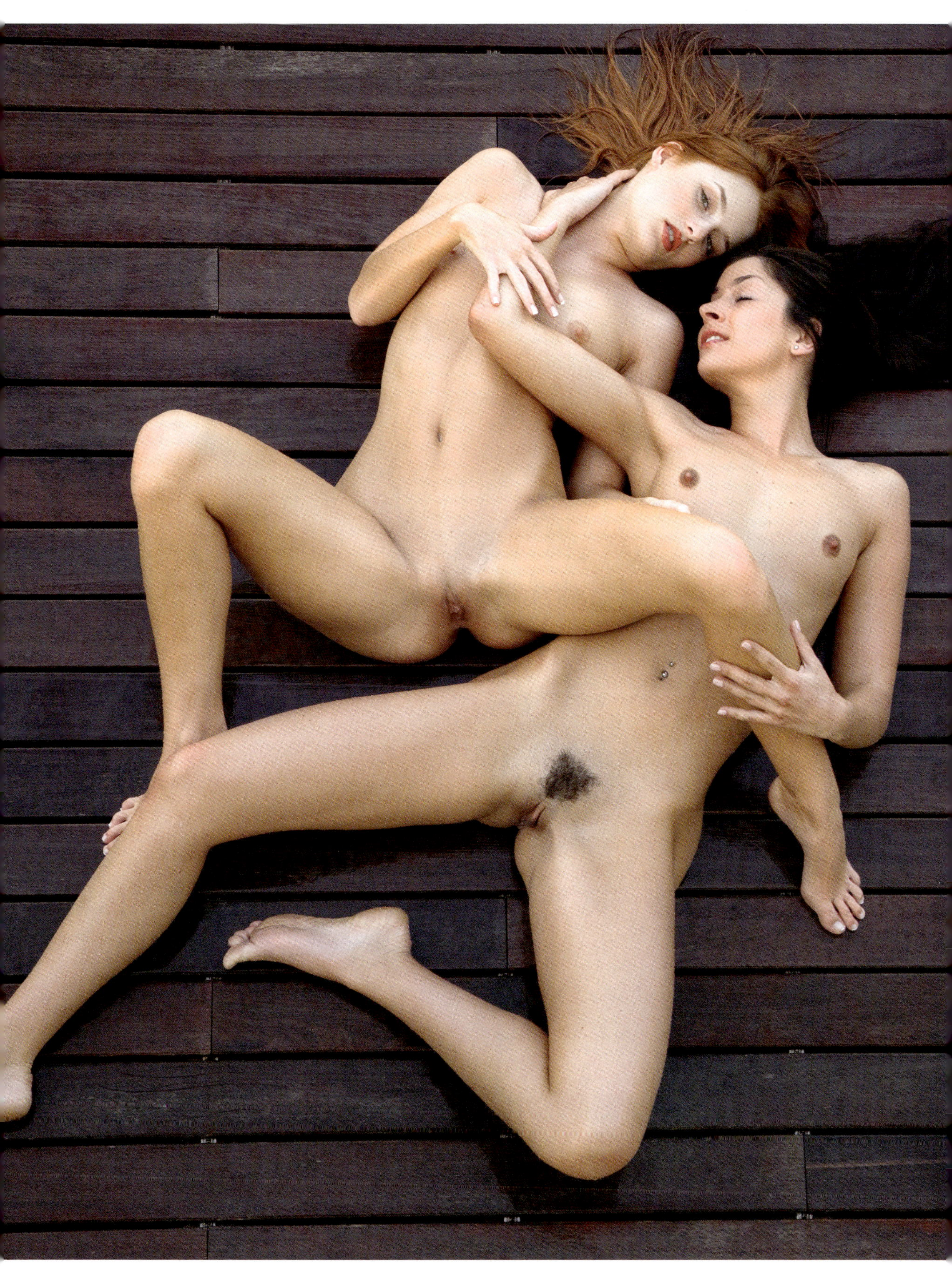

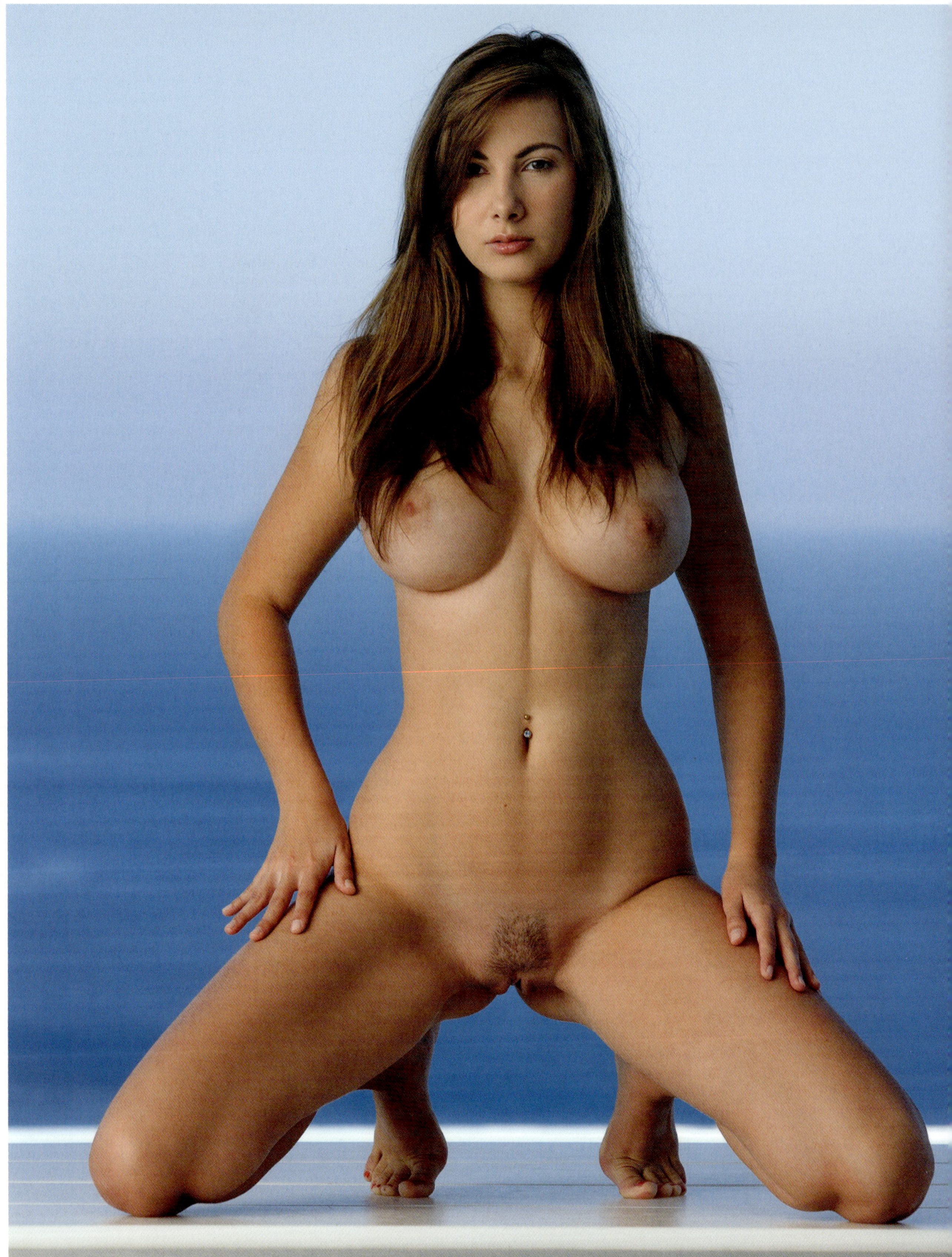

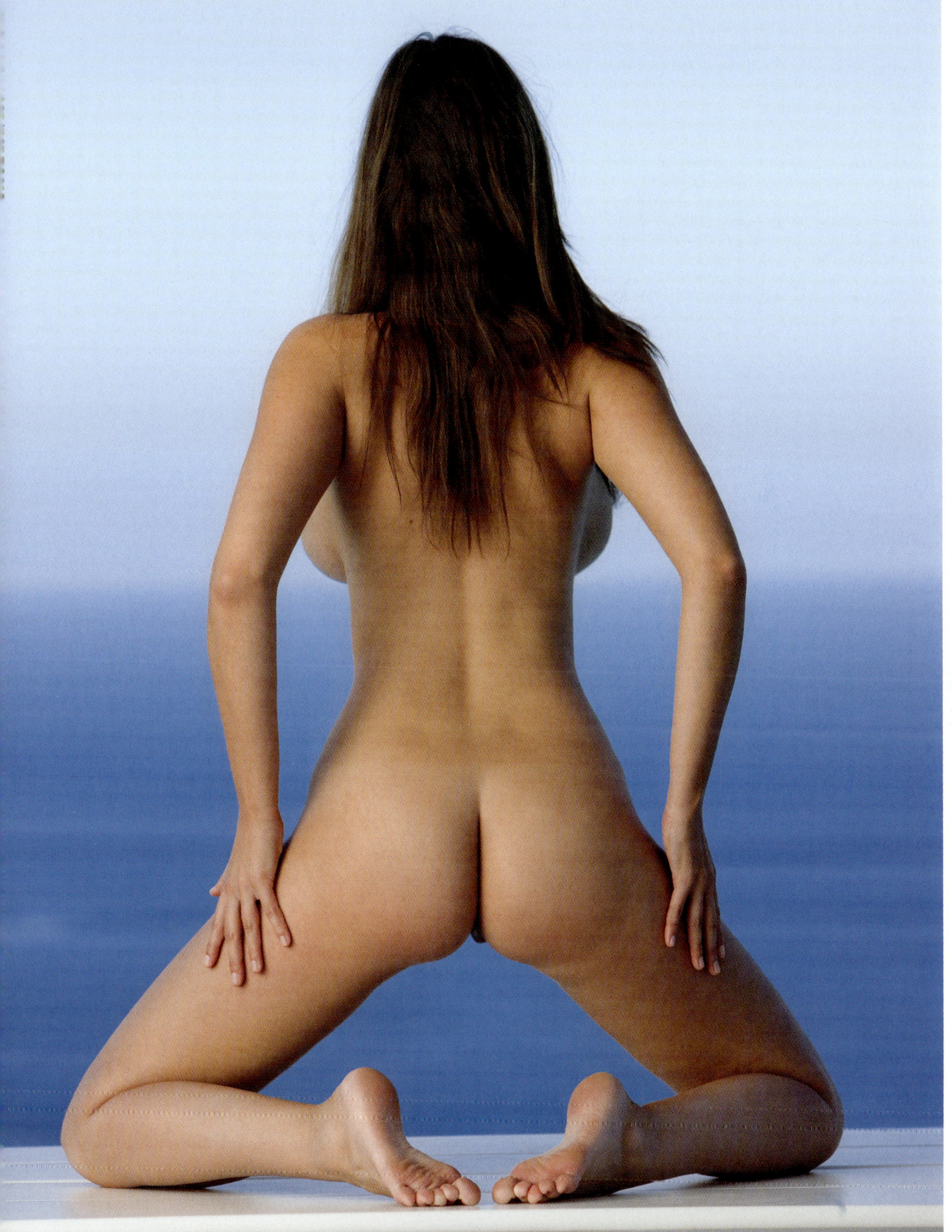

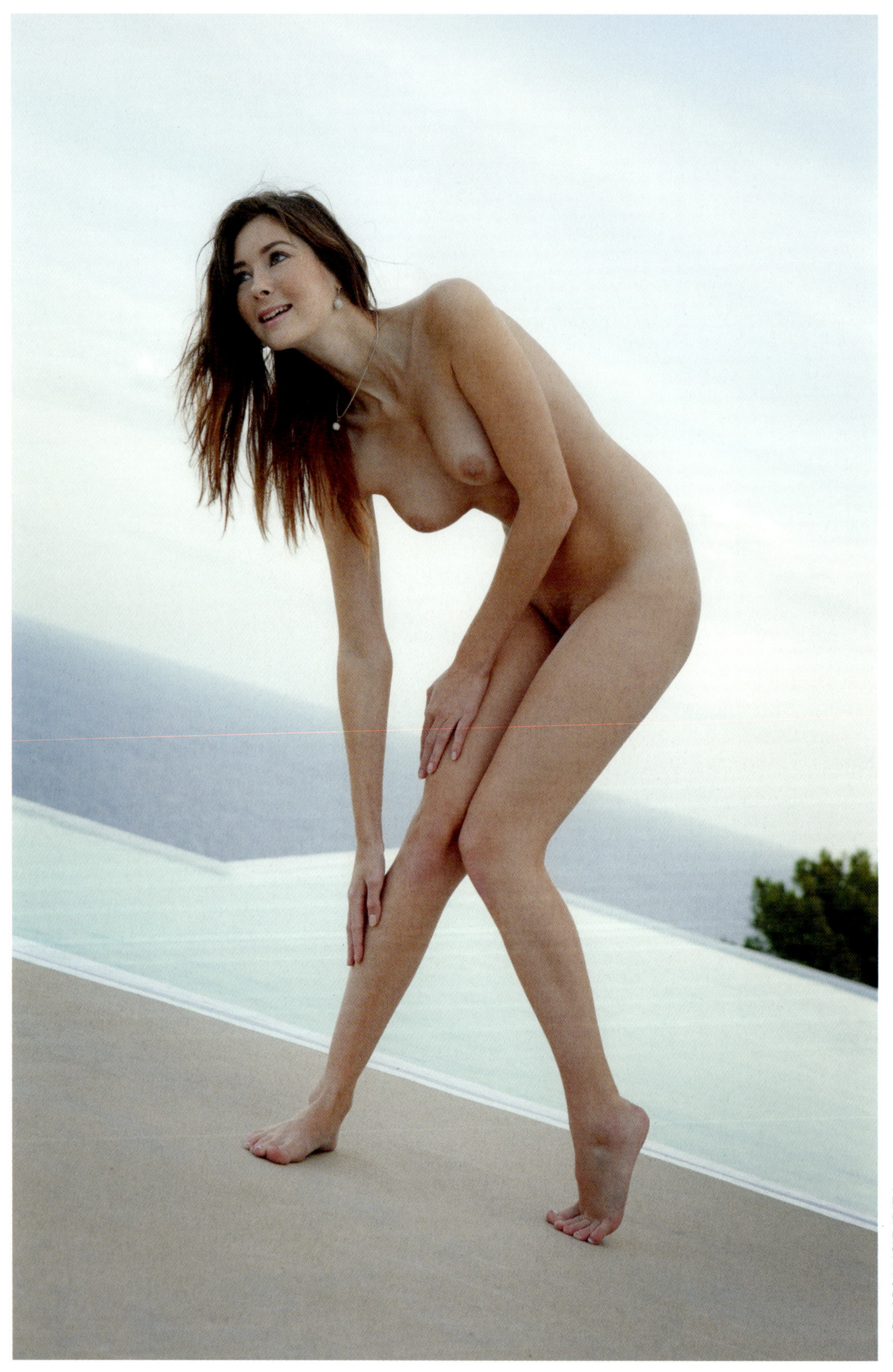

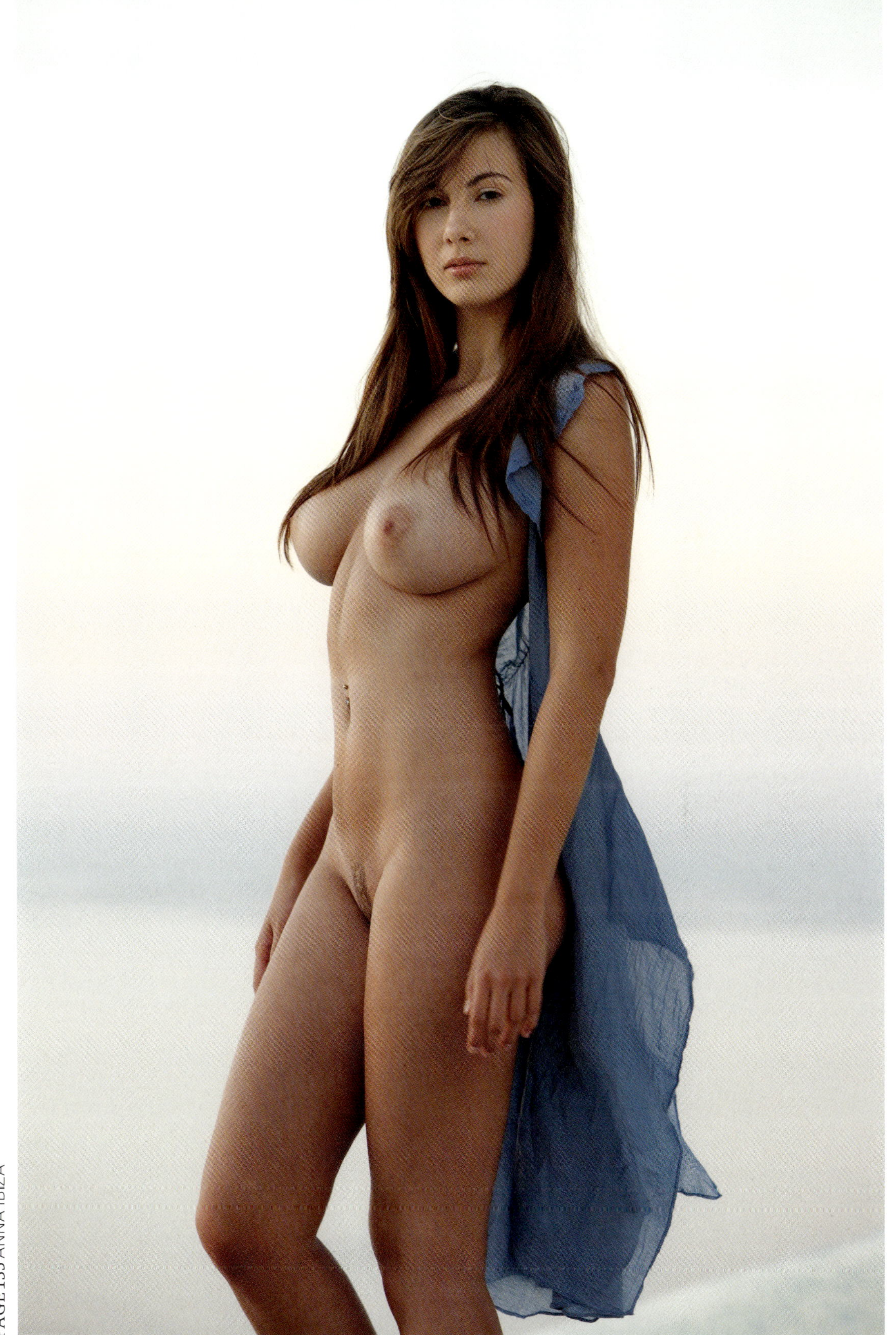

PAGE 136 / 137 ANNA IBIZA

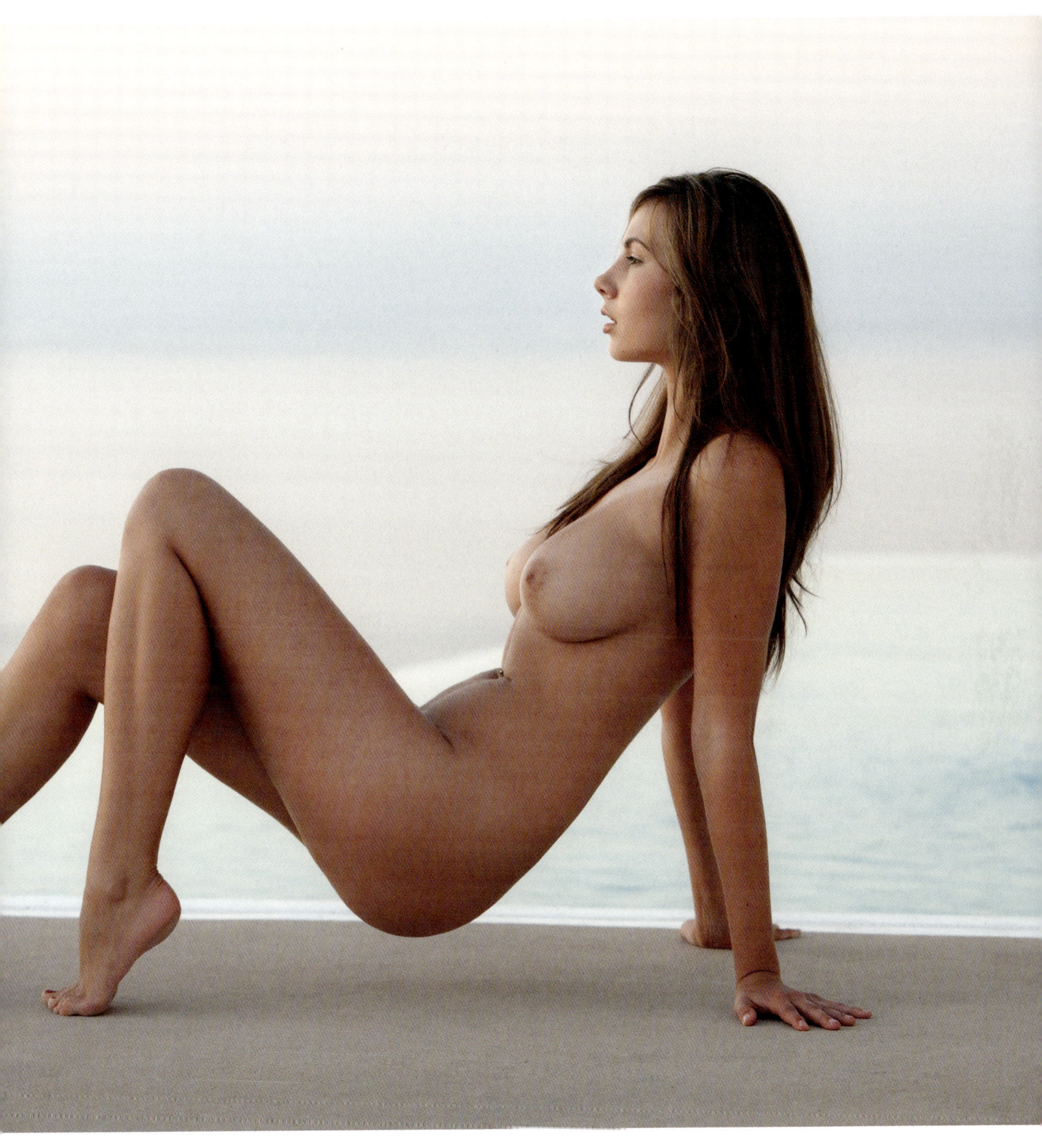

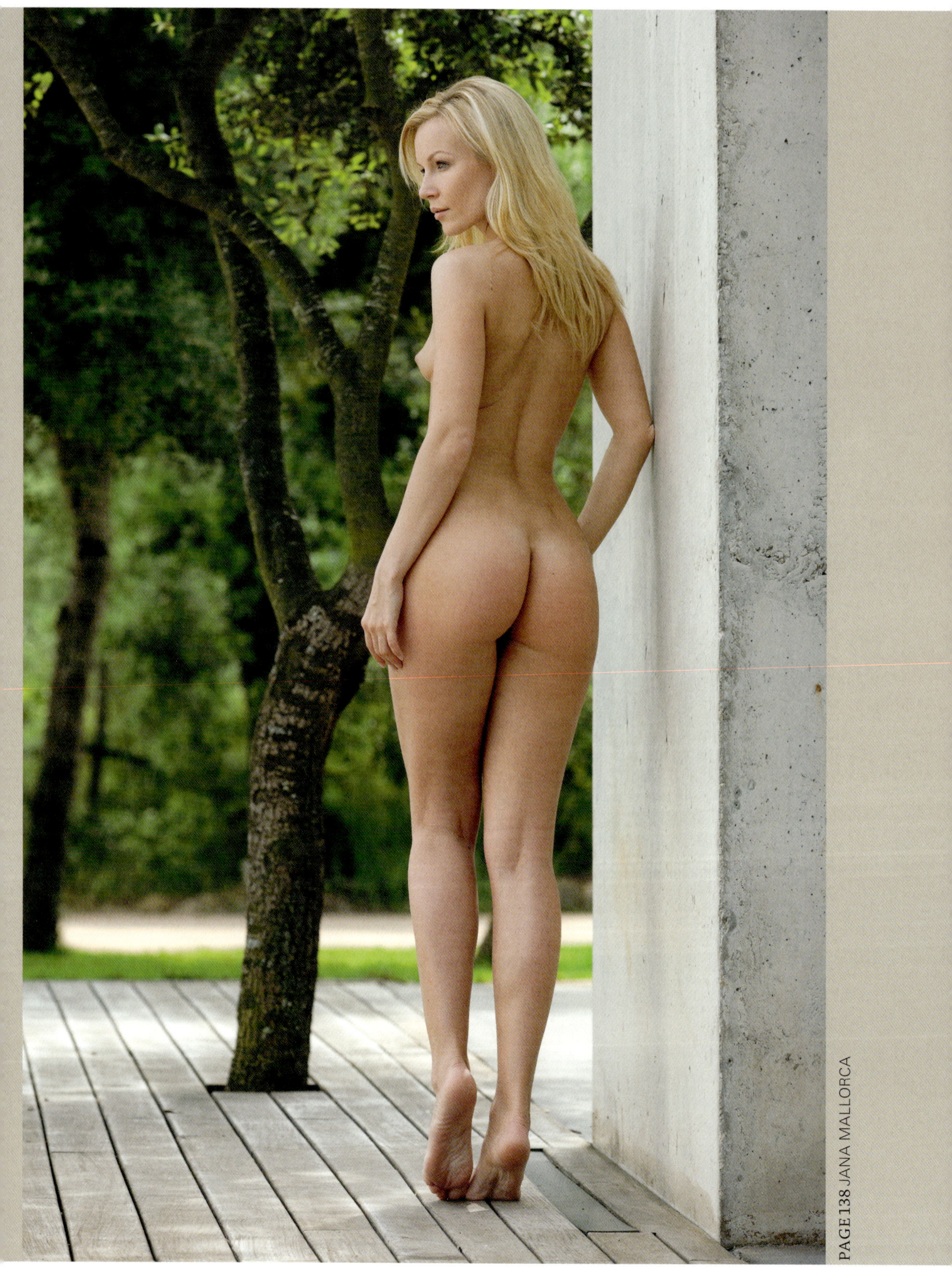
PAGE 138 JANA MALLORCA

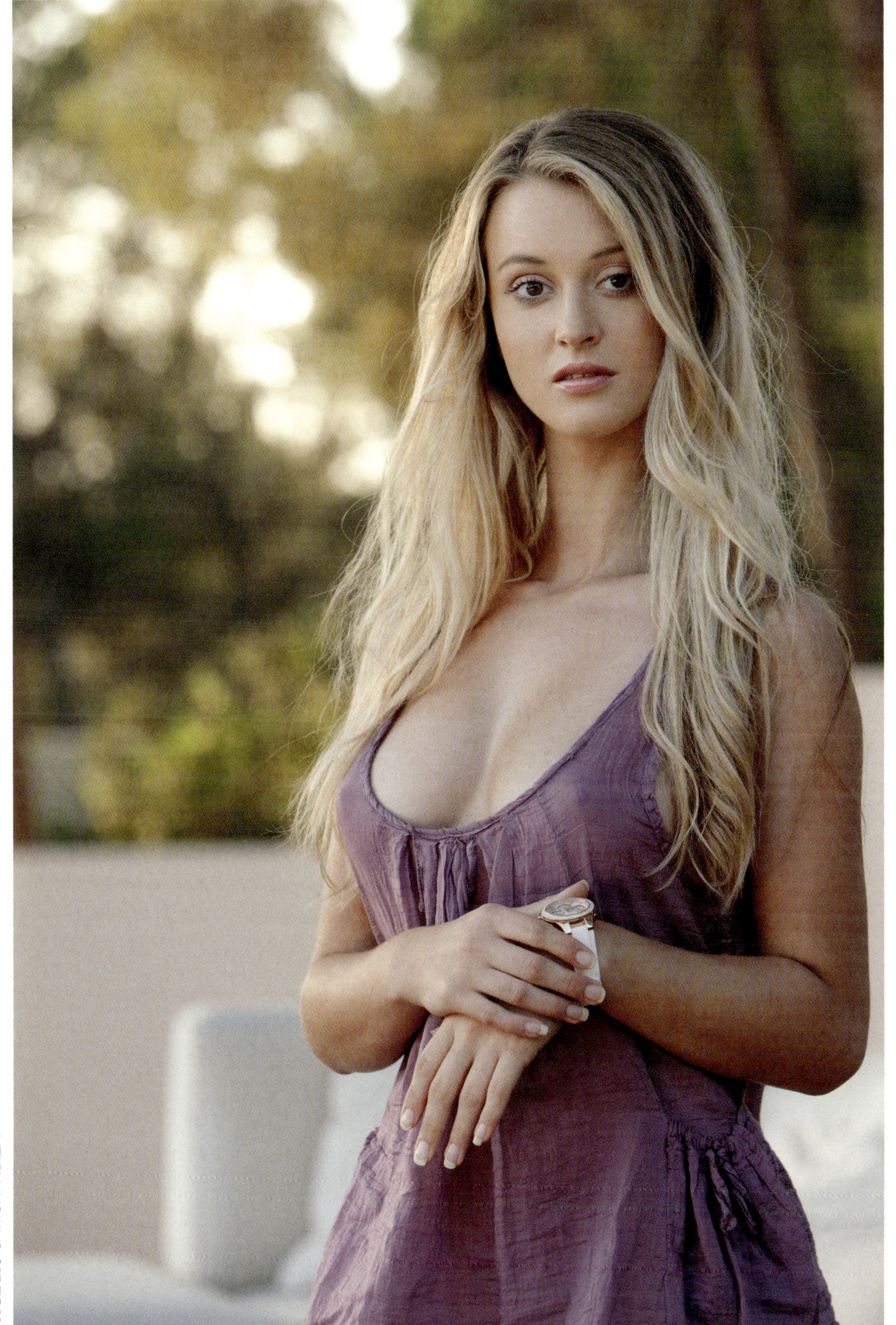

PAGE 139 CARISHA IBIZA

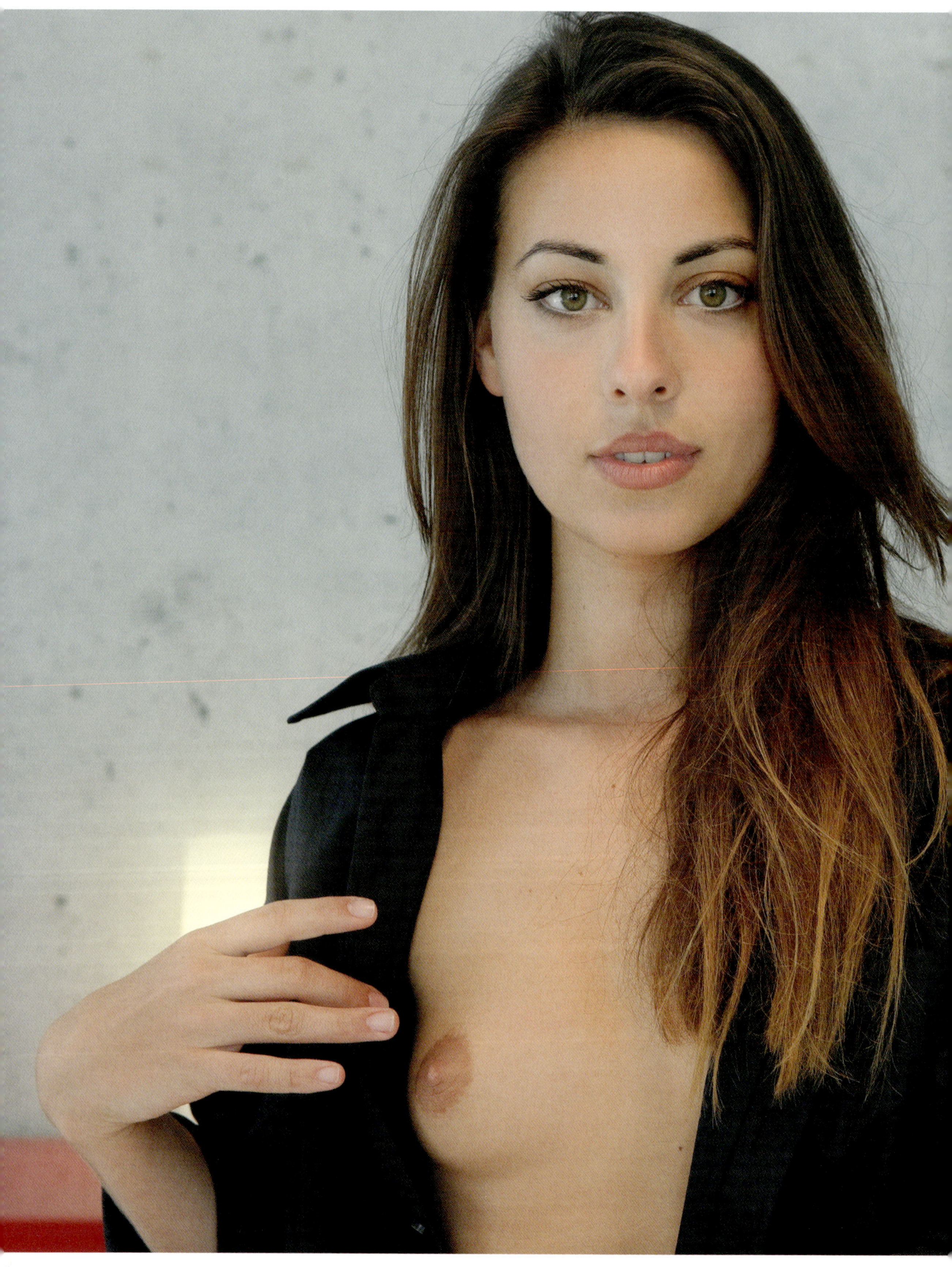

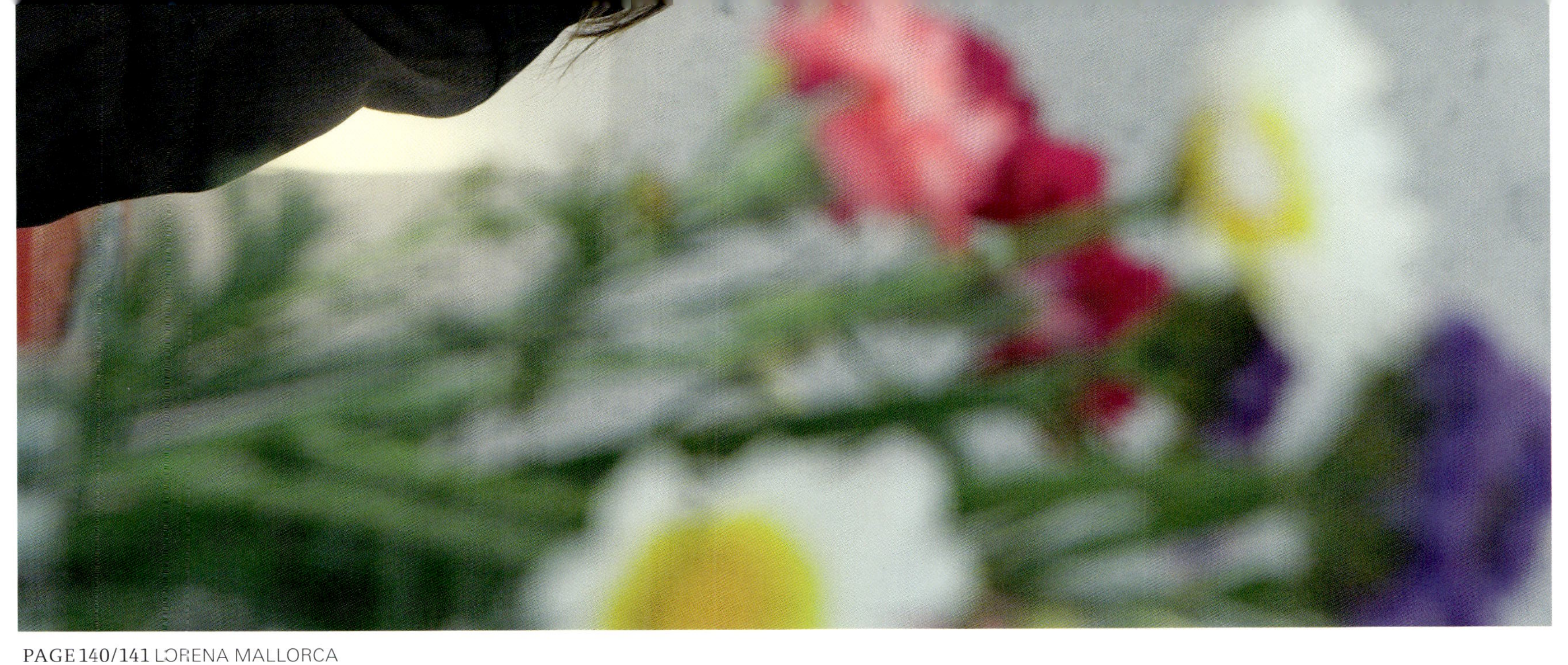

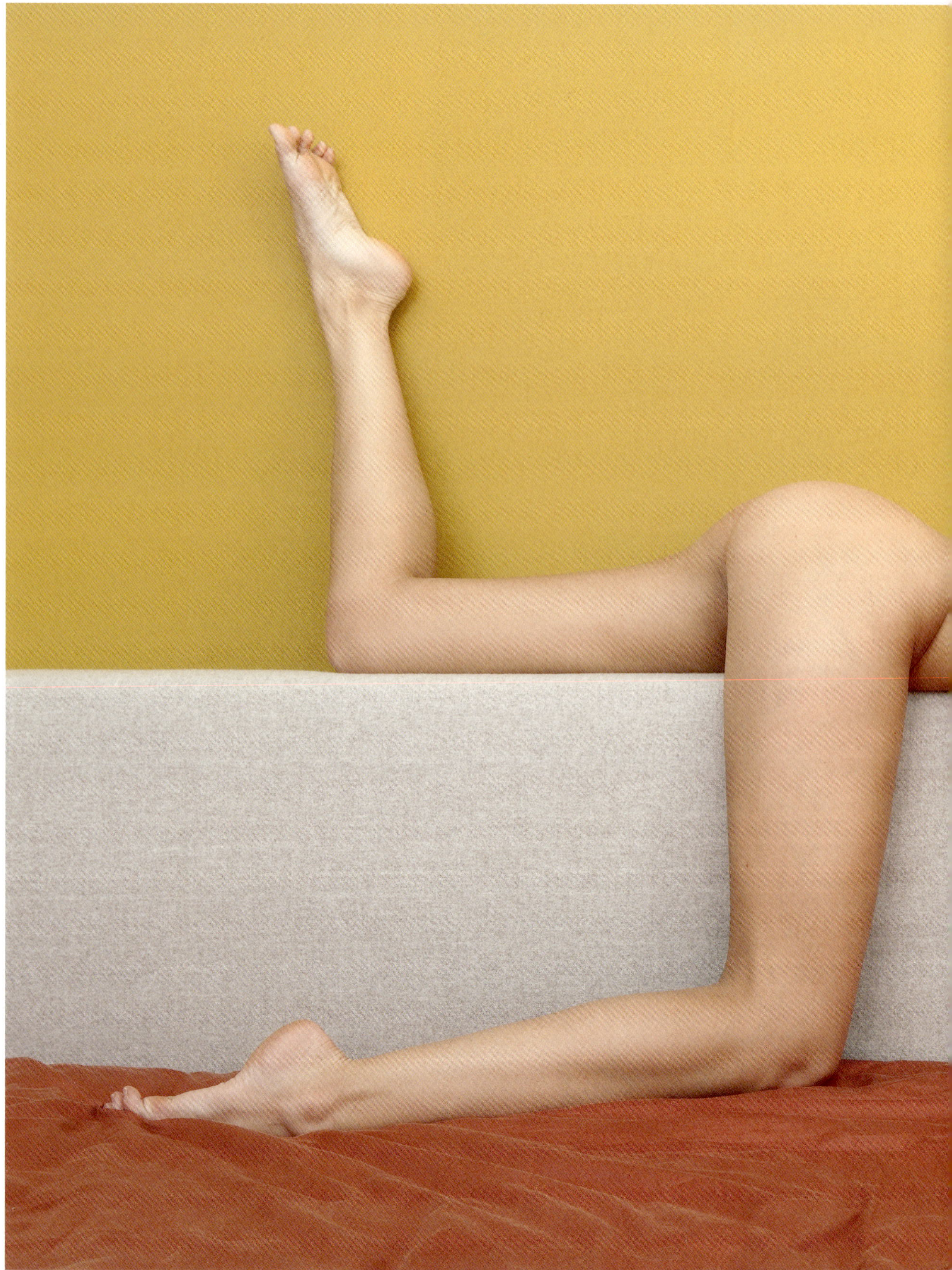

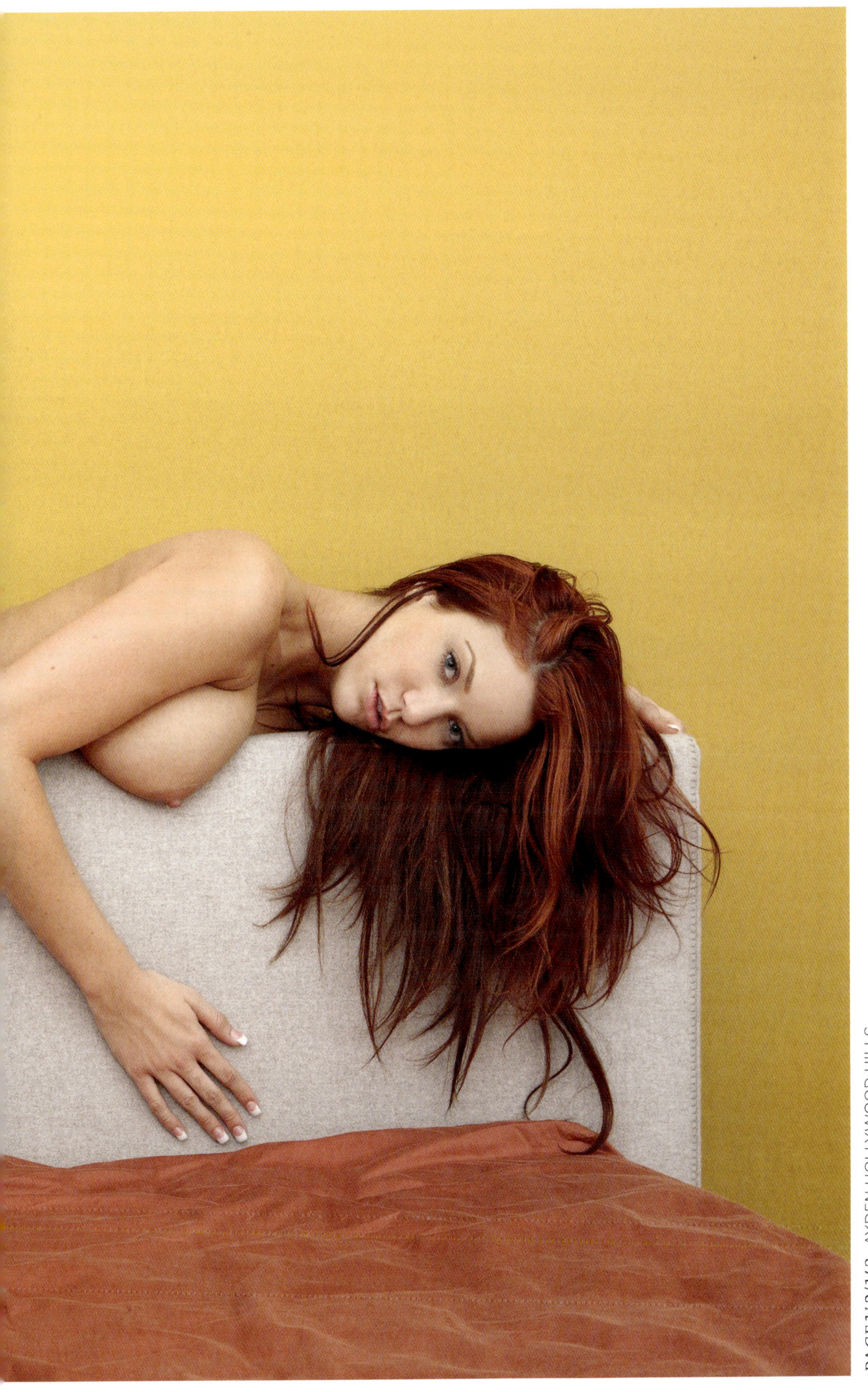

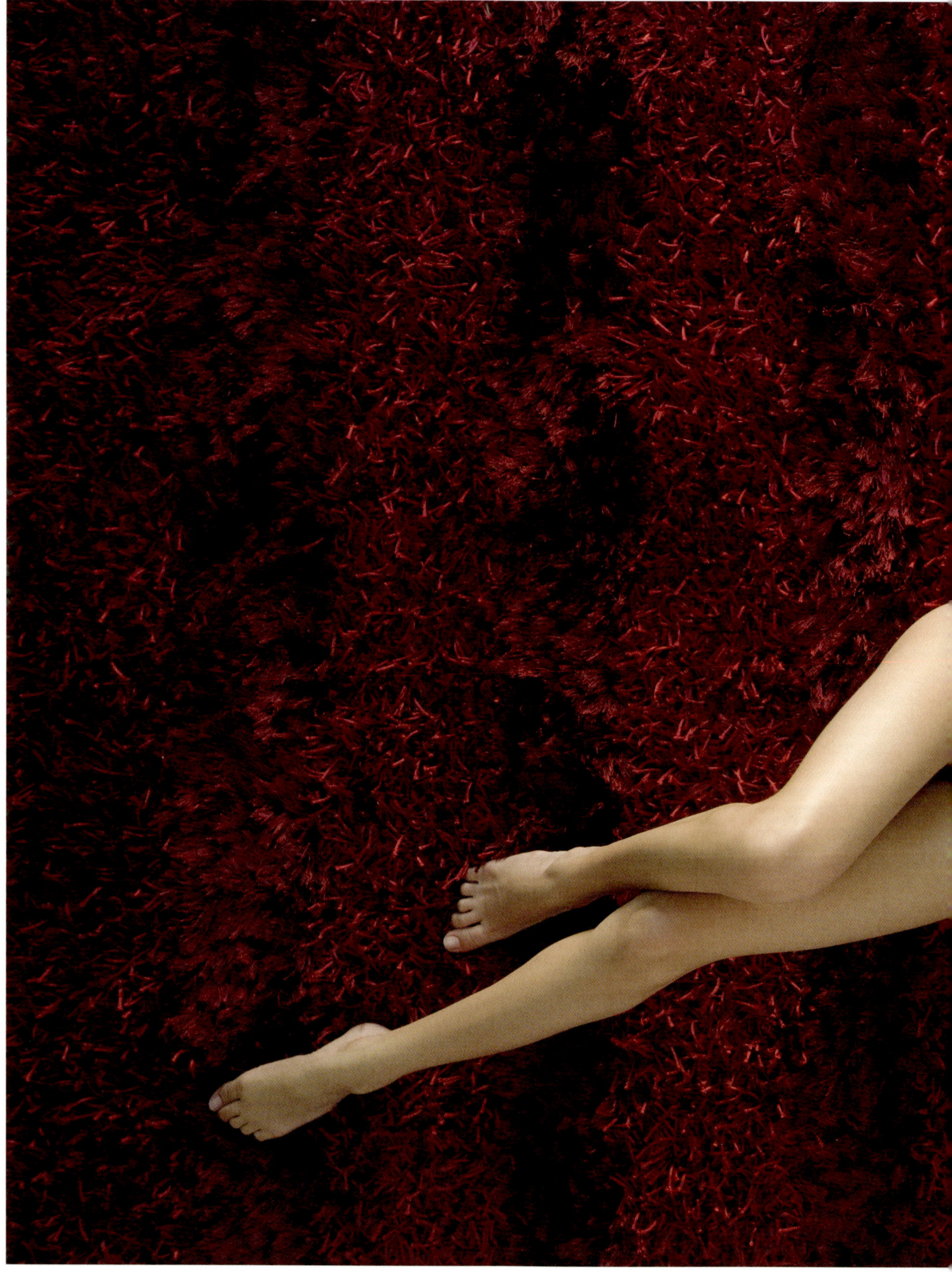

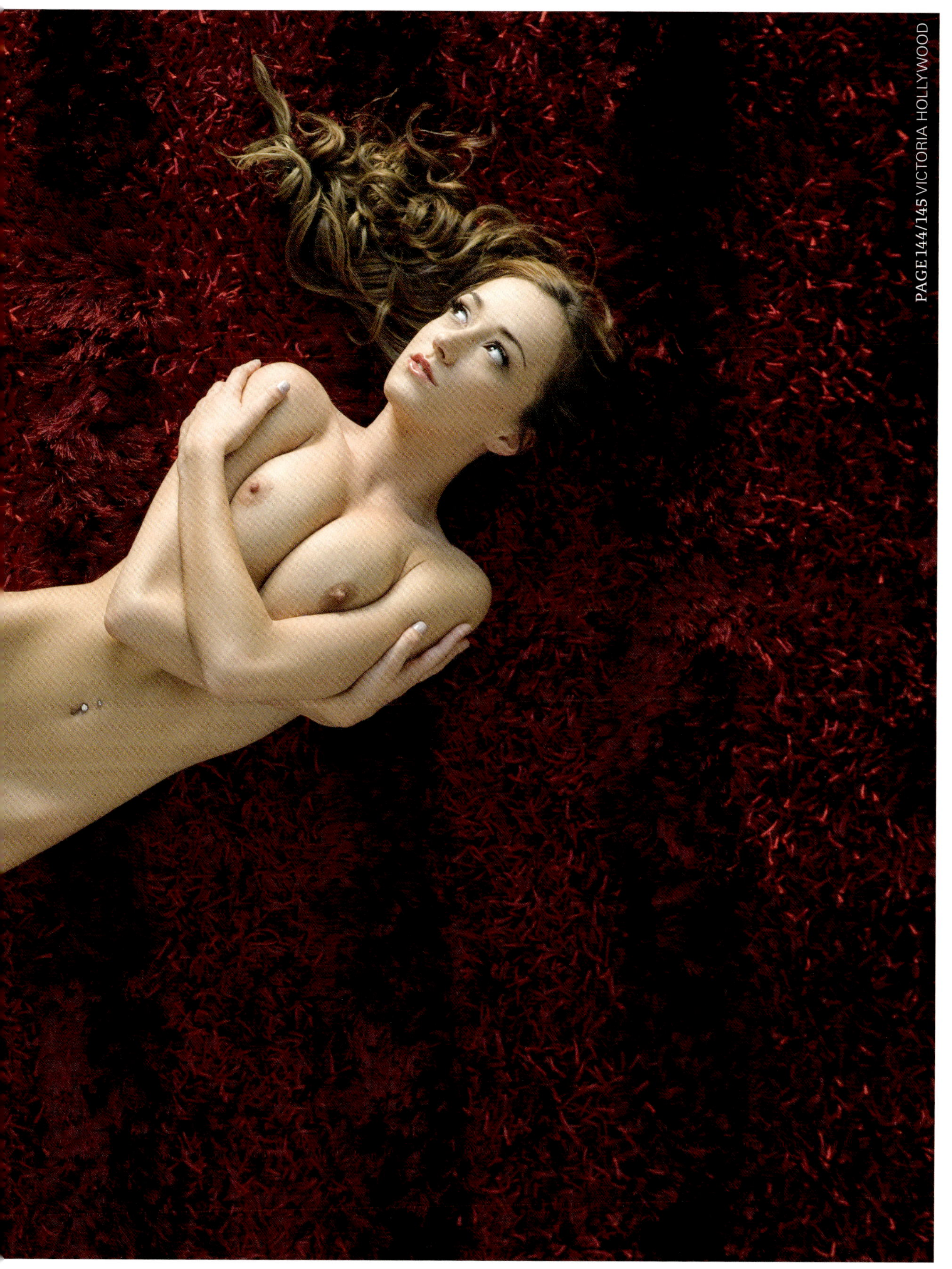

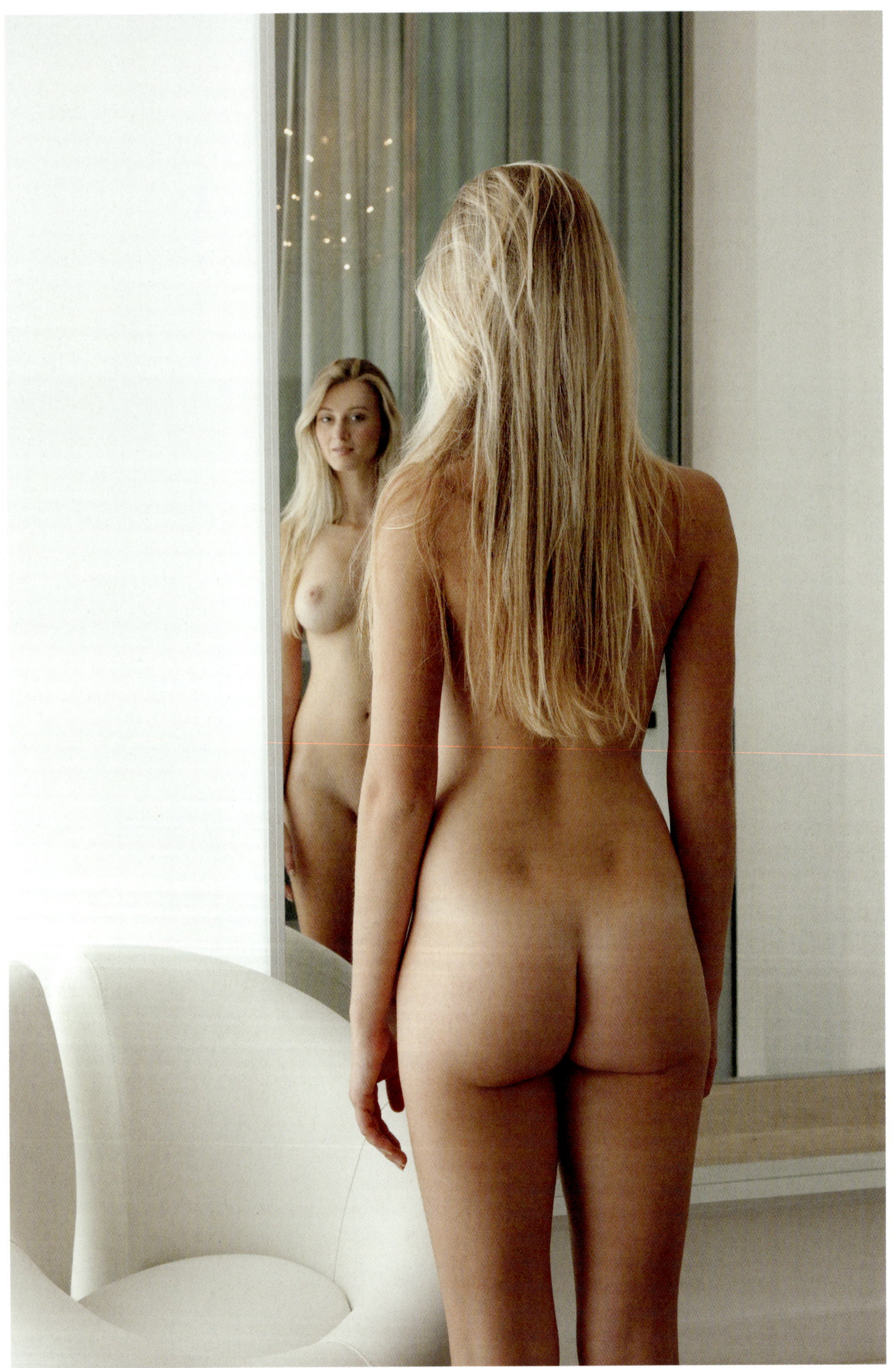

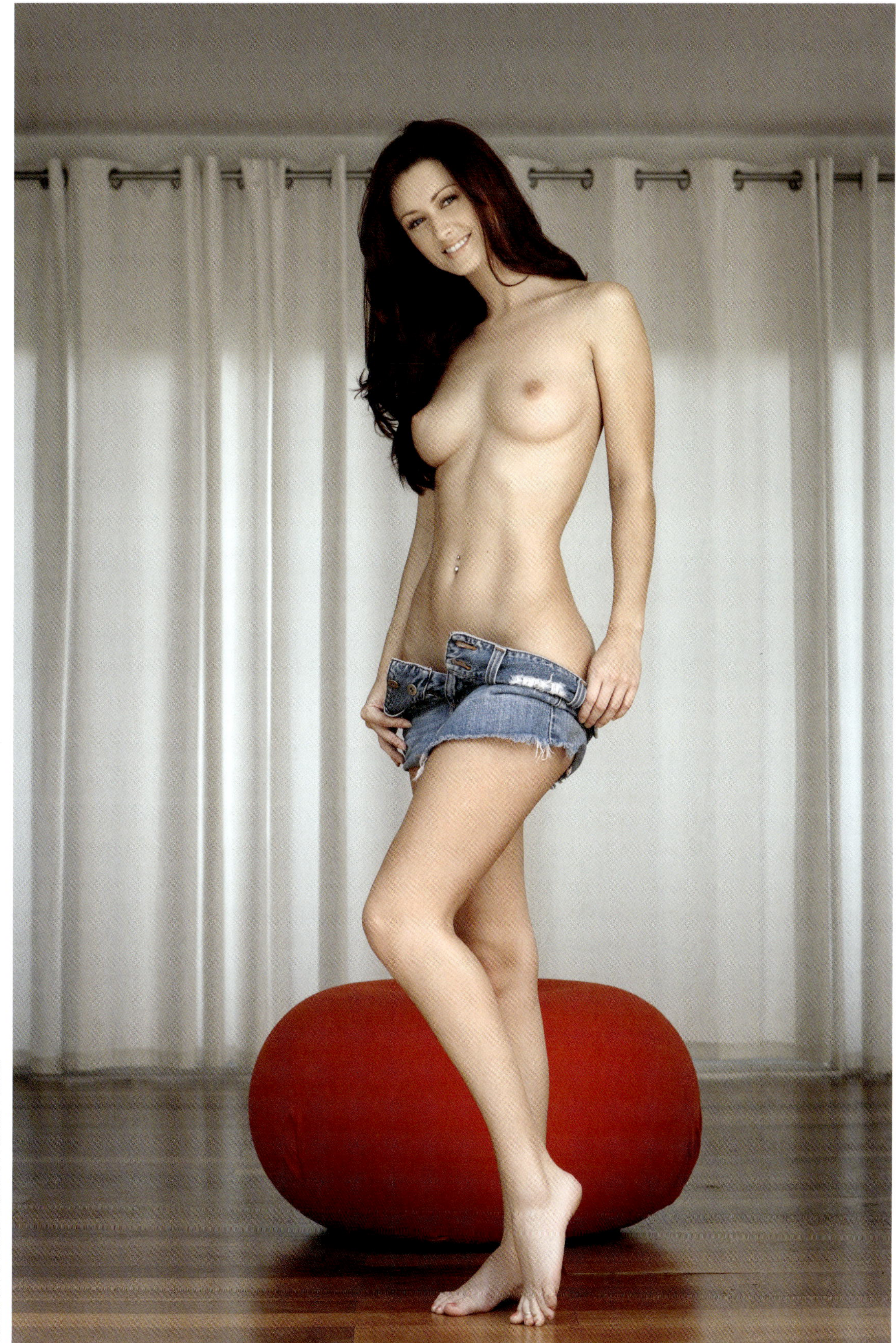

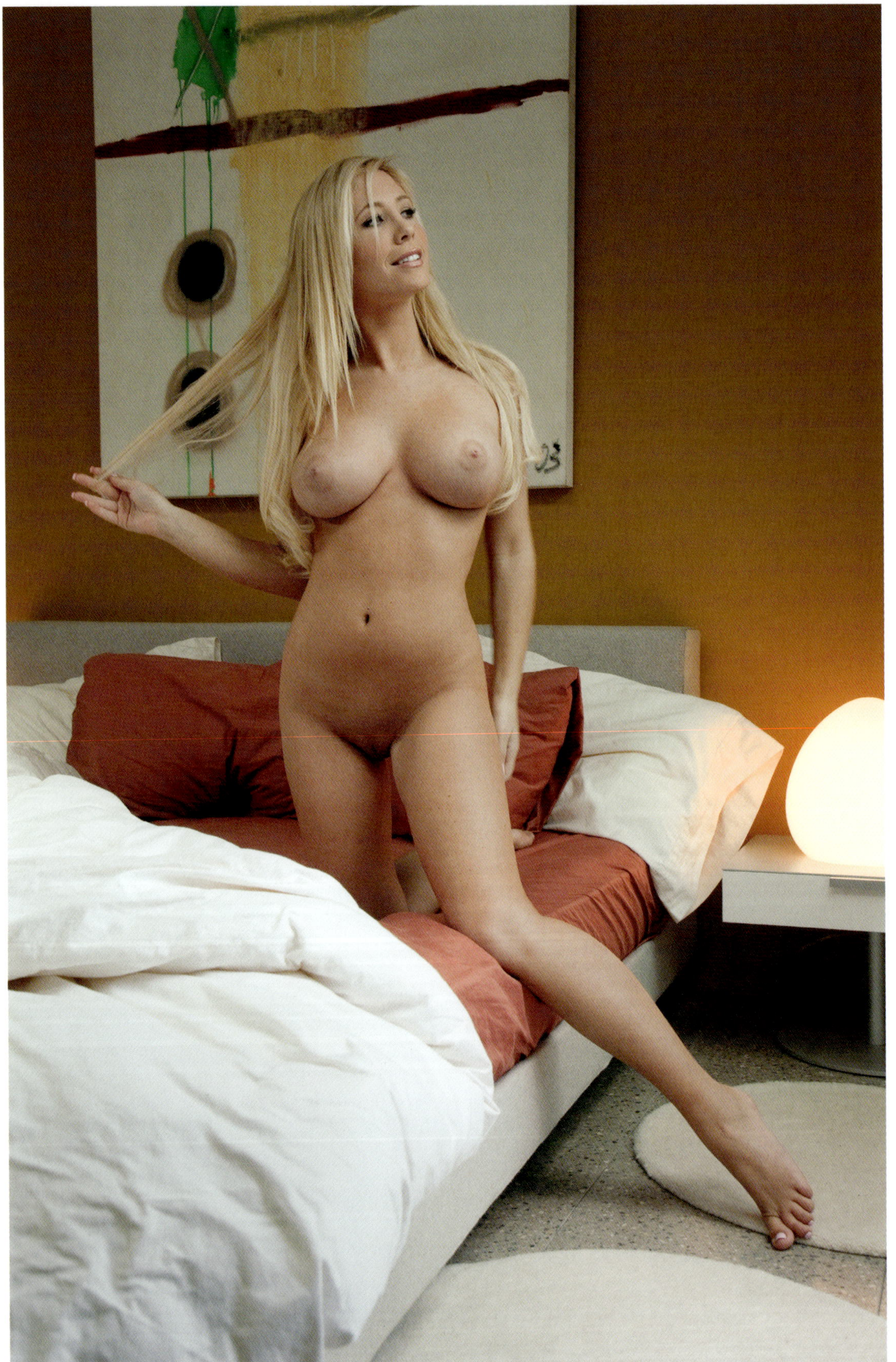

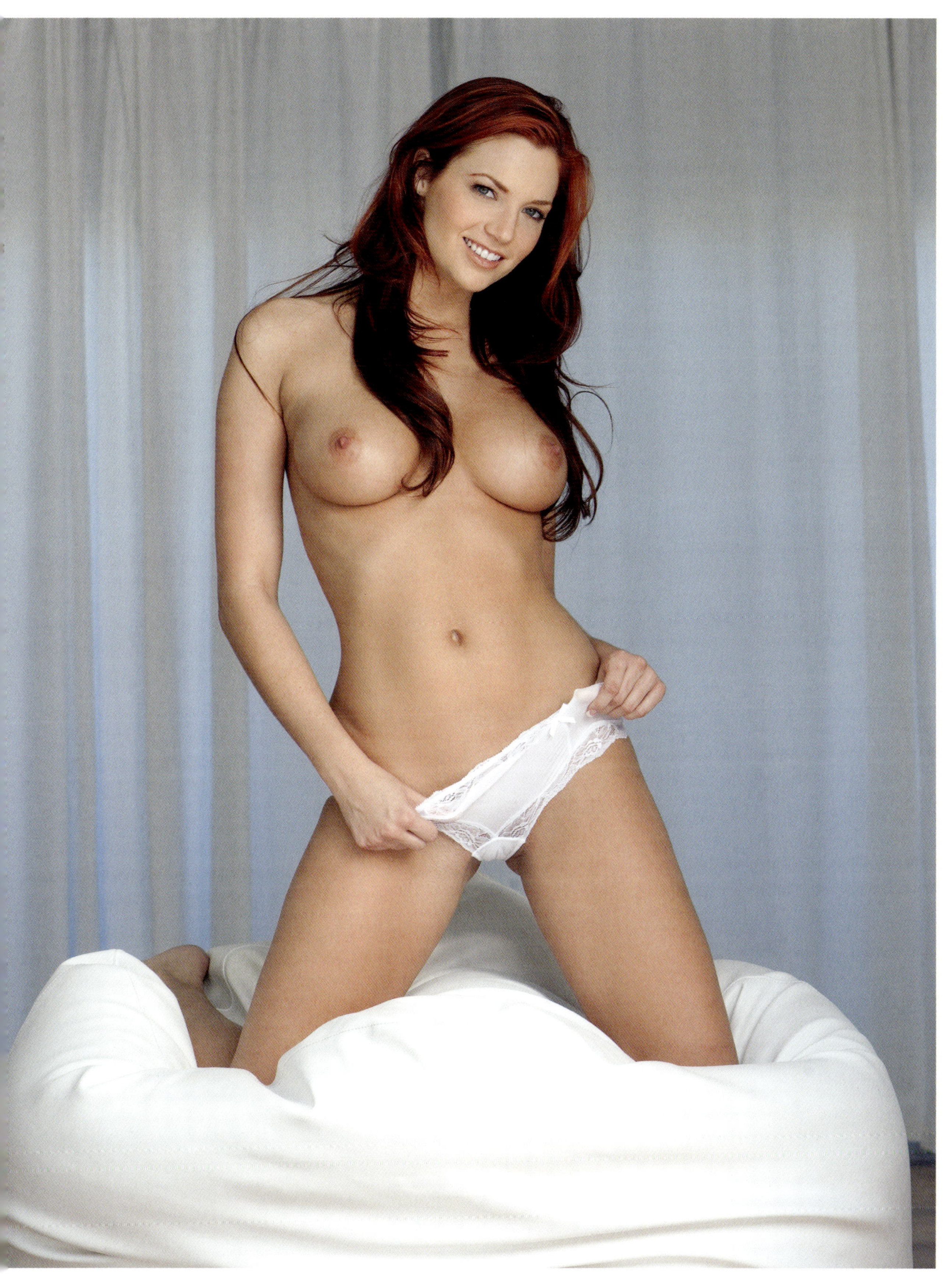

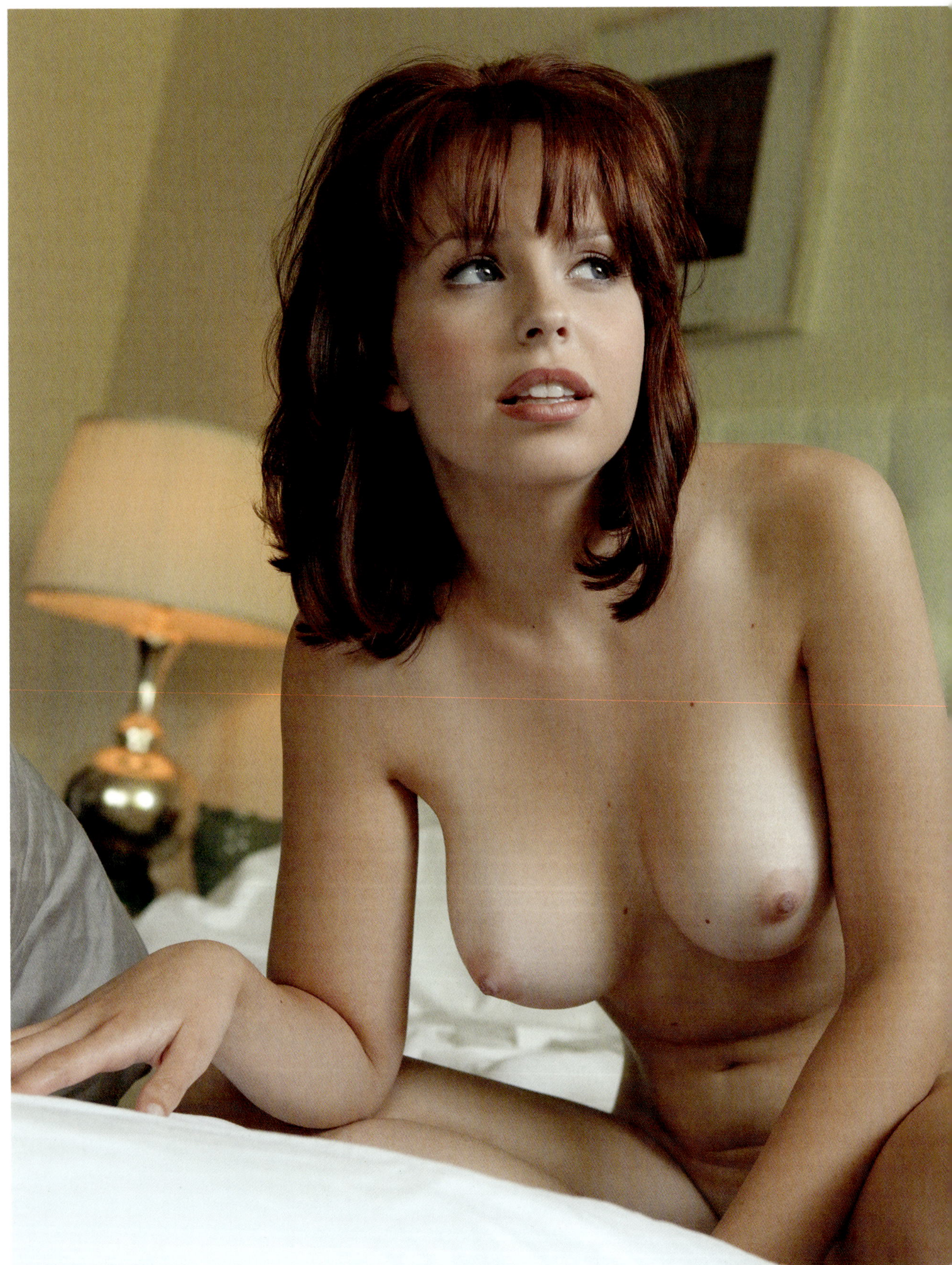

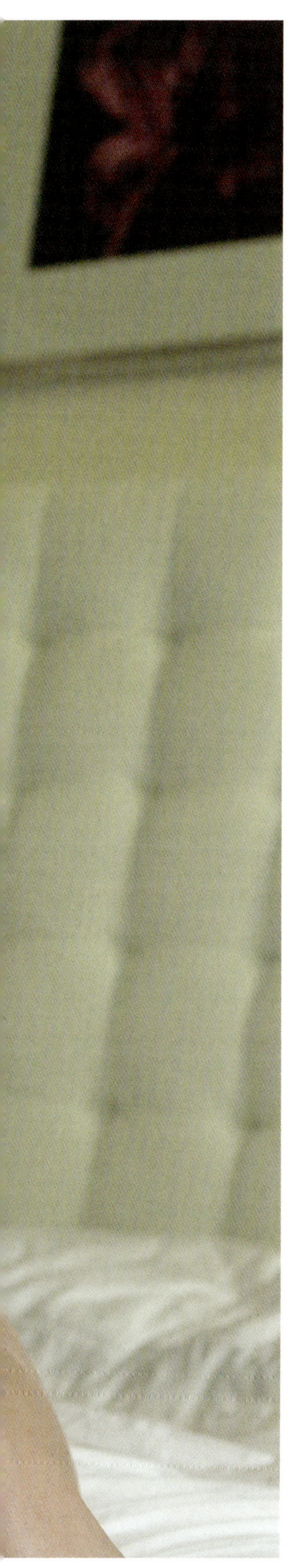

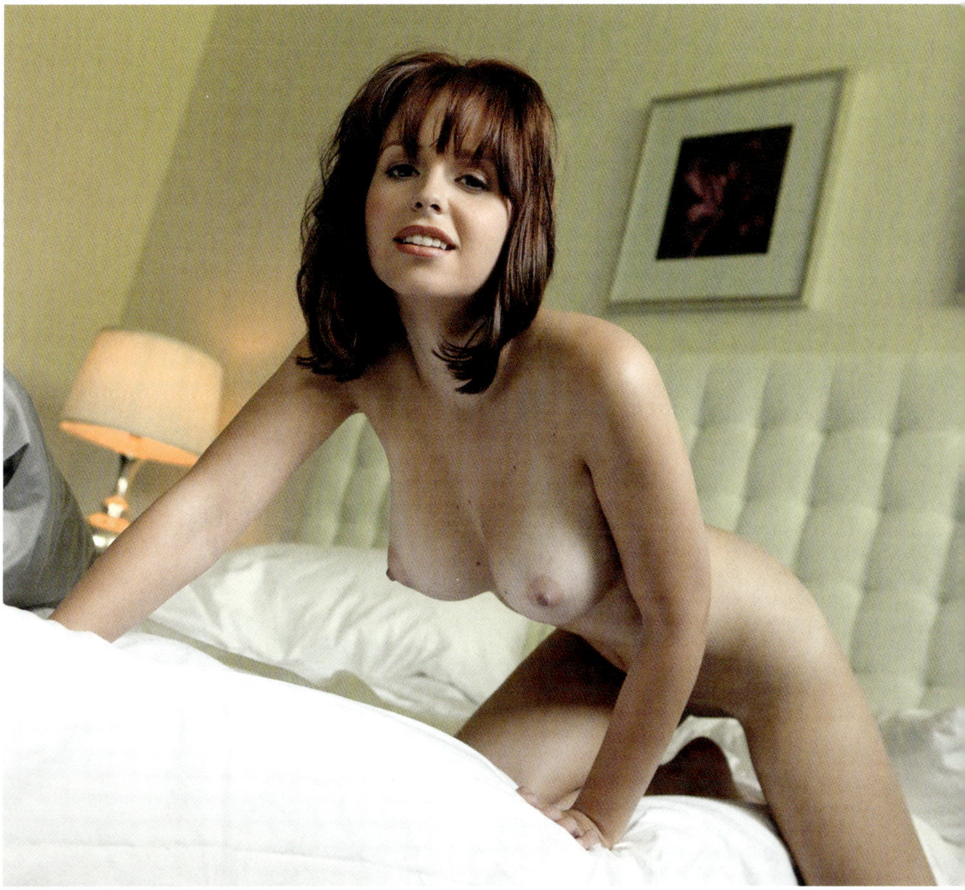

PAGE 150/151 HAYDEN HOLLYWOOD

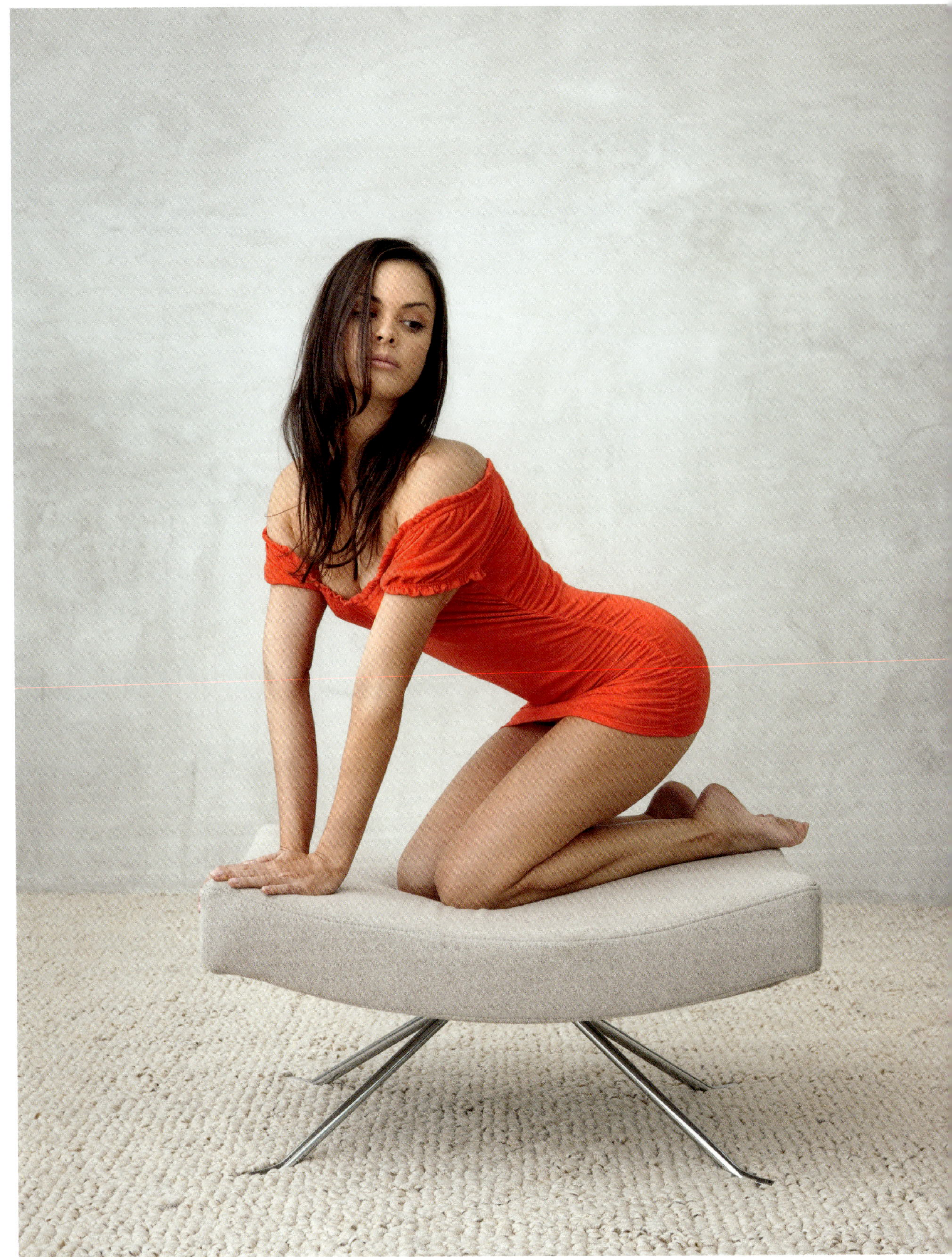

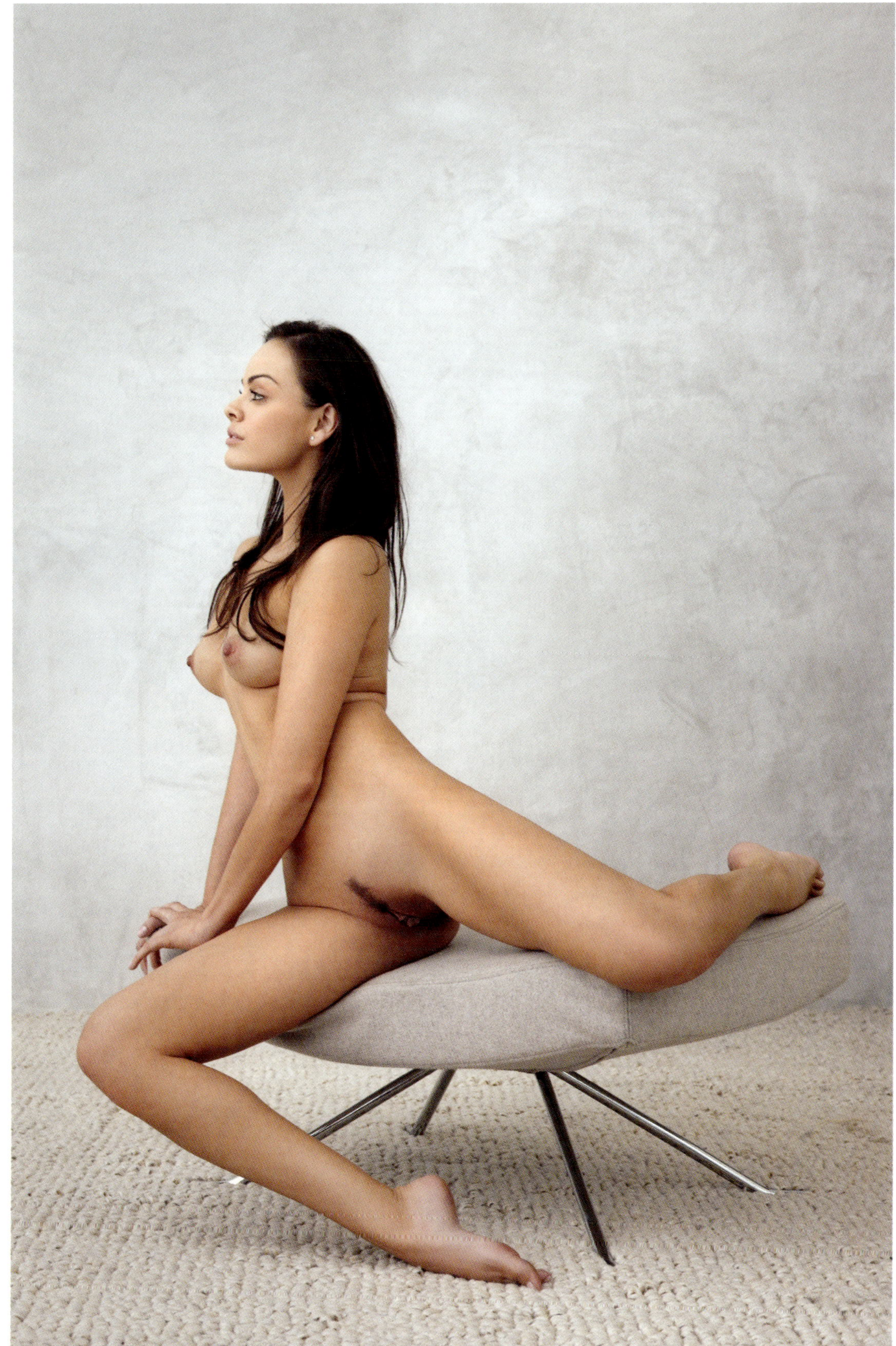

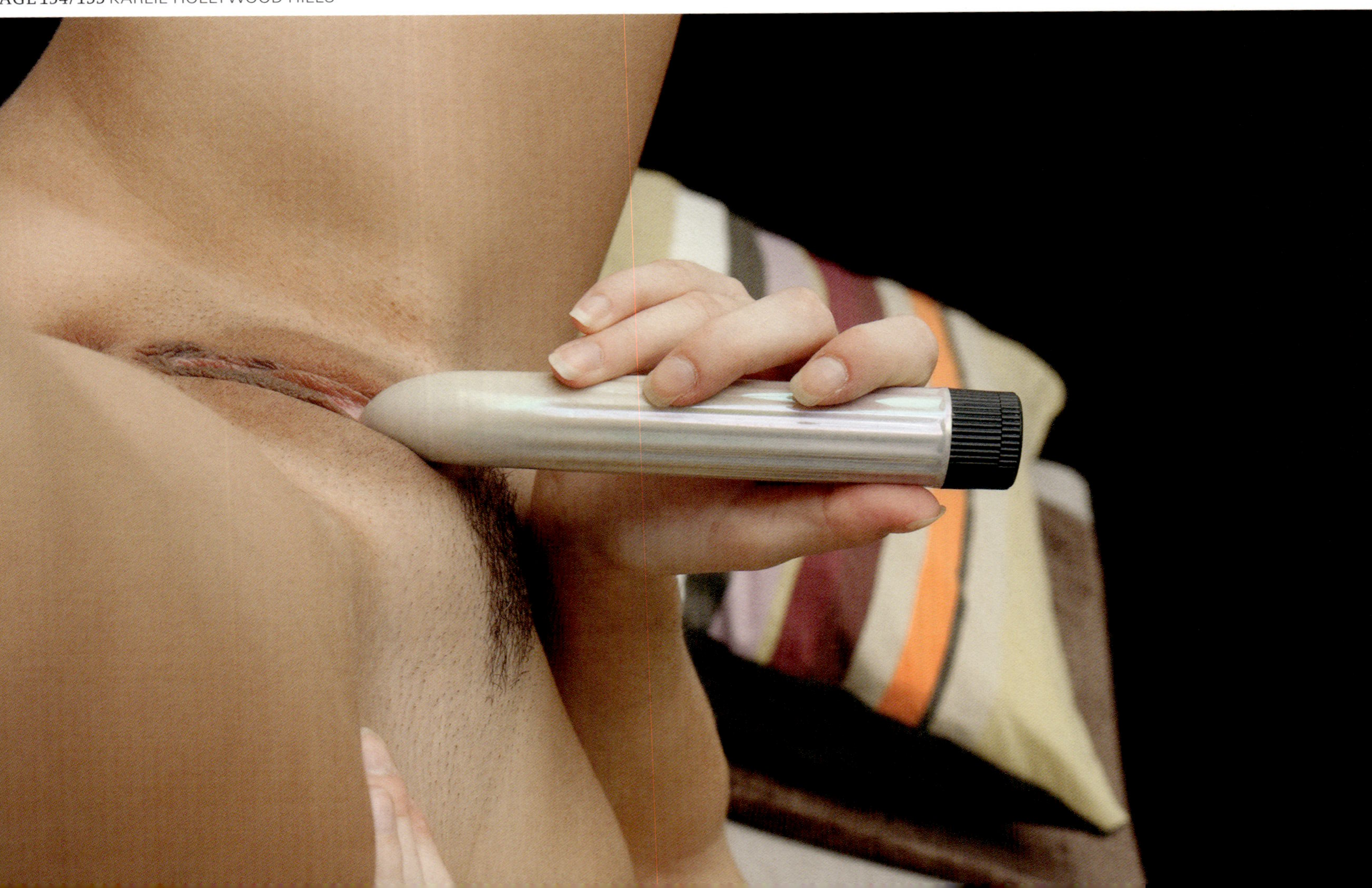

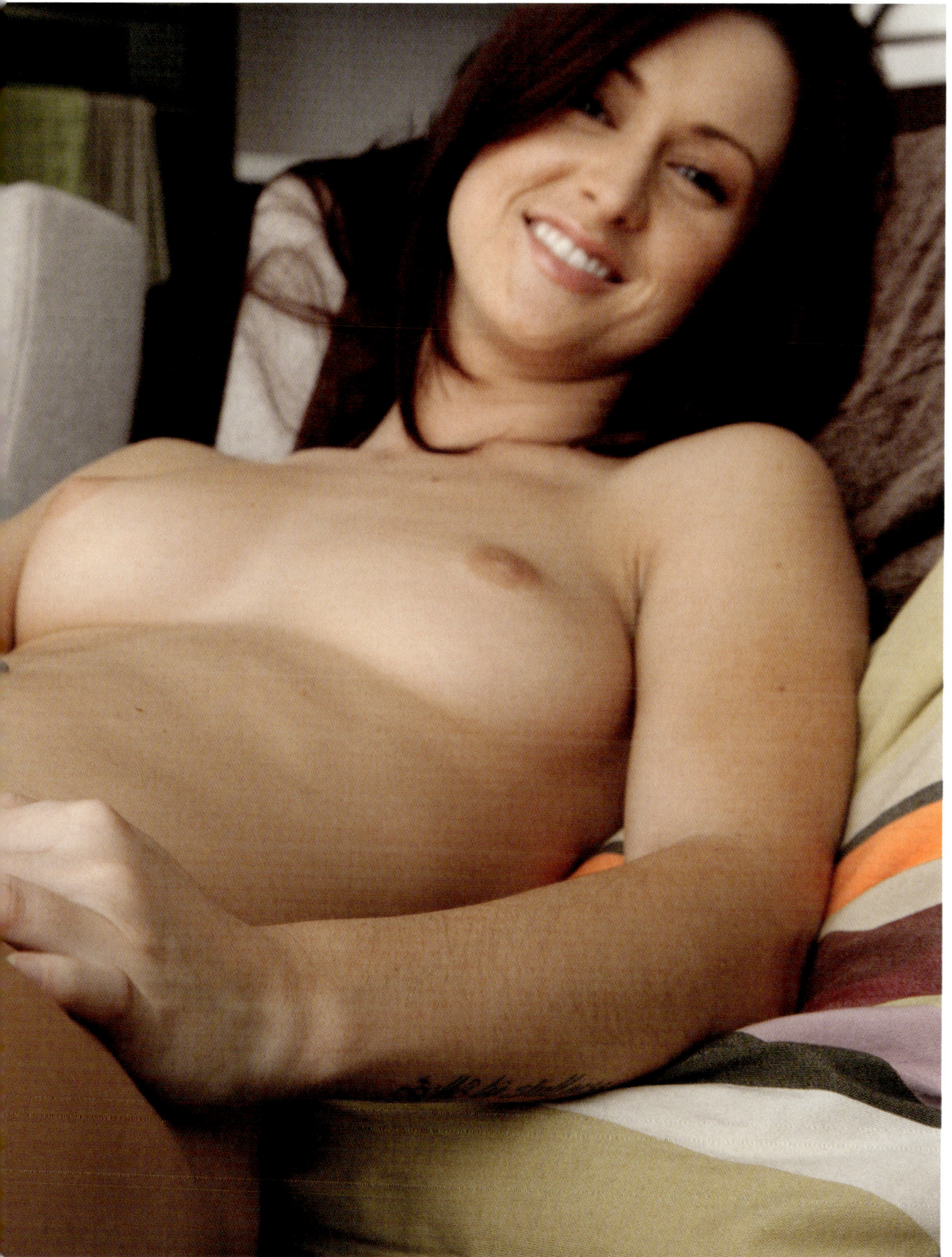

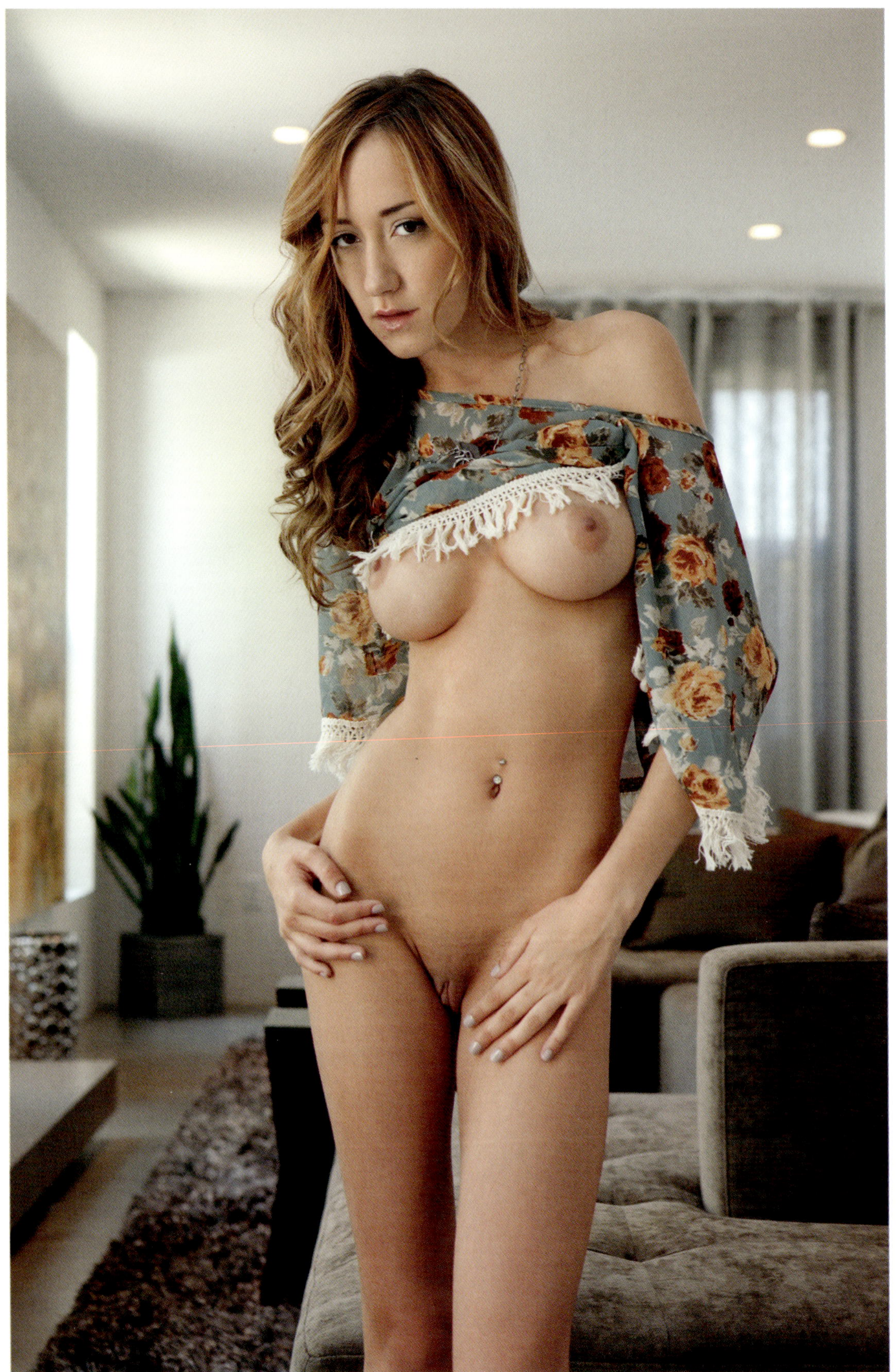

PAGE 156 VICTORIA HOLLYWOOD

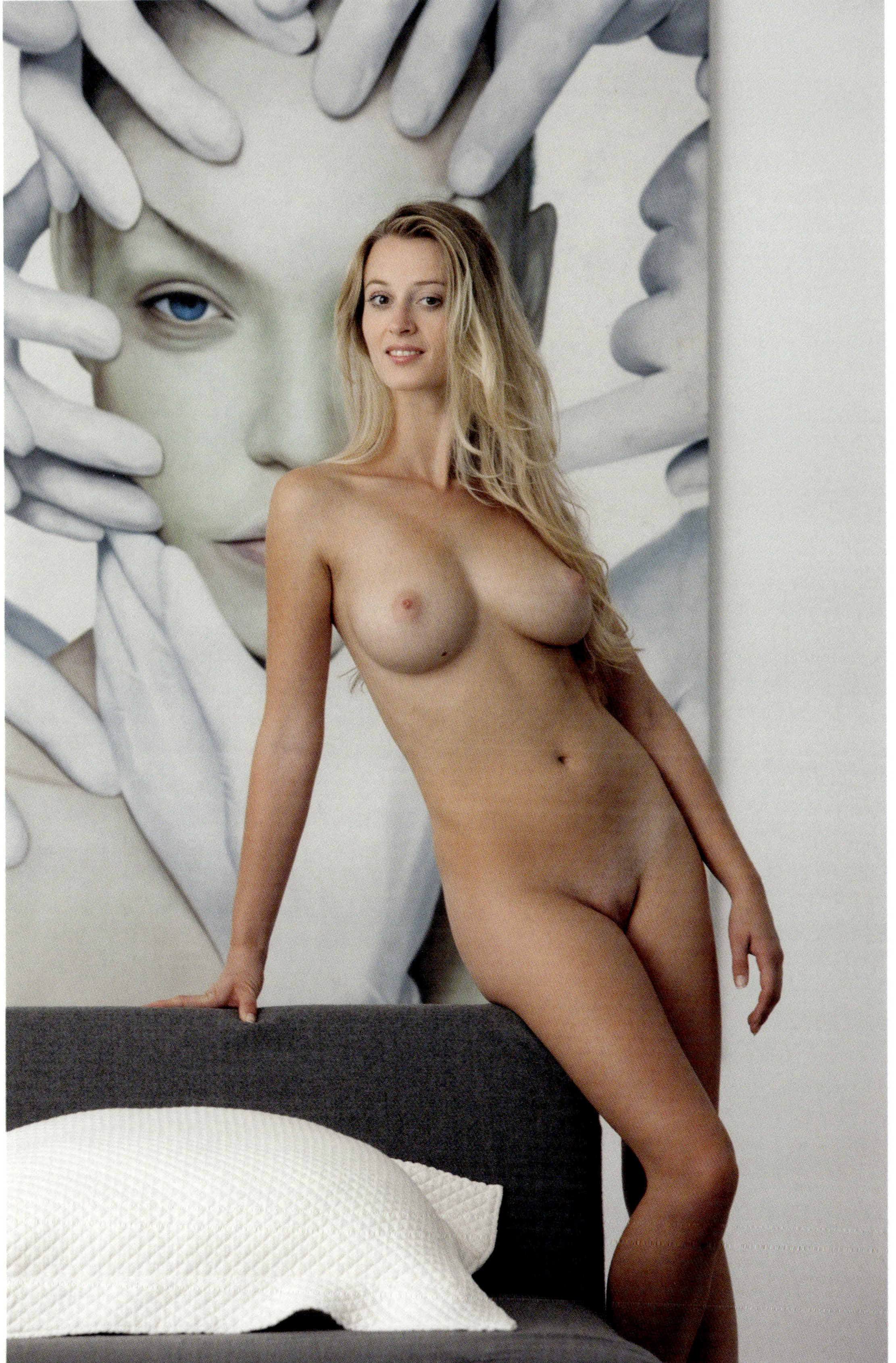

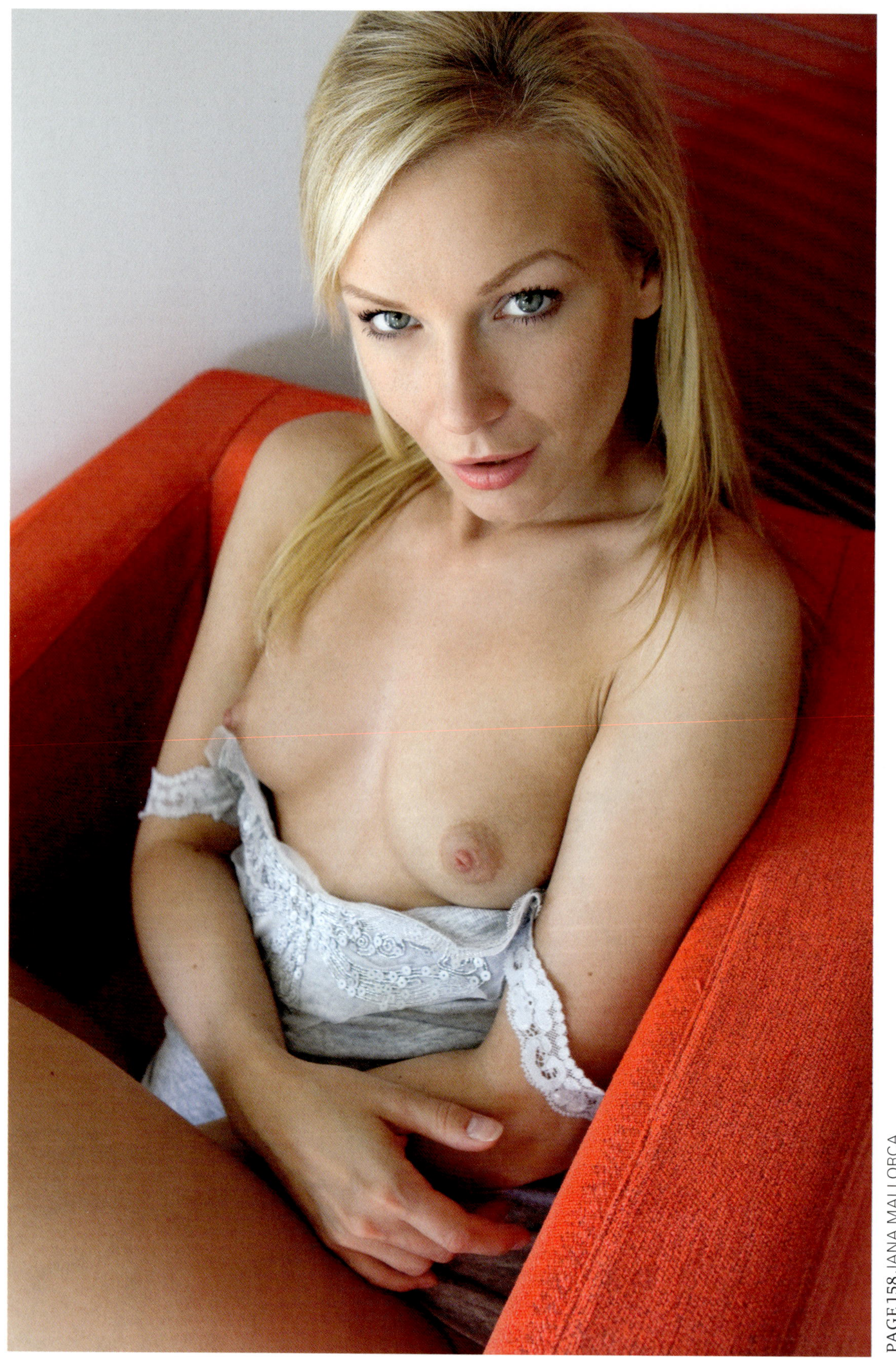

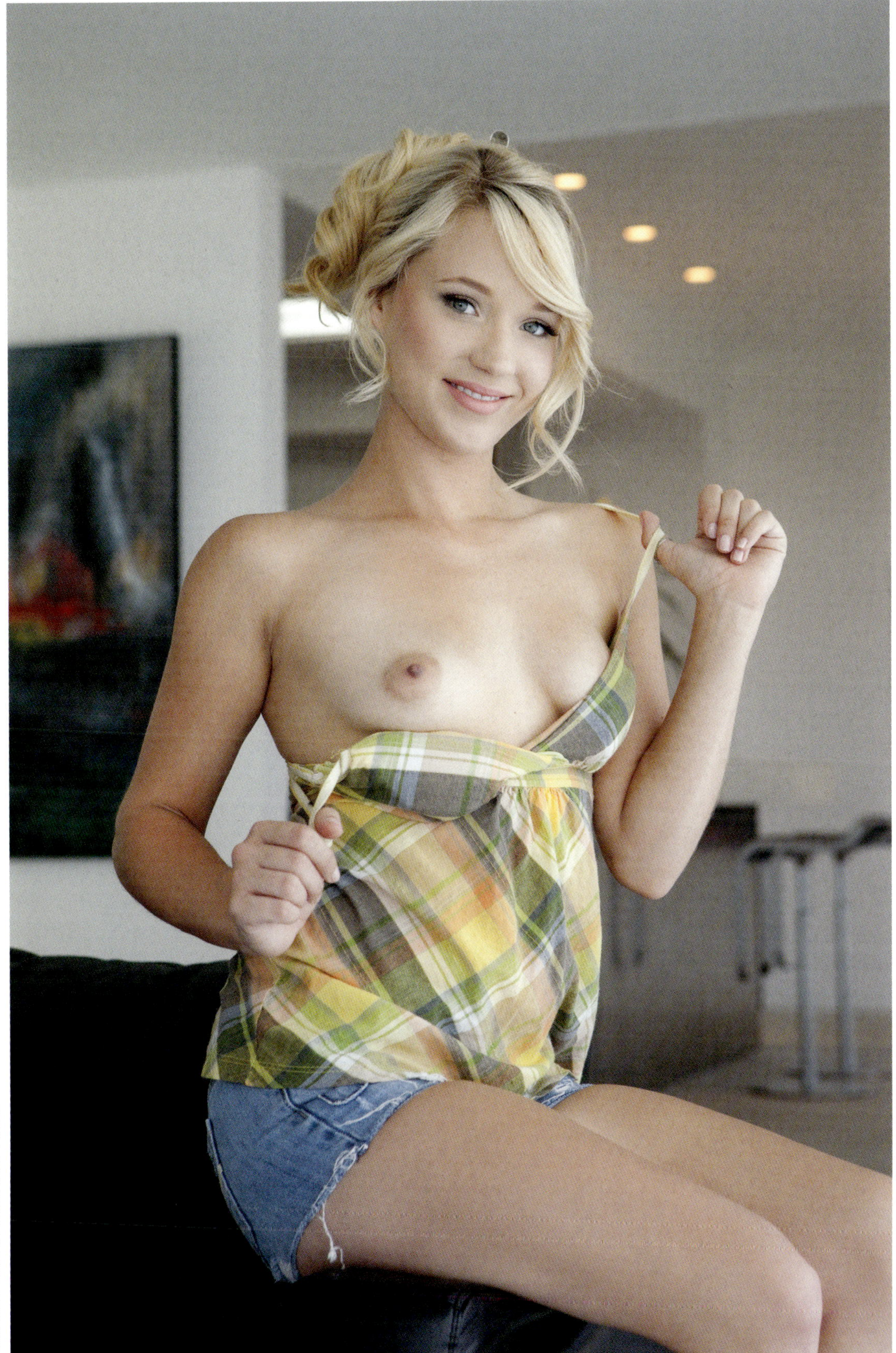

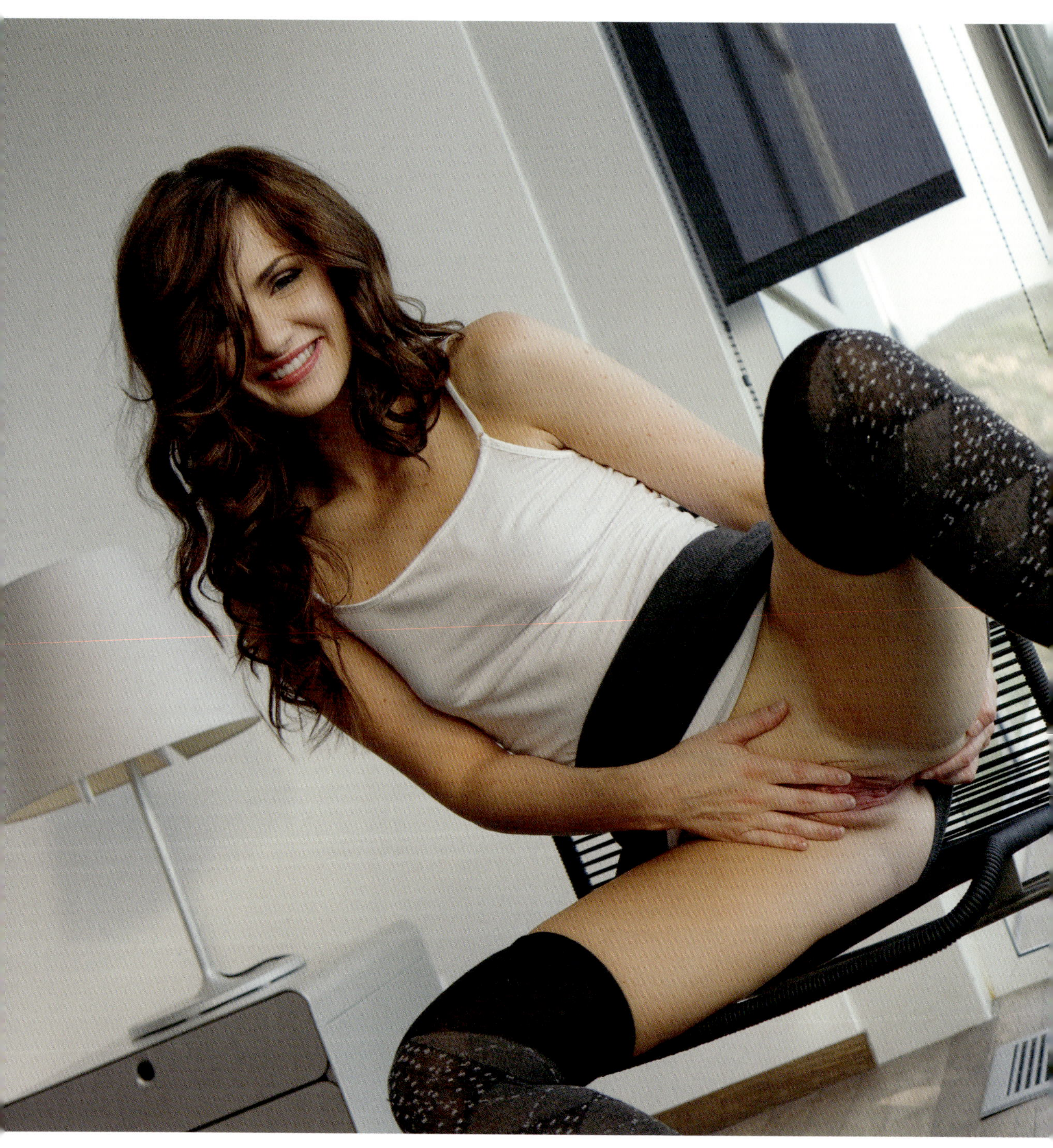

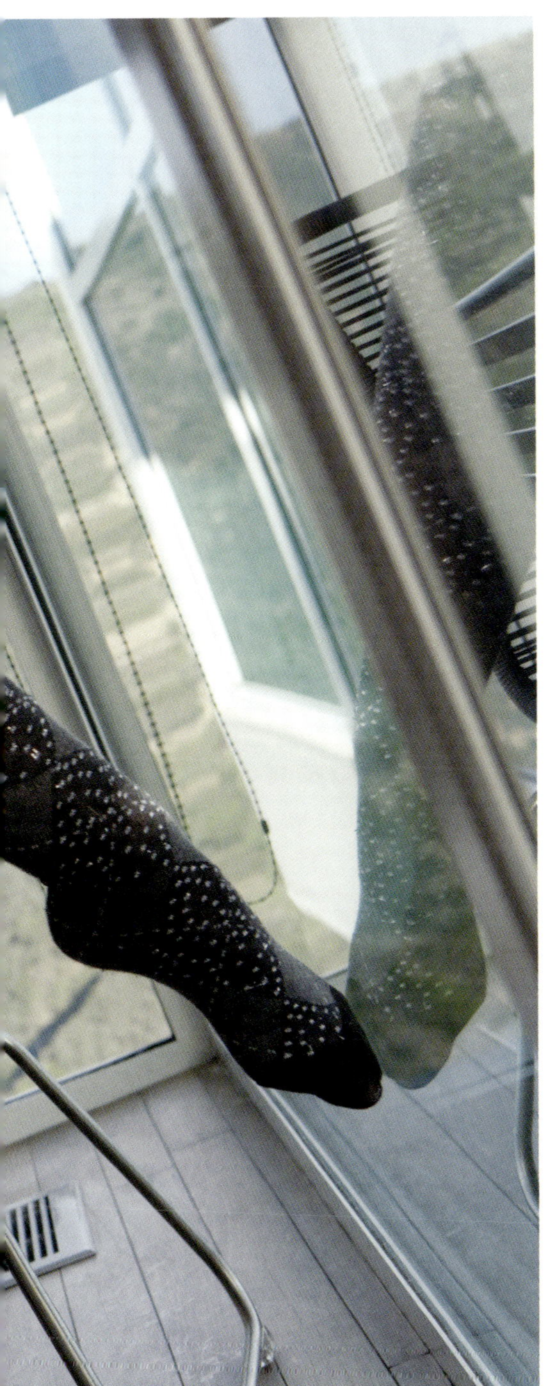

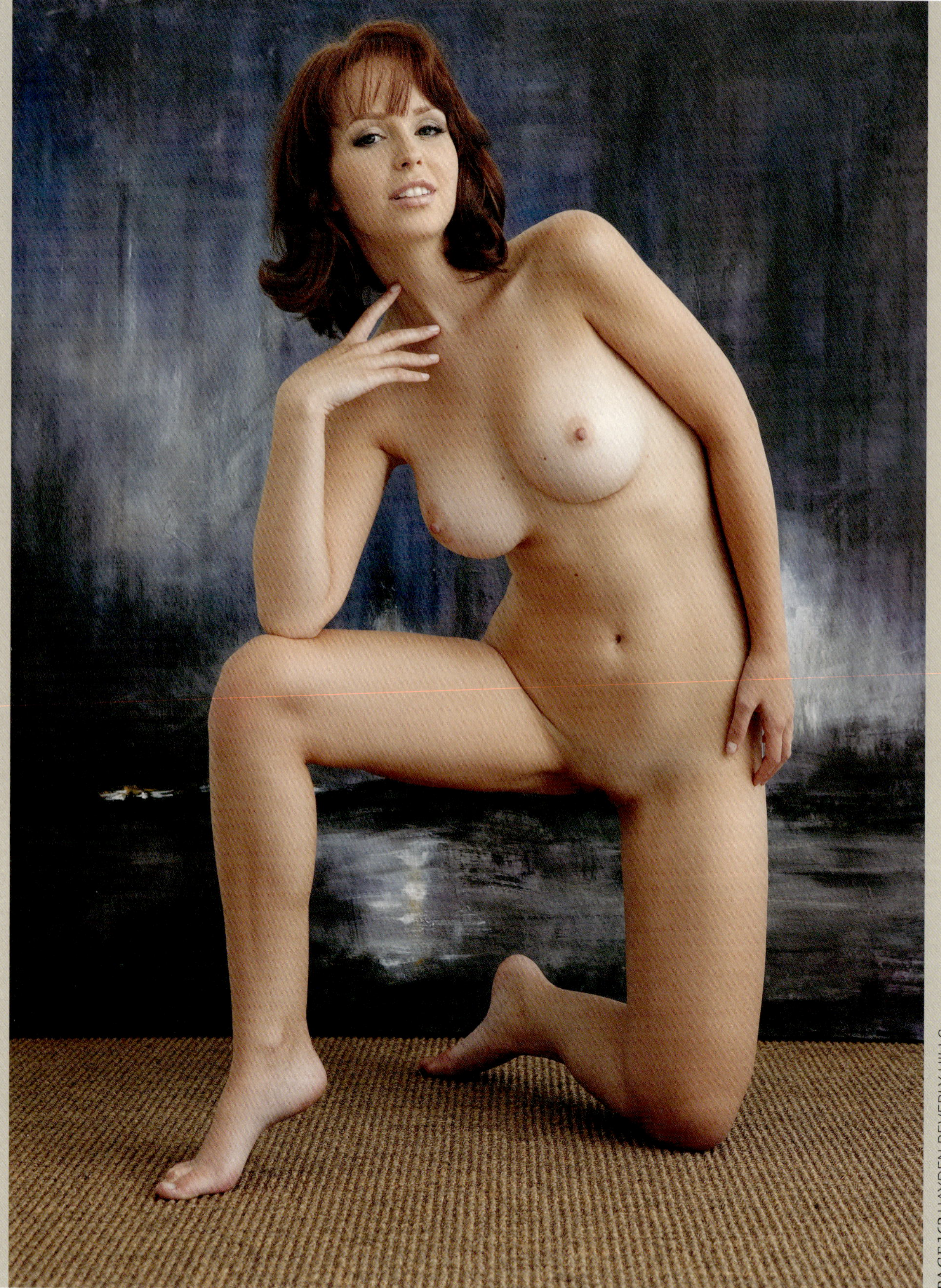

PAGE 162 HAYDEN BEVERLY HILLS

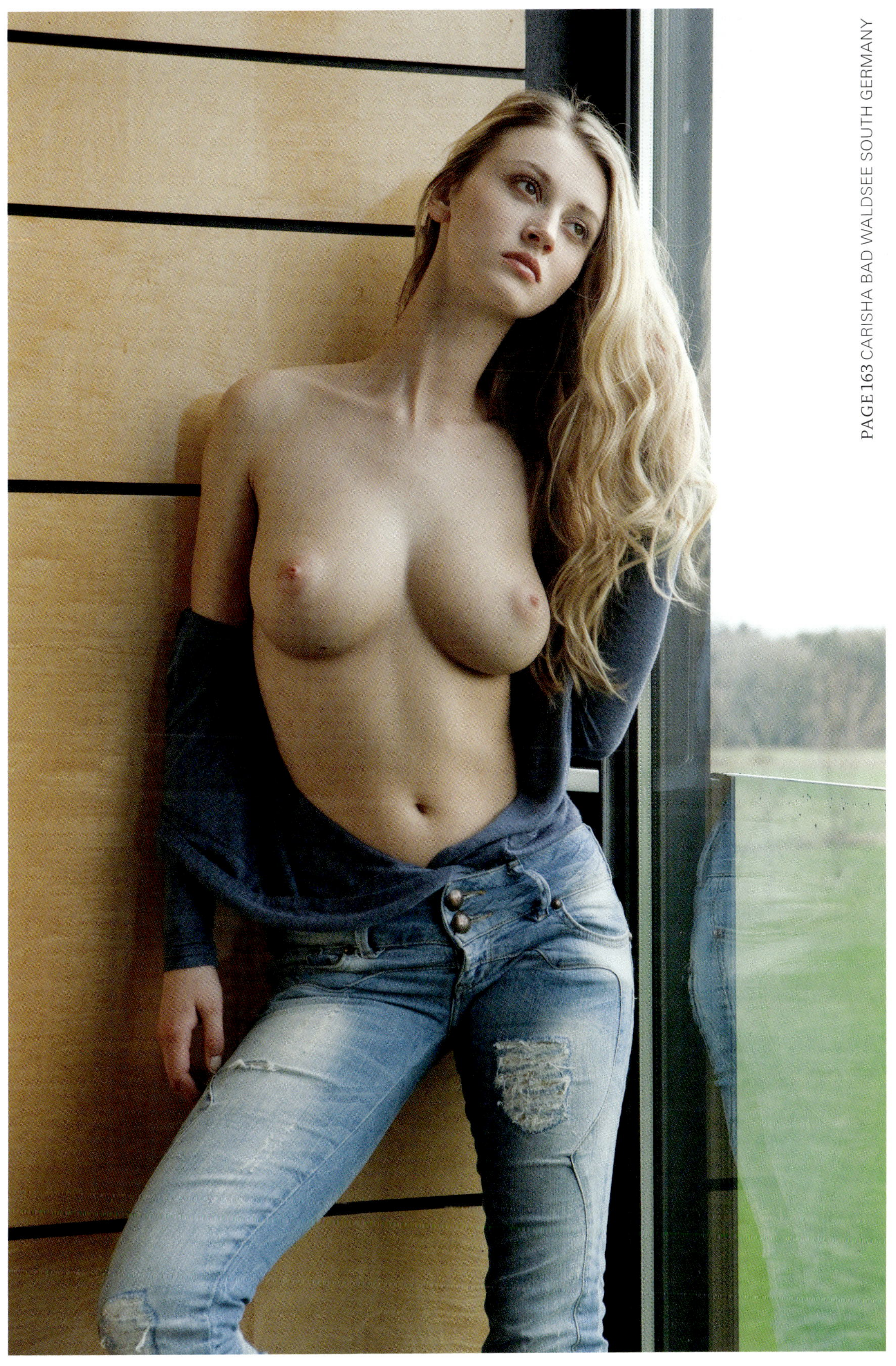

PAGE 163 CARISHA BAD WALDSEE SOUTH GERMANY

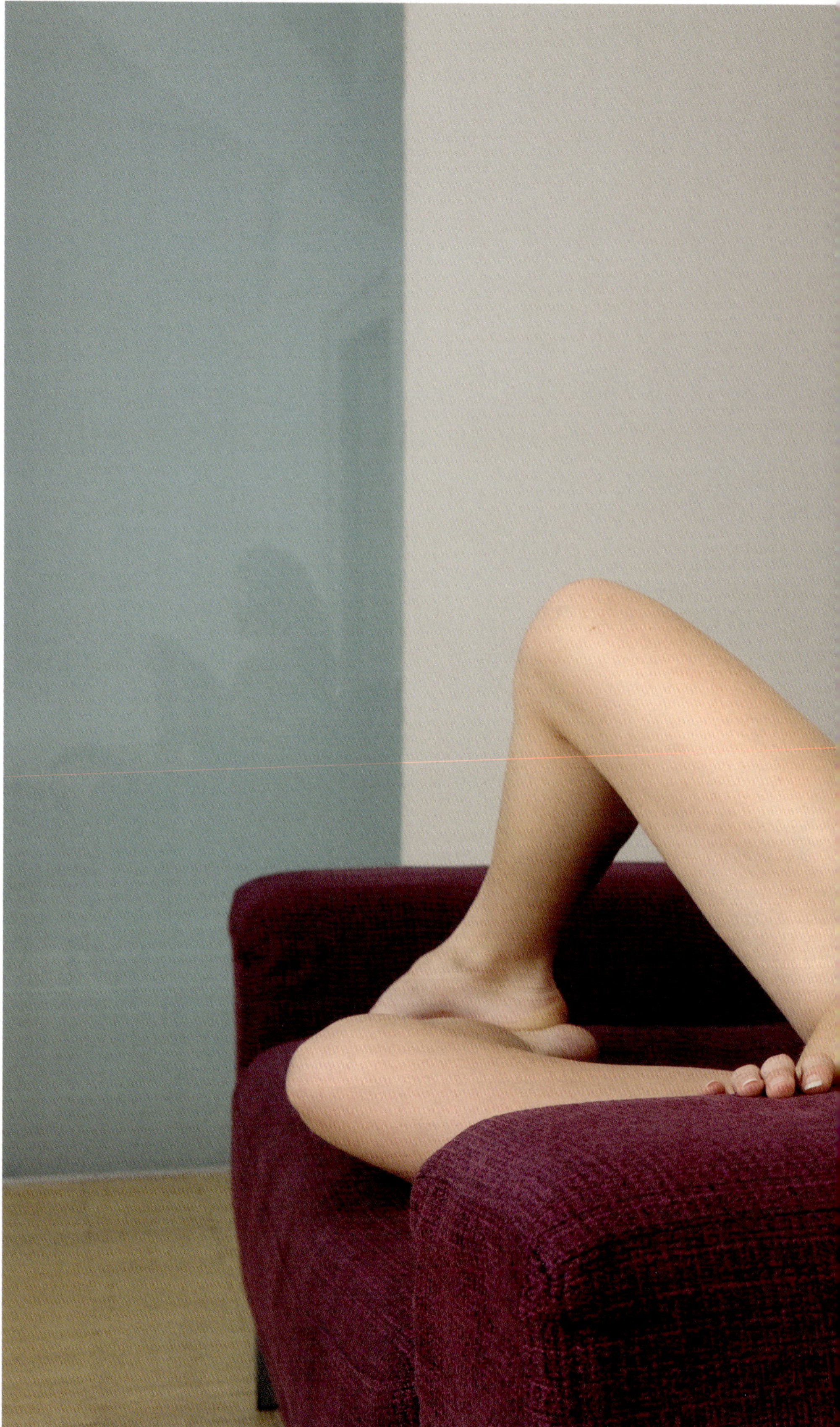

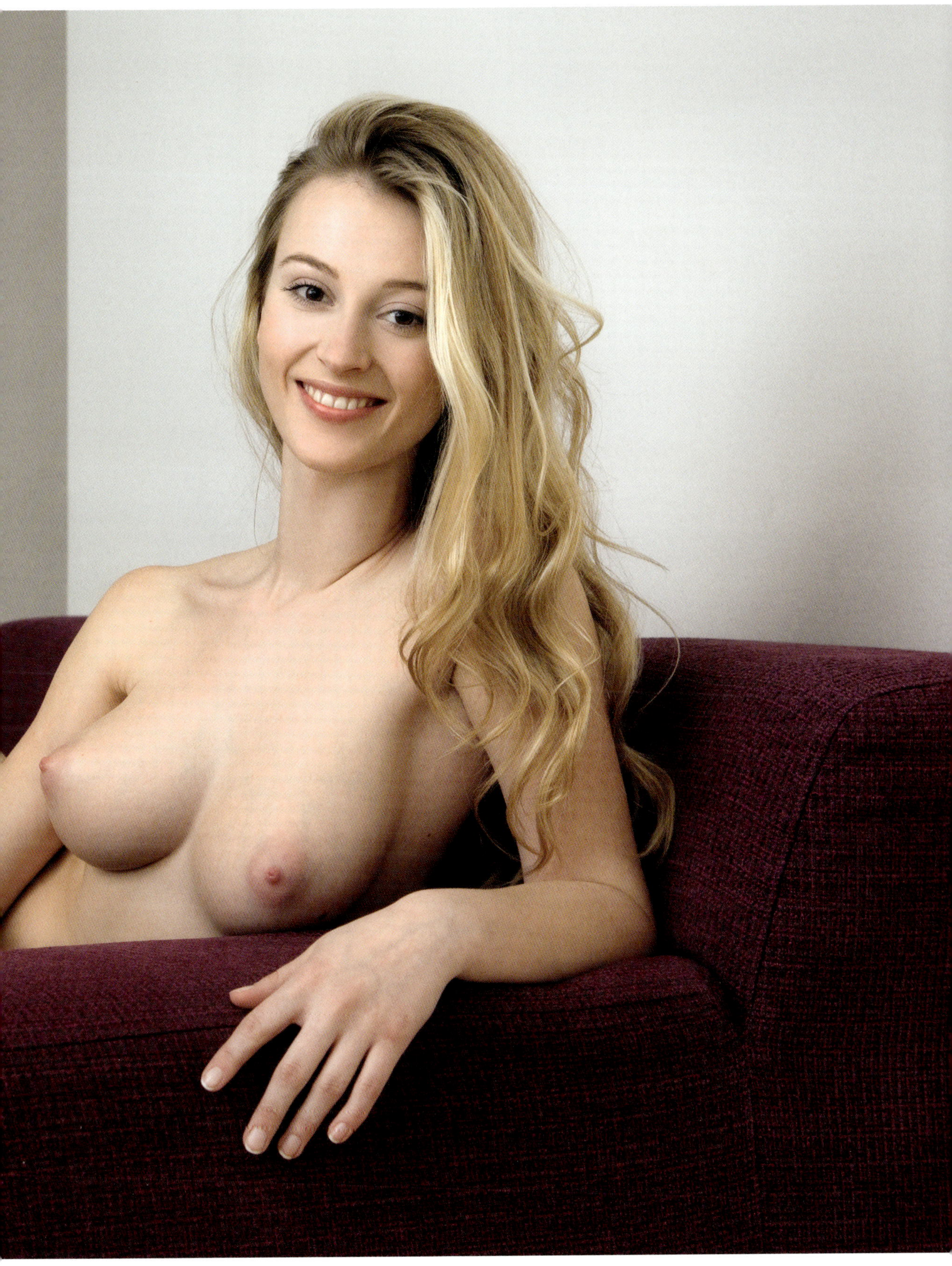

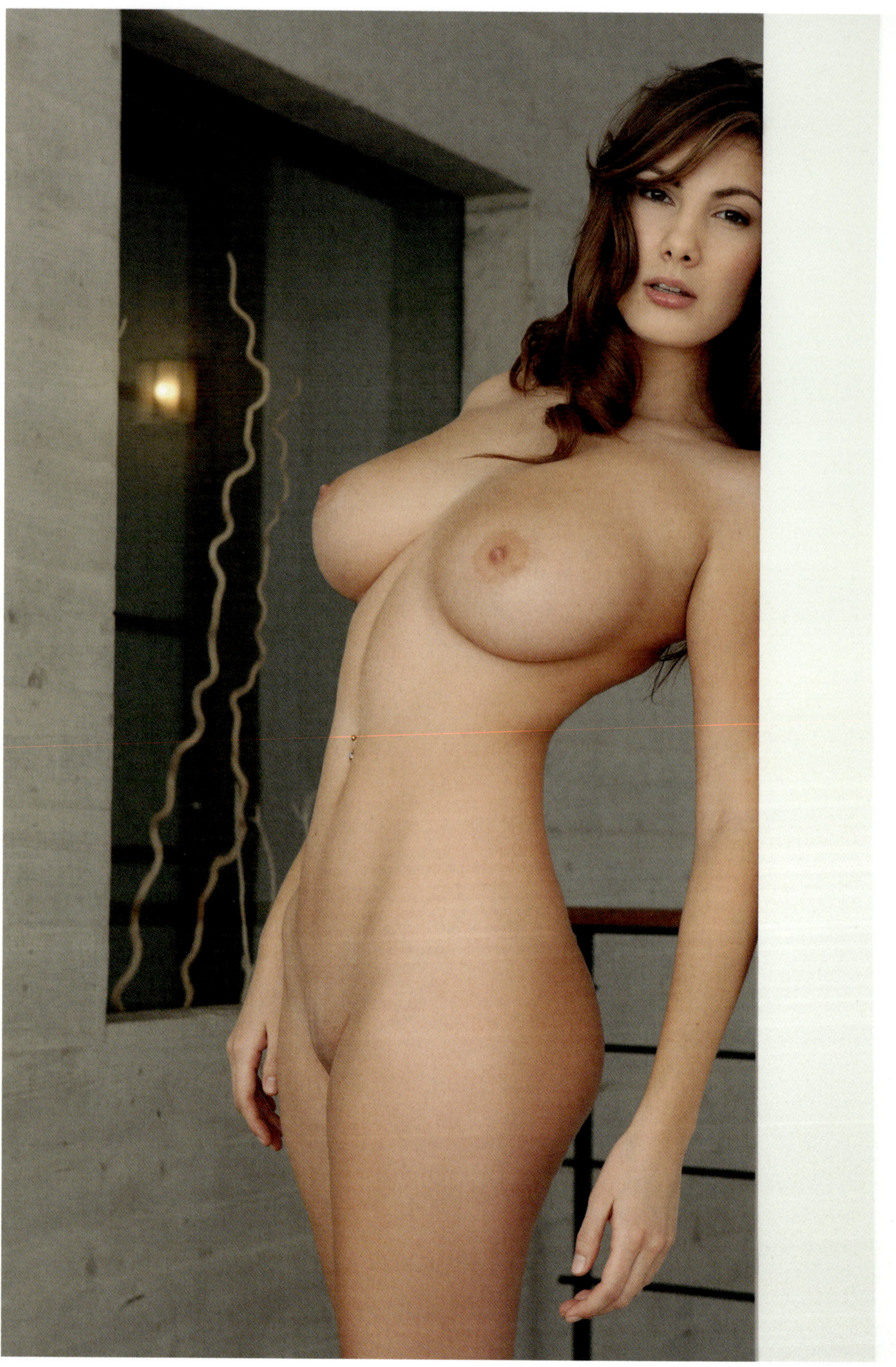

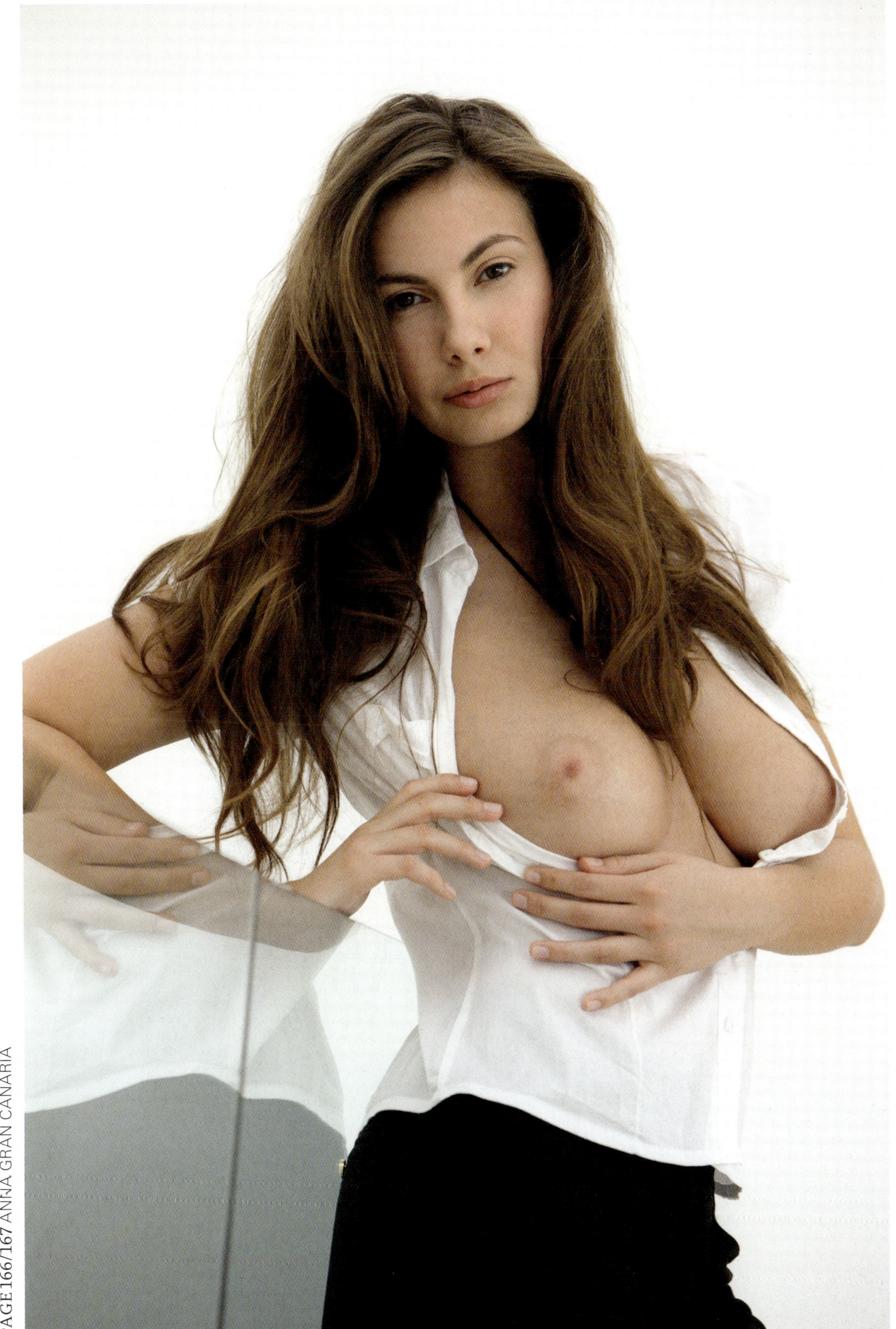

PAGE 166/167 ANNA GRAN CANARIA

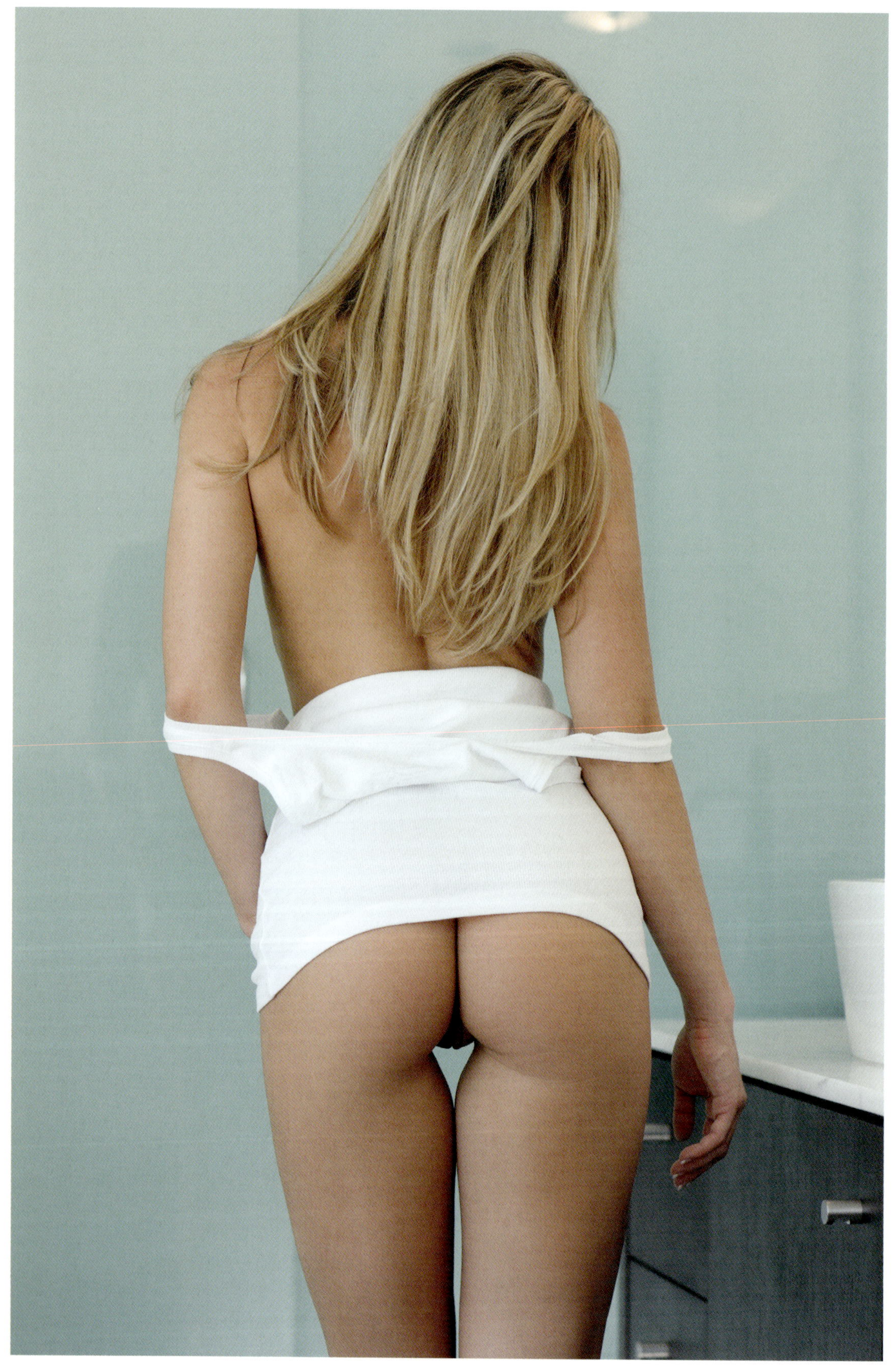

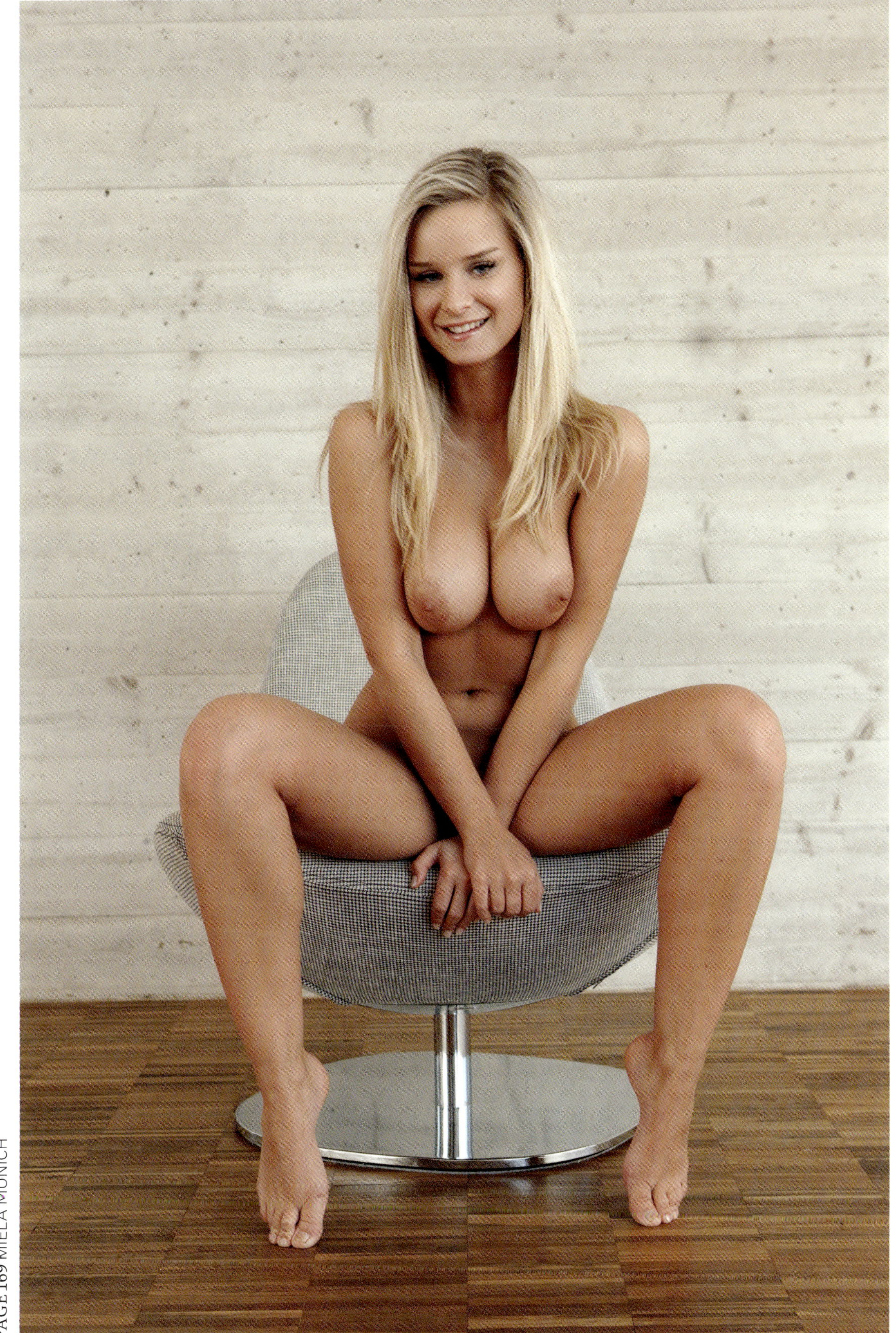

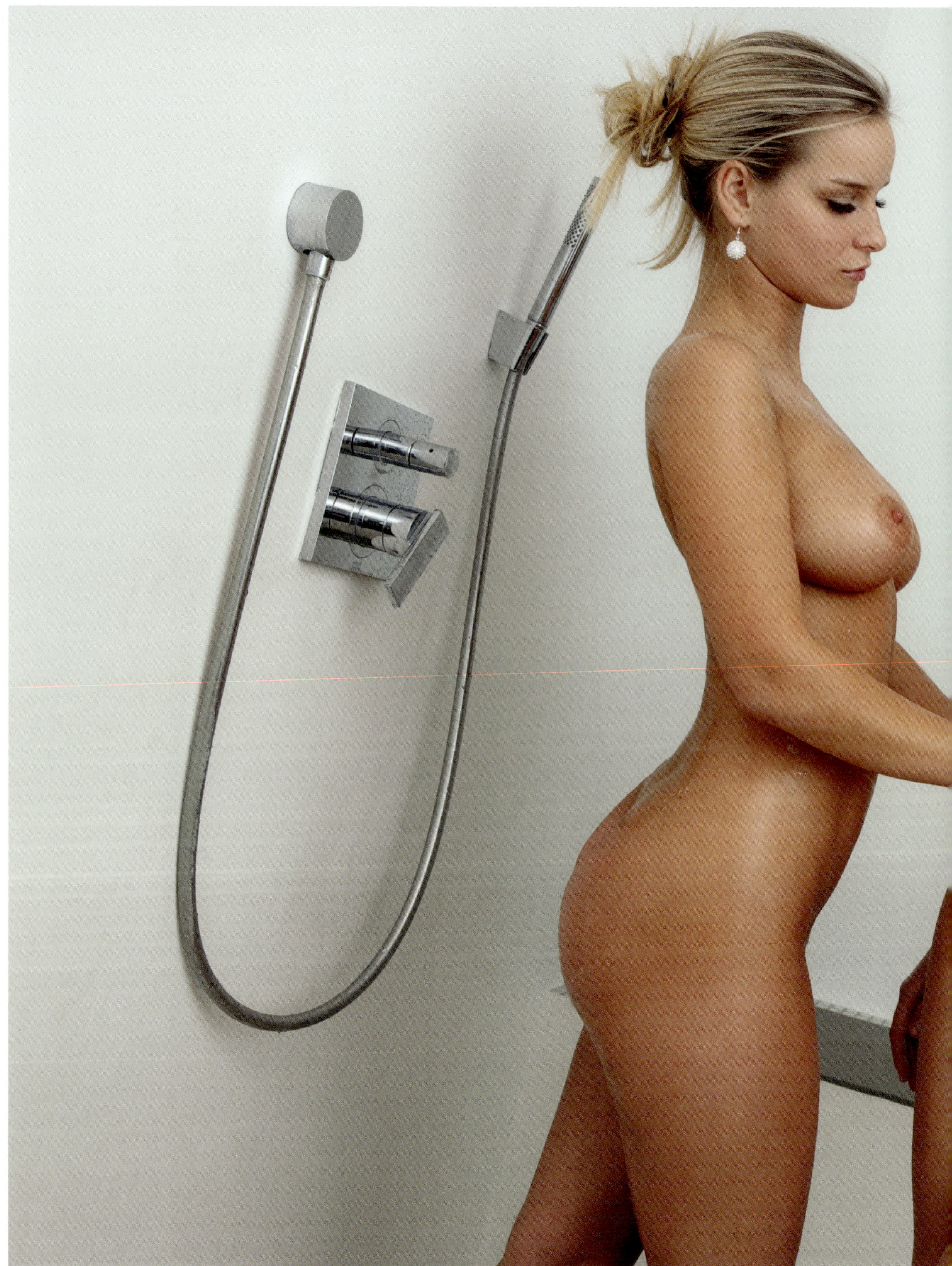

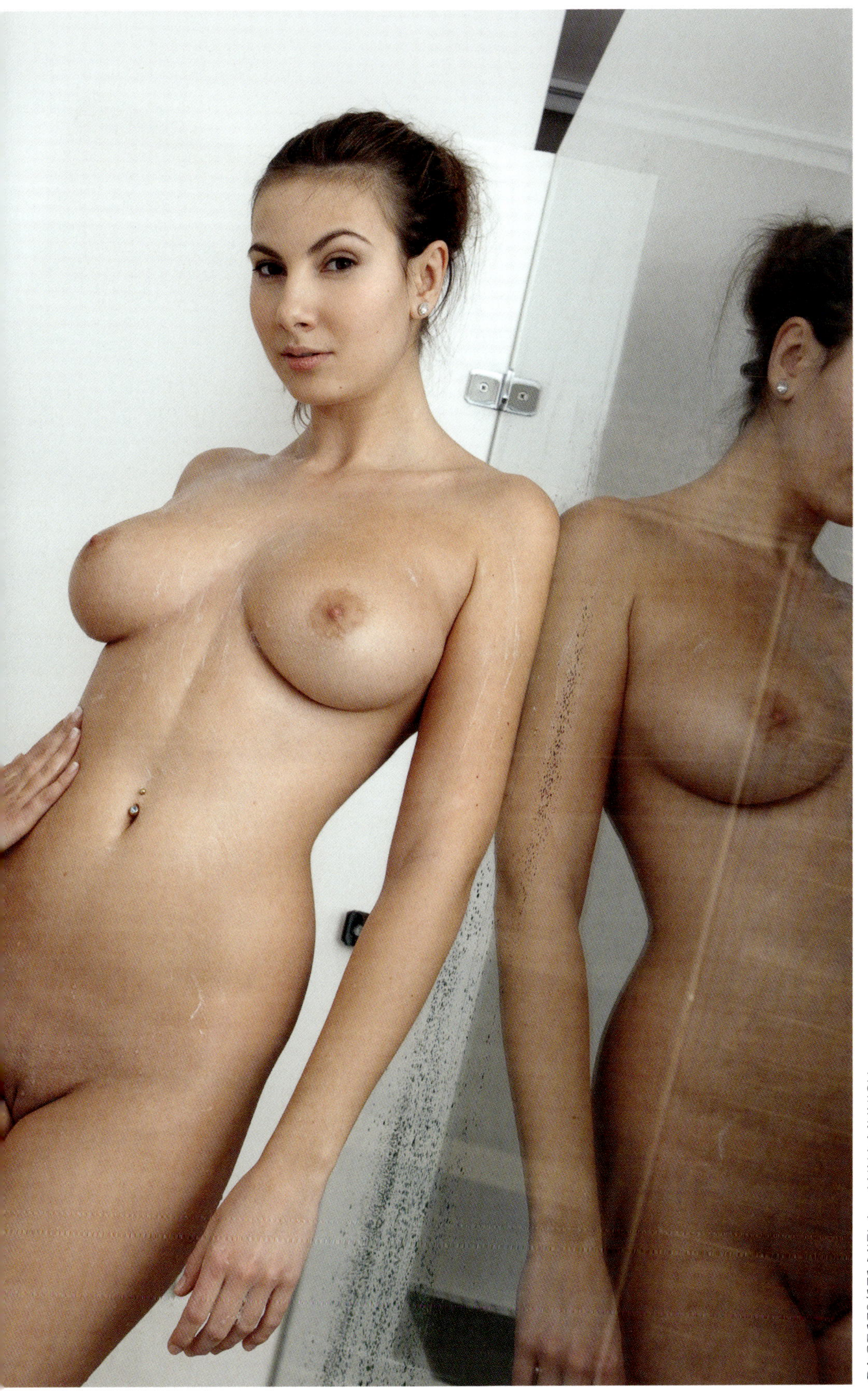

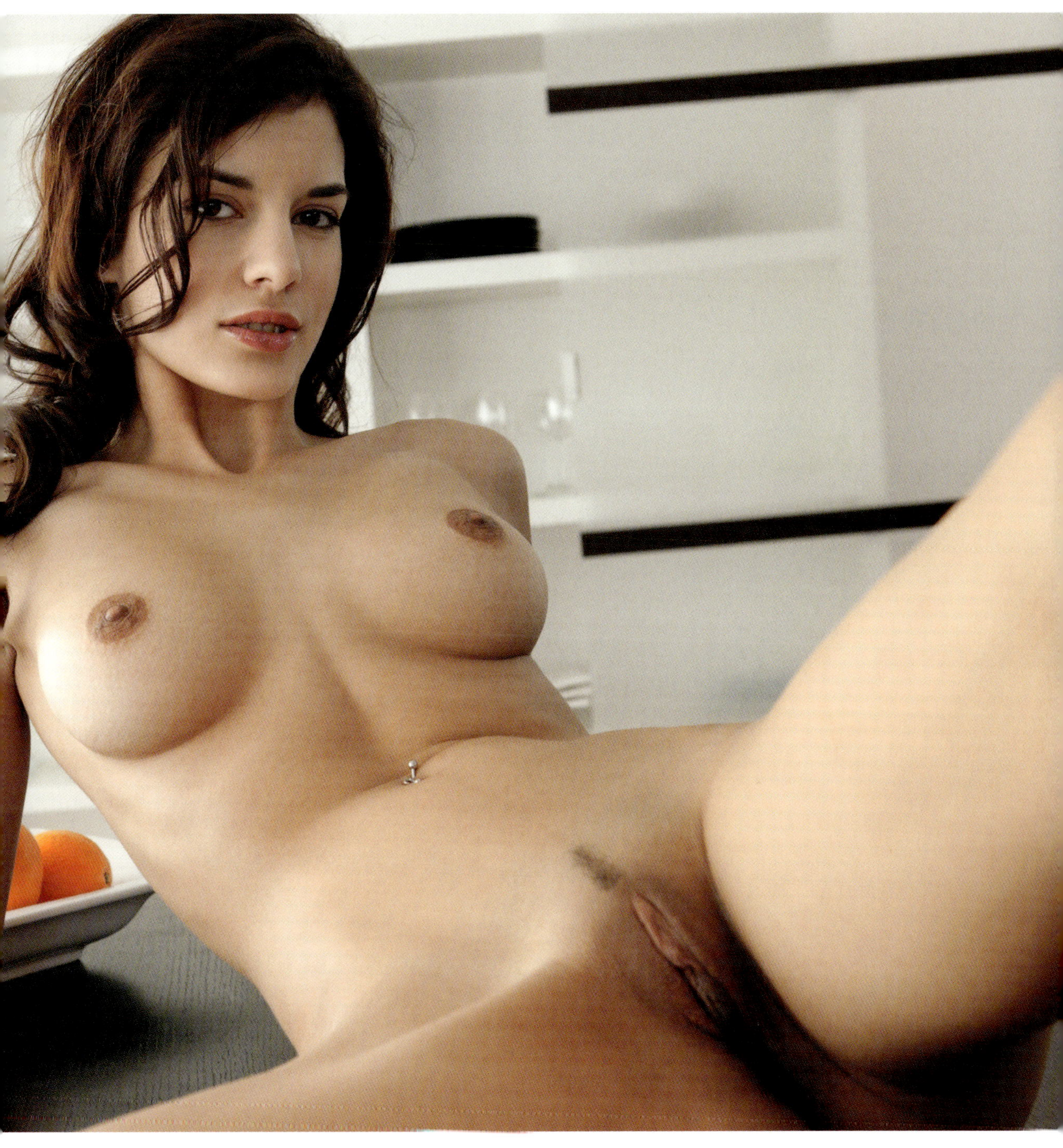

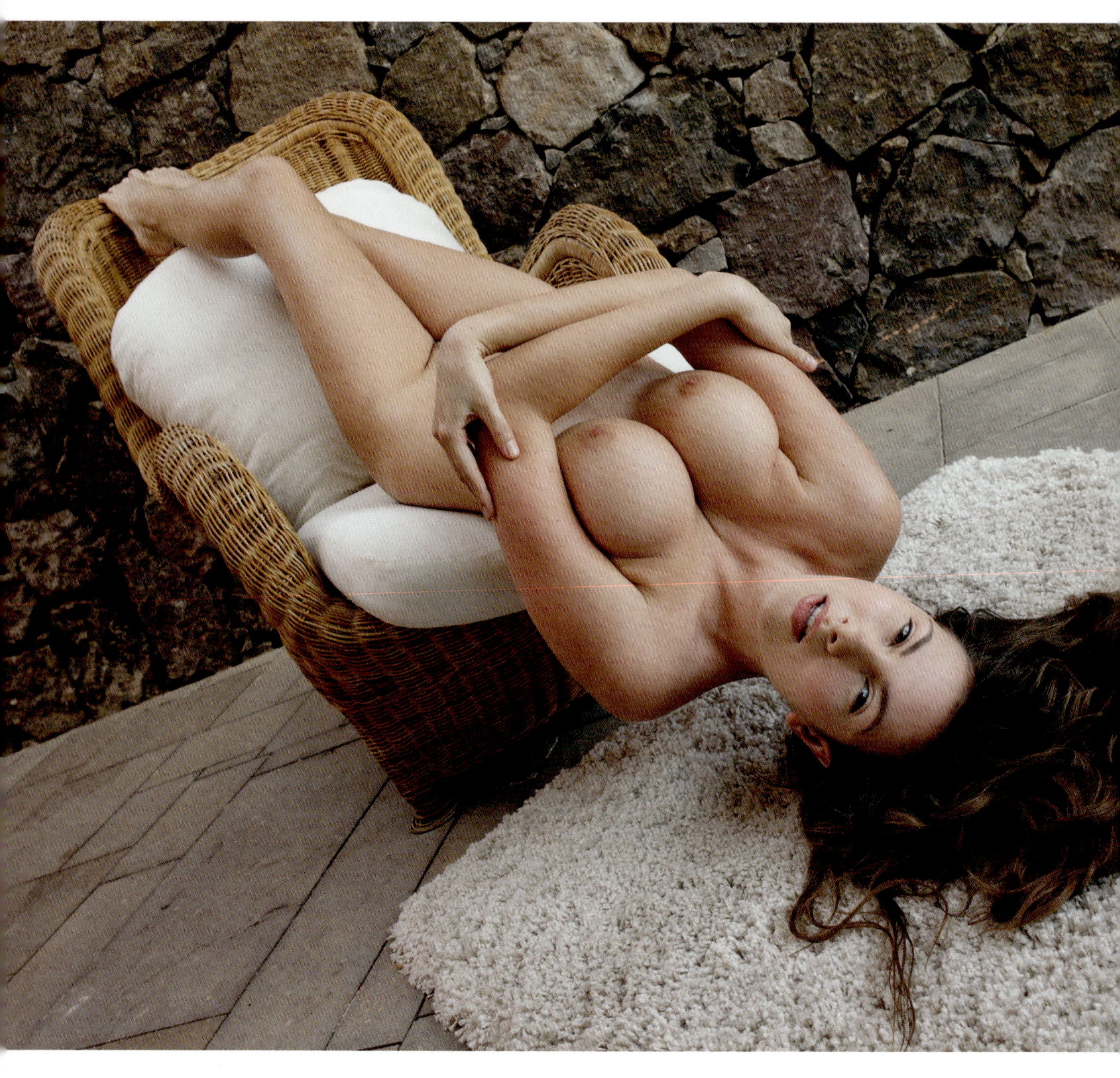

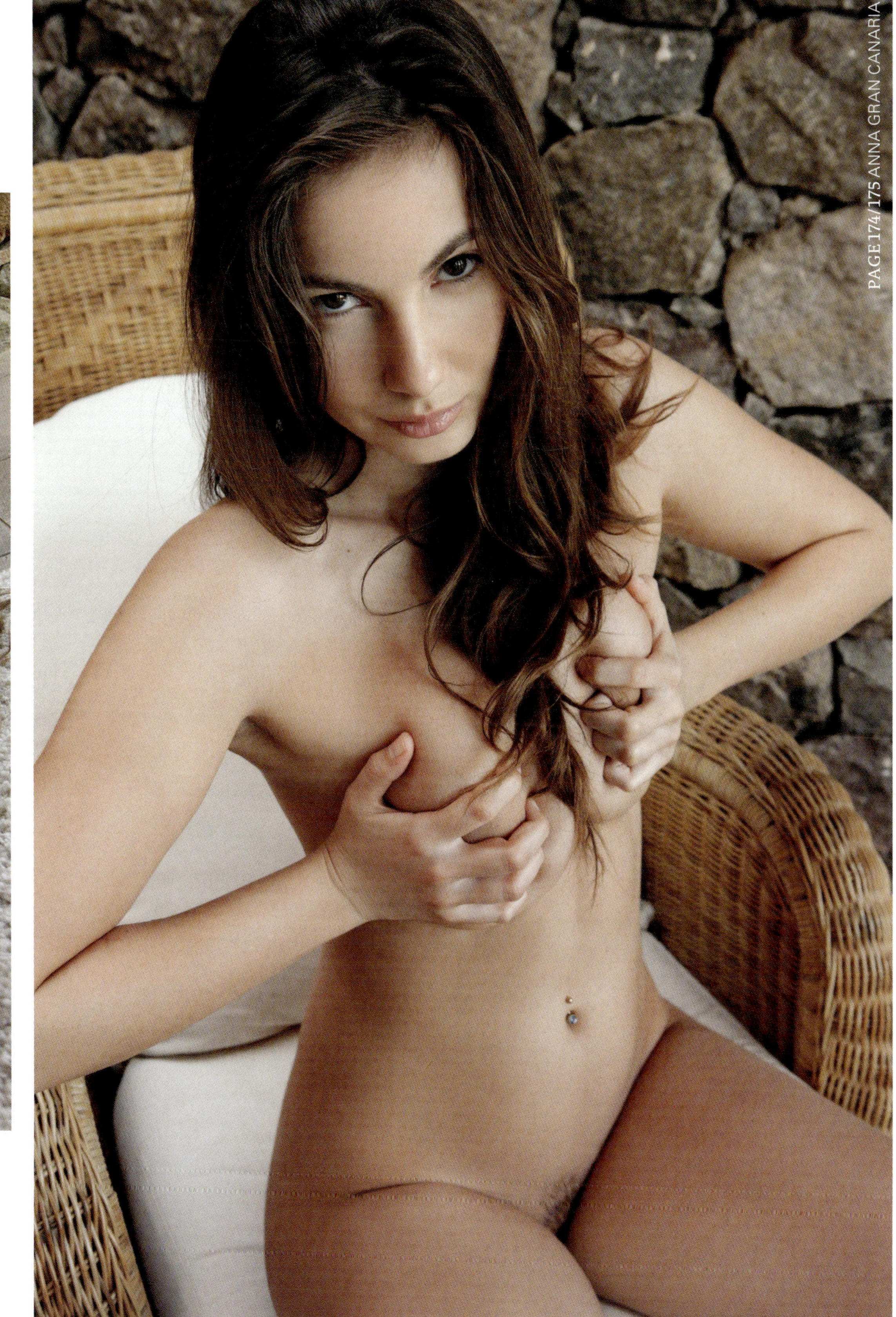
PAGE 174/175 ANNA GRAN CANARIA

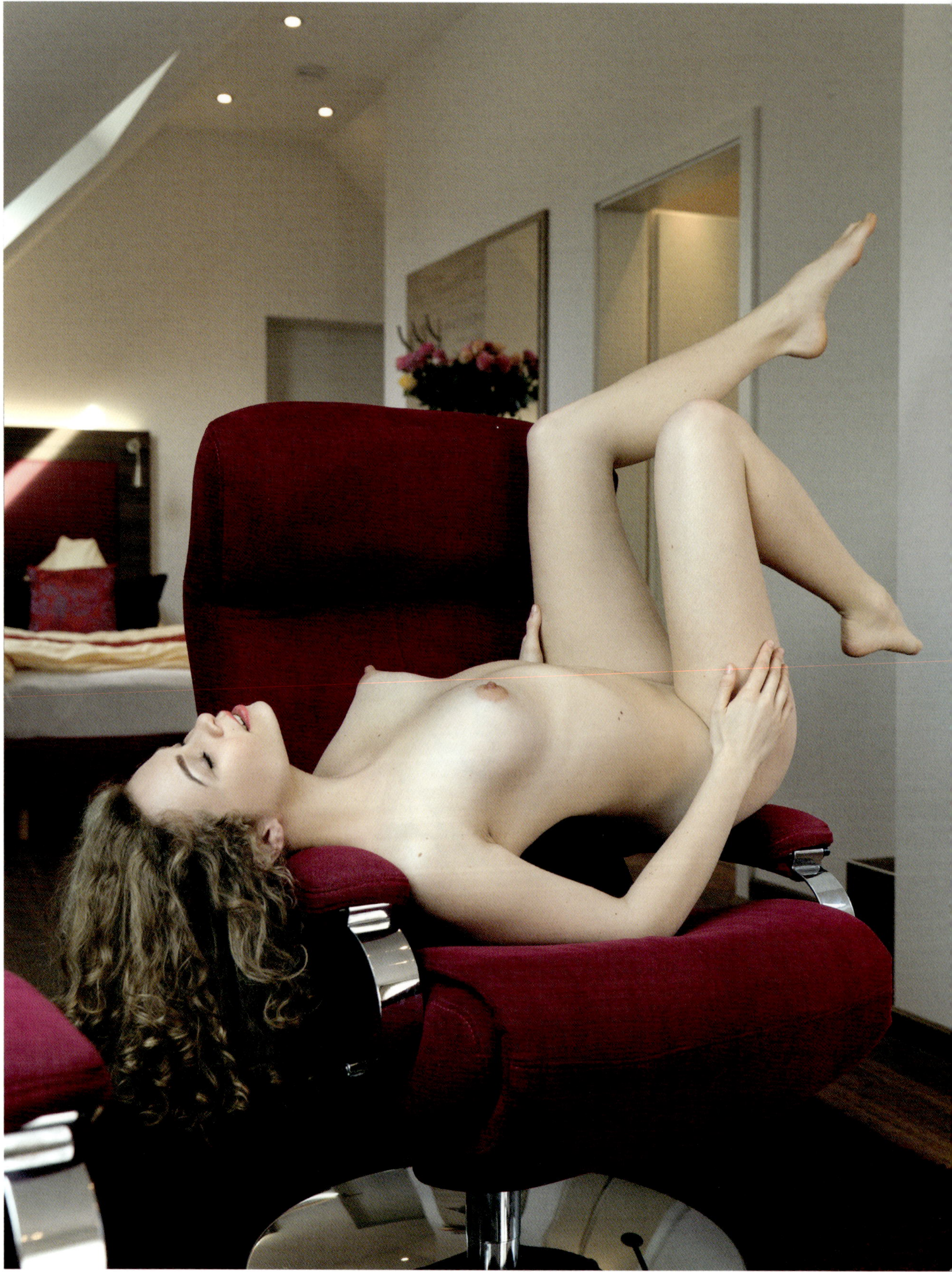

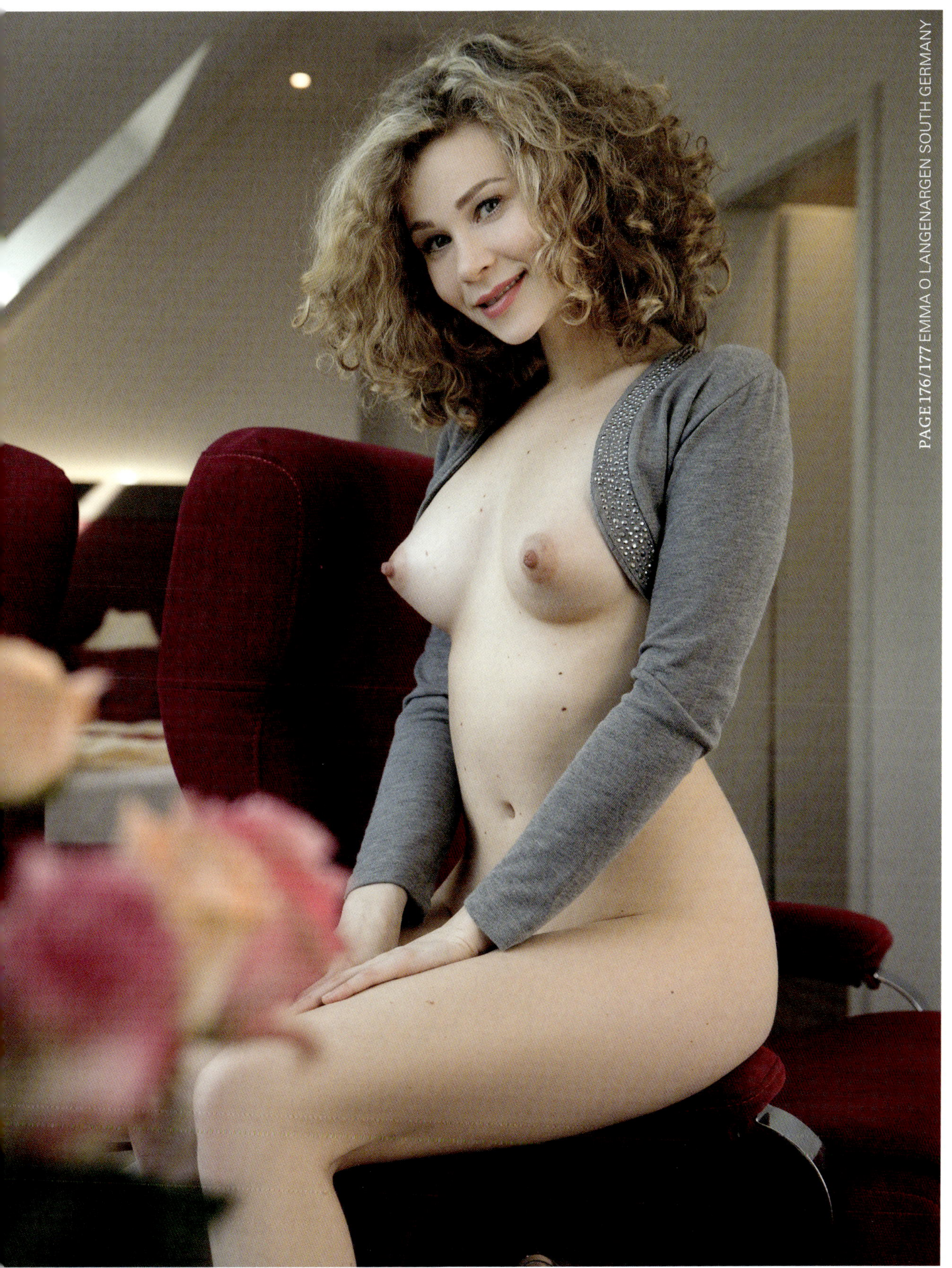
PAGE 176/177 EMMA O LANGENARGEN SOUTH GERMANY

PAGE 178/179 MIELA GRAN CANARIA

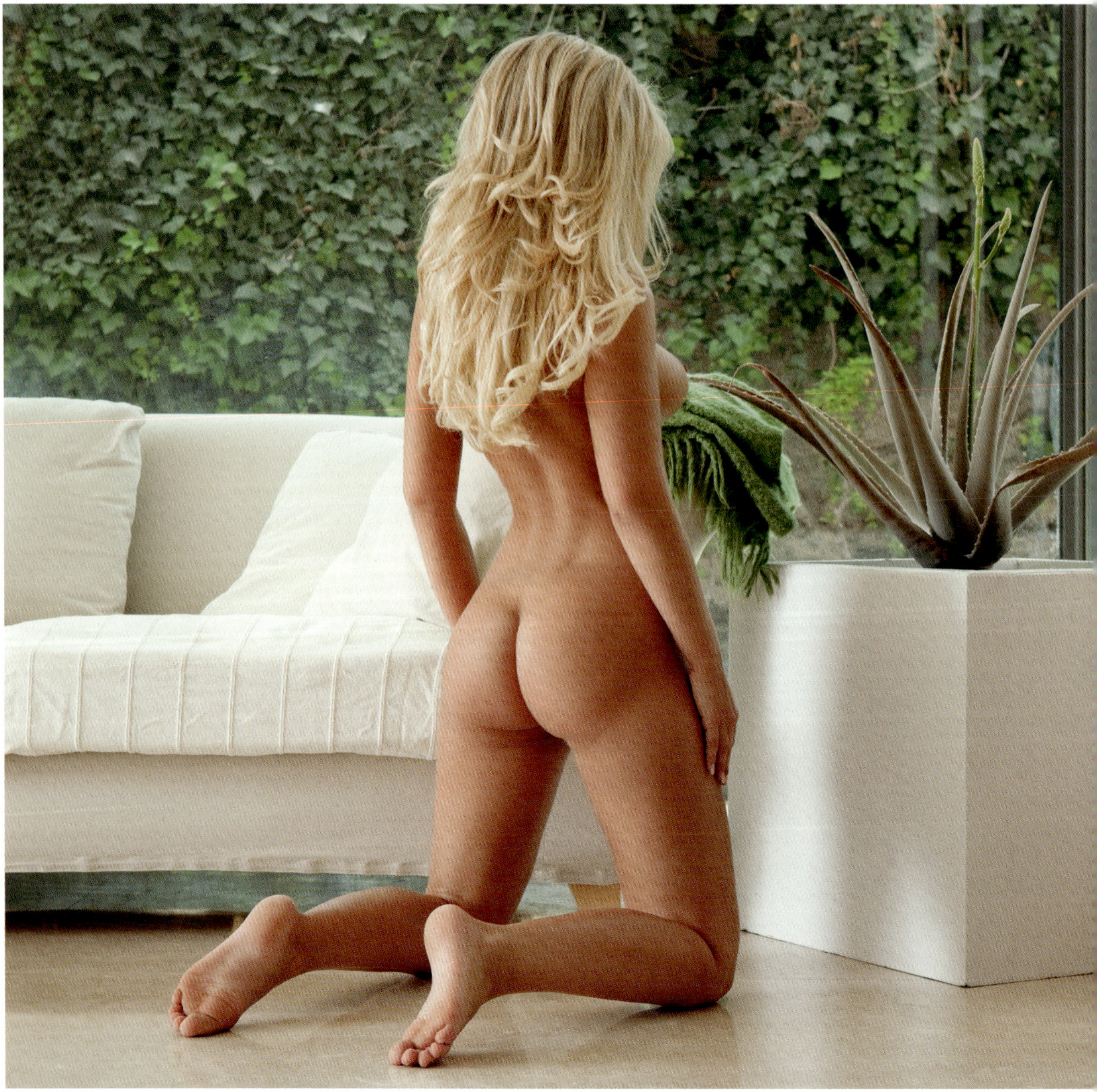

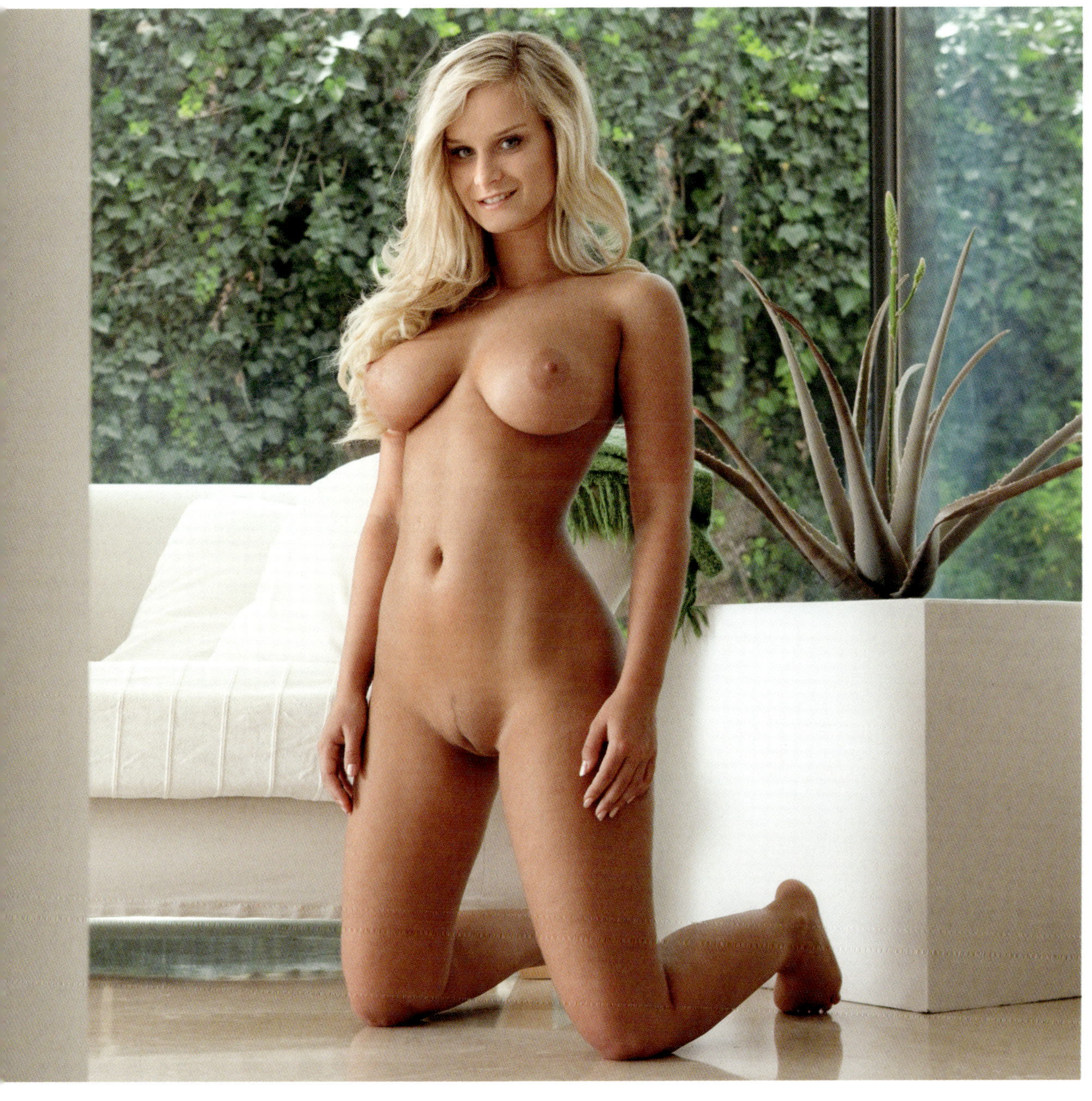

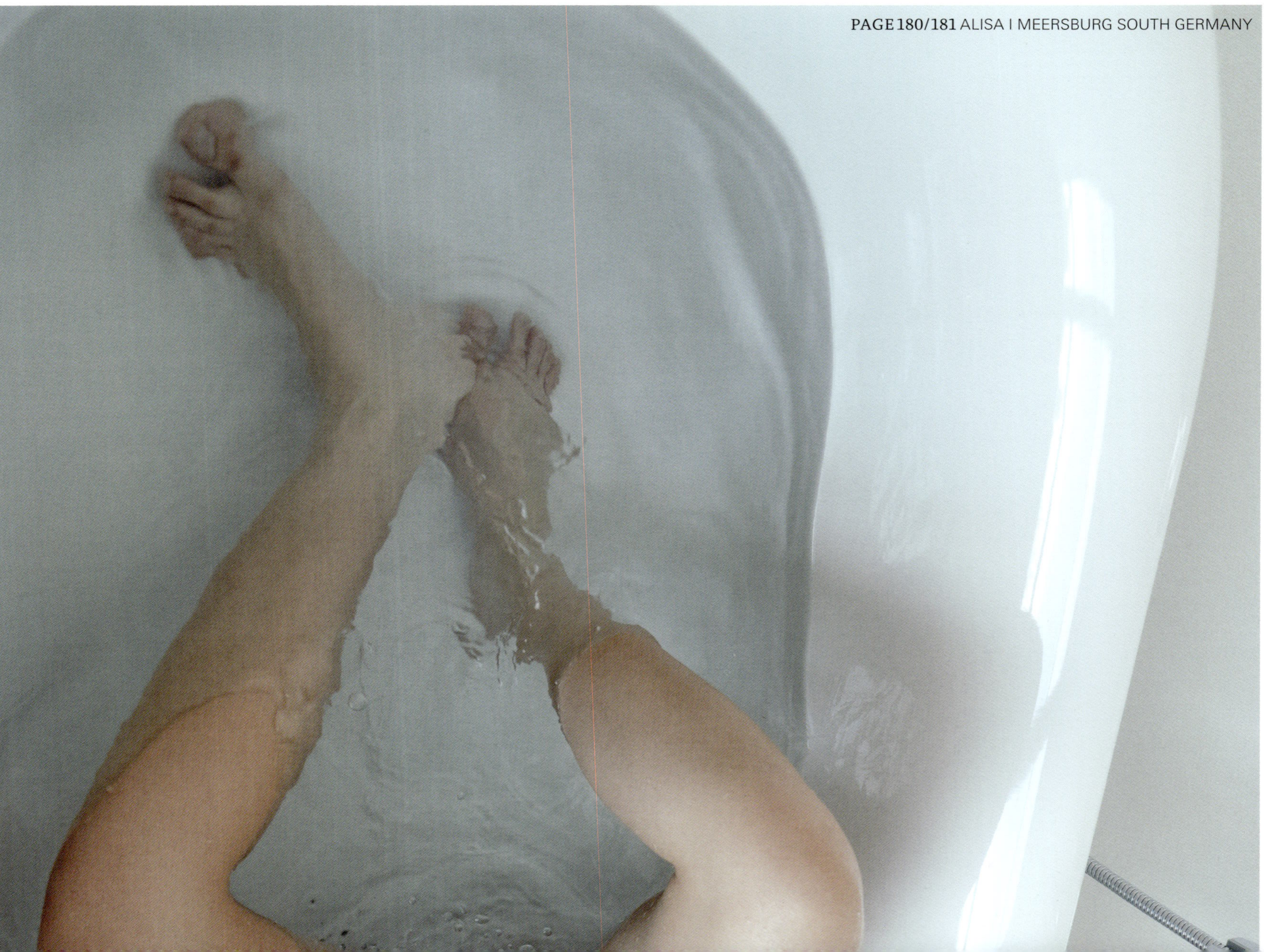

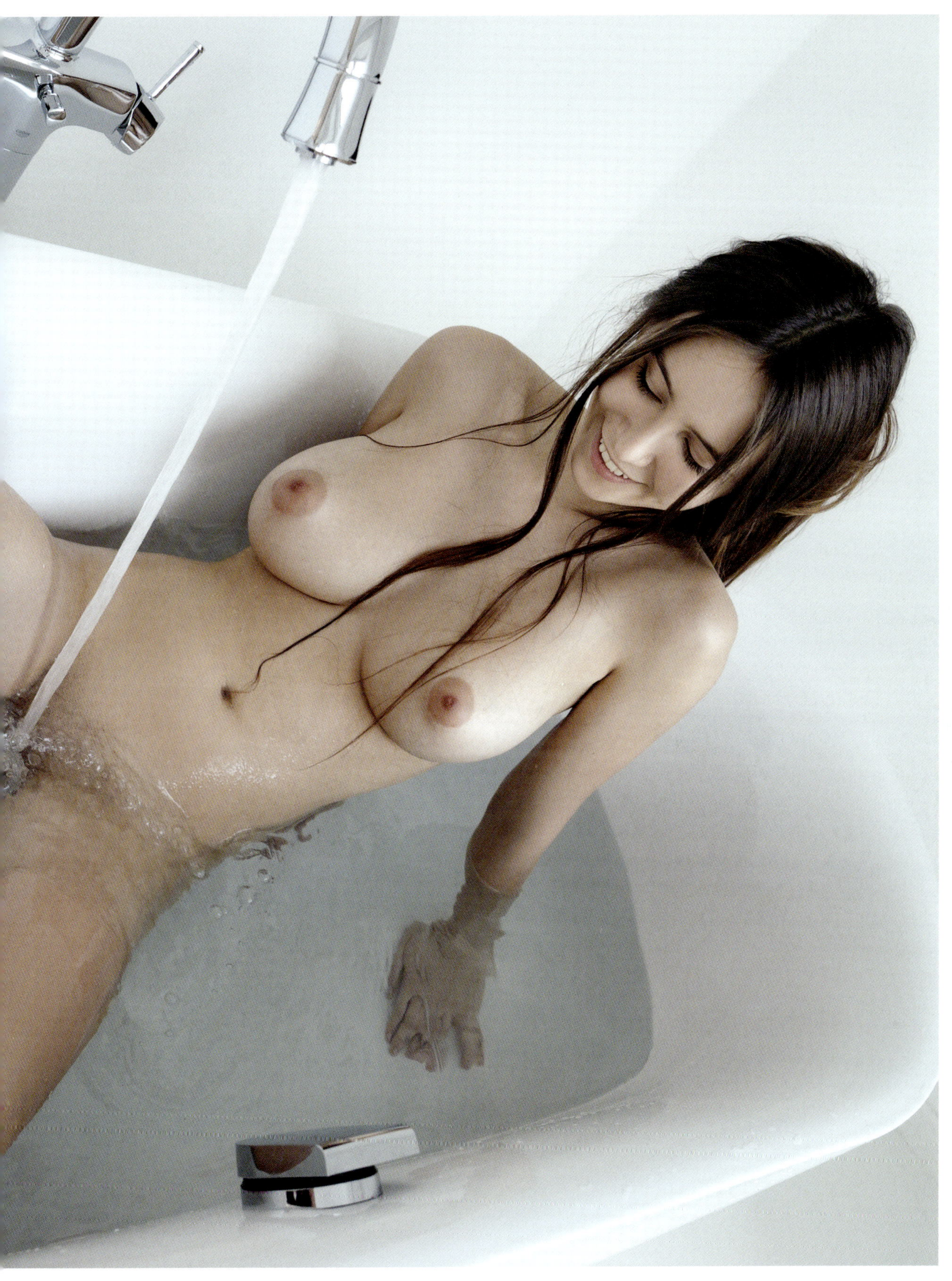

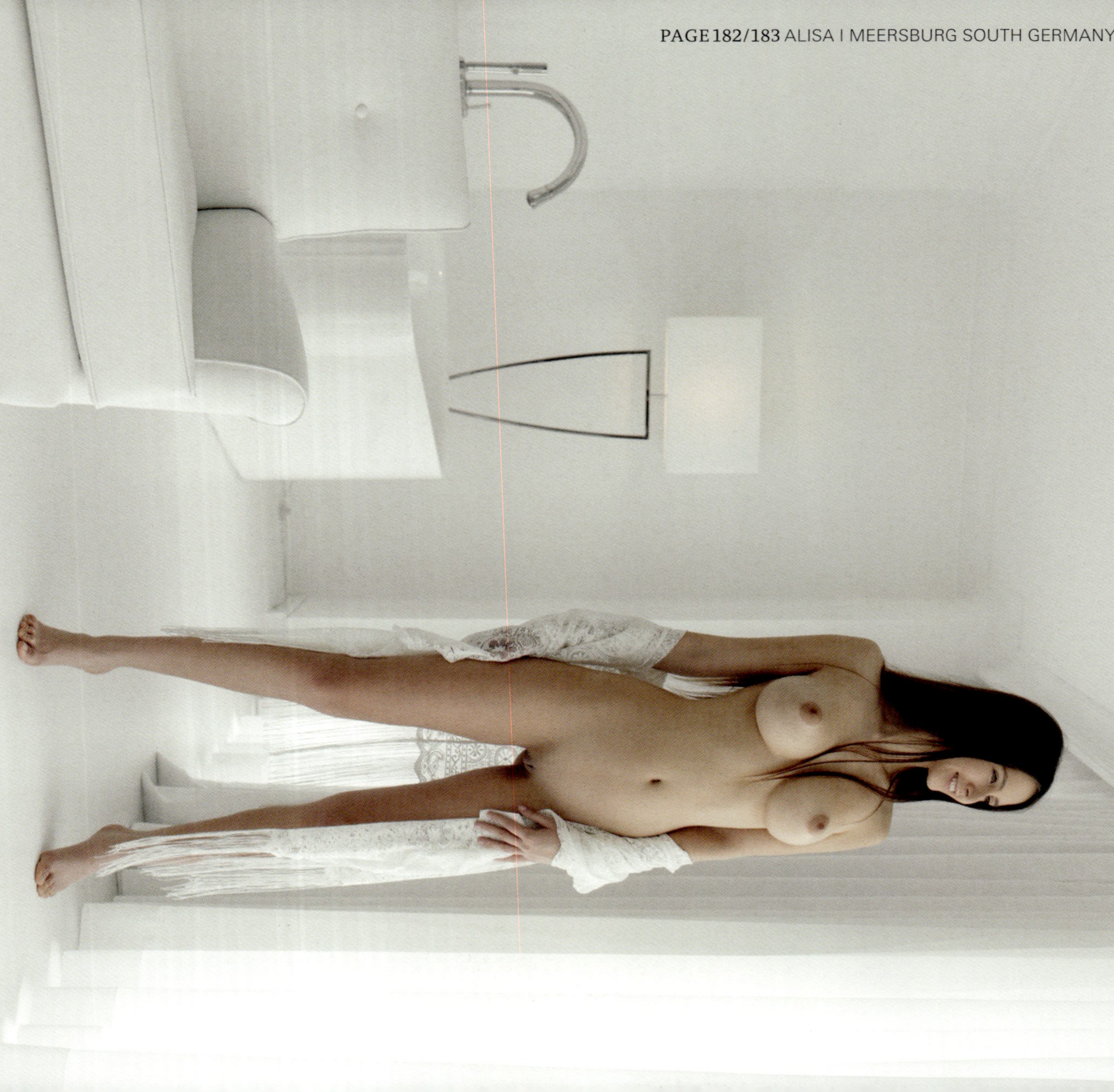

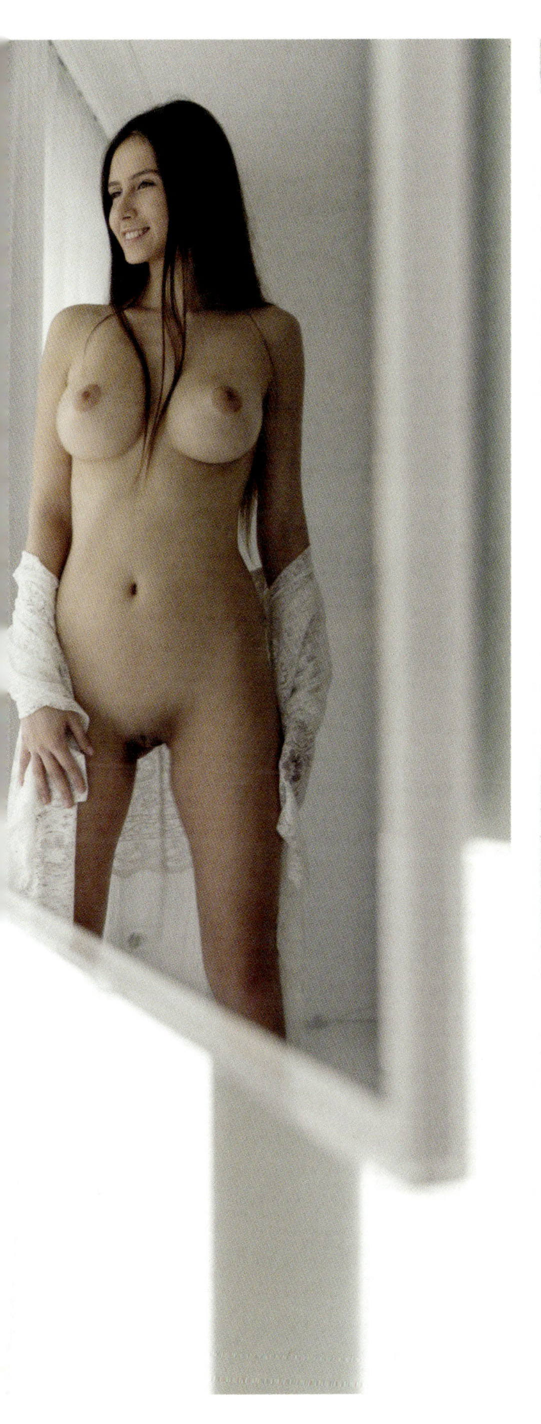

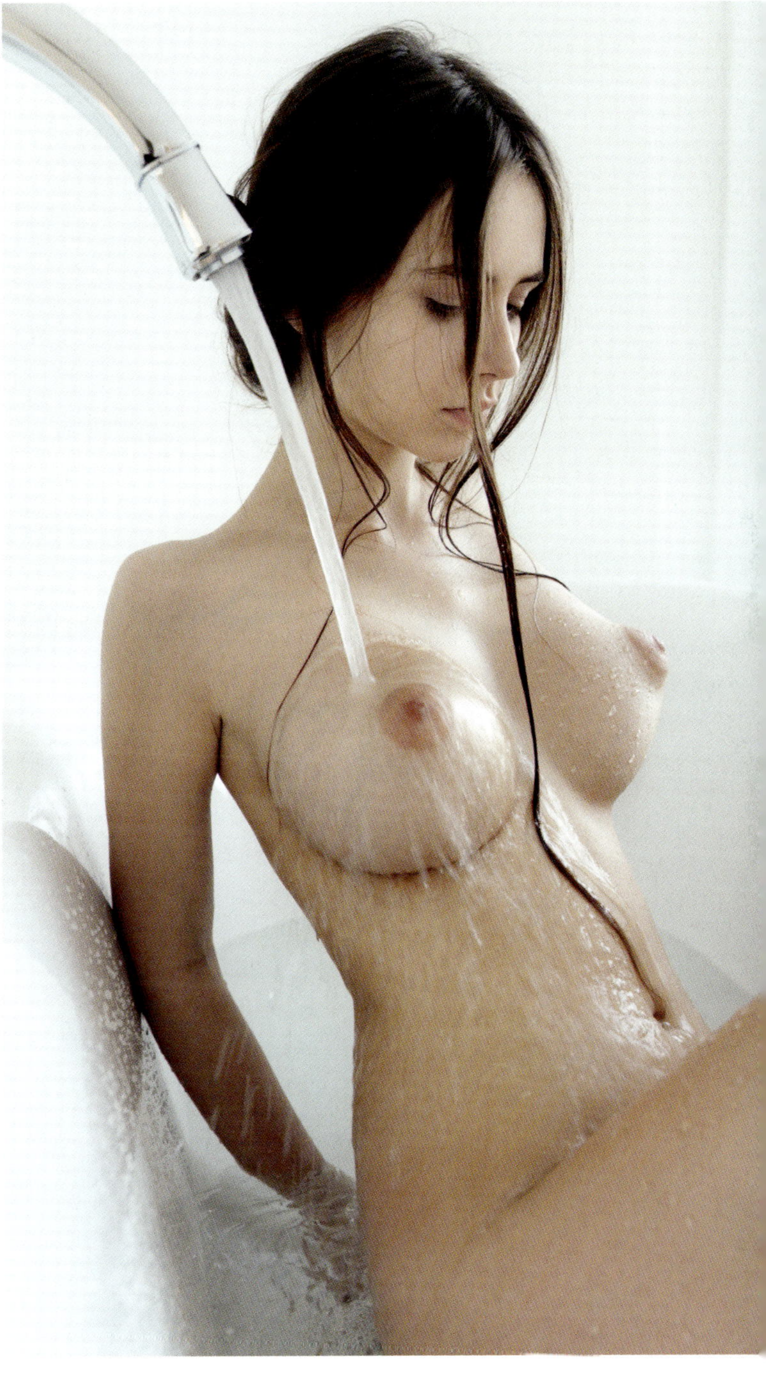

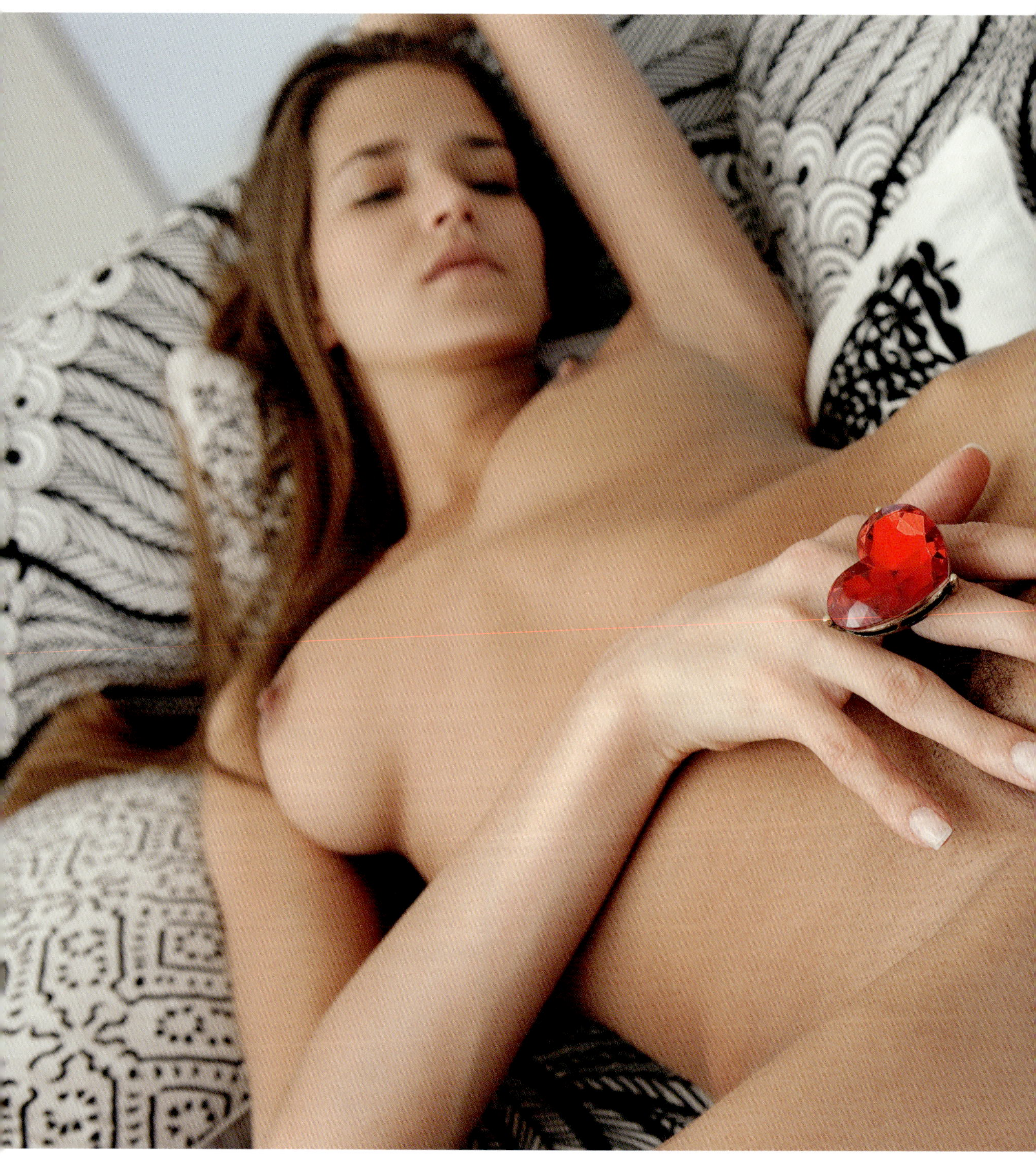

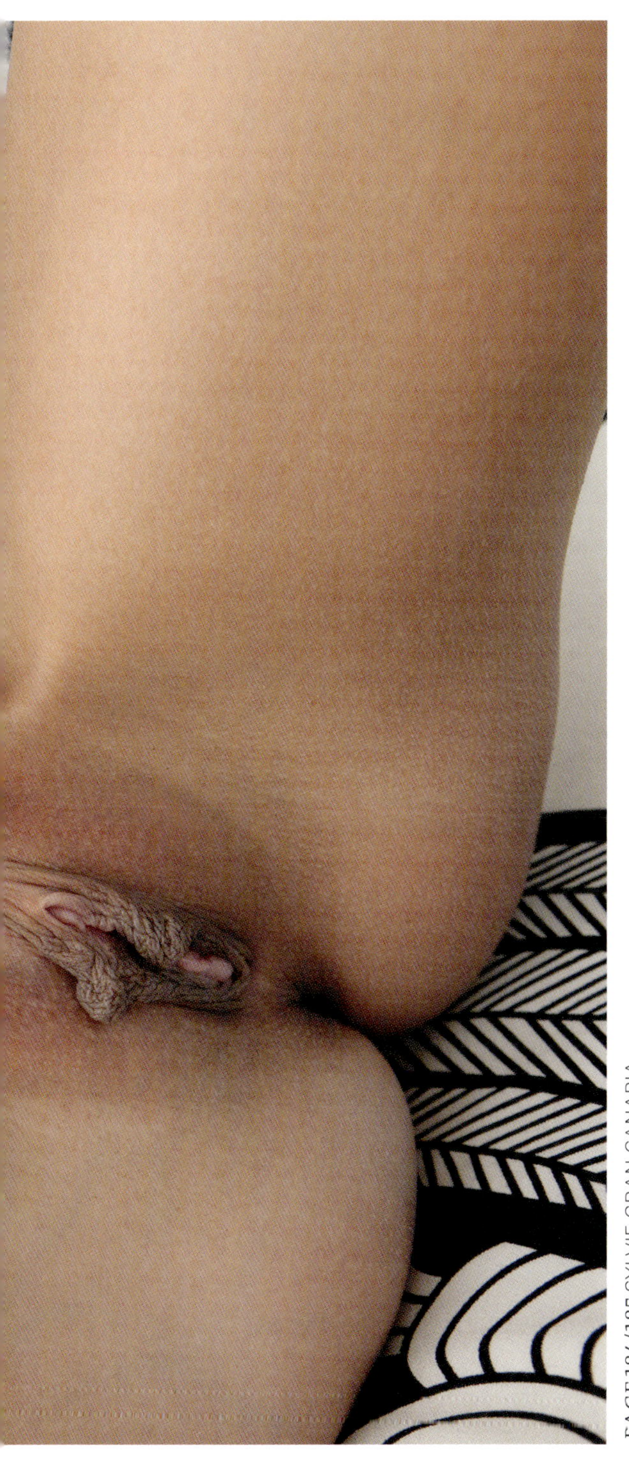

PAGE184/185 SYLVIE GRAN CANARIA

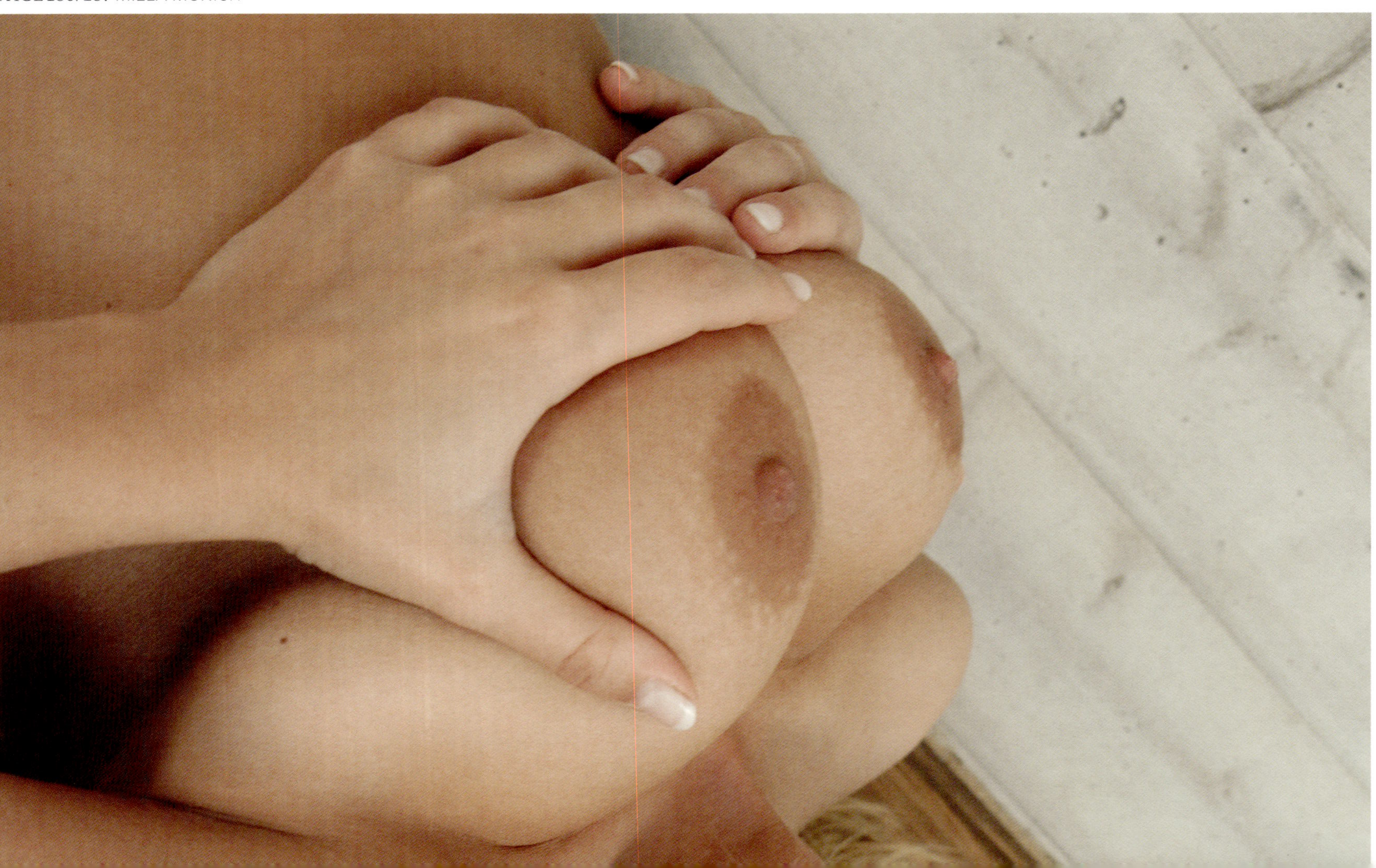

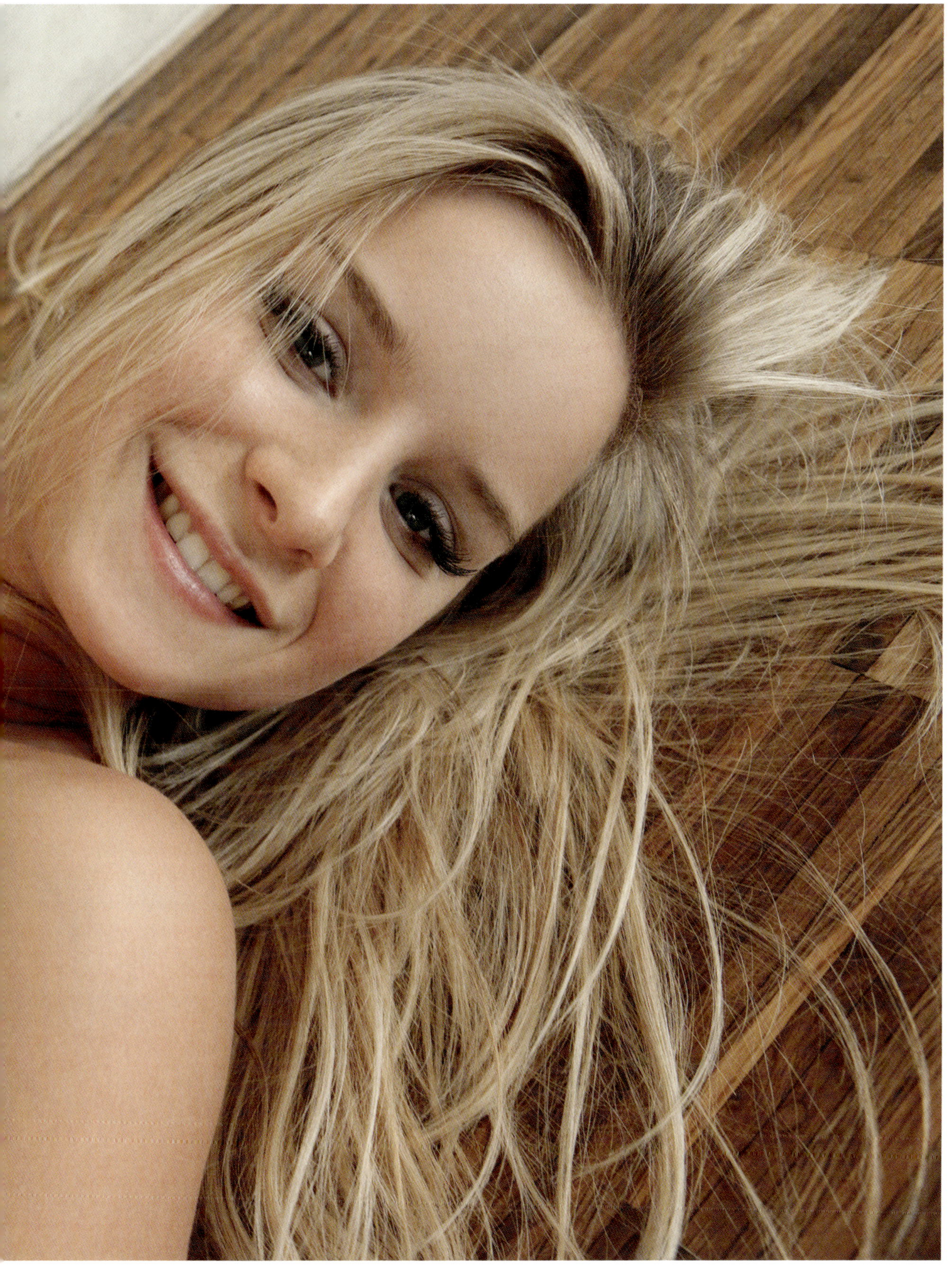

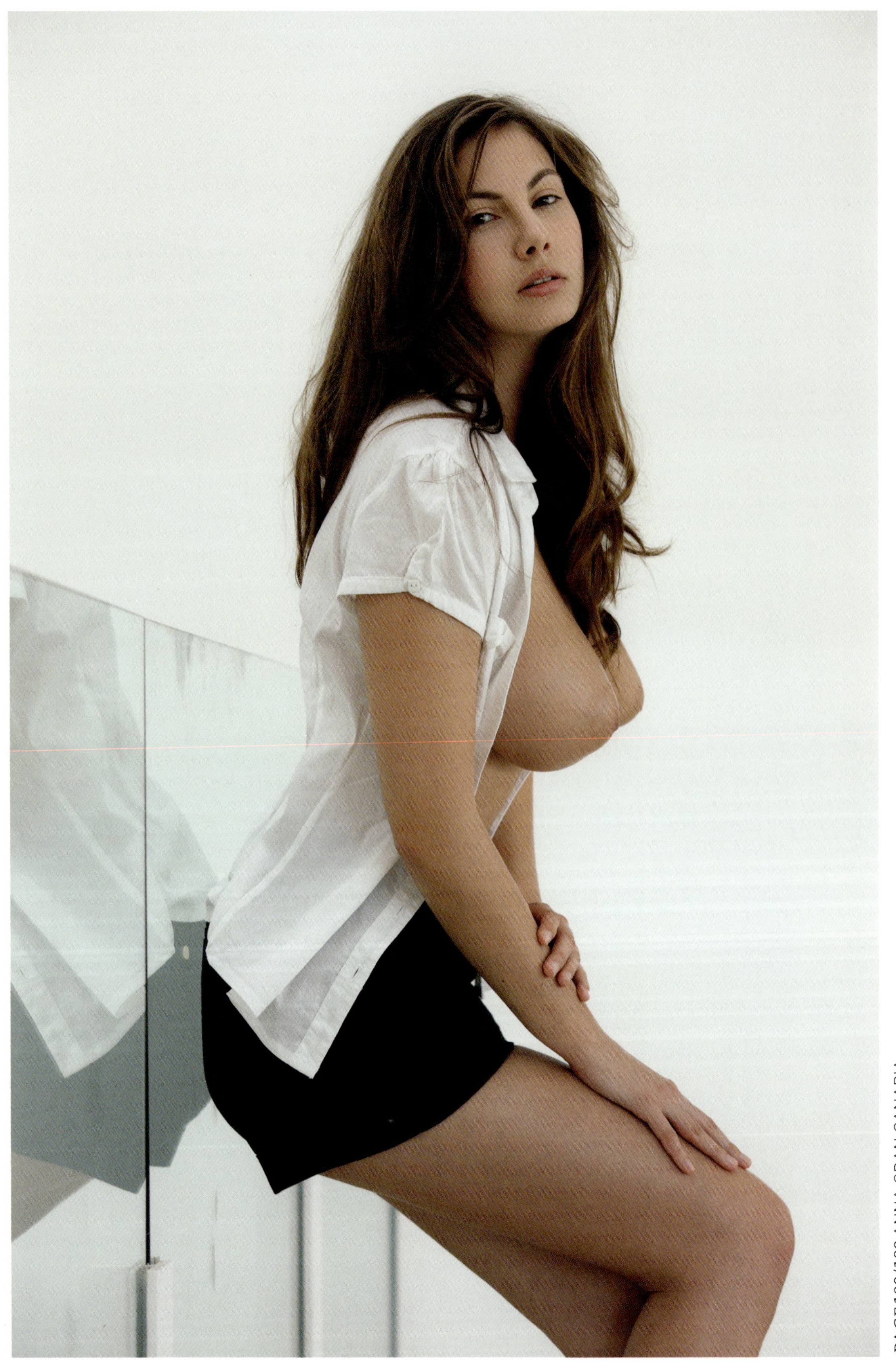

PAGE 188/189 ANNA GRAN CANARIA

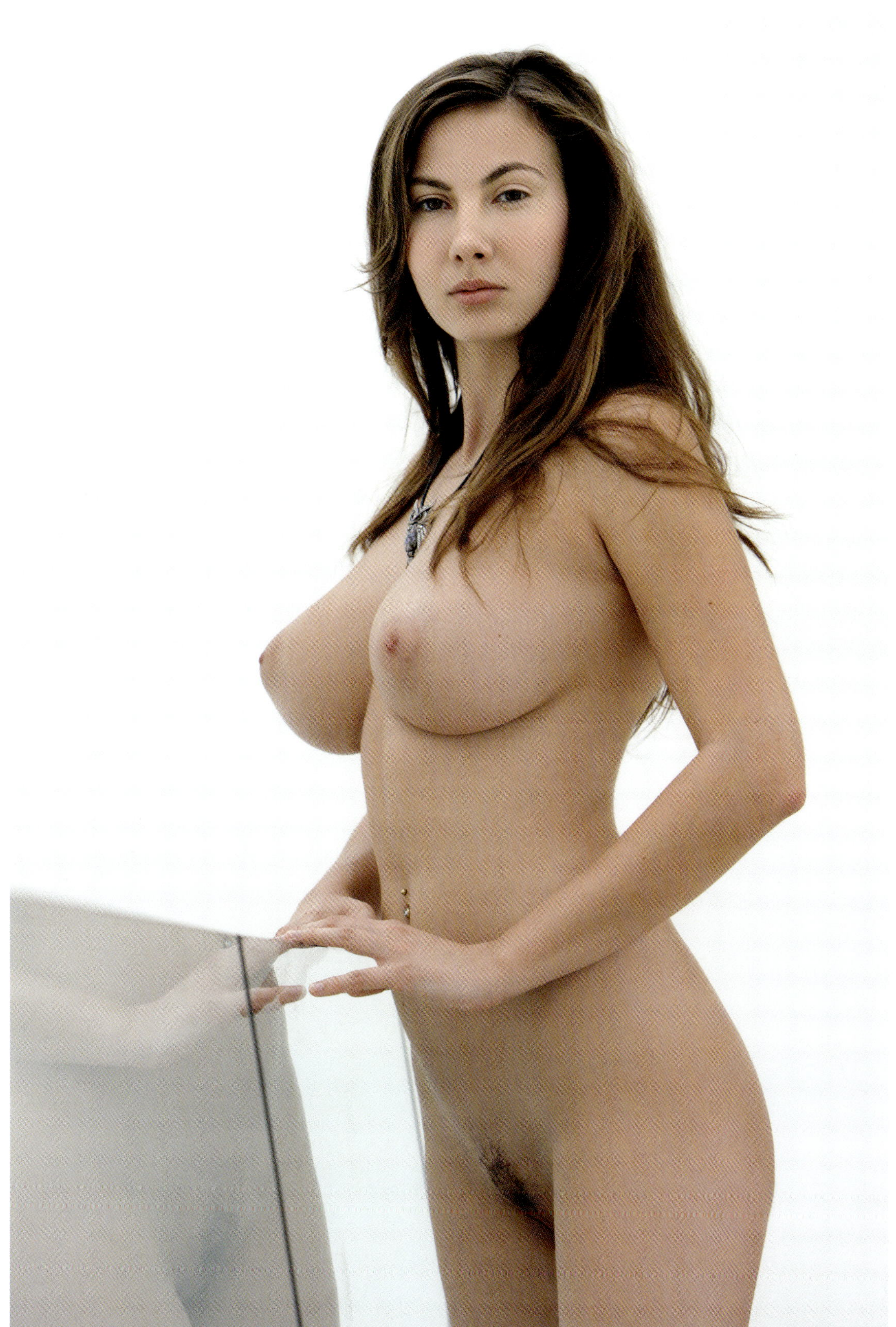

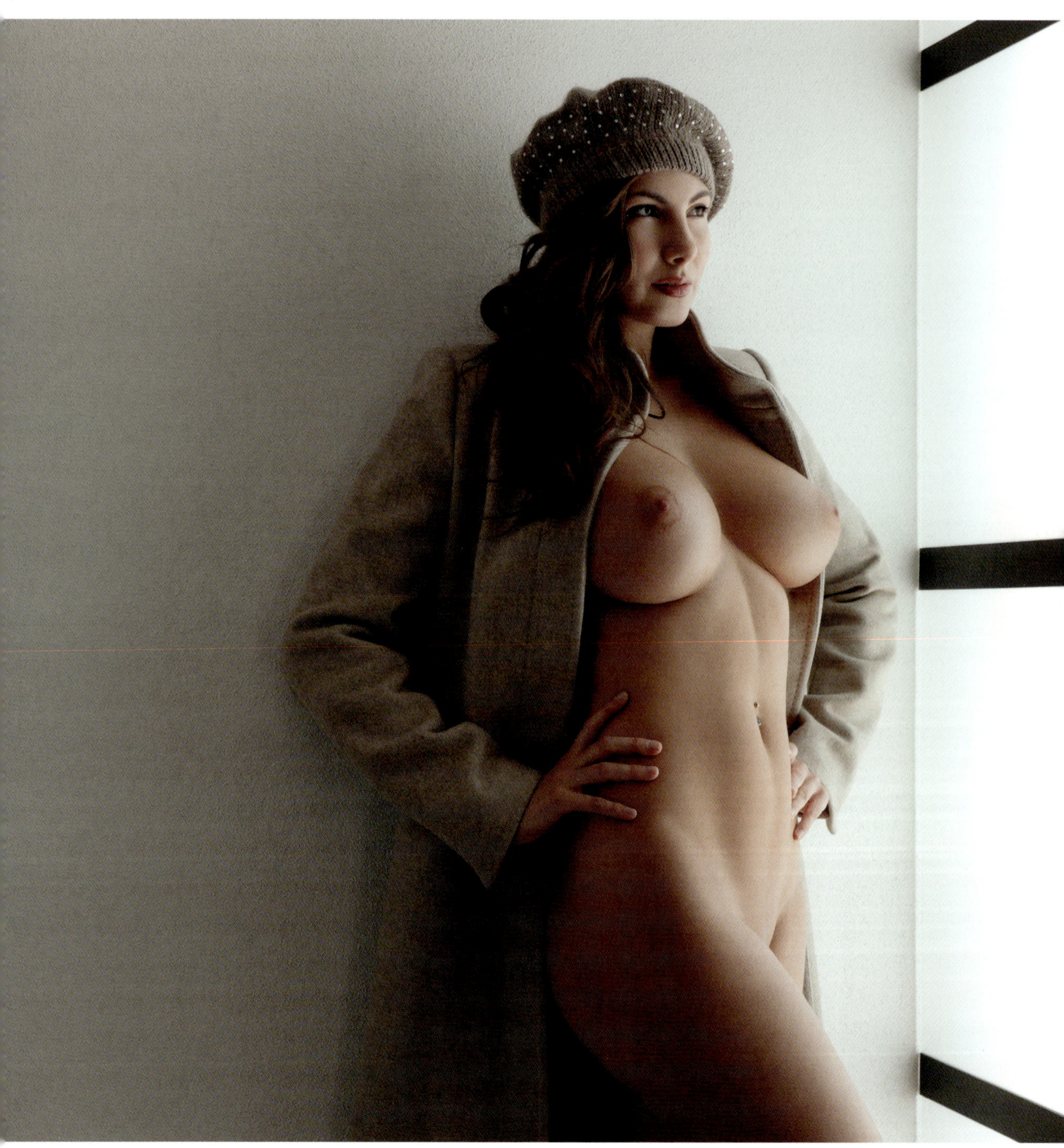

models

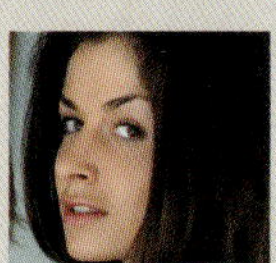

■ Adela
April 10, 1984
age 27, 172 cm,
Czech Republic

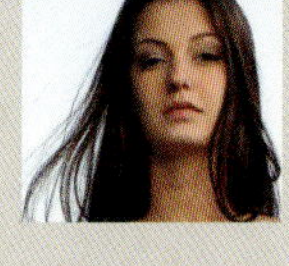

■ Alexis
February 23, 1989
age 22, 165 cm,
Georgia, USA

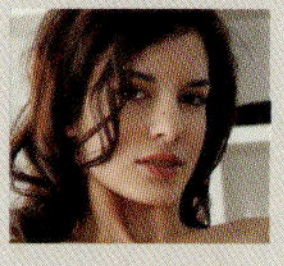

■ Alice
March 06, 1992
age 24, 172 cm,
Czech Republic

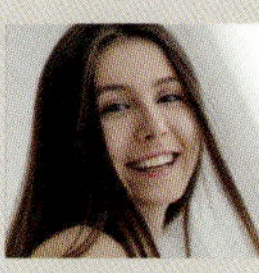

■ Alisa I
March 06, 1997
age 20, 170 cm,
Hungary

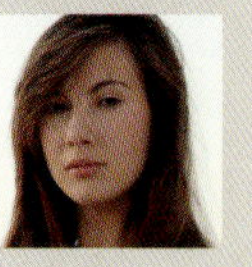

■ Anna
November 24, 1988
age 23, 173 cm,
Czech Republic

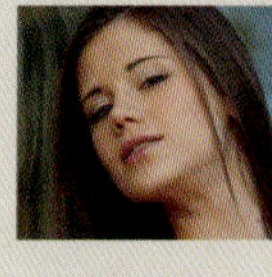

■ Caprice
October 26, 1988
age 23, 169 cm,
Czech Republic

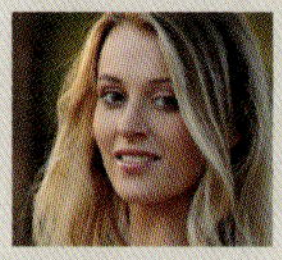

■ Carisha
November 14, 1989
age 22, 169 cm,
Slovakia

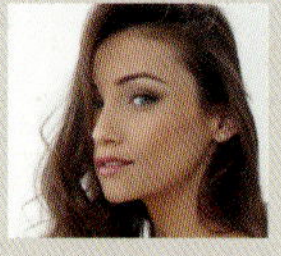

■ Celeste
December 28, 1985
age 26, 162 cm,
California, USA

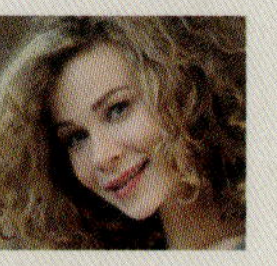

■ Emma O
November 08, 1994
age 26, 165 cm,
Germany

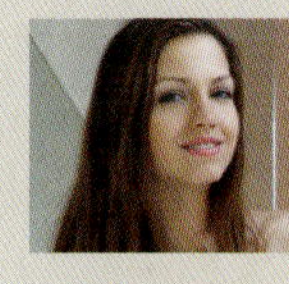

■ Eufrat
July 04, 1985
age 26, 175 cm,
Czech Republic

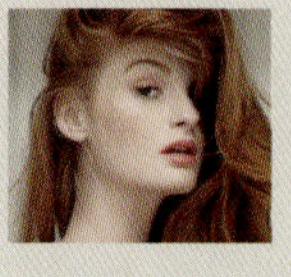

■ Faye
September 19, 1988
age 23, 171 cm,
Tennessee, USA

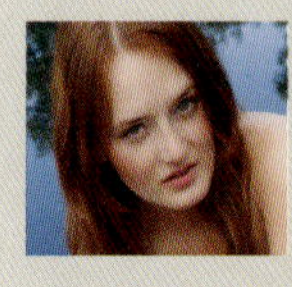

■ Gabriela
January 24, 1988
age 23, 168 cm,
Czech Republic

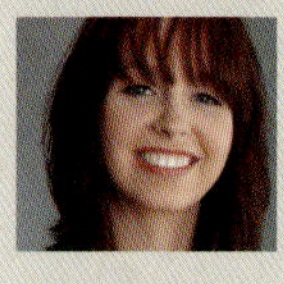

■ Hayden
February 17, 1991
age 20, 162 cm,
California, USA

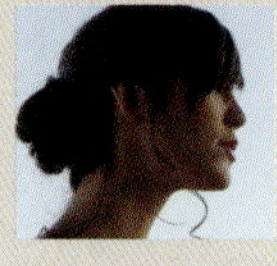

■ Holly
August 16, 1990
age 21, 180 cm,
Arizona, USA

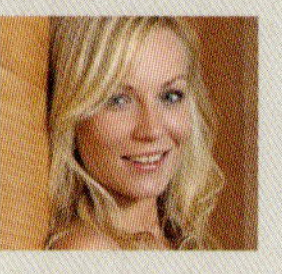

■ Jana
January 04, 1984
age 27, 163 cm,
Czech Republic

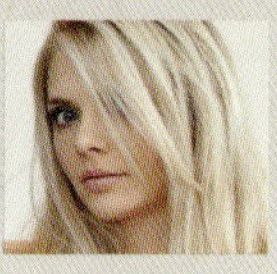

■ Jana
March 09, 1986
age 25, 162 cm,
Texas, USA

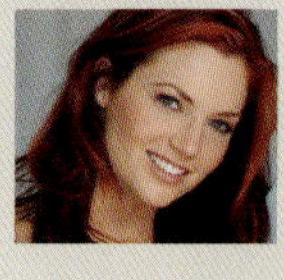

■ Jayden
October 09, 1985
age 26, 168 cm,
California, USA

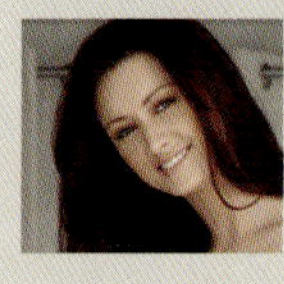

■ Karlie
May 14, 1986
age 25, 154 cm,
California, USA

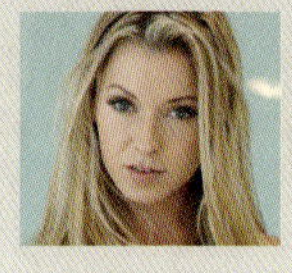

■ Lena
May 12, 1987
age 24, 163 cm,
California, USA

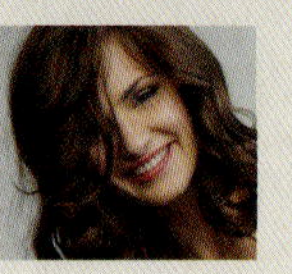

■ Lily
April 15, 1988
age 23, 162 cm,
Oregon, USA

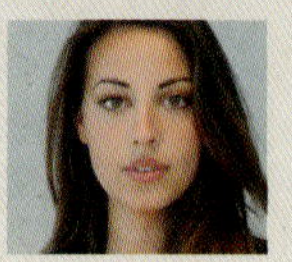

■ Lorena
September 16, 1986
age 25, 171 cm,
Mallorca, Spain

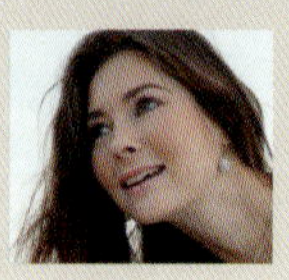

■ Lucie
July 03, 1990
age 21, 160 cm,
Czech Republic

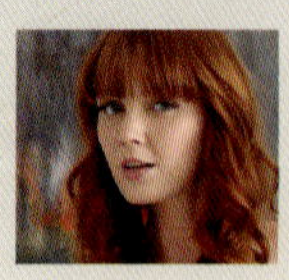

■ Marie
May 21, 1985
age 26, 158 cm,
California, USA

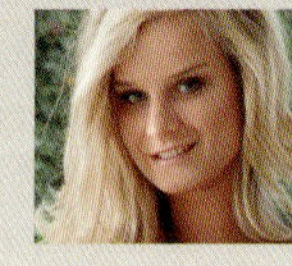

■ Miela
October 20, 1991
age 22, 158 cm,
Czech Republic

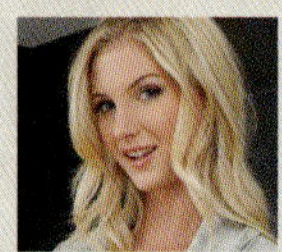

■ Natalie
February 14, 1986
age 25, 178 cm,
Arizona, USA

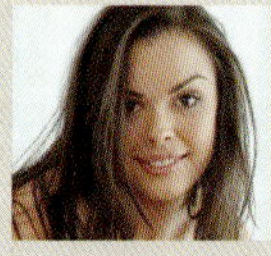

■ Renee
December 08, 1984
age 27, 164 cm,
Nevada, USA

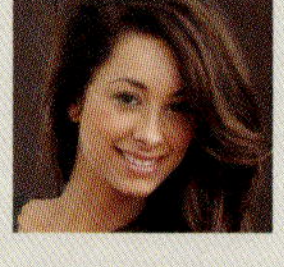

■ Riley
August 28, 1990
age 21, 153 cm,
California, USA

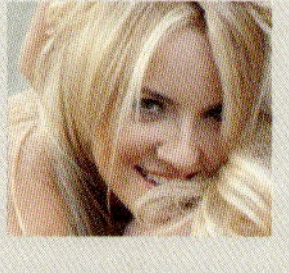

■ Sara
September 18, 1989
age 22, 164 cm,
California, USA

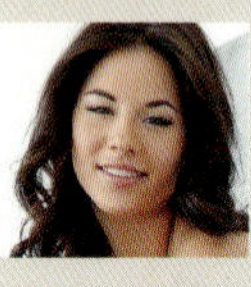

■ Shyla
June 16, 1989
age 22, 158 cm,
Texas, USA

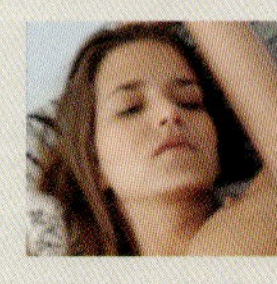

■ Sylvie
December 17, 1988
age 25, 173 cm,
Czech Republic

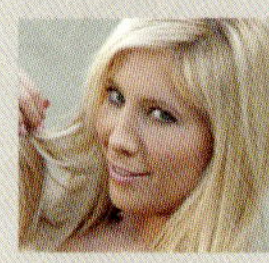

■ Tasha
January 15, 1989
age 22, 165 cm,
California, USA

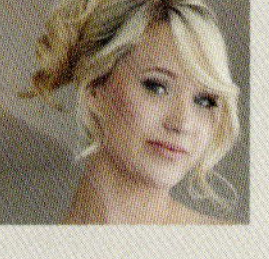

■ Tegan
June 30, 1990
age 21, 165 cm,
California, USA

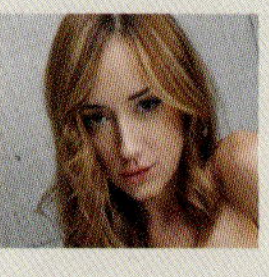

■ Victoria
August 30, 1988
age 23, 179 cm,
Wisconsin, USA